Date Due

ZUR Nov81			
GOR Sep92			
NOV 09 '94			

Cameron, Elspeth, 1943-
Hugh MacLennan : a writer's life / Elspeth Cameron. Toronto : University of Toronto Press, c1981.
xv, 421 p. : ill.
Includes bibliographical references.

1. MacLennan, Hugh, 1907- 2. Authors, Canadian (English) - 20th century - Biography. I. Title.
0802055567

1298372 NLC

Hugh MacLennan: A Writer's Life

ELSPETH CAMERON

Hugh MacLennan

A WRITER'S LIFE

UNIVERSITY OF TORONTO PRESS

Toronto Buffalo London

Toronto Buffalo London
Printed in Canada
ISBN 0-8020-5556-7

Canadian Cataloguing in Publication Data

Cameron, Elspeth, 1943-
Hugh MacLennan

Includes index.
ISBN 0-8020-5556-7
1. MacLennan, Hugh, 1907 – Biography.
2. Authors, Canadian (English) – 20th century – Biography.* I. Title.
PS8525.L45Z62 C813'.54 C81-094364-6
PR9199.3.M334Z62

This book has been published with the help of a grant from the Canadian Federation for the Humanities, using funds provided by the Social Sciences and Humanities Research Council of Canada, and a grant from the Publications Fund of the University of Toronto Press.

To Paul Lovejoy

Contents

Preface

I was first introduced to the work of Hugh MacLennan in high school, where we studied *Barometer Rising* in an edition that had been purged of those passages deemed unsuitable for sound moral development. Like a similar approach in contemporary Health classes, which by urging temperance spurred some of us to experiment with liquor, this presentation piqued my curiosity to find out what he *really* wrote and left an indelible impression that he must be a racy and even an irresponsible fellow.

It was therefore almost incomprehensible to discover in Canadian literature courses at university that critics from the higher echelons of education thought MacLennan a somewhat dull and stolid writer whose stories barely made it across the boundary from social history into fiction. That was in the mid-sixties, when university English departments fairly hummed with excitement about the 'New Criticism': the names of I.A. Richards, Cleanth Brooks, and Northrop Frye were mentioned with hushed reverence in almost every literature course I attended during those years. Professors who insisted on providing historical context and biographical details about literary figures were generally considered to be hopelessly old-fashioned and quite beyond redemption. The argument went, as I remember it, that an artist's creative self was his best self and bore more or less no significant relation to the humdrum self that propelled him through each day: the better he was as an artist, the more thoroughly he had sloughed off the dross of the everyday to release his artistic soul, with the aid of technical talent, to strive upwards into the empyrean of universal archetypes and images. Such attitudes were not likely to encourage biography.

So it was that when I came to McGill University in 1967 I had two irreconcilable views of Hugh MacLennan: that he was a daring and vigorous writer who had put Canadian fiction on the map with *Barometer Rising* in 1941, but also that he was an insipid and uninspired moralizer whose work was valuable mainly as social history.

MacLennan himself was teaching in the Department of English at McGill at the time, having been there since 1951. For a number of reasons, not the least of which had been the sage advice of scholars in the then unfashionable field of Canadian literature that one needed 'a second string to one's bow' if one already had, as I did, an MA in Canadian literature, I never took a course from him. But the comments about him that one inevitably heard in those days did little to resolve the diametrically opposed views that had by now become part of my cultural baggage. Students and staff alike were divided in their opinions: to some he was the most stimulating teacher or colleague yet encountered; to others he seemed dreary to listen to and almost ridiculous in his obsessions. The only common denominator between these groups was the vehemence which informed their reactions. No one then, or even much later when I had the opportunity to interview so many people who had known him personally or professionally at one time or another, ever simply said 'who is he?' or 'I never gave that much thought.' MacLennan apparently mattered.

Who was this man who mattered? Why did he matter? How did he come to write what he wrote at just the moment he had chosen? Or had he chosen anything? Why such radical shifts in public opinion about his books? If academics really believed that he was a poor writer, why did they continue to assign his works on literature courses with such predictable regularity? These and a host of other questions remained unanswered, even after I had read the critical material that was readily available on MacLennan and his work.

Such questions were not uppermost in my mind in 1974 when I attended the Canadian literature sessions of the annual Learned Societies meetings at the University of Toronto. But I heard there an impassioned speech by the west coast poet Frank Davey, about the deplorable way in which critics of Canadian literature had overlooked the two important areas of bibliography and biography. The fashionable 'New Criticism,' he maintained, in concentrating on the text alone, had resulted in predominantly 'thematic' criticism. He regretted that this exclusion of fundamental factual studies (which elsewhere provided the very foundation upon which thematic criticism had arisen), had resulted in a somewhat superficial, and at times flippant, interconnection of image patterns and thematic concerns among Canadian critics. I trust I do not misrepresent Frank Davey here; this, at least, is my recollection of his talk of seven years ago. Above all it impressed upon me the need to balance the thematic studies then so popular in my field with some work of factual substance.

It was only a few months later that I wrote to MacLennan asking his permission and co-operation in writing his biography. His immediate pledge of assistance betrayed a generosity of spirit that he was to continue to provide throughout the full six years of research necessary to bring the project to fruition.

Nothing could strike anyone so forcibly as a biographer's realization that the truth about someone else's life is an elusive and relative matter. As Sigmund Freud once scathingly observed to a friend: 'Anyone who writes a biography is committed to lies, concealments, hypocrisy, flattery and even to hiding his own lack of understanding, for biographical truth does not exist.' Increasingly I have felt that any other person considering exactly the same set of documents, the same mass of correspondence, the same recorded interviews, and the impact of MacLennan's physical presence might have come to different conclusions. Indeed, at a different stage in my own life I might have picked this letter rather than that, shaded one thing more strongly than another, overlooked certain episodes in favour of alternatives. None the less, relative as it can only be, this version of MacLennan's life has been tested against all materials available to me, against the views of himself he has tirelessly shared with me, and against characteristic patterns of action in his novels which, in my opinion, bear a profound relationship to the course of his life.

The question might well arise as to why MacLennan has not tackled his own life story. Readers will observe in the course of reading this biography that at the time he began *The Watch that Ends the Night*, in the early 1950s, he did contemplate an autobiography, but only briefly. It would be 'too cramping,' he confided to John Gray in 1950. He felt the same about biography itself: possible subjects were proposed to him from time to time, notably William Lyon Mackenzie King, but he always drew back on the ground that, as he once put it, 'I would tend to fictionalize too much.'

This single remark is significant. MacLennan, as I see him, is a born writer. The frequency with which he wrote letters, even after the telephone virtually superseded the typewriter, and the quality of those letters, testify to a belief that the written word *is* reality. The persistence with which he initially kept at his poetry and fiction for over ten years without tangible reward suggests that it was more than a peripheral activity; it was an obsession.

Neither Frank Davey's timely remarks nor MacLennan's reliable co-operation would have been of any avail had the Canada Council not responded unstintingly to my request for a three-year research grant, which carried the heavy burden of my expenses. For this grant from 1975 to 1978, as well as for an additional leave fellowship from the Canada Council for 1977-8, I am grateful. Loyola College also provided a summer research grant in 1976. These awards owe much to the people who not only recommended me to the Canada Council but were also keenly excited at the prospect of the biography and unsparingly gave helpful advice: two McGill professors, Joyce Hemlow, herself author of the award-winning biography of Fanny Burney, and Louis Dudek, well-known poet and critic; MacLennan's long-time friend from North Hatley, then curator of the McCord Museum in Montreal, Isabel Dobell; and Patrick Holland, then chairman of English at Loyola College. These funds enabled me to hire three able research assistants, Judith Ackerman, Helene Golden, and Beverley Allix, who helped me at various stages to speed up the project by assembling materials and assisting me to compile a massive bibliography.

The students in my Canadian literature class at Loyola College in 1976, which dealt entirely with MacLennan's works, did much to stimulate me with their discussions and projects in the earliest phase of my research. Additional help for short periods was given by Bettina Fournier in Calgary and Laura Corwin in New York City.

Once research got under way, a wide range of people came forward to offer different kinds of assistance. Foremost among these was MacLennan's sister Frances, who in the kindest way possible shared with me the MacLennan and MacQuarrie family histories, provided access to photographs and to her brother's favourite childhood books, and located two plastic shoebags full of MacLennan's letters home from Oxford and the Continent. In addition, she introduced me to other members of the family and to friends of MacLennan's dating back as far as his high school days. Her tour of the various places in and around Halifax that once assumed significance in her brother's life gave me a 'feel' for his past that was invaluable. Isabel Dobell, with equal hospitality, most generously provided me with an exploration of MacLennan's summer life at North Hatley: she regaled me with anecdotes, and took me round to meet an astounding number of summer residents who seemed thoroughly to enjoy recalling events from his many summers there, first with Dorothy Duncan and then later with Tota.

To the late John Gray, who was undoubtedly MacLennan's closest friend as well as his editor from 1951 on, I owe a very great deal. He provided access in 1977 to the lengthy correspondence MacLennan held over the years with Macmillan's in Toronto, material that eventually formed the heart of this book. Moreover, he reminisced at great length and offered quiet encouragement. For drawing my attention to the letters from MacLennan and Dorothy Duncan to William Arthur Deacon, I am also grateful to John W. Lennox who, with his colleague Clara Thomas, was currently examining Deacon's correspondence.

The staffs at various libraries in which research was done were always co-operative and cheerful. At McGill University the assistance of Gerald French, Elizabeth Lewis, and Victor de Breyne in the Department of Rare Books and Special Collections, of the reference librarians, and of the inter-library loan staff was greatly appreciated. At the University of Calgary Ernest B. Ingles, director of the Special Collections Division, was especially helpful, as were his assistants Appollonia Steele and Jean Tener. I would also like to thank Stanley Triggs at the McCord Museum in Montreal; Alicia Black at the Oriel College Library, Oxford; Nora Robins, special collections librarian, Concordia University; Olive Cameron, Archives Department, Harriet Irving Library at the University of New Brunswick; Charlotte Stewart and Bruce Whiteman, special collections librarians, Mills Memorial Library at McMaster University; Maureen Bradbury, assistant, Special Collections Library at the University of Alberta; John Bell, Archives, Dalhousie University Library; Richard Landon, head, and Rachel Grover, Thomas Fisher Rare Book Library, and Ingrid Epp, Laidlaw Library, at the University of Toronto; Mrs D.F. MacDermaid, acting university archivist, and George F. Henderson, assistant archivist, Douglas Library at Queen's University; Dido Mendl and Beth Stewart, CBC Archives, Toronto; L.C. Chipman, CBC, Montreal; Ellen S. Dunlap at the University of Texas at Austin; and Patrick M. Quinn, university archivist at Northwestern University in Evanston, Illinois.

I am especially grateful to those who made their personal letters from MacLennan available for my use. To Marian Engel, whose letters from 1956 to 1962 were especially significant for their discussions of literature in Canada, my thanks. I am also particularly indebted to Gloria Ingraham, MacLennan's first cousin, for giving me copies of letters from the years 1930 to 1972. In addition, I want to thank Audrey Berner, E.D. Blodgett, Ronald Bottrall, K. Jean Cottam, Douglas Gibson, J. Francis Leddy, Patricia Morley, Mrs M. McPhail, Gordon Roback, Frank A. Upjohn, and Mrs John Gray, among others, for the letters and other material they lent me.

It would be impossible to name all those people who in conversations, ranging all the way from lengthy formal interviews to remarks made on casual social occasions, have contributed to my understanding of MacLennan. Chief among these has been MacLennan's wife Tota: on numerous occasions she has with the warmest hospitality shared anecdotes of their life together and observations about her husband's habits and personality which have been extremely helpful to me. Many, too, whom I have never met, have freely given time to respond to my queries in letters or by telephone. Other members of MacLennan's family have assisted me, especially with their reminiscences about his parents: in particular I would like to thank Robert A. Marsh, MacLennan's first cousin, and Mrs G.S. Macdonald and Mrs James A. Doull, his aunts, for unexpected insights. Dr C. Lamont MacMillan helped give me an understanding of the life of a doctor in Cape Breton during the early years of this century. Light was thrown on MacLennan's Halifax years by Ewan S. Clarke, Jean Coward, Dr Harold A. Scammell, Dr C.J. Macdonald, Gertrude Tratt, Sub-lieutenant Rose-Marie McLellan, and Allan F. Duffus. For their recollections of MacLennan's years at Princeton, I am indebted, in particular, to Colonel Charles P. Stacey and to Israel Halperin, James Sinclair, and John Tuzo Wilson. I was able to obtain an excellent sense of his years at Lower Canada College from the late Dr Stephen Penton, enhanced by the recollections of Walter McBroom, R. Storrs McCall, Robert A. Speirs, and Francis Allen.

The summer months MacLennan spent at North Hatley were described from various points of view, all of which I found useful. Outstanding were John Bassett's recollections, but I am also grateful to Craig Wylie, Raleigh and Louise Parker, Eloise Bender, Moira Bassett, Yvette Meagher, Valentine Edgar, Charlotte Deutchen, and Frank and Marian Scott. The Scotts also contributed a great deal to my knowledge of MacLennan's life in Montreal, as did Victor and Miriam Block, Dr Gertrude Kalz, Michael Gnarowski, and Isabel Lebourdais. For their literary assessments of MacLennan in the context of personal acquaintance, I am grateful to the late C.P. Snow and Pamela Hansford Johnson, as well as to Northrop Frye, Robertson Davies, Margaret Laurence, Ronald Sutherland, William Ready, and Robert Weaver. For her helpful analysis of MacLennan's proposed screen play on Halifax I am indebted to Jane Dick; and for his comments about his ballet *Pillar of Fire* I am grateful to the American choreographer Anthony Tudor. I would also like to thank Fred Matthews for his suggestions and Paul Swarney and Leonard E. Woodbury for their assistance with the Classics.

The business of typing the manuscript was done with remarkable speed and efficiency by Secretarial Services at York University; to Doris Brillinger, Linda Yuffe, and Nadia Muzzatti, my thanks. I appreciate also the help my father D.S.F. Cameron gave with the index. The book design was done with skill and care by Antje Lingner.

No one could have been more helpful in the preparing of the manuscript than my editor Gerald Hallowell; far beyond the ordinary duties of an editor, he read trial portions of it and from then on offered incisive advice in an encouraging way. Others, too, despite their extremely busy lives, gave the time to read the manuscript and make suggestions. Paul Roazen offered advice as a reader from outside the field entirely; Frank Watt and Claude Bissell made some suggestions as readers directly in the mainstream of Canadian literary history; J.L. Granatstein criticized the manuscript as a Canadian historian and made a number of helpful suggestions; finally, my mother, Bertah Cameron, gave advice from the point of view of the common reader. Above all, I am grateful to my husband Paul Lovejoy, who has accepted the presence of Hugh MacLennan into our household and who has on so many occasions found just the right way to help.

E.C. January 1981

Dr Sam MacLennan and
Katie MacQuarrie
about the time they met

Hugh, age eight
the year his family moved
to Halifax

Jean Shaw,
MacLennan's girlfriend
in Halifax

MacLennan at Oriel College
Oxford, 1931

Maritimes singles tennis champion, 1929

In the old Studebaker, summer 1935

MacLennan toasts John Gray at his retirement dinner Toronto, May 1973

Dorothy and Hugh with Gwethalyn Graham at the CAA branch meeting in Montreal, 1946

Anthony Tudor's ballet *Pillar of Fire*, 1946, with Nora Kaye as Hagar (right), the inspiration for *The Precipice*

'Girl on a swing lost in a joy of colors' by Dorothy Duncan, 1956, the painting attributed to Catherine in *The Watch That Ends the Night*

Hugh MacLennan: A Writer's Life

Chapter one

From the Misty Island

Glace Bay, in the middle of the last century, was a primitive place, a stark and lonely outpost at the northeastern edge of Cape Breton Island. On top of the black cliffs overlooking the sea, a single path had gradually become a road along which the coal miners had built their crude wooden cabins, surrounded by long, dry grasses flattened by the winds. As yet, no churches asserted order and sanctity, no schools imposed discipline and human values; there were only a number of rum shops to service the souls and warm the bodies of the eight or nine hundred inhabitants, as damp, enveloping mists rolled in from the sea or stiff Atlantic gales hurled themselves against everything that God or man had created there.

By 1895, when a young man called Samuel MacLennan took up his first job there as a colliery doctor, the town had changed very little. Although there were now good public schools, several churches, and a busy harbour with ships sailing in and out for coal, there was still no hospital, nor would there be for seven years more. To Dr Sam, as people called him, it seemed a barbaric place, and it struck him as forcibly as the cold winds that swept onshore across the flat, tawny fields that he was stuck with 'a ferociously difficult practice among the drinking and squabbling miners.'[1] From time to time, when accidents occurred, he would have to risk his neck descending into the crater-like mines; otherwise his main job, distasteful in the extreme to a teetotaller like himself, would be to patch up the men after their drunken brawls each pay-day. Surely his grandfather Neil MacLennan, who

Katie with Frances, five, and Hugh, eighteen months, Glace Bay had so stoutly set sail in 1832 from Applecross, a misty Scottish village across the water from the Hebridean Isle of Skye, had not pinned his future hopes on such tasks in such a place. The MacLennan clan slogan, *Druim nan deur*, 'The Ridge of Tears,' might well describe the hardships of the old country, but here there ought to have been better fare for the generations to come.

But something in their stern Highland temperament owed little to the environment. Neil's son Duncan, who was Dr Sam's father, had worked his way to straight-laced manhood as a tailor, with dry Conservative politicians and thorny Presbyterian ministers as his closest friends. Marrying late, he and his wife Mary (McPhee) did not produce their longed-for son until Mary was well into her forties. So it was an occasion for whatever celebration the sober Duncan allowed himself when she gave birth to a healthy boy in 1868. Appropriately, he named the belated child 'Samuel' and dedicated him to his own puritanical God.[2] Something of the stern Calvinism in which the old man raised the boy can be glimpsed in the dedication he inscribed on the copy of Thomas Babington Macaulay's *History of England from the Accession of James II* which he gave to his son on his fifteenth birthday: 'With best wishes for his future usefulness.'[3] Useful indeed Sam was to become.

One of the more useful things Dr Sam did, after putting himself through medical school and spending a few years as colliery doctor in Glace Bay, was to marry and settle some distance from the rabble in town in a small house, encircled by a brook, perched atop a grassy knoll a mile or so inland from the coast. Family legend has it that when he first met Katherine MacQuarrie, the local girl he was to marry, the first thing she said was 'Well, Dr MacLennan, I hear you're very brave' – to which he is said to have replied, with a short cough and characteristic brusqueness, 'Oh, nonsense.'[4] It was not long before they were married, on 26 November 1901: within ten months, on 22 September 1902, their first child appeared, Frances Annie Stewart; five years later, on 20 March 1907, their only other child was born, a son named John Hugh.

Dr Sam had chosen for his wife a woman who stood in relation to himself somewhat like a photograph to its negative. In himself, virtue was cast in his family's tradition: abstinence, caution, self-denial, piety, discipline – these were his strengths and they were formidable; his classmates, on his graduation in 1888, had summed him up in the *Dalhousie Gazette* as the one who 'will stay at home – like the good boy.' But in Katie, herself of Highland Scottish blood modified a little by her mother's United Empire Loyalist ancestors, these virtues were turned inside out to their positive form. Whereas Dr Sam turned his energy inward with strict control, Katie, with equal intensity, radiated vitality and warmth outward to those around her: in her, abstinence became a concern for everyone's well-being, caution became a love of fun and society, self-denial was transformed into an attachment to lovely things, piety expressed itself in religious song, and discipline was replaced by sympathetic understanding. Early photographs, sepia like the landscape that formed their daily backdrop, show the two of them in striking contrast: Dr Sam, stiff and serious, his lips pursed, his fair hair neatly brushed, his clothes impeccable; Katie, smiling and dreamy, a dark-haired beauty, wearing the small-waisted, romantic, filmy dresses of the time.

Into the two children, in different proportions, were funnelled the main characteristics of the parents. From the MacLennan side came the clan's temperamental melancholy and the conservative, unbending values of the Presbyterian: the doctrine of work, the exaltation of education, and the principle of self-denial. From the MacQuarrie side came an artistic nature that loved music and story-telling, a sense of down-to-earth fun, and sheer enjoyment of the society of others. Although approached from opposite directions, the main goal, held entirely and reverently in common, was the pursuit of 'civilization.' To Dr Sam this meant, quite simply, the Classics of Greece and Rome. Although he had not excelled in his classical studies as an undergraduate at Dalhousie, he was deeply convinced that a familiarity with ancient literature and history enhanced life immeasurably. Before his marriage, he had spent many a quiet evening at Glace Bay with his cousin Ed Macdonald, 'a very silent person,'[5] translating the Classics with the sense that no matter what the barbarians might be up to in the streets outside, he at least would preserve civilized values in his own home. After his marriage, oblivious to the fact that throughout North America classical education was beginning to give way to the social sciences, he persisted in his private studies. To Katie, 'civilization' meant more generally an acquaintance with the arts – music and literature in particular.

A true inheritor of that temperamental sadness expressed in the ancient clan slogan 'The Ridge of Tears,' Hugh, as he was immediately called, was to write much later: 'Memories, somehow, are always sad.'[6] His first battle was simply to survive the attack of bronchitis that struck him at the age of three weeks, leaving him with a large hollow, mid-chest, which would impede his lung expansion for life. Beyond that, there was the loneliness. Dr Sam, in raising his children outside the town, had wished to protect them not only from the vulgarities of the mining community but from further ill-health as well. On coming home from his patients, he used to string his outer clothing on a line far into the woods behind the house so that no risk of infection would occur. Such isolation was no doubt 'useful,' but it left the two children to devise their play as best they could on their own.

Katie did her best, alone with them so much. She loved to read stories and poems – Stevenson's *A Child's Garden of Verses* especially, and Tennyson's *The Princess* – sections of which she encouraged them to memorize.[7] Like her own mother, with whom they sometimes visited, she also made up stories of her own: dramatic adventure tales in which a girl and boy escaped in boats with fairies or fended off predators in more familiar farmyard surroundings. Everyone who knew her praised her magnificent contralto voice; a favourite for solos in church and at social gatherings, she loved to sing, especially the alto solo from Handel's *Messiah* 'He Was Despised and Rejected,' the 'Twenty-third Psalm' from the Scottish psalter, and folk songs such as the Gaelic *Fhir a Bhata No Ho Eile* (about a woman watching the sea and waiting for her husband to return) and *The Nut Brown Maiden*.[8] She wrote poems as a hobby, a pastime that eventually resulted in a small selection of poetry published in 1956.[9] Throughout these poems her values reverberate: the comforts of home, family loyalty, love of children, reverence for God's created world, thankfulness for the gifts of life, and, as a leavener, a rollicking, hearty sense of humour. Story, song, and fun were her gifts to her small family.

Like his mother, Hugh also began to invent the world according to his own inner reality. An imaginary friend called Bo-Clee-Clee lived in one of the factory smoke-stacks visible from the house. To this friend he attributed his misdemeanours: all the mischief done, the lies told, the accidents that inevitably happened. In one incident his sister recalled, the logic of a small boy's inner world superseded reality: at his grandparents' farm nearby in Glace Bay he planted an egg in the ground, as he explained 'to make more eggs grow.' Like his mother, too, he was venturesome. While Frances was shy and cautious (like her father, she would be the 'good girl' who 'stayed home'), Hugh first struck out at age three when he ran away from home: his life ambition at the time – he intended to become a coal miner – reveals his resentment at being shut away from the wider world he was just beginning to understand.[10]

Although Katie was a strong personality in her own right, there was never any doubt as to who headed the MacLennan household; as Hugh declared much later: 'I am a neurotic, [like] all novelists and artists, because of [my father].'[11] Dr Sam had been brought up in a rigid Victorian style and had not rebelled; on the contrary, once on his own, he had driven himself with even greater determination to become a doctor. Moreover, he now had his eye on becoming a medical specialist so that he could get out of Glace Bay once and for all. His children, he must have decided early on, would also 'toe the line'; they too would work hard and succeed. As Hugh later remarked: 'Calvinism ... was bad with me when I was young.'[12] His 'rebellions' against his father's strictness and perfectionism – the invention of Bo-Clee-Clee, his plans to become a miner – were early signs that all would not be smooth sailing.

By November 1912 Dr Sam had saved enough money from his colliery practice to sponsor further study. As soon as he could, he set off for Edinburgh, Vienna, and Berlin to take courses towards the completion of a specialist's degree in ear, nose, and throat medicine. The following spring, Katie and the children joined him in London. That sea voyage in 1913, when Hugh had just turned six years old, constitutes his earliest coherent recollection.[13] In the cold fog, looking through a latticed window, he saw a garland of flowers fly down past him to hit the water with a splash, and heard the ship's orchestra playing *Nearer, My God, to Thee*; the date was 15 April 1913, the occasion a service commemorating the first anniversary of the sinking of the *Titanic*.

In London, the MacLennans rented a house in Golders Green for a few months, thus affording many opportunities for the exploration of British history from a child's point of view. Dr Sam, perhaps surprisingly for a Scot, was a passionate Anglophile, and wasted no time passing on an unqualified admiration of everything English to his children. Frances began a scrapbook of the royal family; Hugh toured with his mother as many historical points of interest as could be covered during their stay. Something of the vividness with which this London sojourn impressed him as a boy of six can be glimpsed in the fact that fifteen years later, when he returned to London on his way to Oxford in 1928, he could by memory find his way around the area where they had first stayed. While there, he attended a kindergarten from which he emerged, temporarily, with an English accent. The family then travelled north from London, spending August with friends in a canal farmhouse at Bloxwich in the Midlands; having failed after several years to develop a new mine in Glace Bay, the Drabbles had returned to succeed at a similar enterprise in England. After this visit the MacLennans travelled north to Edinburgh, before returning to Nova Scotia in early October.

That fall, despite the fact that he was so anti-American that he had refused to buy what he thought was the best kind of car, a Pontiac, for the simple reason that it was named after an *American* Indian,[14] Dr Sam left for New York to complete his specialist's degree at Columbia University. Leaving the children with their MacQuarrie grandparents, Katie spent the fall with him – her surprise return on Christmas Eve being characteristically dramatic. When Dr Sam completed his degree and returned in January 1914, he moved the family to Sydney, where he intended to set up practice; however, by the end of that year, with the world now at war, he decided instead to settle in Halifax.

This move in September 1915 marked a new stage in the development of Hugh's consciousness. Now eight years old, he was at the ideal age to make of wartime Halifax a heroic world of impressive ships and brave men. The old garrison town had taken on new life in response to Britain's needs. From the top of Citadel Hill, which dominated the setting, ships from all over the world could be seen gliding in and out of the harbour. Men in uniforms jostled up and down the hilly streets, making the most of their free time. Dr Sam had assumed an almost godlike stature in his son's eyes by enlisting in the Royal Canadian Army Medical Corps, shortly after they moved into their first home on Morris Street. Frances was sent to Halifax Ladies' College, where her mother had gone, and Hugh was enrolled in the third grade at Tower Road School. From this date on, the details of his life, especially those relating to ships and armaments for the war, became indelibly imprinted: 'The atmosphere was violently patriotic (British) and Halifax in those days was utterly fascinating. I remember very well the morning the first report came from the Battle of Jutland, with the news that so many British capital ships had been sunk. On a fine Saturday morning, June 1, I was on my bicycle and met another Tower Road School boy called Ashley Robb, who lived on Victoria Road. We both began talking about the battle and agreed that the report was not to be believed. So many ships came and went that I knew the names and dimensions of nearly all of them in the British and German navies. I still remember them ... Troops were repeatedly passing the school on route marches, and the dust they raised puffed out from the columns.'[15]

Not only did he derive this sort of information first-hand, but he was also reinforcing his knowledge by reading. *Fleets of the World 1915*, an official compendium of naval statistics, especially intrigued him, containing as it did a glossary of naval terms, comparative tables of the large-calibre guns of the great fleets of the world, a list of ships lost between 5 August 1914 and 15 April 1915, and illustrations of the major ships currently at sea.[16] As for the Battle of Jutland, he acquired a romantic view of it from the pages of the *Henty Boys* series, whose main character, an American boxer named Kent Templeton, and his friend Cradwick managed to survive the battle in which their boat was destroyed. In the British annuals, *Chums* and *Boys' Own Paper*, he followed the events of the war with a high-pitched, chauvinistic enthusiasm, seeing it as an ideal arena for heroic action. These serials, which he got to read each Christmas only after they had been briskly appropriated by Dr Sam 'to make sure they were keeping up the standard,' reinforced the idealization of England already instilled by his father. In an essay he wrote many years later, he recalled that the heroes of these journals 'troop through my memory like the blond gods of an Olympus where everyone spoke with perfect grammar and knew enough private slang to fill a dictionary. Clean of mind and body, unconscious that "the opposite sex" even existed, they threw all of themselves into "the life of the school." And when school was over, what did they do? Some went to Oxford where they won the boat race. A few (failures I gather) set a new tone in Dawson City.'[17]

Other books read by the hero-dazed boy eventually included Robert Louis Stevenson's *Kidnapped* and *Treasure Island*, Sir Walter Scott's *Ivanhoe*, the Greek and Latin Classics adapted for children, Sir Charles G.D. Roberts' many collections of animal stories, and, for humour, Joel Harris' *Tales of Uncle Remus* and Jonathan Swift's *Gulliver's Travels* – also, and as a matter of course, the Bible. MacLennan's tastes in books as a child must be regarded as important, for in his own opinion the world of fiction he encountered as a child was 'almost more valuable than school.' 'The books we read when we are young,' he wrote in later years, 'are the most important books we will ever read ... If I had not read books when I was young I would never have written any when I was older.'[18]

The curriculum at Tower Road School during the war remained largely unchanged from the beginning of the century: physical exercise and military drill, vocal music, hygiene and temperance, moral and patriotic duties (including 'good manners'), nature study, spelling and dictation, reading and elocution, English, writing, drawing, arithmetic, geography and history, and manual training (optional). So that the older students could take advantage of Halifax's new-found importance, classes in the 'Present War' and 'Canadian History' had been added.[19]

Heroes in books and convoys from a distance cruising in and out of harbour were wonderfully exciting, but to be directly touched by the war was quite another matter. So Hugh found out on Christmas Eve of their first year in Halifax, when his father was called out by the skirl of the pipes playing *The Blue Bonnets* to serve overseas with the Dalhousie Medical Unit.[20] This occasion, as recollected in 'Christmas without Dickens' (1952), came to stand for the first 'break in the normal pattern' as his romantic fantasies of heroism began to be eroded by reality. Now given proof positive that life might indeed be, as his Scottish ancestors had summed it up, 'The Ridge of Tears,' his memory of that evening was profoundly sad: escaping the evening's events through his imagination, he sat in a corner, day-dreaming that he was witnessing the Nativity itself:

> The hills on which the shepherds watched their flocks were the hills about Halifax. The Star was the bright Dog Star that had blazed in the sky the night before the fog came in, and the Child was every child that had ever been born. God knows about it, I thought, and I felt sorry for Him because He did know, for that meant He knew how frightened people were and all about the war and the submarines under the water with the sailors in them pretending to be merry for the sake of Christmas while an officer squinted through the periscope to see if there were any ships on the horizon he might stalk and sink. I thought of the three kings walking very slowly beside their camels because they wanted to be kind to their beasts on a day like this, and finally of the Child in the manger feeling comfortable in spite of Herod and all the frightful things that were going to happen to Him when He grew up. A feeling of relief, the kind of pure happiness that arises only out of loneliness or despair, entered the house like a presence. That night I went to bed sure that somehow everything was going to turn out all right.[21]

To Hugh, his father's disappearance to serve overseas as a doctor in Shorncliff Hospital, a Canadian medical unit in Folkestone on the south coast of England, meant insecurity and fear. Daily, other boys at school were hearing that their fathers had been killed in the war. He must have imagined the worst.

When his father returned shortly before the next Christmas, invalided home because of an infection of the right arm he had contracted through a slit in one of his operating gloves, Hugh was ecstatic. Katie had rented a house in Halifax, sight unseen, so they could all move from Cape Breton, where they had been staying with her parents. But joy at the soldier's return was soon to be qualified. Five minutes after the reunited family walked into their new house, it blew up. Dr Sam, in an attempt to look into the source of what smelled like a gas leak, had descended the basement stairs with a lighted match; the resulting explosion smashed half the windows along the block, and the tremor, like that of an earthquake, was heard a mile away. 'When my father was able to talk,' MacLennan recalled in 'An Orange from Portugal' (1947), 'which he couldn't do for several days because the skin had been burned off his hands and face, he denied the story about the match ... This denial should have precipitated my ... plunge toward neurosis, for I had distinctly seen him with the match in his hand, going down to the basement to look for the gas and complaining about how careless people were.' This dramatic event settled Dr Sam's reputation in Halifax once and for all. As a former medical colleague put it: 'The public at large knew him as the doctor who went searching for a gas leak in the basement of his home with a lighted candle ... Out of this evolved an idea that he was either impractical or lacked ordinary good judgement.'[22] There is no evidence that this widely held view interfered with his practice, as he and his family feared it might; on the contrary, it probably added a human dimension to the man who was so severe that a good many of his relations recall being 'terrified' of him. From MacLennan's point of view, the extraordinary event was traumatic: it shook his father off whatever pedestal of 'war heroics' he had conjured up during the year's absence, for the home and security he was eagerly anticipating had been inexplicably destroyed by the very person he should most trust.

The family retreated in shock to the Sterling Hotel on Barrington Street where they waited out the winter months before moving in the spring of 1917 into the house at 197 South Park Street which MacLennan would consider his real 'home' for the next decade. Situated near the base of Citadel Hill, just opposite the town's beautiful public gardens, this charming house (later renumbered 1583-5) was typical of the domestic architecture in Halifax during the late 1880s: mid- to late Victorian in style, two-storey, it had a mansard roof with an ell at the back and dormer windows with pedimented roofs and scroll brackets at the base of the window architraves. To this large and substantial house, Dr Sam soon added his 'surgery' on the north side. His reasoning, as MacLennan remembered it in 'My Surgeon Father' (1959), ran along the lines that having his surgery at home would enable him to relax between patients; but, like all Presbyterians, Dr Sam was not schooled in taking time off: 'his idea of relaxation between patients seemed to me a very peculiar one. He used to rush from his surgery, seat himself at a desk, and with a huge lexicon beside him he would grimly translate pages of Latin and Greek classics.' It is more likely that having his surgery at home enabled Dr Sam to keep an eye on domestic arrangements. As he got his practice under way, life fell into a predictable round of events. With a maid from Newfoundland called Sadie Giles to help with the chores, and Hugh and Frances at school, a more or less 'normal' routine began.

As a Presbyterian, of course, Dr Sam was 'a formidable keeper of the Sabbath.' 'In my childhood,' MacLennan recalled, 'I had a Jewish friend who looked at [our] household with awe.'[23] Twice each Sunday the family attended St Matthew's Presbyterian Church on Barrington Street. This church featured a rose window copied from Chartres, a high pulpit typical of early Scottish churches, the 'Old Kirk Fiddle' used before the installation of an organ, and a special pew for the lieutenant-governor (later to be covered with a portion of the blue carpet from Westminster Abbey used at the coronation of Queen Elizabeth II). The MacLennans' pew was number 47, in the third row from the back. Katie, of course, sang in the choir. To give Hugh his musical training, she arranged for piano lessons with the church organist, Allen McKenzie Reid. Though he had a good ear for music, and could read fairly well, he did not like to perform: 'I hated it and couldn't do it, and I've never liked doing anything if I couldn't do it well.'[24] Both children attended the Sunday School which preceded church. The combination of this school, the Presbyterian sermons, Katie's prominence in the choir, and their own informal gatherings for religious song at home meant that Hugh was thoroughly indoctrinated with Christian principles in general and Calvinist doctrines in particular. Despite his strong Calvinist beliefs, Dr Sam was on the visiting staff of the local Roman Catholic hospital, the Halifax Infirmary; according to one distinguished patient, it was generally believed that 'his motive in working there was not – as he claimed – to secure the help of better nursing, but to convert the nuns to the Presbyterian Church.'[25] The Army Hospital at Camp Hill was just being completed when the MacLennans settled into their new house and Dr Sam, still a major in the medical corps, was on the appointed staff. He was in the operating room, just about to anaesthetize a patient for surgery, when a great explosion shook the entire town.

Tower Road School opened at 9:30 a.m.; only nine schools in Halifax opened at 9:00. For this reason, when the *Imo* and the *Mont Blanc* collided at 9:06 a.m. on 6 December 1917, causing the greatest man-made explosion in human history before the atomic bomb, Hugh was in the bathroom of his home on South Park Street washing his knees. His mother had caught him as he left for school and considered that in the short pants that were regulation dress his knees were simply too dirty. To MacLennan, who must have been instantly reminded of the explosion only a year before in which his father had levelled their house, the experience was terrifying. Katie and Sadie, the maid, grabbed him and disappeared into the basement, where they fell to their knees and prayed for salvation. Frances, safely arrived at the Halifax Ladies' College, joined the rest of the girls on the floor under furniture. Dr Sam and his staff whisked their patient off the operating table and onto the floor and took shelter themselves. No one had the least idea what could have happened.

The magnitude of the disaster gradually became clear. For Dr Sam it meant an astounding test of his stamina and medical skill as the Camp Hill Hospital was soon flooded with victims from all quarters; 1200 wounded were admitted that day.[26] As an eye specialist, he was in particular called upon to deal with the vast numbers of eye wounds and extractions that resulted when windows all over the city shattered in the blast; with buckets that filled up with eyeballs beside the operating table, he himself dealt with hundreds of eye and facial wounds.

When the final reckoning was made, nearly 2000 people had been killed, 9000 injured, and over 200 survivors were completely blind. Thousands of homes, factories, and offices had been laid flat, and many of the remaining buildings caught fire. Part of the *Mont Blanc*'s heavy iron anchor, weighing half a ton, had flown through the air two miles before landing.

As for Hugh, he roamed the streets, in much the same way as Roddie Wain was to do in *Barometer Rising*. What he saw there finished once and for all any idea that war was fun. Carts carrying victims to hospitals and homes turned recovery stations, people in terror and agony, a boy his own age dragging himself to the side of the road to bleed into a gutter – such images turned the war from a heroic adventure into a sickening reality. The explosion, combined with the stories his father had brought back of the waste of life and the sheer brutality of the war overseas, made the sensitive boy a pacifist. 'For years,' he later confessed, 'the very name of [Field-Marshal] Haig has made me almost physically ill, and now ... it seems to me far more important to discover how such a man could act like that than to orbit a hunk of metal around the sun. In their own way, those first war generals have always seemed to me more frightening than Hitler, who at least was mad.'[27]

Only two months later, after Tower Road School had resumed operations, accommodating classes from three other schools either devastated by the explosion or designated as emergency hospitals, another explosion threatened: 'A false alarm in February, 1918, a bitterly cold day, brought some empty ash sleighs to the school and we were driven off and told to set down behind a hill on the golf links. We were told that an ammunition ship called the Picton was on fire at dock in the New Ocean Terminal, very close to the school. Or that there was a fire in the shed itself, which was filled with shells.'[28] Although no blast occurred, the experience further jolted Hugh into the realization that his world was profoundly threatened.

Perhaps it was the traumatic nature of these events, perhaps it was simply a boyhood fancy, that led him to take an odd decision the following summer. He literally moved out of his home at the age of twelve and slept in a tent in the back yard, summer and winter, until he graduated from university and left for Oxford in 1928 at the age of twenty-one.[29] It all began naturally enough as a result of attending his first summer camp with the Young Men's Christian Association. This camp emphasized the toughness and self-reliance that such camps often uphold; his training there was, moreover, a confirmation of his father's notion that he must soon begin growing up. His letters home suggest that he thoroughly enjoyed the strenuous athletics, and had sufficiently taken to heart his father's parsimony to confess that rather than spend money on the bus fare to New Glasgow on his day off he had asked a friend to buy him twenty cents' worth of items he needed in town.[30] The camp featured tents, and when he returned home after a month he and his father got out the old fishing tent from the basement and pitched it in the backyard. His Spartan father approved of the whole idea, thinking it would toughen him up, and made no objection when Hugh decided to continue sleeping there past Labour Day. The onset of winter forced special provisions against the cold, but still he showed no desire to have the comfort of his bed indoors. His mother urged him to come inside, but from then on, except for rare nights when he was sick, the tent became a way of life. Sadie, quite sensibly, refused to go out in the cold to wake him up, so a ship's bell was installed, strung by a cord through the kitchen window, and every morning not only Hugh but neighbours for some distance in every direction woke to its clanging at seven. Dressed in a special red beret which some friends had brought him from South America, a skating sweater upside down so his legs could go in the arms, several layers of clothing on the upper body, and long socks, he ate cornflakes and milk before retiring and took with him hot potatoes or irons in bags to keep himself warm. To deal with the ice that formed on his chin as his breath froze during the night, he took along a strip of sheet which he tucked around his neck and shifted sideways whenever he woke. According to Frances 'he felt independent out there.' As far as MacLennan can remember, it was a wonderful experience, especially in the summer, reading by the light of the one candle he kept on a table beside him. Something like Milton's *Il Penseroso*, which later became one of his favourite poems, he loved the melancholy solitude in which to contemplate the Classics.[31]

Whether to prove he was tough and thereby win his father's approval, whether to enjoy the solitude itself, or whether to get out from under a mother who was too solicitous and a father who was too arbitrary, MacLennan's tent-sleeping over such a long period was a remarkable thing. Had he simply wished to escape, there was reason enough. His father had accelerated his interest in his children's education. Since education for him meant studying the Classics in the original Greek and Latin, he had unilaterally decided that both Frances and Hugh would study this subject at university. In the meantime he sent off to Eton College in England for their Greek and Latin texts, plus the teacher's 'key.' Both children were subjected to such long evenings' work over these books that each in turn rebelled. MacLennan's later recollections of these sessions concentrated not on himself but on his sister, for whom he felt great pity: 'Father treated Frances without wisdom. She was more sensitive than I. He tried to make her a scholar; I think he drove her far too hard. He wouldn't let her do a lot of things she would have done spontaneously. What she wanted to do was take Honours in English and French; he insisted that she take Greek, which she hated. She would cry when doing her lessons and he would come in and help her. I think for a time he was quite hard on me too.'[32] As Frances remembered it, she was 'tense and nervous and tired' from so much studying: initially they 'used to rave against their father,' a tactic that met with no success; later their mother admitted to her that she should have stepped in to protect them – especially Frances, who actively disliked the Classics, whereas Hugh eventually enjoyed them. Other relatives agreed unanimously that Katie would have been too afraid to interfere with Dr Sam's plans and methods, obsessive as they were. As many people who knew him agreed, he would not for a moment entertain an opinion contrary to his own, and was often rude and unmannerly to those who offered one. MacLennan's lifelong tendency to be angry when his point of view was either ignored or misunderstood – 'the feeling of total frustration which comes when you have tried to be clear and discover that you might as well have been talking another language,'[33] as he put it in later life – may have its roots in his father's dogmatic stance.

And yet Dr Sam had his warm and playful side. One of Hugh's cousins, who came to stay there for a year while at school, recalled that when Katie took her first bath in the splendid new 'Silent Filler' tub they had bought, Dr Sam stripped down, jumped in, and 'roughed her up.' Impulsively, he gave to this cousin a whole shelf of his books (Sir Walter Scott, Carlyle, Thackeray) for repairing an ear irrigation pump. With impish humour he also arranged to take the same train on which Katie's sister Flora and her husband had set off on their honeymoon to Niagara Falls; when the couple arrived conspicuously late for breakfast, Dr Sam was there, grinning, waiting for them.[34] And to the working men who could not afford his fees, he often kindly extended his services free of charge or for greatly reduced payment. Both Frances and Hugh recalled that he could, when the mood took him, be warmly affectionate to them. But on the subject of Latin and Greek he would brook no complaint. As a Halifax doctor, a contemporary of Hugh's and junior colleague to his father, put it: 'he was one of those parents who seeks to have a clever son do the thing he would have tried to do himself had he been given the opportunity. He designed Hugh as a classical scholar. Such parents do not "give in" easily, and I can well imagine that Hugh's youth was not a "rose garden."'[35]

By the fall of 1921 Frances had lost her battle to study English and French. She was enrolled at Dalhousie University in Honours Latin and Greek. Her handwriting on the registration slips for the three years she was there is hesitant and unsure. A better student than her father had been, she earned all first and second class marks in her first two years. In third year, weary of studying so hard towards a goal she wanted no part of, never having been out to mixed parties like other girls her age, she came down with tuberculosis and had to drop out of Dalhousie. With extra work at home on her own, she eventually took special examinations and graduated in 1928 with distinction. Meanwhile, she was off to Calidor, a private sanitarium near Gravenhurst, Ontario, for four long years. According to her brother, 'Frances felt she could never win father's approval. His driving her so hard was one of the reasons she cracked up. The tuberculosis was caused by psycho-somatic reasons.'[36]

As for Hugh, who by 1922 was in the eleventh grade at age fifteen, Dr Sam had decided that he would not only study Honours Latin and Greek at Dalhousie but, on graduating, he would also become a Rhodes scholar. Grooming for this meant a great deal of hard work and private tuition at home. Fellow students remember that Hugh often could not come out to join them, for he was too busy translating the Classics.[37] Fortunately, he reacted to this regime much better than Frances had. He actually liked the Homeric adventures and myths he was called upon to memorize. In fact, one of his favourite books in his teens was the *Classical Dictionary*, 'an old volume with a black cover published in New York around 1870 by a Dr. Smith [Sir William Smith] who looked exactly like the Smith Bros. of the cough drops.'[38] On some occasions at least he preferred to read: his sister recalled, for example, that when he visited the home of Dr Clarence Mackinnon, to see his friend Gordon, he would often seek out the doctor's library and spend hours there reading while the other boys played outside.

On the other hand, MacLennan followed another of his father's ambitions for him, sports, which did get him out into the open air. At twelve he began to learn how to play tennis at the Waegwoltic Club, where Dr Sam kept a small row-boat (he considered canoes unsafe). He apparently applied himself to mastering tennis with exactly the same kind of persistence he had been applying to a mastery of the Classics.[39] Practising specific shots hundreds of times while other boys were satisfied they had learned enough after half an hour or so, he gradually developed into a formidable player, despite the fact that his lung capacity was inhibited by the cavity in his chest. He was, above all, determined to win. In athletics in general, for which he had a natural ability, and in tennis in particular, he discovered that he could win both games and his father's approval by means that also provided a physical release from tensions. In fact, as he later realized, he could act out on the tennis court all his pent-up anger against his father for working him so hard and expecting so much of him: '[The tennis player] doesn't merely hit [the ball]. He pounds it, he smashes it, volleys it, slices it, chops it; he also flubs it and curses himself for having done so, and in the process he becomes thoroughly exhausted. After such a concentrated fury of released aggression against an inanimate object, who is there left in the world he wants to hit even if he has the strength for it?' In 'Confessions of a Wood-chopping Man'

(1956), he revealed the same pattern of releasing aggression through physical 'acting out' – in this case, chopping down trees – wryly linking his actions to his hostility towards his father: 'Perhaps the psychiatrist who lives below me on his own tree-enclosed acreage, hearing the crash of my falling oak, thinks I am ridding myself of aggressions, too. He may even think I am slaying a father-image.' At the age of fifty he looked back and remarked: 'One of the best things in my fifty years of life has been the game of tennis, chiefly because on the tennis court experience atones for a lot of lost youth.' Tennis also provided him with an outlet for the sexual frustrations of adolescence. In 'The Pleasures of Tennis' (1968), he brought to conscious theory what, as a teenager, could only have been unconscious instinct: 'After a five-set match even Claudia Cardinale is just another object, and couldn't compete with a cold beer. A tennis player may be a lusty man, and a lusty man may be a good tennis player, but you can't be serious about both things at the same time or even in the same tournament week.'[40]

MacLennan had grown into a handsome young man. Just under six feet in height, weighing about 165 pounds, he dressed neatly in expensive clothes and kept his dark hair clipped short. Always more like his mother's side of the family, he combined her lively good looks with a certain set of the head that recalled his father's sterner authority. It was not surprising that girls should be attracted to him, and they were. One girl in particular became his favourite from his mid-teens in high school. Jean Shaw was a tall, dark, vivacious girl who, like Katie, had a remarkable gift for dramatizing and music; eventually she was to become assistant director of the Dalhousie University Orchestra, in which, when she was not directing, she played first violin. According to one contemporary, 'Hugh had an extraordinary notion of Jean Shaw'[41] – he idolized her. This view is borne out by the appraisal he contributed to the *Dalhousie Gazette* in 1927 beneath her graduating picture, in which he lavishly compared her to Aphrodite:

Jean Alexandra Shaw

'Wit and grace, and love and beauty,
In an constellation shine.'

A description of Jean is a gilding of refined gold. She is the laughter-loving Aphrodite of her class but her laughter does not keep her from serious thinking. In manner charming, in conversation at once witty and wise, and in character wonderfully sympathetic, she is justly popular. She is vice-president of the Glee Club, sings, and plays both violin and piano with equal excellence.

With the benefit of hindsight and an acquaintance with Jung, he later claimed that she was 'for a very young man [in love] ... an anima for seven years.'[42] His idealization of Jean Shaw found expression in romantic poetry, a strong taste he had picked up from his mother. Not only did he quote to her long passages from Shelley, Byron, and Keats, but he also made up his own verses, which were often taken by those who heard them as being lines from the English Romantics themselves.

He was not the first, nor will he be the last, young man to express his love in romantic verses. But his imagination was always vivid. Looking back on this stage of his life more than a half-century later, he cast himself in the role of St Paul on the road to Damascus, struck by the mystic revelation that he would become a writer:

> [My commitment to writing] began in the form of what Lewis Mumford called an 'apparition.' I was sixteen years old; it was a night of wind and tumbling clouds about a full moon and a lonely shore outside Halifax. And suddenly the whole world I lived in seemed like a moving and visible fragment of millions of other worlds, and a whole multitude of unknown worlds inside of myself ... I always sensed without knowing it, what scientists have proved only recently, that all of us have a genetic inheritance formed hundreds of thousands of years ago, an 'instinct bank,' combined with another mysterious agent, discovered only last year, which Freud called 'memory traces on the subconscious.' You don't know what they are, but they are *there* ... Some poets and writers and artists, usually without knowing it, seem to be in tune with the few scattered fragments of this unknown past, and I think in some of them, strange fish are exploded to the surface from this abyss ... [From this 'apparition' I felt] a sense of vocation ... to understand it, to understand where I was, the search for identity was really what you'd say today.[43]

Although MacLennan, in these comments in 1971, shamelessly mixed together fashionable references to Freud, Jung, and the New Biology, and then played off his Celtic self-dramatization against the sure knowledge of what his career had become, there is every reason to believe that he was given to such visions and vague imaginings as an adolescent. The world of the imagination, stimulated by literature and fed by his own sensitivity, was more engaging than the world outside.

In 1924, when he graduated from the Halifax County Academy with a University Entrance Scholarship and the Yeoman Prize in Latin and Greek, his father took him aside and said: 'You are the fifth generation [on your mother's side]. You have a chance to belong to civilization and now you must work.'[44] By the phrase 'belonging to civilization' Dr Sam, of course, had three very specific things in mind: studying the Greek and Latin Classics, winning a Rhodes Scholarship, and completing his classical study in England.

When he entered Dalhousie University in Honours Latin and Greek that fall, he had an enormous task before him: not only must he fulfil his father's ambitions – ambitions for which he fortunately had at least some taste – but he must somehow reconcile this pursuit of the Classics with his inner vocation to become an artist. For the time being his course of study and sports took precedence over the artistic instincts he had inherited from his mother. Applying himself with almost superhuman concentration, he excelled at university. Rumour had it that even when he was not feeling well his father insisted he attend his classes.[45] From the fact that he set off quite opposite reactions in two of his teachers there, it can be deduced that he had already become a definite personality. His Classics tutor, who had earlier trained him at the Halifax County Academy, was J.W. 'Lucky' Logan, an older, thoroughly 'Victorian,' ex-army officer, who in many ways combined the enthusiastic good humour of Katie with the high standards of Dr Sam. With him MacLennan enjoyed a full and profitable relationship; in his later tribute to this favourite teacher, he praised the qualities he was being raised to exemplify: solid scholarship, concern for other people, love of life, athletic pursuits (Logan was the rugger coach), and a passion for the Classics.[46] At the same time, he had more than his share of run-ins with the head of the Classics Department, Professor Howard Murray,[47] who found him too 'inquiring,' and bullied him as a result.

In his Latin and Greek courses, MacLennan received nothing but first class marks, right through until his graduation in 1928. He did moderately well in English, which he studied under Archibald MacMechan, and in mathematics and history; his marks in physics and philosophy were undistinguished. His performance in Classics, however, won him the Studley Club Prize in his first year and the Khaki University Scholarship in the next. Dr Sam's vigilance had paid off. Controlling his son's destiny even to the point of deflecting other scholarships and awards to more needy students, which he was able to do by serving on a number of university boards,[48] he was saving Hugh for the final glory of the Rhodes. In 1928, at graduation, it must have looked as though the plum was well within his grasp. The summer before, as a member of the Dalhousie tennis team, Hugh had won the men's doubles championship, first of Halifax County and then of Nova Scotia; he had excelled in basketball and rugger. He had been a member of the student's council and president of his class. Now, in his graduation year, he took the Governor-General's Gold Medal for Classics.

It was a severe blow when the Rhodes Scholarship for Nova Scotia was awarded to Ralph C.C. Henson, an outstanding student taking three majors at Dalhousie, economics, philosophy, and education (later he would have a successful business career in Toronto and Regina, mainly with the stockbroking firm, Wood Gundy, Limited). But all was not lost. In special circumstances – if an award holder died or a provincial scholarship was not taken up – a scholarship could be awarded in a national competition.

Returning home one wintry day, MacLennan saw a telegram on the polished table in the dark, wood-panelled hall. He snatched it up avidly and devoured its contents: 'CONGRATULATIONS. RHODES SCHOLARSHIP FOR CANADA-AT-LARGE AWARDED TO JOHN HUGH MACLENNAN.' Filled with relief after the certainty he had lost all chance of fulfilling his father's determined hopes, he sensed he was not alone. There, in the doorway to the front room, stood Dr Sam, looking not at all pleased. 'Go and shovel the walk, Hugh; it badly needs it,' he said dryly, and with his short cough turned and disappeared into the inner darkness.[49]

In a front-page report of Hugh's success, the *Dalhousie Gazette* on 20 January 1928 proudly announced: 'Mr. MacLennan will go into residence at Oxford next fall; a brilliant career is predicted for him.'

Chapter two

The Voyage Out: Oxford and the Continent

On 17 September 1928 the *S.S. Devonian* set sail for Liverpool, numbering among her passengers Hugh MacLennan and his mother Katie, both spellbound by the apparently limitless range of possibilities the future promised. The day before the ship left Halifax, Dr Sam had offered his twenty-one-year-old son some characteristically brief advice. 'According to him,' Hugh later recalled, 'Money, Women, and Liquor were the three problems of every man who ever lived, nor were they (according to him) insoluble. With the first I was to be thrifty; the other two I was entirely to avoid.'[1] Armed thus with Presbyterian ethics against life's tidal waves of troubles, the young man turned his attention to the immediate question of his life's work. At this point he was passionately committed to classical scholarship. Now, he thought, all those hours spent with Dadden, mastering the basics of Latin and Greek, will help to open the doors of civilization itself. The opportunity to attend Oxford, and from there to travel to the Continent and explore the countries that had founded Western culture, would be the culmination of everything he had been brought up to value. Almost as if he were his father's emissary, MacLennan went up to Oxford to fulfil the ambitions he had by now adopted as his own.

Although his studies and his future as a scholar were uppermost in his mind, he had not abandoned all thoughts of writing. The romantic and creative Katie continued to encourage his efforts at poetry, and shared with him her own strong emotional reactions to the seascapes

On the Acropolis, Athens, March 1931

and landscapes they saw as they travelled. As MacLennan recalled in the early 1960s, in 'On Living in a Cold Country,' he also met on board ship an older writer with whom he passed many hours in conversation. Although this man never became famous, and MacLennan soon forgot his name, his influence was important, for he was the first Freudian he had ever met. After hearing a description of the young man's life so far, he forecast that his father's puritanical mores, his sleeping in a tent in such a cold climate, as well as his personality as displayed in their conversation, added up to sleepless nights ahead and the sweet torture of creative writing. He told MacLennan that he had an Oedipus complex, thus drawing attention to the psychological phenomenon that would lie at the centre of his later work. This trip marked his initiation into adulthood, a voyage into the wider world that was to become his stage.

Disembarking at Liverpool and taking the train to London on 26 September, MacLennan and his mother settled comfortably into their hotel at 24 Craven Hill Gardens in Bayswater.[2] The following day began a fortnight's sightseeing and preparation of the young man for Oxford: a suit must be tailored at Harry Hall's; 'flat silver and oddments' acquired at the 'Thieves Market' (the Caledonian Market); china purchased for use in his room; a trunk bought to hold his belongings. With formidable energy the two of them explored London, MacLennan stubbornly refusing to use the guide-book his mother had purchased. In fact, Katie allowed her son to feel like a man on their excursions. 'I let him take the lead in everything,' she wrote home to 'My dearest Sam,' 'paying the way and even when I know he is taking the wrong turn I still let him find his own mistakes. He plans out nice economical lunches and teas. You'd be surprised.' It was almost as if she were the girl and he the adult. 'We have been having a wonderful time,' Hugh wrote home to Frances. 'Mother is as sprightly as a young kitten. The trip is doing her a tremendous amount of good.'[3] In the daytime they went to St Paul's Cathedral; by bus to Golders Green, where Hugh knew his way around from recalling his visit at the age of six; to St Martin-in-the-Fields in time to see a wedding; to the National Gallery, where both admired especially Honthorst's *Christ before Pilate*; to Westminster Abbey, the Zoo, the Tower, Gamages, No. 10 Downing Street; to Foyle's Bookstore to send off a Greek grammar to Dr Sam; Chancery Lane, the Victoria and Albert Museum, the Embankment at Chelsea, Carlyle's house in Cheyne Walk, Windsor Castle, and Hampton Court. By night they attended plays and concerts: *Bird in Hand*, a light comedy by John Drinkwater; *Such Men Are*

Dangerous, featuring Matheson Lang; a promenade concert; and a piano recital in Queen's Hall by the Polish pianist and composer Paderewski. Despite the hurly-burly of these activities, they both found time to record their impressions and write home often. Katie's diary shows unflagging high spirits and excitement at most of what she saw, mixed with the occasional critical comment about the expense of shopping and the odd habits of the English, including their incessant smoking and early morning tea. Hugh's letters reveal a young man dazzled by a world decidedly the best of all possible worlds, a full-hearted enthusiasm for the traditions of history and literature, so tangible here in sharp contrast to their absence at home.

While in London, MacLennan went to see Sir St Clair Thompson, his father's former chief surgeon, in order to have his left ear examined. At fifteen his father had drained an infected ear, and there seemed to be a small perforation in the eardrum as a result. Dr Thompson reported, both to MacLennan and to his father, that a small opening did indeed exist, but it was probably the result of natural causes. Although the doctor pronounced his hearing sound and equal in both ears, he warned that the left ear would be vulnerable to infections, and precautions must be taken never to get it wet.[4]

On his way to Oxford at last on 10 October, Hugh waved goodbye to his mother, 'very keen to get on with his new life and his new work.' 'We cannot be thankful enough,' Katie recorded in her diary, 'for such a good boy, kind and upright.' Sad as her son was happy, and for the same reasons, Katie spent another week in London, where everything seemed to remind her that he was gone. Even at Temple Church on Sunday, four days later, the organist played Chopin's funeral march, one of his favourite pieces. 'The organist's interpretation was a bit different to Hugh's,' she noted, adding with some pride: 'but nonetheless, Hugh had made no mistakes in time or notation.' A three-day trip to visit their old family friends the Drabbles near Birmingham helped to cheer her, and then a two-day visit to Hugh at Oxford put her mind at rest about her son's general well-being. She found his rooms under the bell-tower in the first quad at Oriel College 'wretchedly small.' 'You reach it from a staircase via a little ladder placed flat against the stone wall,' she reported in one letter home, 'open a door, and there you are. There is a study and tiny bedroom, and in the study a fireplace about as big as a vegetable dish that you'd put on the table at dinner time.' From the window of her room at the Mitre, Hugh pointed out some of the landmarks of Oxford; then they toured the university town together. Noting in her diary that her son was 'second to none' among the boys she met there, Katie departed for London, and then for Nova Scotia aboard the *Regina* in the company of Dr and Mrs Clarence Mackinnon, fellow Haligonians and parents of Hugh's childhood friend Gordon.

Nothing anticipates disillusionment more certainly than idealization. Though he dealt with the situation courageously and patiently, MacLennan did not find life at Oxford quite as he had imagined it would be. He moved into his 'digs' which he shared with Robert Lasch (later editor of the *St Louis Post-Dispatch* and winner of a Pulitzer prize for journalism), an American Rhodes scholar reading Modern Greats (philosophy, politics, and economics). He donned the truncated, waist-long black gown that set the 'commoners' off from the scholars, exhibitioners, and dons, whose choir-like black gowns were knee-length. Then he faced the hard facts about his courses.

MacLennan had enrolled in Honour Moderations and Literae Humaniores (Greats), considered in those days to be the most difficult course of study at Oxford and the toughest of its kind in the world. Honour Mods., in which a student was awarded a class grade (first to fourth), was entirely classical and intended as preparation for Greats; the latter resulted in a degree and involved the study of ancient history, philosophy from Plato to Alfred North Whitehead, and more classical work based on a number of Plato's dialogues including the *Republic* and Aristotle's *Ethics* and *Politics* – all read in the original Greek. As MacLennan soon discovered: 'We were supposed to write prose as good as Demosthenes and Plato (if they had an off day) and as Cicero and Seneca likewise. One paper (translation only) was based on all 48 books of Homer and more than half a dozen major Greek orations. Another was based on the entirety of Virgil and about 20 orations of Cicero ... Papers also on Greek Tragedy (Aeschylus, Sophocles and Euripides) and on Aristophanes, required not only a knowledge but an actual recollection of the textual criticism with any suggestions of one's own that might be appropriate. Also papers of a similar kind on Catullus and Propertius, Horace and Juvenal, Plautus and Terence and a General paper.'[5]

He had been in Oxford only a week when he wrote home in despair to warn his father that any expectation he would do as well at Oxford as he had at Dalhousie must be scaled down. In mid-October he sat his first college examination, one of the 'Collections' held at the beginning or end (or both) of each term to test the work recently completed with individual tutors; after getting back the results, which, being seconds, placed him just about the middle of his group, he wrote again: 'I may as well say now, that at present I am hardly up to some of the scholars. I have read as much as most of them and more out of the way reading perhaps, but these fellows have been trained for Oxford work by Oxford men for about 12 years and therefore they have necessarily a big advantage over anyone from overseas. As a product of cultured humanity, however, I count myself a bit ahead of most of them for these chaps – they run between 18 years of age and 20 – know practically nothing else ... The Mods exams are a good way off still, but I may as well say here and now that if I get a second in Mods I shall be satisfied.' Two weeks later he reiterated this warning to his father, adding: 'If you had not set me going I would be completely swamped.' In pages and pages home he recorded the daily progress of the staggering workload that was expected of him. Much later he recalled: 'The Old Man ... was not a scholar; he was a student. He completely under-rated the difficulty of handling a field like [Classics] in Oxford ... I never worked so hard in my life ... I couldn't face this ... Those Englishmen could do one of those prose compositions in 2-3 hours; it took me 2½ *days*, and then they'd be bad.' As a result of the shock of having to adapt to pushing himself to the very limits of endurance in his academic work, for marks that would still be unsatisfactory to his father, he 'almost had a nervous breakdown in that first term.'[6]

Nothing captures MacLennan's feelings during this period so vividly as the painting at the National Gallery that had so struck him two days after his arrival in London – *Christ before Pilate* (later renamed *Christ before the High Priest*) by Gerrit van Honthorst. In it, Pilate and Christ face each other across a table on which lies an open book. Though Pilate is seated while Jesus stands, authority informs the former, whose admonishing finger gestures as he interrogates the quiet, passive prisoner with bound hands before him. Two civil servants, arms crossed, and a handful of soldiers, look on indifferently; there is no one to turn to for help. MacLennan's identification with the helpless Christ, called to account for himself before Pilate's judgement, must have been instant; his feelings of paralysis in the face of a powerful authority, especially in regard to open books, could not have been otherwise.

Although eventually he came to be close friends with his Mods. tutor, Ernest Ely Genner, his first impressions were not good. Like MacLennan's father, Genner was a puritanical teetotaller, and he had incredibly high standards for the boys working under him. 'Genner is not a particularly lovable man,' he wrote home; 'Like so many other very devout people his standards are so high that there is not much of the milk of human kindness evident on the surface ... He has made all knowledge for his province if anyone has, and in his bowed and wrinkled old head above his dried up little body, there is stored up a tremendous amount of stuff ... [He] gave us two most frightful pieces which I know would absolutely floor Howard Murray and Nicolls [his former professors at Dalhousie].' Genner, in short, was an intensified version of Dr Sam himself.

Another cause of MacLennan's distress during his first term at Oxford, and one he never fully overcame, was the climate. For him, English weather – muggy on bad days, balmy on good ones – was enervating and made him feel much less like working than he otherwise would have. 'The climate is awfully relaxing beyond a doubt and it is hard to work on many days.' Near the end of that term, fortunately, at a dinner given for Rhodes scholars, the distinguished colonial historian Professor Reginald Coupland gave him some advice: 'He said that exercise heavy enough to make one perspire thoroughly was necessary every day, if one was to do good work in Oxford.' Taking this advice to heart, MacLennan began running every afternoon around Christ Church Meadow, took up rugger and, a little later, tennis. The rugger games he enjoyed especially, for they were played much more for the pleasure of it than they had been in Canada: 'We get far more fun out of the game as it is more open, and not so bruising or dirty as at home'; often, he commented, no one even knew the score at the end. Tennis, on the other hand, was a serious business, and he felt at a distinct disadvantage, for he did not like the grass courts after so many years of mastering his techniques on the hard courts in Halifax. Throughout his four years at Oxford, MacLennan was to continue this regime of strenuous exercise, commenting every now and then in his letters how much it helped him to cope physically with the climate.[7]

This exercise doubtless helped him to sublimate his feelings as well. Although he kept a photograph of Jean Shaw in his rooms, along with some familiar photographs of Halifax scenes taken by the Nova Scotian photographer MacAskill, women were to be absent from his Oxford existence for the next four years. Not only had he taken his father's advice on his departure seriously, but he had also understood for some time that he must not even think of marriage until such time as he could afford to support a wife. This notion had been a particularly strong idea of Dr Sam's, and he had made it quite clear that his son would sacrifice his further education, his potential career, and his family's respect if he were to 'engage the affections' of anyone before he were well established. Oxford, at that time, had but a few women undergraduates, who were restricted to women's colleges; so MacLennan had also to adjust to what he called this 'monastic' life after the mixed society he had enjoyed at Dalhousie.[8]

Not only did he miss the presence of women in general, and Jean Shaw in particular, he was also profoundly homesick. He wrote frequent letters home – at least one a week – and expressed often how much he liked hearing from the family. Although he dealt bravely with these feelings, and did not mention them directly, sadness crept in at the fringes of his letters, especially those written around Christmas.

His acknowledgement that he must not become involved with any woman until he could support her was just one reflection of his sensitivity to the fact that his father was supporting him. His letters are full of financial accounts, invariably explaining why such-and-such was a bargain or the lengths to which he had gone to save money. As he remembered it: 'I was determined as far as I could that [my father] shouldn't spend any money on me. He had to stake me to my last year because a Rhodes Scholarship was only for three years.' Even in London with his mother before going up to Oxford, he had felt it necessary to report to his father in this way. 'We are really not spending so very much money after all,' he wrote on one occasion. 'Our clothes and so forth are necessary and are much cheaper and mother made a marvellous bargain in linen. Indeed for every penny we spend we seem to be getting something substantial in exchange for it. We have only been to three theatres. One cost nothing (Harry Hall gave us complimentaries) the others were about 2 s. each.' Later, after he had travelled more widely, he angrily reassessed this London sojourn, coming to the conclusion that he and Katie had been staying at a hotel that had been far too expensive.[9] Because of his financial dependence on his father, his thoughts were never far from his accounts, lest he be accused of being spendthrift or self-indulgent. In fact, he subjected himself to considerable discomfort on later trips by travelling third class in conditions that revolted him physically.

He had also to adjust to the fact that he was once again a freshman in a large institution. Even Rhodes scholars, who were some three or four years older than the other freshmen there, were shown little of the sort of attention their efforts at home had generated. Dr Sam's Anglomania had prepared his son to like and to fit in with Englishmen; even so, for an initial period at least, he felt isolated by the cool condescension with which the other students treated all freshmen. 'In first term,' he recalled at the end of that year, 'everyone treated the other with a restrained courtesy.'

Aside from plunging headlong into his work and exercising strenuously, he took other steps to keep his mind off his homesickness. He attended and eventually joined the Newlands Club, which met to read plays aloud, his first dramatic role being that of the queen in *Cymbeline*; later he sampled roles in many other Shakespearean plays and in modern works such as those of Eugene O'Neill. In November, after consideration of the expense involved, he decided to rent a piano, which proved extremely difficult to manoeuvre into his rooms; he played for relaxation – his favourite piece, and one over which he acquired reasonable mastery in time, being Beethoven's *Appassionata* sonata. He also sought out Mr Rusk, the closest Presbyterian minister, and attended St Columba's Church.[10]

From the letters he wrote during his voyage to England and his first term at Oxford, MacLennan's future as a writer can be glimpsed. Almost without exception he saw sights, then and later, through the literary experiences he had already had; real occasions, for him, often seemed reflections of the more intense experience in books. Not only were his impressions filtered through literature, his own descriptions of events and scenery displayed a literary quality. His account of the *Devonian*'s arrival at Liverpool is only one of many possible examples: 'Toward noon we passed the Isle of Man, the scene of Sir Hall Caine's novels, with great purple hills billowing up and rolling into each other and rugged grey and brown cliffs of stone splashed with white spray ... The voyage has been quite uneventful. Off the banks we saw about twenty whales spouting all around us and schools of porpoises vaulting over the rollers like rows of hurdlers, all together ... When we landed tonight it was dark and we could see very little of Liverpool. It was covered with a twilight haze – all purple and yellow and rose, with a moon like an uneven honey-comb rising over the rows of docks and lights all subdued and glowing very softly.' A little procession of swans on the Thames between Windsor Castle and Hampton Court reminded him of Spenser's *Prothalamion*; the castle itself, he recorded, was '"bosomed high in tufted trees," as Milton described it in L'Allegro, which he wrote at Horton only a few miles from where we were.' On the bicycle he acquired in October he cycled around Oxford and the neighbouring countryside, writing home to say, on one occasion: 'I passed the famous *Scholar Gypsy Inn* where Arnold, Newman and their friends used to walk out to tea.'[11]

By the end of the first term he had made at least a partial adjustment to his new life. As he left for his first 'vac,' to be spent with the Oxford ski club at St Moritz in Switzerland, he reported: 'Today was very crisp with a hoar frost in the morning and I was half sorry to leave Oxford for I have grown to like it very much and feel quite at home in the place now ... I am more than thankful every day that I chose *Oriel*. *Everyone* in Oriel is reading for some sort of honours. The provost won't accept anyone who is not. The result is that the *tone* is about as high as one could get and the college is considered the soundest all through of any in the University, although Balliol always has enough fine scholars to top the class list.'[12]

There is other evidence that he felt he was beginning to fit into Oxford life, though his assertions sometimes lacked conviction. From about November on, his letters were increasingly filled with the jargon and English speech mannerisms he was hearing all about him: 'chaps,' 'I daresay,' 'rather,' and many other such words and phrases began to appear. The beginnings of an English accent are almost audible.

By the time he arrived in St Moritz at the beginning of December 1928, however, he was far from sorry he had left Oxford. Travelling by train with Charlie Briggs, a wealthy and lively Rhodes scholar from Cleveland ('Oriel without Charles would be like salt without its savour'), who had suggested the trip in the first place, and another Rhodes scholar named Fowler from Australia, MacLennan had his first taste, or more accurately his first smell, of third class travel. His description of the 750-mile trip reveals a turn of phrase and a sense of humour that showed that Katie was not the only one in the family who could tell a good story: 'In one carriage, trying to sleep, were huddled Briggs ... an Australian Rhodes scholar, myself and an Italian plumber, who claimed our friendship on the grounds that he had mended pipes in Balliol. He also slept with his shoes off – a factor that made sleep desirable but impossible.' MacLennan regretted that the train passed through the war zone at Amiens at night when he could not see it. Characteristically, he felt the significance of the places they were passing through his prior knowledge: 'I remember that we stopped at *Laon*, where the Huns first fired at Paris with Big Bertha. We also made a stop at *Châlons* where the famous battle between Christendom and the Saracens was fought out ages ago.'

He found St Moritz overwhelmingly beautiful, elegant, and invigorating: 'I am more and more glad that I came here. The only effect of the high altitude is that I feel very vigorous and ready for anything. I am doing the set portion of work every day in much less time and much better than I ever could at Oxford. In fact, St. Moritz seems almost ideal for work and play and lastly, the beauty of the place is beyond any description.' Skiing came easily. He wore his ordinary clothes, and bought a pair of heavy boots, which, he guiltily rationalized to his father, 'can be used for rough work for the rest of my life.'

With the dreaded Collections awaiting him at Oxford, however, he spent a good part of each day at work. Keeping to a set routine, he studied from 9 to 10:30 a.m.; skied until lunch at 1 p.m.; worked again until 3; skied from 3 to 4:30; took tea while an orchestra played classical music; studied again until 7:30; bathed, changed into a dinner jacket and black tie for dinner at 8; then did a final two hours of work before bed at 11. After a week of this life he wrote to Frances: 'for grandeur, I'm afraid, the Engadine has even Cape Breton beaten.'[13]

During this year Frances provided a striking contrast to her brother. While he was living the life of the most privileged young men of his age, she was still struggling in convalescence, recovering from tuberculosis; in addition, she was working on the final stages of the Classics BA she should have had in 1924. Despite the abyss that separated their fortunes, she loyally wrote regularly to her brother; in return, he too wrote often, asking with great concern about her health.

At the end of his two-week stay in St Moritz, tanned and fit, he exclaimed: 'This Alpine trip has been a wonderful tonic and I shall likely come out here next year if all goes well and if the ski-club can get as good prices as we are getting now.' Just before he left, however, the 'season' began, and wealthy tourists started arriving. As he wrote to Frances, he disliked these idle rich intensely, and without hesitation expressed his preference for the ordinary people working around the palatial hotel: 'The hotel is filled up now with every nationality under the sun, most of them very wealthy and most of the women American and German. We shall probably have a bang-up Christmas dinner, but for my part I think I shall go down to one of the little inns in the plebeian part of the town afterwards. David Tod, one of the young Englishmen [here], has been down several times with me, talking with the Swiss guides, who all speak a broken English. I like that sort of person much better than the hotel crowd, who are gross materialists every one and out for money and little else. The fare [rates] we are getting for 15 fr. costs 70 fr. in the season.'

In order to avoid the temptation to spend money, MacLennan carried only two francs in his pocket. After an excursion to a dance in the lower town, with some girls Charles Briggs had known in the United

States, his penuriousness proved to be embarrassing: a shrewd driver refused to return them to the hotel for less than ten francs. With surprising aplomb, MacLennan solved the problem: 'There was a sort of roulette wheel business going on in the lobby and on the off chance I put my 2 franc piece on the nearest number and won 16 francs with it. I then placed it on the next nearest and won 16 more ... The numbers I had backed had tremendous odds against them and I shall certainly leave the machine alone in future, as it will "rook" you nearly every time.'[14]

When he arrived back at Oxford, he wrote his Collections immediately. Once again he found the climate disagreeable. 'The air has a caressing balminess about it that immediately lulls the wits asleep. I feel mentally lazy already,' he wrote to his father four days after his return. As for the Collections, he rationalized his inability to get a first class with great care for his father's benefit. The top scholars, he pointed out here and elsewhere, 'are the two men most lacking in personality and general intelligence and self-reliance in the whole college.' He predicted that he would get a second class, but assured his father that he 'worked harder than most and really enjoyed what I was doing, which is the main thing to me, after all.' By this time he had had a chance to compare notes with some of the other students, and to his chagrin he found that the only other Canadian Rhodes scholar studying the Classics that year, Moffatt St A. Woodside at Corpus Christi College, was doing much better. 'Ontario sends over the best, as is to be expected. The fellow from Toronto Varsity this year is named Woodside and is writing off his Honour Mods this spring. He has had four years under Maurice Hutton personally, and as Hutton used to be an Oxford Don and is unquestionably one of the best men in the game today, Woodside has been well-prepared. He should do extremely well. His prose is very strong, as he has been doing 2 a week for Hutton for four years. I have read far more Mods work than he, as he has done no Demosthenes, Cicero or Homer and but little Virgil, which will force him to do much hard reading. On the other hand he puts very little time on his prose, has studied, textually, most of the set places, and knows the *Republic* nearly by heart.'[15] MacLennan correctly sensed that he was not in the same league as Woodside, who would go on to a distinguished career as a professor of Classics and as a top-level administrator at the University of Toronto.

Nevertheless, he threw himself into the next term's work with a grim determination reminiscent of his father. By Easter he was nervously writing the 'Divvers' papers (Divinity Moderations, a minor requirement), with a touch of the flu and a bad case of pink-eye which had swept the college in an epidemic.

Directly afterwards, he prepared for his second vacation: this time to Italy for a month via Paris and then home through Innsbruck and Munich. In London, before he left, he and Charlie Briggs saw 'a marvellous War play,' *Journey's End* by Robert Sherriff. Taking along his 'vac' reading – six books of the *Aeneid* and five of Cicero's orations – he set out for Paris with an IODE scholar from Nova Scotia, Alfred MacDonald, again braving third class train travel with 'four Frenchmen who looked and smelt like Apaches.' They took a room at the famous Hotel Sélect in the Latin Quarter, and with only fifteen minutes sleep in twenty-four hours, 'set forth eagerly to CONQUER PARIS,' a noble enterprise that consisted of a walking tour to the usual highlights, Notre-Dame Cathedral, the Louvre, the Tuilleries, and the Eiffel Tower. MacLennan decided he liked France more than he had expected, more in fact than London. As usual, he measured what he saw against what he had read: 'when we were standing there it was impossible to picture it as the Place de la Révolution, with the guillotine, and the knitting women and the howling mobs about it, as it was a century and a half ago.'

Crossing the Italian border in late March 1929, the two young students had to contend with 'a French tramp who represented the lowest dregs of humanity' who came 'sprawling into the carriage dead drunk' and fell asleep on the bench. At Turin, a three-hour wait for the train to Milan afforded them their first view of an Italian city. MacLennan was not impressed: 'Turin was a mass of flags, troops and Black-shirts ... The inhabitants ... looked frightfully dirty scum. And the soldiers with feathers in their hats and flowing cloaks so strutted about that they made us almost irritated. They were a miserable looking body of men, and apart from the clothes, looked shoddy. A half regiment of Tommies would make a terrible mess of them.' In Milan 'there was a Fascist Jamboree on of some sort,' but MacLennan's attention was distracted from politics for the remainder of this trip. In Lerici, which he always considered the loveliest place he had ever seen, he and Alfred relaxed thoroughly, swimming in the warm turquoise Mediterranean daily. Once they took a car into the mountains to visit the ancient castle where Dante had written several cantos of the *Inferno*. At Pisa they climbed the famous tower.[16]

In Rome, MacLennan delved deeply into the classical history about which he already knew a great deal, reporting each excursion in detail to his father. One of the highlights for him reflected his Scottish heritage: in St Peter's Cathedral he stumbled across the tomb of Bonnie Prince Charlie and wrote home proudly that the Roman Catholic Church had honoured the leader of the Highland clans at the tragic Battle of Culloden with an official plaque. Most of his experiences in Rome, however, related directly to his studies: 'I stood on the rostra where Cicero stood, just in the shadow of the Capitoline, with the arch of Sept[imus] Severus and the wreck of the Senate House on the left. The marks where the beaks of the ships were set can still be seen in the front; you can also see the spot on which Marc Anthony exposed Julius Caesar's body when he made his funeral speech from the rostra. On the spot where the temple of Vesta stood there are nearly a dozen statues of Vestals remaining with inscriptions at the bottom on which you could see the names of the gens: the Claudian, Scauran, etc.'

Of all that he saw in Rome, he liked best the Palatine, once the site of the palaces of the Caesars but which was now a luxuriant garden among the ruins. It 'has a restrained beauty about it,' he wrote romantically to his mother, 'an air of keeping back some tremendous secrets, that, in the late afternoon at any rate, is very manifest ... One could almost *feel* the silence of centuries closing in ... The dark cypress trees ... which Browning said grew in Italy "like Death's lean, dusky forefinger" seem to symbolize and sum up the whole scene.' Reading Hugh's richly descriptive letters from Rome must have filled Dr Sam with inordinate pride and satisfaction; largely through his dreams and practical efforts, his son was now tasting the best fruits of civilization.

Working hard on his Collections each day, MacLennan had almost finished his assigned reading by the time he and Alfred reached Florence on 16 April. 'Although I had read much of it before,' he wrote to his mother, 'I had done so in such a hurry (reading with Dadden in the evenings) and so long ago, that I had forgotten it completely.' If MacLennan had been an excellent guide in Rome, now MacDonald proved to be his equal in Florence, since the Renaissance was his specialty in the Honour School of Modern History. For five days they explored the ancient town. MacLennan found that it 'carries the burden of its history with a rare grace that even Oxford cannot manage, and it is the very lightness of its manner that seems to bring all its great men closer.' Although he paid great attention to the city's landmarks and the astounding works of art to be seen in the Pitti Palace and the Uffizi Gallery, he also noticed, as he had in Turin, the military presence in the town.

I don't think there is much hope for European peace being at all permanent. I have talked to a good many students who have been at German universities, and while the old Hun feels quite well disposed to England, he is leading his infants to the altar, as Hamilcar did Hannibal, to swear them to an eternal hatred of France. I met a fellow in Rome who had been a year at Heidelberg, and he said that Germany is still a pretty military nation. France, of course, has soldiers around everywhere, and as for the admirable people in whose country we are at present, they are strutting round in twenty different kinds of uniform; police like Napoleon; military in grey, brown, blue, black, green, silver and yellow, with everything on their heads from an ostrich feather to a brass hat that glitters like a searchlight when the sun hits it. They love it and are still patting themselves on the back for the fine job they made of shelling Corfu five or six years ago. And in the middle of them 'il Duce' who struts higher than them all, whom they all feel envious of, but all follow like sheep. All over the place plastered on buildings and lamp posts are his pictures, in all his latest poses, with 'Viva Mussolini' underneath ... I really think that if Mussolini declared war on France tomorrow (I don't think for a minute he will) all these people would be behind him to a man. It is very funny to people like Alfred and me, and I can't help thinking I'm more of a Christian than I had thought I was. These people simply think in terms of war and can't understand anyone who doesn't. It seems so utterly stupid and makes one think that Christianity can't have any hold on Europe at all.

After a day and a night in Venice, in which he saw 'the Rialto ... where Antonio rated Shylock on his monies and his usances,' he climbed St Mark's bell-tower and saw below him all Venice, described perfectly by Shelley as a 'peopled labyrinth of walls.' He smuggled out of Italy a length of silk for his mother, wrapped around his waist, and some tobacco for his father.[17]

Regretting that his holiday was over, delighted to have spent only £31 for the entire six-week trip, he returned to Oxford in late April, ready for his next Collections. His work, as he described it, pursued 'the even tenor of its way' – which is to say, he was still getting second class in his proses for Genner. He had by this time, however, scaled down his expectations and was no longer worried about his work. Nor was he any longer feeling isolated: 'in the [second] term we grew more or less used to each other and now have become a large and cheerful and more or less united family with old Charlie Briggs easily the darling of the college.' In fact, with 'Eights Week' under way, which meant girls visiting to watch the rowing competitions and to attend the accompanying round of social events, MacLennan actually became quite lyrical on the subject of Oxford: 'Spring has not come yet and will not come for another year. But summer has arrived in its stead and is sitting down snugly in Oxfordshire today, with all her usual accompaniments of purple haze, green grass and leaves and trembling waves of air from heated walls ... Oxford is transformed ... Last fall the countryside looked dull; in the winter to have called it drab was to flatter it; but now it is beautiful and greener than anything I have ever seen. The view over Christ Church meadows is glorious. Rich green grass like a soft carpet in which the cattle stand swishing away the flies with their tails; and all around it ... those great limes and elm trees, which join overhead and make even the broadwalk a tunnel of green leaves and chequered sunlight.'

As for the visiting ladies, MacLennan complained that he was out of practice: 'It is so long since I have talked to any female for more than five minutes consecutively, that I almost felt embarrassed, but fortunately one of the girls had been out to Canada for six months and had had most of the rough edges smoothed off, so that it was possible to talk about other things than the weather, the greenness of the grass and how one liked Oxford and how quaint the barges looked, as I very likely would have been reduced to otherwise.'[18]

Although Dr MacLennan was pressuring his son to stay abroad and spend his 1929 summer vacation in Germany, Hugh decided to come home instead. Feeling a little guilty about wanting so much to return to Canada, especially since his father had made him the lavish gift of $1000 for his birthday in March, his rationalizations were lengthy and convoluted: Heidelberg was supposed to be unattractive; he could accomplish more reading at home than on a trip; he had three years ahead in which to do more travelling on the Continent; it made more sense to go to Germany after Mods.; and so on. The truth was that it had been a difficult year indeed, much more difficult than he had ever really confessed in his letters. The closest he came was a statement he made not long before he left: 'I hope you will not be too disappointed, but it is really not so easy to plan years ahead a schedule and follow it out exactly ... Perhaps it would do me more ultimate good if I stayed there all alone this summer, but I am afraid I am not Stoic enough to relish a summer spent without exercise by myself in a strange country, and Germany of all countries in the world is the grimmest.' He had made a go of it, but now he needed to come home and gather strength for the struggle ahead. By 19 May he had arranged for a summer membership at the Waegwoltic Club in Halifax and had booked his passage on the *Arabic* to New York. In his last letter home in June he wrote: 'I'm so glad to think that I shall be soon seeing you all at last ... that nothing else seems to matter very much.'[19]

Dr MacLennan met his son at the pier in New York, and was in a surprisingly relaxed mood. 'Dad is a wonder for energy and vigour,' Hugh wrote to his mother, 'and he seems able now to do what he has never done before – to take it easy on occasion, and not try to do too much.' Dr Sam's means of relaxation was a whirlwind tour of New York with his son, a day trip out to see Princeton, and a flying visit to his sister-in-law Ethel in Baltimore. The strong anti-Americanism of the father was clearly reflected in the son; while Dr Sam deplored Manhattan as 'a cemetery where everyone tried to have a tombstone larger than his neighbour,' Hugh sounded like an echo: 'The streets are just as noisy as everyone has always told me they were, the crowds just as conglomerate, the traffic just as badly managed. But there *is* something amazingly raffish about New York, even on Fifth Avenue. Even the shopmen on Oxford St. try to look like public men. Here the public men seem to be trying to look like shopmen.' As for Princeton, where they visited Professor A.C. Johnson of the Classics Department, whom they had met the year before at Dalhousie, Hugh did not particularly like it: 'Although very new, [it is] lacking that elusive something that makes Oxford at once so lovely and so baffling.'[20] The observations of the two of them in the United States sound a little like the comments of the country mouse visiting the town mouse.

Once back in Halifax, at home on South Park Street, MacLennan settled into serious study and some good tennis at the Waegwoltic Club; by the end of the summer he had improved his form to the point of winning the 1929 Maritimes singles tennis championship. It was a summer to recharge the batteries, to gather enough strength from familiar surroundings to meet the demanding and radically different life he would face once more in Oxford.

Despite a gloomy fall term, the wettest November for seventy years, his second year, spent in new rooms in the Tudor section of the third quad on Oriel Street, was more enjoyable. Again the workload was extremely heavy; at the end of the first term, he sent one of his frequent 'progress reports' to his father: 'For Dadden's benefit I will set down what reading I did last term: *Cicero: Pro Sestio; Pro Flacco* (the hardest I have read); *In Verrem* I; *Pro Roscio Amerino. Demosthenes: Naval Boards, 3rd Olynthian; Peace; Chersonese; Rhodian Freedom; Megalopolitans*; and about eight private speeches the names of which I can't remember. Anyway I have now done all Virgil, all Homer, all the

Demosthenes except *Leptines* and all the Cicero except *Verres Actio* 2, which I will only do for Mods in spot passages ... I also read over the first book of the *Annals*, and went over the *Antigone* once more.' Even so, he wrote: 'I have been very happy and busy and have had loads of exercise.'

By this time his tutor was able to assess his work more accurately than in the first year, and he found his performance inconsistent. 'It all seems to depend on the mood I am in when I do a prose or an unseen [passage], which makes me very erratic,' he complained.[21] He could also be counted on to make at least a couple of 'howlers' in each piece of work. Although at last he was obtaining the occasional first on his proses, his marks stayed pretty much where they had been all along – in the middle of the second class; he was not among the three Classics men chosen by Genner to represent the college in the competition for the Ireland Scholarship.

At Christmas 1929 MacLennan set off again for St Moritz, this time in the company of a Lowland Scottish fellow-student called 'Jock' Waldie, who had never been outside Britain before. The channel crossing was a nightmare, and MacLennan's vivid description of it occasioned great anxiety when his mother read it: 'I spent the most terrible three hours of my life on the channel boat, between Dover and Boulogne ... Great waves were breaking over the mole at the harbour mouth, and when we got outside the breakwater a monstrous breaker took us full on the beam and laid the ship flat. I was sitting on my bags as near the middle of the boat as I could get. A long bench ran along the opposite rail, lined with people and suitcases. As the sea struck us they all were lifted; in a perfect semi-circle they flew across the little bit of deck and landed with a crash together. A little, bearded Frenchman landed on top of me. As he leaped up and began to apologize profusely the ship righted itself and he was flung violently backward to the exact spot he had left. – For a little while it was rather fun. It was certainly a glorious sight to see the colossal seas and hear them crashing on the decks fore and aft.'

After breaking the trip for a couple of days in Paris, where he found that 'the dinners tasted like pure ambrosia after Oxford,' he proceeded alone to St Moritz. With his skiing a little better, and the mountain air again exhilarating ('the air is like champagne ... [It] makes one feel like jumping'), he once more enjoyed a wonderful holiday. Not that it was a break from work: putting in five or six hours of study each day, he prepared again for the Collections that would await him in Oxford. His prejudice against the wealthy tourists who frequented the famous resort, especially the Americans, was even more deeply imbedded: 'Some products of the U.S.A. and Southern France finishing-schools are beginning to trickle in, disturbing somewhat our self-satisfied, monastic calm. They are quite the usual type of polished inadequacy who will go home and tell their friends who have not been here, that St. Moritz, which they will carefully accent on the last syllable, is simply marvellous, that Giocondo is simply marvellous but not quite so marvellous as Raphael ... Lord knows you can't very well blame them, least of all in America, where there are so many half-educated people who think they have education, and therefore are almost impossible to do anything with.'[22]

Among what he called 'the ubiquitous influx of Americans' were a number he singled out as particularly distasteful: Richard Barthelmess, the film star, who struck him as 'a very little unimpressive fellow, slowly tending towards corpulence, studied in every motion and affected in voice'; and the tennis star Lili D'Alvarez, 'the most selfish and conceited little woman that ever stepped on the courts.' Most of all, he was appalled at an American heiress from Chicago: 'One of our visitors is the proper heroine of the modern English holiday novel. She is the daughter of Armour, the famous meat packer, who has a corner on the Chicago slaughter houses and "Orange Gut" for tennis raquets. I expect she is one of the richest heiresses in the world.' Later, after dancing with her, he somewhat modified his opinion, but he felt none the less that she 'was not a patch on the average college girl of Canada in charm or intelligence.'[23]

On his way back to Oxford he made a side-trip to the beautiful Lerici for a few days, after stopping briefly at Milan, 'one of the ugliest cities on the globe.' To his digust Shelley's house in Lerici had been turned into a cinema.

Under the laurelled tablet set in the wall, engraved with Shelley's magnificent [lines]

> 'The One remains, the many change and pass;
> Heaven's light forever shines, earth's shadows fly;
> Life, like a dome of many-coloured glass,
> Stains the white radiance of Eternity
> Till [*sic*] death tramples it to fragments!'

Under that is a lurid movie advertisement – 'Giovanni Gilbert, "Buddie" Arthur e Clara Bow. Quella e voi, Bambino.'[24]

Once in Oxford, he threw himself into his work and athletics with characteristic vigour. He was not among the top fifteen rugger players who comprised the college team, but he continued to play on an informal basis. Early in 1930 he became secretary for Oriel's tennis club, using the signature 'J. Hugh MacLennan,' and was responsible for scheduling games and making arrangements for the new courts then being built. In hopes of making small excursions beyond the few miles his bicycle could manage, he bought a motorbike and named it Rosinante after Don Quixote's horse. On weekends he began exploring further and further afield, but as the term drew to a close, with the dreaded Mods. exams at hand, the workload became overwhelming and prevented him from doing anything but study. So great was the strain of studying for these exams that he was to recall thirty years later: '[Final examinations] are horrible things. I never minded them much at Dalhousie, but at Oxford they were so awful that still, about once a year, I wake up in a sweat knowing I have been unable to cover half what they require. I couldn't either.'[25]

After these exams, from which he emerged 'numb' in mid-March 1930, he had no thought but to escape from Oxford: 'Some idea of the mental blank I was in can be gathered from this: I had the fixed idea of getting out of Oxford as soon as I possibly could. The wind, rushing steadily past my ears and into my face at 30 miles per hour, would refresh me. The steady throb of the engine beneath my haunches would slowly shake me back to natural life again. And so, notwithstanding a cold breeze and an inky sky, I set out. I had no particular idea where I was going.' On the whim of the moment he biked to Devonshire; on the next day to Bath and Wells; and the following day set off back to Oxford, soaking in the physical sensations so long denied through closeted study. Then he was off on 19 March to Germany, stopping in Paris on the way with the fun-loving Charlie Briggs. From there he wrote home apologetically: 'My few days in Paris were rather extravagant, I'm afraid ... after such a long spell of scorning delights of all kinds, except the pleasure of hard work, a little fling seemed almost necessary. But from now until the end of the vac I expect my living will be fairly reasonable.' 'It was a grand feeling,' he added, 'to just sit still and see the people go by, after months of working even at one's meals.'[26]

As always, MacLennan saw new scenes in a literary context. After a rhapsodic description of the woods among the high hills behind Wiesbaden, he concluded: 'There is also the occasional ring of an axe where some woodcutter is at work. It would be unfitting to call him a lumberman – an insult to his green smock and dignified beard and mustachios. Again, if it was not for the crunch of breakers on the shingle that I was longing, I would admit that all this was very wonderful; that the dove-grey quietude of these sombre woods was letting me into another little chamber, full of old recollections, and making kiddish dreams come true. I probably would have clear forgotten Hans Anderson & Co. if the atmosphere here had not brought them up from the hinterland of my mind. Therefore I *had* to call the lumbermen "woodcutters." And I am quite sure there must be the odd charcoal burner around too.'

His study of German proceeded in a more or less desultory fashion as he allowed his mind to unwind after the Mods. Away from his work, having escaped from the determined, hard-working, puritanical side of himself that had of necessity surfaced in preparing for these exams, he blossomed. Here in Germany the more artistic and physical side of his nature had an opportunity to express itself; wandering around Wiesbaden, taking long hikes through the delightful woods surrounding the city, simply sitting drinking beer in the evenings, he made up for the time he had lost in study. With a new image to match these 'halcyon days' he grew a moustache, and, playfully defiant, he told his father: 'After four days [my moustache] could be seen across the room; a shadow admittedly, but manfully asserting itself. Now, after ten days, it has become formidable. In another fortnight I hope to have the ends waxed. And then, as I swagger down the Wilhelmstrasse, I shall think myself the devil of a fellow; (I look rakish already) And if I stop off in Paris, on the way back, Jacques Bonhomme should certainly scratch his head and mutter – *voilà, un homme*! And if you were to see it (which you never shall) you would certainly say, (with much truth) "Lord, Hugh, that does look awful. Shave it off."'

Naturally his thoughts turned to the young women of Wiesbaden, but they were not much to his liking. He considered them far too heavy and unattractive to compare with Canadian girls, who, he asserted, 'have the highest average of good looks in the world.' 'Here,' he wrote, 'the Frauleins tramp the Wilhelmstrasse with the port of a soldier. Groups of them surge along arm-in-arm, and I swear they make a clamber like the Thundering Herd. They are like the men – symmetrical; evenly squared off, fore and aft. To quote a vile phrase that Charles culled from an auto ad: they are "built for comfort, not for speed."' Summing up his holiday state of mind for his father's benefit, he wrote: 'It may faintly interest you that your son has become temporarily a cabbage, but beyond the mere statement of fact, there can be no further comment on that.'[27]

MacLennan had arranged to meet another Oxford friend in Wiesbaden a week or so after his arrival. John Nason, also a Rhodes scholar, was from the American mid-west (he later became president of Swarthmore College, then head of the US Foreign Policy Association, and finally president of Carleton College in Northfield, Minnesota). They had settled on Wiesbaden because it was reported to have an excellent tennis club. After almost a month of playing tennis daily with Nason, just walking around, picking up what German he could (which was quite a bit), and generally enjoying life, MacLennan returned to Oxford after paying a quick visit to the Drabbles in the Midlands.

The perspective gained on this long and relaxing holiday marked a new stage in his discovery of himself. In the first place, with the second class marks he received when the Mods. results were released in April, he was able to accept, once and for all, his limitations as a scholar. 'I'm afraid an Oxford "second" is about my limit,' he wrote home. 'I'm sorry. But that's the best I can do here in Classics.' 'A first was beyond my mental powers.' From what he had observed, he was not too displeased with himself: 'I am half glad I have not the mentality that takes with easy readiness to an exam like Mods. It is a bit finicky.' At the same time he was positive about what the course had done for him so far: 'It is a stiffener and foundation for "Greats." I think it has done me a great deal of good. It has made me pay attention to detail and has tidied my mind up as nothing else would have done. I daresay that you can see ... a greater tendency towards conciseness ... in my letter-writing.' His tutor apparently knew how much his student wanted a first, and wrote a personal note to soften the blow: 'I had thought that your results would have been a bit higher, for your work in the past term made it seem likely that you would score heavily on your books. At any rate you may feel that you yourself are in no way to blame.' After all, MacLennan pointed out to his father by way of excuse, only three of the twenty-five Oriel men who wrote the exams got firsts.[28]

At this point also he was able to reassess the puritanical values his father had tried to transmit to him. For the first time he began to consider several factors: the obvious differences in attitude between his mother and his father; his own personal obervations of English, Swiss, French, Italian, and German customs; his own feelings about the puritanism forced on him by the need to study so hard for the Mods.; and the needs he now recognized he had for physical release, natural beauty, fun, and artistic expression. In a roundabout way, through a series of comments on Genner, MacLennan made his own position clear to his father: 'Genner is the perfect example of the highly emotional man, who has repressed his emotions all his life, in every channel but one. He once told an undergraduate that when [he] was up at Balliol, two things only interested [him] – work and religion ... There is something about Genner that one can't help pitying, in a way. His father was an iron-monger. He goes out of his way to tell people that ... I believe all his life was a fight to secure himself ... The old Puritan, as I really believe, is half afraid of human friendships for fear it will lessen his friendship with the Deity. I'm afraid I'm a Greek at heart. I can't avoid the moderate in all things. Puritanism, on the one hand, seems to me as much a waste as does Hedonism on the other. I haven't the iron in my will that Genner has.'[29] Despite this criticism, as much an evaluation of Dr Sam as of Genner, MacLennan continued to attend the Presbyterian church and occasionally the Oriel College chapel. He was defining his own religious feelings as being more mellow than those of his father.

With these new principles in mind, he confessed: 'I'm making the most of the society of my fellow beings this term, having made a bit of a hermit of myself during the last two terms.' One form this socializing took was the 'pub-crawl,' which he described in detail in one of his letters home in May 1930. 'Such a thing as a pub-crawl,' he hastened to add to his teetotal family, 'is "an excellent entertainment of a calm evening" as an old scholar of Merton hath writ. It is not a dissipated evening (this for Frances' benefit) nor are the men that sit on the old beam seats at the Bear and Turf either drunk or hilarious. They are just spending a quiet evening at their club.' Some aspects of his gradually widening experience with drinking, however, did not find their way into his letters. A 1952 essay, 'Orgy at Oriel,' describes a 'bump supper' celebrating his college's success in the boat races; the level of intoxication would have appalled his family.[30]

Although MacLennan had resigned himself to a second in his academic work, he still had high hopes for his tennis. He turned his attention to the competitions from which a team for the university would be chosen; the top six players of the year would be awarded the highly coveted Oxford 'Blue.' As the new term began in May 1930, his letters were filled with details of matches as he attempted to raise his standing from one of the lower echelons of the top ten. While he remained a 'Penguin' (one of the top fifteen), not a 'Blue,' he nevertheless enjoyed playing and was not really disappointed; he had practised hard and on one occasion had even resorted to playing in his socks to get a grip on the wet turf, but he had to conclude that 'I do play below par in Oxford ... Whether it is the climate or what, it seems that I can't go all out for a whole match.'

He had, in the end, come to enjoy the translation from Greek and Latin that formed the Mods. portion of his course of study; but he now turned with much greater enthusiasm to those courses in Greats which would be done in English. The work was comparatively less difficult. Essays on subjects such as 'Greek colonization' and 'democracy versus oligarchy' were fascinating to research; fun to argue out with his new history tutor, the famous epigraphist Marcus Niebuhr Tod; and satisfying to complete. 'The more I read of Greek history, the more it is possible to trace modern parallels,' he wrote in excitement by the term's end.

As he finished the year, before leaving for his second summer vacation in Germany, he felt well and happy: 'Oxford in summer time, in one's second year "living-in," with "Schools" just behind one's back and much leisure on one's hands, is certainly among the good things of life.' 'I understand now what Rupert Brooke meant, when he said that in the beauty of the New World he missed the voices of the dead.'[31]

Before leaving for Germany, however, he made a few excursions on Rosinante around the English countryside. Having heard from Jean Shaw that she would be visiting Edinburgh briefly, he biked north and met her there for the day. While there, he recounted for his family's benefit a sample of the Scottish temperament which must have amused his mother and struck a familiar chord in his father: 'I had purchased an ounce of tobacco in a small shop, when the shopkeeper, with scrupulous care, pinched up a tiny grain in his fingers and called me back. "Indeed noo and it's noe use for ye tae be trowin' this away; nae use at aw."' 'From scenes like this old Scotia's grandeur springs!' he wryly commented. His side-trips on his motorbike culminated in a day at the tennis matches at Wimbledon, which he described fully in a later essay, 'Have You Had Many Wimbledons?' (1958).

Probably to spare his mother the anxiety she would have knowing he was travelling all the way to Germany on Rosinante, he was vague about his plans until the last minute. Then, sending his suitcase ahead of him, he set off on 9 July on an eventful ride over the cobbled roads of Belgium, from Ostend, up the coast to Blankenberge, inland to

Bruges, Eeklo, and on to Ghent. In Liège, en route, he recalled knowing a little about the town 'having read a thrilling yarn about the [German] siege [of 1914] in the *Boys Own Paper* years ago. (The B.O.P.'s were a pretty good investment).'[32] As he completed the last lap of this section of the trip from Aix to Ghent, he exclaimed: 'My opinion of Browning's horse has gone up tremendously.' Partly because he temporarily lost his way, and partly because the motorbike broke down, it actually took him a day longer than Browning's horse to complete the journey.

Once in Germany, at last past the rough, cobbled Belgian streets, he followed the valley of the Rhine from Cologne down through Bonn, Koblenz, Bingen, Mainz, Worms, Mannheim (where he stopped the night), Heidelberg, Rastatt, Baden-Baden, and finally into the city of his destination, Freiburg. 'Here,' as he wrote home, 'my luck was with me.' Through some Oriel College men that he met there as arranged, he found his way into a German Catholic family who, by providing a wonderful context for his German studies, were to help make Freiburg the favourite of all his European haunts. The household of Herr Professor Holtzmann took him in as a paying guest for the next two months. With three Wagnerian daughters ranging from nine to thirteen years older than himself, he had ready-made company and incessant German conversation, for the Holtzmanns spoke no English at all. Sharing their delicious and gargantuan meals, accepted warmly as another member of the family, he spent a delightful summer there, studying the vast amount of material for his courses he had come by now to regard as normal.

At the end of his time in Freiburg, he drove Rosinante to Bremen, shipped the bike back to Oxford where he was to sell it on his return, and boarded a ship to Halifax to spend five weeks at home. Not only did he need to see his own family again to steady himself, but he had also discovered at Oxford that he had developed periodic bursts of sea-fever. 'Unquestionably it is *the* thing and nothing else,' he explained, 'that never fails to stimulate my imagination.'[33]

When he returned to Oxford for his third year in the first week of October 1930, he at last felt fully comfortable in the place. 'I'm a senior man in the college now. A funny lot the English are. The seniors are infinitely more unreserved than the Freshers. One meets the Freshers still full of that absurd dignity – and not yet devoid of all the silly prejudices their public schools have procured for them.' He was now able to claim confidently: 'In the 2nd, 3rd & 4th years there are hardly a dozen men whom I don't know by their first names. Such is Oriel.'

The human comedy now commanded his attention, and more strongly than before he wanted to mix with all sorts of men. 'Why is it,' he mused on one occasion, 'that I am no respecter of persons?' – by which he meant that he himself found it odd that the snobbery of Oxford, with its emphasis on the élite, had not made its imprint upon him as it had on others. One Canadian in particular had gone in quite the other direction, and he deplored the affectation of this man, even to the point of refusing a casual invitation to join him for tea on the grounds that 'I don't feel I could stick an hour and a half of Walter's new voice': 'The honest man of destiny, I fear, has degenerated into an affected ass. What a voice! I only hope my "English accent" doesn't sound like his. At least mine was unconscious ... I never came in for such a patronizing before ... Pon my soul, as Dadden would say.' For him, conversation was interesting with all types of people, not just with the élite he was being educated to join: 'I'm afraid – again – I'm rather hopeless. I like talking to all manner of people even if I don't particularly like or admire them. "Getting their reactions" I should say, were I a Yank.'

This curiosity about human nature, various dialects, and different circumstances was later to stand him in good stead as a writer. Even at this point his ability to present a number of incidents through dialogue, description, and wry observation indicated an unusual talent, like that of his mother, to find interest in the everyday. On the ship from Halifax to Oxford that autumn, for example, he had been as attracted by a Scottish miner, whose drunken conversation about philosophy and theology revealed a 'mind and ideas [that] were by no means ordinary,' as by the wife of a retired major, Mrs Wood, who was '100% snob'; his record of a conversation that begins with her condemnation of the miner shows his developing ability: 'Mrs. Wood wanted to know "Who that person was"? On being informed she remarked that she thought he was drunk. I agreed with her and said so and was asked how I could associate with such persons. Following enlightenment, theology and philosophy seemed inadequate. For Mrs. Wood, being an ardent churchgoer (Church of England), naturally thought such subjects a little intimate if not indecent. She disliked Gen. Johnston and asked me if I didn't think him rather common. I didn't, of course, and said so. The fact that his father was a baker was supposed to mark the difference ... "Knowing one's place" was her philosophy of life.'[34]

In fact, a great number of the incidents that took place during these Oxford years of intellectual growth and travel were to form the basis of his later characters in essays and novels alike: retired colonels met at Cheltenham, his experiences in Germany, a nude swim in Lerici unwittingly located in front of a convent, tennis matches at Wimbledon, eccentrics encountered at Oxford, a chance meeting with Albert Einstein while running around Christ Church Meadow.[35] His letters home, almost like journals, recorded these happenings for future use.

As far as his academic work was concerned, he had evolved a new attitude: work, but no more overwork such as he had undertaken his first year. He continued his dramatic readings with the Newlands Club, his roles including Cassius in Shakespeare's *Julius Caesar*, Selein in James Elroy Flecker's *Hassan*, the sergeant in G.B. Shaw's *The Devil's Disciple*, Joxer Daly in Sean O'Casey's *Juno and the Paycock*, the murderer in Elmer Rice's *The Adding Machine*, Maurrant in Rice's *Street Scene*. He also joined the Bryce Club, an international club which gathered to hear important speakers and discuss their ideas. And he began to write poetry quite seriously when the mood took him. Now into the more enjoyable part of his Greats course, he thoroughly relished the tutorials with Marcus Niebuhr Tod in history, with W.G. Maclagan (later to become regius professor at Glasgow) in philosophy, and with Sir David Ross, provost of Oriel and a leading Aristotelian scholar. His main tutor, Tod, was a tremendous change from Genner: 'Life under the benign regime of Marcus is such a startling change that I haven't yet grown used to it.'[36] Students in these tutorials were expected to present arguments in debate with their tutors, and MacLennan delighted in this Socratic process.

In these sessions he developed a style of argument that was to become increasingly turgid and 'scholastic.' Two of the discussions he singled out himself in letters home give a good impression of the sort of training he was now receiving; they also reveal his convictions on war and religion, subjects that were to be of tremendous significance in his later life. The question of war arose out of a discussion of Aristotle's *Ethics* during a tutorial with Sir David Ross, who, to draw out his students, had claimed that ethics were relative.

I asked him: 'If then, everyone in the world but yourself were a liar, and you knew that, thro' their falsehoods, the machinery of society was being clogged, would you still hold it unnecessary for you to tell the exact truth to them – unnecessary ethically, that is?'
Provost: 'Yes.'
I (*sic*): 'Then wouldn't it follow from that position that individualism and self-interest formed your criterion of conduct?'

Pro: 'No, I hardly think that is a fair way of looking at it. Suppose a case of war. Is a general compelled to tell the truth to his opposing general?'
I: 'Isn't that a confusion of circumstances? I mean, war being the most complete negation of all principles of society – that we know, can an analogy drawn from there have any real weight as applied to a world of society proper?'
Pro: 'I think your statement far too sweeping. Do all rules of society go by the board in time of war? What about loyalty to one's country and to one's general? Again, does it not happen, in time of war, that the machinery of the nation runs generally smoothest of all? How then can you maintain that war is a negation of society?'
I: 'I'm not sure that I can agree with your suppositions. You say that loyalty etc., being rules of society, are in great force in war. I grant you. But *Society* in general, or the *Social Cosmos* has clearly been cut in two and is at war with itself. Therefore the principles of society cannot have a general application.'
Pro: 'Don't think me an advocate for war, MacLennan. Perhaps I *have* overstated the case for it. My original case I call, (for want of a better name) Ethical moderation. I say that I am not wholly bound to tell all the truth to a man who is clearly telling me an untruth and will use my use of the truth against me. (Comment: The Scotch Christian, *nicht wahr*?) I say equally that there are certain rules to be applied to war. e.g., poison gas. The man who uses poison gas is clearly more wrong ethically than he who does not.'
I: 'Theoretically speaking, Sir, I can't agree. In fact, if we are to set up theories and stand fairly up to them without trimming, I should say that once a condition of war exists, that once a man has allowed himself to be drawn into it, the man who uses poison gas is more ethically correct than he who doesn't.'
Pro: 'How do you justify that statement?'
I: 'If a man *chooses* to fight, and if his choice is a *moral* choice, it surely implies that he considers his side of society – the cosmos having been shattered – the better side. Therefore, it follows theoretically, that the other half is not society at all: that it can be considered as much a hindrance to society proper (his own) as disease. And if gas is the only thing to stamp it out effectively he is morally bound to use it.'

Just as MacLennan argued strongly and with personal conviction against any ethical justification for war, he presented the case for Christianity, as the opposite of war's 'individuality and self-seeking,' in a paper for W.G. Maclagan. His subject 'How did history succeed in achieving an ethical standard?' inevitably involved a definition of virtue, and he argued that 'the strength of Christianity was that it was able in Christ to create a definite, real and objective standard [for virtue].'[37]

As a result of these 'hair-splitting' exercises, even his personal correspondence became infected with a dry scholasticism often totally unsuited to the subject at hand. One of his cousins, Gloria Ingraham, the daughter of his mother's sister, who had met him once in Halifax when they were both about eight, had written to congratulate him on his acceptance at Oxford. From that beginning a remarkable correspondence had developed between them in which they both tried out their ideas and thoughts on the other. In his letters to Gloria, MacLennan indulged in extravagantly long and tedious discussions on subjects he did not broach with his parents: above all, he was interested in finding out what constituted the feminine mind. A typical letter from this period illustrates perfectly the scholarly turn his mind had taken:

In Oxford the world in which women move seems somehow remote. And yet I am now prepared to admit that its plane is a higher one. It is not right that it should be higher, of course. Man being of the Earth, is quite clearly earthy. I don't see why he should try to exalt women above the earth (in his own imagination). The average man would be most embarassed [*sic*] in heaven and should really hate to ever have to go there. But he is by no means so reticent in setting the women that he likes in heaven. The more animal-like a man is, the happier he is, provided his instincts serve him aright. The trouble with female society is that it makes him dissatisfied with his condition. He then will commit the crowning folly of all and fall in love. By the sheer act of doing so, he ceases to be an animal. He will very possibly find that the object of his folly is pure animal herself and so will be dissatisfied. He is lucky, of course, if she is. For if she is not: the two of them will live for a time in fairyland. And there, of course they will both be heartily miserable, for fairyland is a most unnatural and uncomfortable place to be in. Then, having at last shaken themselves out of it, they will go back to the normal existence of eating sleeping and drinking and thereby fulfil their proper function on earth. While doing so, and being quite happy about it, they will complain about the loss of that glorious, carefree rapture that once was theirs: altho' they had been very uncomfortable when they actually had been in that state. It's all very amusing and disconcerting. Smugness is surely the most perfect bliss in the world. And yet it is not only held a vice but a man will be mortally offended if he be called smug. In other words, object to having his happiness detected. Love has long been advertised as the crown of life. And yet, the chappie who looks for it seems to forget all about the proverb that tells him how uneasy will lie his head if he get the crown he desires. Smug content is a subjective good and an objective evil. Love is definitely a subjective evil and is supposed to be an objective good. It's hard to know which is the more choice-worthy. A little while ago I should definitely have said the former. Now I am in doubt. And why? Because a little while ago something reminded me of the scent of a girl's hair, the gleam of a curving limb and a voice breaking thro' the darkness of a quiet evening. Three of the worst reasons conceivable! And yet they were marvellously persuasive. So now, you who are responsible for some of this, tell me which is the better part – the masculine security of pipe and dressing gown over the embers of a dying fire (the ale of life); or the pretty pretences, the charming self-delusions and general unearthlyness [*sic*] which are the peculiar attendants on female society (the champagne of life). They say that lack of confidence in love's efficacy augurs cynicism. I so far question that as to say that belief in *love* absolutely proves a man a cynic. Why? Because it constitutes an escape from the earth, love being itself unearthly; and it furthermore assumes that such an escape is a good thing. And so, as my parents and instructors have always told me that cynicism (disapproval of the world) is a bad thing, it surely behoves me to have as little as possible of female society lest I should become a cynic. However, I should like your opinion on the question. Bacon has said: 'The Light of the Reason is never dry' (i.e., 'is never unbiased'). And your letter, I fear me, was quite a shower of water on *my* reason.

In his letters to Gloria, who must have been a paragon of patience, the first samples of his own poetry appear. At the end of each letter he either quoted from his favourites, such as Bliss Carman (whom, ironically, he had discovered at Oxford), Milton, Shelley, and Keats; translated bits of romantic poetry from *The Oxford Book of German Verse* or of Virgil and the other classical poets; or he wrote out poems of his own. He found translation more difficult than writing his own poems: 'You really can't translate poetry. I've tried Greek dozens of times and it's always been dog English instead of Sappho or just plain Hugh MacLennan, both of which were equally bad.'[38] The book he remembers liking most at the time was Palgrave's *Golden Treasury*, which, in the early twentieth-century edition he read, included poets like Tennyson and Rupert Brooke. His taste was still for the unabashedly romantic – whether classical, German, English, or Canadian. Although he was vaguely aware that new styles of poetry were coming into vogue, he was unfamiliar with both T.S. Eliot's *The Wasteland* (1925) and the poetry of W.H. Auden, who was himself still an undergraduate at Christ Church the year MacLennan had arrived in Oxford. He dismissed any post-romantic poetry he had read as too cynical, finding it on the whole distasteful. As he remarked to Gloria: 'If I write you any more of my products, I shall try to include some cynical ones. It seems to be one's duty to be cynical these days.' Inspiration to write, as he described it, seized him unaccountably and from without, in much the same way as he had experienced so-called 'apparitions' during his teens.

I hadn't written a line of poetry for ever so long. But it's something one can't escape, no matter how far one runs. And today it seems to have caught me up with a vengeance. It just came and I can't explain its lucidity – I mean lucidity in coming, you know, not of expression. The one starting 'The rain fell softly all the day' represents about 18 minutes work: I suddenly saw the picture before my mind and ... my pen moved.

The rain fell softly all the day
And evening came & found the sky
All bright & clean & like the bay
Sail-prankt with clouds; and lightly they
Did wheel & run & upward fly
Dissolving in the sunset's ray
Till naught remained but sea & sky
   And a robin's liquid singing.

So may we two, on whom did fall
A tangled world's vast mystery,
Find that our tears have washen all
Clean as the sky; and turn & call
From soul to soul across the sea
Of all between; and rend the pall
That blinds our lives & leap & be
   Re-born in the robin's singing!

His subjects, perhaps typical of a young man of twenty-four, included unfulfilled love, the horror of modern cities, the beauties of the natural world, loneliness, war tragedies, and so on. Later, in 1940, he confessed to Gloria: 'The Oxford stuff was pretty poor, even though I guess I once thought it good and certainly got a kick out of writing it.'[39] Much later he recalled: 'I was a terrible poet; I wrote a lot of awful sonnets.'[40]

Even at the time he had very definite reservations: 'I'm sending you the fruits of my labours, three of which are translations and worse than they'd be anyway, and the others packed full of faults and quite undistinguished. No, it's not mock modesty. I haven't many illusions left. And if one of them doesn't resemble Oxford landscape, don't forget that poetry consists largely in recollection.' Two of these poems are worth setting down here: the first reveals his feeling for the Nova Scotia landscape, the second his profound sense of the tragedy of war.

'Peggy's Cove'

On the grey rock the waves and villages meet
  Far in the strange, grey sea;
The mist close wraps them in her winding sheet
And thro' the liquid stillness drones the beat
  Of the eternal sea.

No forests stir; no birds in springtime sing
  – only the rollers drone;
Only in Autumn nights the heavens ring
With the bleak cry of wild geese, voyaging
  Over the world alone.

Yet are you symbol of my sea-borne home
  Grey village in the waves;
Strong in your strength, your sons the whole world roam;
Still must their thoughts forever homeward come
And question not, but watch your strong winds coam [comb?]
The sea's grey, flowing hairs; and hail their home
  Grey village in the waves!

'These Laid the World Away'

('We buried them together, our officer and an English Lieutenant')
German soldier's letter, July '17

Here lie two youths, once beautiful and swift
That knew the music of the summer sky;
But, being young, they squandered nature's gift
And wrought great deeds because their faith was high.

O Faith! God's mightiest boon that moveth mountains,
Take here these two, our cheapest, easiest gift,
Forgetful of their earth, its hills and fountains
And of themselves, once beautiful and swift![41]

On his next vacation, in December 1930, he returned to the Holtzmanns' for a German Christmas. He had brought back from Halifax a

German grammar, published in Saskatchewan of all places, and he had spent an hour or so each day learning vocabulary. On arriving at Freiburg he found he now understood about ninety per cent of the family's conversation. His main difficulty was shyness, but, warmly welcomed as he was, this difficulty was soon overcome. By the end of this second visit he was proclaimed 'honorary brother,' which further broke down formalities and allowed the sisters to speak more freely. 'Looking back to my earliest recollections which are all of the war, I find it rather amusing,' he wrote to his mother. 'Had any one told me – or you – then, that I should one day become an honorary member of a German family within the next fifteen years, I fancy we should both have been surprised. Had we been told also that the son of that family was a belligerent in the host of baby-killers opposed to us, I suppose the surprise would have been more than doubled.' He noted that Germans prided themselves on saying exactly what they believed, and found the English, by contrast, dishonest hypocrites for their politeness. From this new vantage point, he learned something more about women; as he wrote later to Gloria: 'This past vac in Germany let me into more crannies of the feminine mind than I believed existed. No – I didn't fall in love. That's a prospect that I view with dismay. But my three "sisters" – aged 37-33 and open-minded as children – spoke all their thoughts and aspirations like any devout Catholic to his father-confessor. I can't say I'm cynical about "this thing called love." But I'm very distrustful.' None the less, he confided: 'The lonely *voyageur* need have no fears for a lonely evening in the average German town – if his tastes incline in the proper direction! ... When the darkeyed little lady looms up from the shadows of Cologne Cathedral and whispers *kommst du mit*, I have an enormous advantage over her. Should the thought strike my mind – that she would wish to strike it – "This is a bad thing, to go with you," I should immediately wish to go. The wish would, in reality, be no whit less noble than the wish that made Columbus set out to the Indies. It would merely be the lure of adventure. If anyone were asked whether he would prefer a voyage to "the good lands" or "the bad lands" he would not hesitate for a moment. And so, being thus armed, I can look at the lady and say "Fraulein, your nose is a bit too long, your eyes are quite attractive, but your mouth is too full. On the whole, I think a glass of beer would be preferable. Would you care to join me?" And not infrequently she does and for a few minutes at least, can be quite interesting.'[42]

On his way to Freiburg he had stopped for the first time in Berlin, and found himself disgusted by the city's immorality and decadence:

'The French artistic sense does its level best to make a sacrament out of vice. The Berliners accept it and slobber in it with a cynicism that is rather terrifying if it were not also disgusting.' 'Berlin is now the gayest city in Europe. By "gayest" one generally means "most vicious."' Thus, he concluded: 'Berlin seems like a compromise between Paris and Imperial Rome, with a good bit of New York thrown in after dark.' This decadence, he felt, was related to a falling-off of Christianity among Protestants: 'The only countries of Europe containing practicing Christians are Catholic. The Protestants of Germany are for the most part careless of agnostics and very cynical. They are also beyond doubt the most immoral lot I have ever seen.' Despite his natural tendency towards Christian ethics, he was finding the formalized expression of Christianity increasingly disappointing, mainly because of his scholastic training in debate; even a visit to the college by the Archbishop of York during the subsequent school term was a let-down, for in his address 'Is There a Moral Standard?' 'he marred his effect,' as far as MacLennan was concerned, 'by making a childish fallacy on a vital point through ... a loose statement that the pulpit seems to compel almost everyone to that mounts it to make.'[43]

That winter at Oxford was a particularly cold and muggy one. MacLennan turned to rugger and tennis for relief: 'without Rugger I should unquestionably perish,' he wrote home. He had developed new skills that led to his playing wing-three-quarter instead of fly-half as before. 'It is delightful,' he insisted, 'to bury one's face in the cold wet turf, while the feet of both sides are scrumming on top of you; to get really soaked and muddied and into a close personal fellowship with the earth. And after that a rare old English tea and a quiet pipe. Such is the masculine tranquility of Oxford at Michaelmas!'[44] In the tennis trials he now stood eighth on the university ladder, with a good chance of winning a 'Blue' or 'Half-Blue' at the final trials in June. But before that he would use his last trip abroad to visit Greece.

In mid-March 1931, disappointed that his father could not join him as previously planned, he set off on what he thought of as 'wanderings worthy of Odysseus.' The timing could not have been better. He had just completed the section of his studies on Greek history before this Easter break; 'and with it fresh in my mind,' he wrote home, 'I think it would definitely be the psychological time for the visit.' To Gloria he confided: 'If my profession – as will likely be the case, at first anyway – will be tied up with things classical and Greek thought in particular, I should be a fool to miss seeing the places that gave birth to it all ... And the beauty of this life of mine is that I can take my tools along in a handbag and do my six to seven hours a day in mornings and nights and leave the afternoons free.'[45] So off he went to Paris, spent a grim night in Genoa, down through Rome to Brindisi where he set sail for Athens, stopping at Corfu and passing close to Ithaca en route. Delighted at the cheapness of the trip (the travel alone was only about twenty dollars, a room and breakfast forty-five cents, and a brandy six cents), he found Athens unbelievably dirty, but none the less magnificent. Everywhere he turned he saw evidence of the things he had been studying, but beyond that the splendour of the Greek landscape was overwhelming. 'I am a pro-Athenian,' he wrote to Gloria. Atop the Acropolis, when a young Greek photographer snapped his picture in front of the Erechtheion, where the serene Caryatides grace the Porch of the Maidens, he was ecstatic: 'The Parthenon on the Acropolis seems both as young and as old as the world. I saw it first from the Pnyx, the old meeting place of the Assembly. It was sunset and the sea, four miles behind, was burnished a bright bronze. Westward the Eleusinian hills "had deep pockets in their purple sides"; far in front rode the snow-caps of Parnes and Pentelicon; on the right the great ridge of Hymettus; and in the middle the Parthenon, showing pure white against the dark rock of the Acropolis, seemed almost to float over the city ... Pericles himself could find no words to praise it. He only said "Fix your eyes upon Athens and become lovers of her."'[46]

Greedily he soaked up the atmosphere and revelled in the sense of history. But the trip was marred a little by loneliness; without an emotional centre such as the Holtzmann family had provided in Germany, his travels were less than ideal. None the less, he managed his share of adventures. On one of his jaunts in the Peloponnesus, he set out by foot, with a guide and a donkey 'too lively with ticks to sit on,' to visit a monastery far up the Langada gorge 'through which Spartan spearmen had marched against the Messenians.' Unfortunately, or perhaps not, he got lost, and found himself late at night sharing an authentic Greek peasant meal at Kalamata. 'The soles of my shoes torn and my feet bound up with handkerchiefs,' he later recalled in 'My Most Memorable Meal,' 'I staggered into the town ... at midnight, paid the guide and looked for a place to eat.' The meat? 'An old goat,' his host replied, 'that made so much trouble we killed it last week!'[47]

His final year at Oxford was dominated by tennis and poetry. In tennis, he won the university singles championship during the autumn of 1930, ensuring that he would be picked to play for Oxford against Cambridge and would therefore win the 'Half-Blue' for this year. By June 1931, just before going home for the summer, he thought seriously of collecting some of his poems for publication. As he wrote to Gloria: 'I hope to get them published some of these days, as I have about enough for a small volume. I couldn't possibly get any money out of them, for poets never do make it, but it is really an end in itself and is appreciated, if not paid, as such. It wouldn't do me any harm and in other ways, might do me a bit of good. What surprises me is the trend towards mysticism some of the later ones are taking. One is to a large extent unable to govern the run of any good poem or indeed of any work of art, as I heard Galsworthy say here just last week. I don't think, either, that they can be really termed pessimistic, altho' very few are exuberant. Another odd result is that they have revealed to me quite another side of myself.' One of the poems included in this letter illustrates what he meant:

'Nocturne'

With dropping May the summer night is full.
One with the breeze I hear the river's sigh;
Breathing as one asleep he wanders by
The towers and trees of this town-beautiful.

O Dreams of terror and wild loneliness!
I do not dare unbar your door so soon
To set you free to voyage to the moon
And lose yourselves and me in wilderness.

Wrapped in the night's soft quiet I see friends pass
And intimacy in their accents plays;
Or gather by the door and watch the rays
Of the moon's bright magic creeping thro' the grass.

O dreams, I held you back for loneliness!
No deeper seas or quieter knows the soul
Than here, where men like waves about it roll
And know not how to speak their friendliness.

So forth, O dreams, to Beauty and to Rain,
And smell the May upon the night's warm lips
Go forth: launch to the dark your shapely ships
And lose yourselves that you may find again![48]

In this same letter he seemed to be suggesting also that he had in mind either a career as a writer, for which his degree in Classics would only be something to fall back on to earn a living, or that he fancied his poetry might enhance his career in the Classics, making him a more attractive candidate for an academic position. In fact, his interest in his studies was seriously affected by his desire to write. As he wrote much later to Leonard Cohen, a student of his who was to become a writer himself: 'I remember spending the last two vacations before my Greats, when theoretically everything in my future depended on getting a good class in final schools, and being quite unable to do any studying. I was writing all the time. Mostly bad poetry ... right up to the final schools. I suffered in my results, of course, and superficially I damaged myself, but if I hadn't done that I'd now be a disconsolate don somewhere thinking that life had passed me by.'[49]

Now, in his last year at Oxford, he submitted his work to publishers – first to John Lane and one other publisher in the autumn, and then later around Christmas to Elkin Matthews' firm. All three publishers turned down his manuscript. As far as he was concerned, these rejections were not his fault, but the result of a general depression in the Western economy. Although he was willing to admit that his poems were 'a bit uneven,' and that they had 'a distinct non-English savour' about them, thus putting off publishers who were more used to the English pastoralism of poets like Edmund Blunden, he thought that once he got more business sense about how to aim them at his potential market 'some of them will live': 'I should naturally like to get them out now, but if I can't, I am perfectly confident that when I mature more and get on to the hang of "marketing" it I shall be able to do something with it. Readers are like sheep and read what they are told to read.' With all the arrogance and playfulness of a young man of twenty-four, when he wrote home explaining his failure to publish, he boasted: 'Indeed, I have a very big grudge at the world. Why? Because the best poet that has appeared since the death of Rupert Brooke and James Elroy Flecker is not being given a chance to put his stuff across. It's bad enough to tell a man that his stuff lacks the necessary merit. It's far worse to say "We like your work immensely, as it shows not only charm but also technical ability, but regret that we are unable to make you an offer for them, as there is no market for poetry nowadays." That's what Elkin Matthews said. And so, now that a publication would have done all the good in the world, no one will publish. I think later on that I shall have a chance, if not in England, at least in America.'[50] He hardly dared hope for what he most wanted – to be a successful writer.

Like everyone at the time, MacLennan found his life increasingly intruded upon by politics. When he had first come up to Oxford he had been a 'born' Conservative; assuming more or less automatically the Tory attitudes of his father, he had regretted the Conservative loss in the British election of 1929. Through some of his Oxford friends he had gained some glimmerings of insight into the Labour party and the doctrines of socialism, but he had not pursued these ideas. In Italy he had seen and disliked the rising influence of fascism, with its military trappings, but his real interests lay elsewhere. Now, however, in the early 1930s, the world situation was such that it could no longer be ignored. As the British poet Stephen Spender later maintained: 'From 1931 onwards, in common with many other people, I felt hounded by external events.' Like everyone else in that 'watershed' year – the effects of the Depression now apparent to all – MacLennan began to worry. He wrote in June:

> Things look pretty dismal in the world just now. Germany is trembling on the verge of bankruptcy; Russia has her nose magnificently, if dangerously, on the grindstone; France seems the only really prosperous country left. England is doing as well as might be expected and doesn't whine much over her troubles. I'm awfully afraid that America has been hardest hit of all, except perhaps, the poor old Hun. And the tragedy of it is that she is more largely responsible for her own plight than she can realize. It is a sound paradox to say that no one is more unpractical than the business man. He rarely can see the wood for the trees and the business instinct of seizing the bird in hand leads him far astray in international politics and economics. *Ecce Signum*! American business men have been so rapacious in draining Europe of its last dollar in the war debt that now Europe has literally no money left with which to buy. Hence the industrial depression ... I really think the worst times, if they are not actually past, are on at the present and we will blunder thro'. Economists predict a few years of very hard times, followed by a great reduction in the cost of living.[51]

With the establishment of the 'National' government in the fall of 1931, MacLennan paid more attention to British politics than ever before. Although he predicted the 'Nationalist' victory and was anti-Labour in his sentiments – 'they are no more than clap-trap' – after the election, noting the country had decided 'to stick to the flag,' he worried that the new government might turn out to be mainly die-hard Tory. In the future, however, he felt the socialists would likely return to power, though they lacked experience at the moment. Observing the growth of Communist strength, particularly in Scotland, he commented: 'we aren't ready for it yet. In time, perhaps.'[52]

Of greater personal interest, however, was the news from Germany, since he planned to return to the Holtzmanns' for the Christmas holidays. In the election of September 1930, Adolf Hitler and the National Socialists had made enormous gains, emerging as the second largest party in the Reichstag; since then, the centre of gravity of German political life had moved rapidly to the streets. With the increase of violence and extremism, on the left as well as on the right, MacLennan became anxious about whether or not it would be safe to travel there. None the less, he wrote to his father on 6 December 1931 announcing his plans to go to Freiburg, assuring him that he anticipated no trouble. Once in Germany he was further relieved. 'As the winter wears on,' he reported home, 'the probability of revolution seems less and less. For all who had anything, the manufacturers and the older families, have pretty well pooled their resources to stave it off. Repudiation there will certainly be, but a revolution is not probable unless the French, following the repudiation, enter the Ruhr again.' His German had by now progressed to the point at which he could eavesdrop unconsciously in public, thus enabling him to soak up a good deal of the local atmosphere. He gathered that Thom, the fiancé of one of the Holtzmann girls, had gone off to Innsbruck; later, he came to realize that he had become a Nazi. Certainly he had no liking for the man, nor did Herr Professor Holtzmann since Thom's main trait seemed to be shocking rudeness. On the other hand, he missed his company: 'Life in Freiburg without Thom is rather quiet. I wish he were here, for argument with him was wonderful practice.'

While MacLennan was in Freiburg, an incident occurred that shook him and brought home to him some of the realities of the times. Someone threw a brick at the professor's house and broke the window, leaving MacLennan to calm down the three hysterical daughters. Eventually it was explained as a political gesture: 'The breaking of the professor's window has been traced to Communists who, not unnaturally, are not well-disposed to the Catholic Church, of which Herr Professor is one of the most prominent members. What good it will do them to smash a ten mark window of his I cannot say. It was pretty dirty and if I could have laid my hands on the lad who did it, I should have given him a warm time. The average Hun who goes Communist is generally the reverse of strong and ferocious.'[53] In the political polarization that was taking place throughout the Western world, MacLennan, at this point, had little sympathy for either the left or the right.

Once back in England, in January 1932, he turned his full attention to his own future. His father had urged him to consider two alternatives: to proceed to a Ph.D. in Classics at either Princeton or Harvard or to attempt to locate a job as schoolmaster in a boys' public school in England. To the latter suggestion he was firmly opposed: 'It would be a rut of the very first magnitude, in which, to be quite candid, I should not even be granted great liberty of thought. And the prospect of working with small boys from 13 to 14, for the next ten years, in an atmosphere in which Cricket and Rugger were the staples of conversation, does not appeal at all and I don't think it would be good either ... I know I should not be happy in their atmosphere.'

The other alternative was only marginally more appealing. After applying to Princeton through a series of letters to Professor A.C. Johnson, whom he had met at Dalhousie in 1928 and had contacted with his father when they had visited Princeton in 1929, he discovered that he would be lucky to obtain even a $400 fellowship towards his first year there. According to Johnson it was 'the same old story of course – the depression.' A few, like Woodside, who had come down from Oxford in 1931 and taken a position at the University of Toronto, were lucky enough to find jobs, but by 1932 the situation was worse. None the less, Johnson advised him to apply, holding out the probability that if he could finance his first year a part-time teaching job would materialize or he would be given fellowships to pay for the remaining time. 'I am awfully sorry,' MacLennan wrote home, 'not to be able to earn next year, more sorry than I can say. But Prof. Johnson says no one a few years ago could have foreseen a depression.'[54]

His guilt and resentment at having to accept even further financial support from his father inform every letter home from his last term at Oxford. One aspect of his guilt involved Frances. Although she had successfully completed her degree in Classics at Dalhousie after her long convalescence, she had tried unsuccessfully to go on to obtain a Master of Arts at the University of Toronto. After recovering once again from two serious breakdowns of health in Toronto, she had resigned herself to the very job her brother could not stomach – that of teaching, in a girls' private school at Compton in Quebec's Eastern Townships where she would remain until 1939 (then, after obtaining a Bachelor of Education in Toronto, and teaching a few years at Havergal College, she transferred to Netherwood School in Rothesay, New Brunswick, where she was to remain until her retirement in 1971). Certainly in 1932, at the time MacLennan was making a decision about his own future, it pricked his conscience to know that his sister had already established her financial independence. 'As Dadden has more or less given me the portion of goods that falleth to me,' he wrote directly to Frances, 'I have about decided to stomach the damned Ph.D. and have done with it, if for no other reason [than] that university jobs, no less than the commercial world, are just as stagnant as they well can be ... As both Canada and the States will at the heel of the hunt prefer a man with a Ph.D., I suppose the sooner I manage the fool thing the better.'[55]

In the end, he was awarded the John Harding Page Fellowship of $400 at Princeton, but he was given no teaching assistantship to supplement it. When at the end of the spring term of 1932 he went down from Oxford, having taken a third class in Literae Humaniores, the occasion was hardly auspicious. Twenty-five years old, with his Oxford BA in Classics, he could not have known that the Depression would deepen and that the field he had worked so hard to master was quickly fading from significance in North American education.

Chapter three

The Voyage Back: Princeton

Boarding the *S.S. Pennland* at Southampton in June 1932 to return home for the summer, MacLennan could have had no idea that one of his fellow passengers was to become his wife. None the less, that summer night, though it was far past midnight, the American woman he would marry four years later was leaning over the sturdy oak deck rail, looking like one of the tall, dark-haired Greek Fates he had been reading about in his studies at Oxford. Her quick, dark eyes singled him out below on the quay, chatting with another man in the intermittent light that fell on them as busy stevedores loaded the ship with cargo. Speculating as to who they might be at that hour, she concluded that the older man was American; MacLennan, the younger, she fancied might be a Dane. 'The other man was younger and obviously as intent on his own conversation as was his companion. His clothing was nondescript – untidy gray slacks, a brown tweed jacket, a scarf knotted about his throat, and no hat. Occasionally, as he moved aside to permit passage of one of the ants [stevedores] trundling a loaf of sugar, he stepped within range of a light. Only for a moment and then out again, but it was enough to show a head of wavy, tousled brown hair and a mobile face that even from a distance I could see broke into laughter as easily as it receded into a frown.'

Attracted by even this glimpse of the 'boyish' figure, curious to discover whether he was to be a passenger aboard ship, even more curious perhaps to discover whether her guess about his national origin

On board the *S.S. Pennland*, June 1932

was correct, Dorothy Duncan was pleased to find, within less than a day, that he had indeed boarded the *Pennland*:

It was the next evening after dinner, when I was reading in a far corner of the lounge, that I looked up from my book to see the younger of the two men from the Southampton dock standing in the doorway, surveying the room and all its contents. He looked us over, one by one, as though hunting for someone who might speak his language, unobserved by the large and small groups who were playing bridge or telling tall tales. He lingered perhaps a full minute while his eyes became accustomed to the light, and then he turned to leave. With his hands on the doorframe he looked over the room once more, quickly, and then I found my stare caught ... as though someone in a movie close-up had turned from his preoccupation and looked straight at me. His eyes smiled though his lips were still, and then he was gone.

I went back to the pages of my book, but instead of reading I began to curse my ineptness with languages.

She caught sight of 'the young Dane' once or twice the next day, but it was not until that evening, returning to the same corner of the lounge with her book in the hope that he would seek her out, that she finally managed to meet him. He invited her to join him for a port, possibly for the same reason he had noticed her the day before – that her resemblance to his Halifax sweetheart, Jean Shaw, was so striking that they might have been twins. Dorothy found the sound of his voice 'utterly charming and the smile that went with it more so.' Pique at her inaccurate guess about his nationality was overwhelmed by relief that they had English in common. Noting both his 'shyness' and equally his 'determination,' she initiated a conversation that rapidly informed each of them about the other. Those few days aboard the *Pennland*, she recalled, were idyllic.

That night and the next and the next we talked, walking the quiet decks after we tired of the lounge. How the inmates of the cabins below must have hated us, when the hours after midnight seemed to us even better for walking than the hours before. They were the most effortless conversations I have ever taken part in, perfectly adapted to the mood of an uncommunicative young woman; for one question or remark on my part would elicit a half-hour's reply, and while it was being expanded I had ample opportunity to observe and listen to the fullness of things not spoken ... What could Nova Scotia be like, that its people gave this name to themselves with such pride in their voices that one felt they were convinced of a superiority palpable to the rest of the world?

The falling stars had made him think of some lines of poetry; and as he repeated them without the self-consciousness an American would have shown, I found myself wondering if they were all as filled and running over with vitality and joy and intensity as this one. His voice rounded the cadences of classical verse as easily as it broke later into a popular New York dance tune which he had lately heard played in the Savoy. It was obvious that all the time he was loving it, tasting it, drinking deeply of it, and learning its ways he was managing to see life whole ... His shyness was as real as his charming manners and his ability on the tennis court, and yet ... too much of him at a stretch was apt to be exhausting, like trying to master a new skill without allowing for the psychological pauses necessary when the human mind adapts itself to something unfamiliar.'[1]

There remains always something mysterious about attractions between men and women – why this one instead of that? Yet Dorothy's account of her first meeting with MacLennan tells us a great deal about the nature of the bond that was forming. First, his youth, a 'boyish' quality about him, appealed to her; she was three years older, and perhaps the impulse to look after him, to protect, possess, or to be proud of him, propelled her to him. His intellectual interests, which he was all too eager to show off for her benefit, as he was later to do for his family, coincided with her own. It is tempting to see in that open book over which they exchanged their first glance, an omen for the future bond of a common interest.

And in Dorothy's account can be seen a large dose of the romanticism MacLennan himself had been expressing in his poetry: it is summer, two young people are aboard ship, walking the decks in the moonlight; as in the song *Some Enchanted Evening*, they exchange their first glance as strangers 'across a crowded room.' To her, MacLennan was a 'hero' and a 'poet.' Above all, she must have been drawn to his strength: not his mere physical strength, though his accounts of his tennis achievements and his fine, good health made that obvious, but that combination of 'vitality' and 'determination' which was summed up in her single word, 'intensity.' An invalid since childhood, she must have wanted that strength to lean on, to draw on when her own waned. And, paradoxically, in her appetite for life she too was intense – keen in her perceptions, full in her sensual enjoyments – to a degree that she found matched in this young man with his gusto for life and his apparently limitless energy.

Dorothy Duncan had been born in East Orange, New Jersey, in 1903 and had grown up in the 1920s in Wilmette, just north of Chicago on the shore overlooking Lake Michigan. Her ancestors had almost all come out from England on the first ships, and although the family had never been wealthy it had developed a high degree of individualism over several generations. Moving south and west out of Massachusetts, members of the family had fought on both sides in the Civil War. Dorothy's grandfather had been a major in the Northern army and had been stationed on the Texas-Arkansas border following the war. There he raised his five sons, of whom Edwin, Dorothy's father, was the eldest. At the age of seventeen, Edwin L. Duncan had run away from home to avoid the military academy his father had chosen for him; ironically, the name by which he came to be known in later life was 'the Colonel,' as the military life he had tried so hard to escape eventually thrust itself upon him as his national duty. Photographs reveal that he was a large, dark, forceful man. As Dorothy remembered him, he was 'eager to move on to new fields, at home or wherever he found himself, ready to try something new.' His first job had been with the United States Sea Post Service; later he became head of the Railway Mail Service in New York at the time Theodore Roosevelt was police commissioner there. By the time MacLennan met him, he was living at Wilmette, working as an administrator for the Union Pacific Railway. Something of his tireless energy can be seen in the fact that at seventy-eight, having retired to Laguna Beach, California, he volunteered for the Marine Corps and served as a guard in the El Toro camp for the last three years of the Second World War.

Dorothy's mother had a background and personality that contrasted dramatically with those of her husband. Where 'the Colonel' was all force, restlessness, confidence, she was all delicacy, quiet, and home-rootedness. Her childhood on the plains near Denver had been dreadful; both her parents had been confined to institutions for the insane, leaving as their only legacy a younger brother for her to raise and the principles of the Christian Science religion in which they fervently believed. Her schooling was consequently 'sparse and irregular.' According to Dorothy, 'my mother always craved the security of deep roots, permanence, the surroundings of long-loved treasures.'[2]

This unlikely couple produced two daughters who, in their personalities, represented their own split in attitude. Dorothy, the elder, resembled her father to whom she was very close. 'He was the only person who accepted me as I was,' she later told friends in North Hatley.[3] Her younger sister Jean, closer to their mother and favoured for her beauty, enjoyed excellent health, but Dorothy was a semi-invalid from childhood having suffered rheumatic fever. As MacLennan later described it: 'both valves [of her heart] were damaged not by one assault of the disease but by four. Never in her life did she know what it feels like to be physically strong ... She discovered early that the young are rendered uncomfortable by the weak and the sick, and she studied early to disguise her symptons ... She loved watching hockey and tennis and baseball and ballet and all the activities of which she herself was deprived.'

This physical weakness, however, belied the strength of her personality. By her own account she read omnivorously, like so many invalids, and was thoroughly acquainted with many of the intellectual and political trends of the day. Attending Northwestern University in Evanston, near Chicago, in the early 1920s, as an undergraduate studying botany, she recalled wondering if she could make it through the geological field trips on the dunes of Lake Michigan;[4] because of her 'past and present cardiac condition' she was exempted from the physical education requirement.[5] As she accustomed herself to becoming one of life's spectators, reading increased her interest and knowledge in literature and the arts. Her best subjects at Northwestern, aside from botany, were English literature, art appreciation, painting, and drawing, in all of which she obtained first class marks.

The Chicago of her day was infamous. She remembered well the football game in Soldiers' Field when the youth of the time gave a standing ovation to Al Capone and his bodyguard.[6] At the worst of the Depression, under the iniquitous regime of prohibition, there was much open crime in the streets, and gangsters brazenly exterminating each other. Signs of the economic slump were everywhere in the winter of 1933, when the unemployed slept wrapped in newspapers under conduits and on the ledges above the urinals in men's lavatories in railroad stations.

Neither the Duncans nor the MacLennans were dramatically affected by the Depression. Sufficiently well off, though by no means rich, both families were still able to afford not only life's necessities but many of its luxuries as well.

After completing her Bachelor of Science degree in botany in 1925, Dorothy had worked at first for a public relations organization in their advertising agency. Later, she had opened a small business of her own in Evanston, and was secretary to the principal of Portage Park grammar school in a poor section of Chicago. Like her father she had always enjoyed travel and adventure: already she had made a trip through the Canadian Rockies[7] and down the west coast of the United States; every summer, when the grammar school closed she had travelled by ship to Europe.

These summer trips constituted for Dorothy 'my own brand of postgraduate course.' In fact, she was in some ways like the visitors to St Moritz that MacLennan had so disliked. 'I was an American,' she explained in her recollections, 'and in those days Europe was a place where our money bought pleasures. Its politics were of little interest and – so we thought – without any apparent relation to ourselves.' As she later summed up the years just prior to meeting MacLennan: 'That was the era when we all went to Europe. I was part of the age of coonskin coats, flappers, the Charleston, bathtub gin and the first trumpet blasts of Dixieland jazz. I was "twenty in the Twenties." We listened to King Oliver at the Royal Garden and stayed up all night to talk about ourselves and the new world being realized by Fitzgerald and Hemingway and Dos Passos, the new world being searched for by John Gunther and Jimmy Sheean and Milton Mayer. They were Chicagoans too, our seniors by several years, but they were all part of us and we were of them. What they could do we were going to do, too.'

That summer of 1932, when she met MacLennan on her fifth trip abroad, she had been in charge of a group of tourists making a European excursion from Chicago.[8] Her job had included responsibility for their passports, tickets, and accommodation, but once they reached the London office of the tourist agency that had given her the job her duties eased off, leaving her free to enjoy the rest of the trip through the Netherlands, France, Switzerland, and Belgium. On the way over to London, Dorothy had fallen in love with a young man who in fact lived wthin three miles of her home, although she had not met him before. Saying farewell to her tourists once they had been collected and deposited aboard their ship home, she had changed her personal booking to the *Pennland*, which sailed later, so that she could rejoin her sweetheart in Switzerland a little longer. They had made a date to meet in Chicago at the end of the month.

So it was by sheer accident that this strong-willed, statuesque American woman and the young Oxford graduate met, for she had changed her bookings at the last minute and he had gambled, like the man she had seen him speaking to on the quay, that there might just be room for another unbooked passage on the *Pennland*.

At the age of twenty-five MacLennan was remarkably naïve about women. His experience had been pretty much limited to his summers with Jean Shaw and his idealization of her from a distance; his encounters with the few women he had spoken to briefly during his thoroughly masculine years at Oxford; and the letters he received from his cousin Gloria whom he did not even remember meeting. As he himself confessed, his greatest understanding so far of the feminine mind had been the result of his visits at the Holtzmanns' where their three daughters, all older than he was, had spoken freely about their inner feelings. But these girls were from a different culture than his own – German and Catholic – and their 'confessions' to their 'honorary brother' were made in another language; furthermore, they themselves had been so sheltered that well into their twenties they had literally believed that the stork had brought them into the world.[9]

Now, however, he fell in love. It was just about the most impracticable thing he could have done at this point. His father's insistence that marriage was out of the question until he had a job, while undoubtedly sound advice, was especially difficult to bear for a young man who knew that jobs everywhere were becoming more and more scarce. Although he had definitely set his sights on a Princeton doctorate before leaving Oxford, meeting Dorothy made him change his mind. Accepting money from his father for his last year at Oxford had already rankled deeply. It would not have taken much to trigger the rebellion that now occurred. Falling in love with Dorothy, a force stronger than his father's logic, was reason enough to abandon the grand plan to go to Princeton. As soon as he got back to Halifax, having waved goodbye to Dorothy, who stayed on the ship bound for New York before taking the train home to Chicago, he began looking for a university post.

To his family, and to his father particularly, MacLennan had reached the zenith of success that summer. A younger cousin who met him then for the first time recalled being overwhelmed by the aura of importance that radiated from the most significant member of the clan:

Hugh came back from Oxford with the richest Oxford accent it was possible to produce with the rough Canadian vocal chords he had begun with. I remember this, for it was perhaps the first time I had ever met Hugh ...

We were all rather overawed in the presence of our own relative, Hugh MacLennan, who had been chosen to go to Oxford to be made into the nearest thing to royalty we had ever imagined. And he seemed to enjoy the role, giving us plentiful dollops of his new speech and urbane attitudes about cultural and world affairs we had never thought about. He had been to Germany, had sung songs there with German students, had drunk BEER, and had the little cardboard circles to prove it. He had worked at music, and played very creditably upon his mother's piano a long passage from Beethoven's *Appassionata* and displayed himself clad in a new style of clothing, expensive soft shirts of a chequered Viyella, I would guess, with trousers that didn't match his jacket. I [a high school boy] was overwhelmed.

This was the summit of uncle Sam's aspirations – his son as English as a Canadian can be made, a man of the new world, healthy in every respect, enthusiastic, full of beans (his mother's phrase) and uncle Sam positively glowed with pride. My God, Hugh had done everything he had wanted to do, and better.[10]

By fortuitous coincidence, a job in the Classics Department at Dalhousie University opened up that summer. The honours he had already brought that university and his solid Oxford degree made his employment there a virtual certainty. But he was rejected. Another candidate had applied who was not Canadian, but English; Lionel Pearson had also attended Oxford where he had obtained a first in Mods. and a second in Greats at Trinity College. As MacLennan was told by Professor Howard Murray, who had been chairman in his day and had never particularly liked him: 'After all, you're a Canadian and he's an Englishman. It makes a difference.' In his later recollection of this traumatic scene in an essay called 'How We Differ from Americans' (1946), MacLennan wrote: 'It was one of those arterial sentences. It went from my brain right through me till I felt it in the back of my legs.' According to MacLennan this decision constituted a personal vendetta against his father: a prominent member of the board later told Dr Sam that he had always hated him and his son, and had been glad of the chance to teach him what the world was like.[11] Ironically, the outcome of the board's decision was what Dr Sam wanted: his son, he had long since decided, would get a Ph.D. from Princeton.

Determined to find a job somewhere, anywhere, MacLennan sat down in the summer of 1932 and wrote applications to each university with a Classics Department in Canada. By the only other university that had an opening he was told: 'two Englishmen are applying for this job and I don't think you'll have much of a chance.'[12] This situation indeed taught MacLennan what the world was like; it was not really much different from what he had already known as 'The Ridge of Tears.' For a man who at Oxford had considered it a good thing that the better Englishmen should be encouraged to come out to North America to take up university posts, this rejection was devastating.

The bitter disappointment and acute frustration with which he set off for Princeton in October 1932 was to continue throughout his entire three years there. To add to his miseries, Princeton was not to provide him with the teaching opportunities he had hoped for. Longing for independence and his own income, tired of being a student and following his father's advice, he came close to having a nervous breakdown, just as he had almost done during his first term at Oxford.

His first impressions of Princeton, when he had seen it with his father in the spring of 1929, were now confirmed. He still thought the place pretentious: '[It] has copied in its architecture ... nearly all the famous landmarks of Oxford and Cambridge, and for good measure has thrown in a replica of the great tower of Canterbury Cathedral. Here is the perfect illustration of *la maladie Américaine*, of the incapacity to accept the fact that a building constructed by monks for the glory of God cannot be copied in the United States and named after the soap baron who put up the money without something happening to its spirit.'[13]

The style of classical study at Princeton was radically different from the methods he had mastered at Oxford, and it could not have suited him less. All but one of his professors derived from the Germanic tradition, which meant that their scholarship consisted of extremely detailed analyses of classical texts and sources – thorough, but unoriginal. The free-ranging discussions of ethics, philosophy, and history – especially the relating of past historical events to present circumstances of which he had become so fond at Oriel – were things of the past. Professor Kelley Prentice, for example, who taught a course on Thucydides, spent the entire semester from early autumn until mid-February on a page and a half of original text. 'I recollect,' MacLennan later wrote to his friend Edmund Wilson, the American critic, 'that he required of me a sixty-page report on a single sentence containing some twelve words. As the sentence was merely a join-sentence I asked him how it was possible to write anything on it at all and he gave me a knowing look and said, "we are more thorough here than at Oxford."'[14] In addition to Prentice's course on Thucydides, in the first two years there he also took the three other courses that were required of all graduate students: a course on Roman drama, Edward Capps' course on Greek comedy, and a tutorial with A.C. Johnson. In his Roman drama course he encountered the same fastidious scholarship offered by Prentice: '[I was] required [to write] a fifty page term paper on the biography of Plautus, of whose life virtually nothing is known. Some fragment [in it] recorded the line, "For ten years I worked *in pistrino*." As Latin has no article, that could be either "in *a* mill" or "in *the* mill." This [had given] rise to a spate of German, and some American, dissertations on where the mill was located. If I remember rightly, a German scholar claimed that the mill was now buried under the Asti Spumante factory. Of course all it meant was "I worked ten years in the mill" – i.e., it took me ten years to learn to be a successful playwright. I pointed out ... that this expression was as common in Latin as in English. I [was told to] repeat all this nonsense about the mill's location.'

Edward Capps was the single professor at Princeton that MacLennan liked and respected. Capps had been associated with the American School of Classical Studies in Athens since 1910, had been ambassador to Greece under Woodrow Wilson, and was the American editor of the great Loeb Classical Library series. His broad outlook and experience appealed to MacLennan much more than the nit-picking of the German-American tradition. As he explained it later, the myopic textual criticism he found characteristic of Princeton was all 'caused by the necessity to "publish."' As far as he could see, many of the 'problems' these scholars concentrated on were specifically manufactured so that their solutions could enhance the reputations of those who explained them. There was, to his mind, no comparison between Oxford and Princeton: 'Genner at Oriel had published only one article in his life, but he knew the field better than the whole faculty at Princeton put together. None of the students could write Latin and Greek above the fourth form level in an English public school.'[15] 'They were saturated in the Germans and were jealous of Oxford and Cambridge which they called amateurish.' Instead of developing the range of his classical knowledge, the 'German-Americanism' of his courses at Princeton and the individually directed readings he did under Johnson's supervision 'came close to killing all joy in the field.'[16]

Princeton at the time was an élitist institution where an attitude of exclusivity made newcomers like MacLennan feel alienated. Graduate students drifted from class to dinner in the great hall like a flock of crows in the long black gowns that set them off from the rest of the university. Another well-known Canadian who was a graduate student there at the same time, the mathematician Professor Israel Halperin, agrees that it was a grim place in which to study; no one took any particular notice of the students. Indeed, he himself almost left the place after his first few weeks since he was convinced that he was surrounded by geniuses and wouldn't make it.[17]

Certainly by the time Dorothy saw him again, eight months after he had disembarked from the *S.S. Pennland* in Halifax, MacLennan was deeply depressed. Meeting him as arranged in New York City on the Ides of March 1933, she was shocked at the change in him: 'the recurrent sense of strain and unrest where he had expected to find a bright certainty had already modified the easy laughter in his eyes. Rather often during the three days of that weekend I felt as though I were seeing a boy who had never encountered meanness or cruelty in his life discovering for the first time that man could be inhumane ... Americans learn somehow to defend themselves from their fellows as early as they can remember. But the world this grown-up boy had always known was like a large and tolerant family, in which it was taken for granted that all its members were men of good will ... It was painful to see this country of mine having a physical as well as an emotional effect upon him.'

On this, his second, visit to New York, MacLennan expressed very much the same point of view that he had shared with his father in the spring of 1929. Now, in the trough of the Depression, he found it more garish and frantic than ever. On this point Dorothy disagreed. To her New York was an exciting city full of wonderful things to do and stores in which she could treat herself to the clothes and jewellery she liked. For the two of them, on this second meeting, the clash of opinions must have been a surprise. As Dorothy recalled the visit in her later book *Bluenose*, MacLennan did not hesitate to criticize the city she so loved:

I enjoyed it as I always had. Only, this time I tried to see the crowds – crowds milling in its streets on their way to nowhere, crowds sitting at restaurant tables through twenty-four hours of every day, crowds buying and spending and trading – through his eyes, as though I had never seen them before.

Automats appalled him and cafeterias made him furious; they were uncivilized, he assured me, and he'd starve before he set foot in one again.

People who shoved things in his face and asked him to buy, people who prided themselves on making smart deals at someone else's expense, people who gambled large sums of money on watered stocks they knew nothing about and then shot themselves when they were cleaned, were suddenly become monstrous to me as seen through his eyes, though subconsciously I still accepted them as natural phenomena ...

I remember that we walked up Fifth Avenue in the late afternoon, engrossed in our own private delving into the mysteries and agonies of the universe. He did the delving, actually, and my eyes had a tendency to wander to the shop windows – to emeralds chez Tiffany, and mink in Revillon Frères, and inexpensive lotions in expensive containers at Elizabeth Arden's. Only when Fifth Avenue is completely destroyed will we find better things to desire than the wares displayed in its windows ... If our backgrounds were different, it was not so much in what is called the social scale as in the wide divergence between the professional world and the world of business and technology. Our approach to any subject or experience was invariably by dissimilar routes – his as the artist, mine as the pragmatist ...

Certainly, the anti-American feelings Dr Sam had fostered in his son were bound to present obstacles in this courtship, but despite MacLennan's prejudice a bond was forming between them. Dorothy, because of her education, her wide reading, her various jobs, her travel abroad, was far too intelligent to take his remarks to heart. She listened carefully and to some extent was convinced by his point of view: 'Though I disagreed with him instinctively when my country and my kind of people were subjected to examination by the penetrating vision of a newcomer and a potential novelist, my common sense was forced to uphold the validity of his judgements and conclusions.'[18]

Fate, however, had intervened to make this meeting a considerably longer one than either had intended. President Franklin D. Roosevelt had closed the banks the day before MacLennan left Princeton; when he got to New York he found the banks closed there too. As a result, he was unable to get enough money to take the train back. With no other alternative, they stayed in a hotel, on credit, for five days until the banks reopened. Thrown into such close quarters with the first woman since Jean Shaw who had stirred his emotions deeply, MacLennan's love blossomed. The consummation of that love during their stay in New York effectively meant to each of them that they were engaged.[19]

Above all, Dorothy seems to have been attracted to MacLennan's artistic ambitions. By this time he really was 'a potential novelist.' After he had failed to find a publisher for his poems while at Oxford, he had decided to try his hand at fiction. It had been there, when he ought to have been studying for his Greats final examinations, that he had begun to work on his first novel.[20] In one of the many letters he had sent to Dorothy since they had separated, he had confided: 'I'm working like the devil, at two jobs, really, research and private writing.'

Dorothy was full of admiration. More than that, she had an instinctive sense that he really had the ability to succeed at it. She was the one, above all, who encouraged his first efforts at fiction and expressed confidence in what he was trying to do. As she recorded the deepening of their relationship: 'That night we heard Schnabel in Carnegie Hall, a stern, gray little man with a very straight back whose power over us for the moment was complete. Out of the isolated pools of consciousness in which we sat our eyes met. His were smiling again ... More important than anything else, the wrapping of aloneness which had insulated me the whole of my life from all other human beings – to my own discomfiture and the despair of everyone who had tried to penetrate it – was now being dissolved by this man who made no effort to do so. Without talking about it, we realized that being together was good.'[21] To MacLennan, who also felt profoundly lonely and depressed, Dorothy's lively, informed conversation and her unwavering confidence in him were just what he needed. Turning away from his family, he directed his main correspondence to her instead. He was beginning to depend on her.

During his three years at Princeton, MacLennan rebelled against a great deal of what he had previously taken for granted. At Oxford he had written home on several occasions to express his sincere gratitude to his parents. He had once written to his mother to say, for example: 'you and [Dadden] have done everything possible for me. I think that between you, you have given me about as satisfactory a bringing up as was possible for anyone to have.'[22] Now, however, he was not so sure. Contrary to his practice at Oxford, he stopped attending church. He paid far less attention to his studies at Princeton than he had ever done before, and threw his best energies into his writing. The news of his attraction to a girl like Dorothy was bound to meet with Dr Sam's disapproval: she was American and older than Hugh; her family were business people; her name 'Duncan' was Lowland, not Highland, Scottish; her religion was Christian Science not Presbyterian; and her damaged heart made it most unlikely she could ever bear children. At Oxford, MacLennan had been able to reject the extremes of his father's puritanism gracefully and without any particular stress, but now there were so many areas of disagreement between them he hardly knew where to begin. He could not any longer be 'the good boy' and continue to follow his father's grand plan without grave doubts about its outcome. As he later put it in an article called 'Couth and Uncouth' (1955), at Princeton 'I continued to study, worked alone at nights, humiliated because I was unable to acquire the independence which alone could have given me a feeling of dignity.'

His rebellion against his father was fed by his early encounters with Freudian theory. Although he had first discussed the Oedipus complex with the writer on board the ship that took him to England, he had begun reading Freud's works in earnest about 1930, a year or so before he came down from Oxford. The widening abyss in understanding between them became absurdly clear when he had attempted to discuss Freud's ideas with his father. 'Freud is no quack,' Dr Sam had dogmatically asserted. 'He was a very competent physician to begin with. And, moreover, as for what he said about the dreams of those foreigners, from what I saw of the morals in Vienna I have no doubt he was absolutely accurate in his deductions. But of course, nothing Freud said could have any possible application for the Scotch.'[23] Even though his father's view amused him, he disagreed. The more he thought about it, the more compelling such concepts as the Oedipus complex, the death-wish, and the symbolic import of dreams seemed to him. Through Freud, he began to recognize the bitterness of his anger against his father. By the time he found himself at age twenty-five attending Princeton against his will, he began expressing it.

Feeling beleaguered and generally hostile, he also found himself increasingly aware of a profound dislike of his physical surroundings. The sight of New York during the Depression, as well as the hideousness of the wasteland formed by the huge, ugly industrial complex between Princeton and the city, further stirred his sentiments against what he had called at Oxford the 'individualism and self-seeking' of the American businessman. In short, he was ready to explore and to be influenced by one of the main intellectual movements of the thirties, Marxism.

At Oxford he had not concerned himself deeply with politics. His Conservative sympathies were inherited and entrenched, and in fact he had sounded just like his father when he wrote home to say that he had met a wonderful old retired colonel at Cheltenham, adding: 'Such is the brain that wins battles, but he was delightful none the less. The sort of Tory one never wants to see go and, I suppose, that one never will.' When he regretted the Tory defeat in the election of 1929 he was in no way unusual at Oxford: the town had given 14,000 votes to the Conservatives, 6000 to the Liberals, and 4000 to Labour. Nor was he unique in regarding the left as something of a lunatic fringe movement at the time, even if temporarily in power.[24]

By his third year at Oxford, however, he had begun to take socialism more seriously. He had moved out of his rooms at Oriel and into an apartment in the Cowley Road with a friend, Geoffrey Wilson, whom he described as 'as obstinate – and I think – as unreasonable a socialist as I have ever met' (Wilson later managed to reconcile himself to becoming an executive in the World Bank and eventual knighthood). The Cowley district southeast of Oxford was a stronghold of Labour support, mainly because of the Morris factory workers who lived there. MacLennan showed little, if any, real sympathy for the Labour party itself, but mainly because of Wilson's influence and his ongoing interest in all classes of men he was increasingly aware of its activities. His sense of political issues at the time is perhaps best seen in his assertion that 'politics seems an awfully stupid sort of game in which 99% of the members are as much at sea as the electorate.'[25]

During his first year at Princeton he was exposed further to left-wing ideas. He shared a washroom off his room, #201, in the Graduate College with another student he had met at Oxford, Geoffrey Bing, 'a hilariously witty man of almost total irresponsibility'[26] (before the war Bing became Labour party whip and afterwards attorney-general of Ghana). The two men, that year, read some of the works of Karl Marx and became interested in communism.

By 1932, and for the rest of the decade, the left had great appeal for many North American intellectuals. During the early thirties Marx' theories seemed to many to provide an accurate analysis of the dynamics of economic change, and helped to explain the Depression that had left millions of workers unemployed. In his *Decline of American Capitalism* (1934), Lewis Corey, a Marxist economist who had been a member of the central executive committee at the time of the formation of the Communist Party of America in 1919, had argued, for example, that the social and economic crisis was caused by the excesses of the capitalist system; as Marx had demonstrated, this property-based system was doomed to destruction by a revolution among the very masses it had brought into being to implement its acquisitive ends.[27] By the middle of the decade, as the totalitarian governments of Italy and Germany became more aggressive, the appeal of the left increased because of its firm stand against fascism.

MacLennan, at this time, was ready and willing to open his mind to left-wing views. Given the conservative outlook inherited from his father, his political 'conversion' constituted a significant part of his current rebellion against many things in his past. The discussions of Marx and his theories with Bing also provided him with an intellectual challenge at a time when he found such stimulation lacking in his academic courses at Princeton.

Although there were other Canadian students at Princeton, MacLennan seems to have had little to do with them. John Tuzo Wilson, who later became an eminent pioneer in the field of geophysics, was there at the time, as were Fred Jolliffe, later professor of geology at Queen's University in Kingston; Loris Russell, curator of the Royal Ontario Museum; C.P. Stacey, eventually the official historian of the Canadian armed forces; and James Sinclair, who became a Liberal member of parliament and father of Margaret Trudeau. Charles Stacey also lived in the Graduate College at the time and recalls an incident that suggests that MacLennan wanted little to do with his fellow Canadians at Princeton. Coming out of Nassau Hall one day, MacLennan passed him, stopped, then turned around and called out saucily: 'I think you're the most Canadian looking person I know.'[28] If Stacey wore his nationality on his sleeve, he reciprocated by regarding MacLennan as a peculiar sort of character who spoke elaborately in a high-pitched voice with a slight English accent, and dressed very much in the tweedy style of Oxford, as did many of the students who had come down from that august institution. Although much later in Canada the two men became good friends, at the time Stacey saw MacLennan as 'a violent Nova Scotian,' who thought Confederation had been a terrible mistake because his 'superior' community was being debased by association with lesser men.[29] As for American scholarship, he remembered, MacLennan often spoke of it with great contempt.

MacLennan did not really fit in at Princeton, either academically or socially. His only close friend among the other students was the Cambridge poet Ronald Bottrall, who had come to Princeton on a Commonwealth Fund Fellowship and was later to join the foreign service. He was a little older than MacLennan and had taught for two years in Finland before coming to the United States. He had also succeeded, where MacLennan had failed, in publishing in 1931 a volume of poetry called *The Loosening and Other Poems*. Bottrall's poetry was 'intellectual' or 'modern' in the mode of T.S. Eliot – a type of poetry MacLennan had already rejected as being too 'cynical' for his taste. For a time, however, he responded to what he later recognized as the 'messianic' personality of the man who knew 'Tom,' 'Ezra,' and 'Wystan' personally: 'I consulted his priestly critics, F.R. Leavis, Cyril Connolly and T.S. Eliot himself, dutifully said farewell to many of the poets I had loved and joined the column that trudged off into the wasteland. It never occurred to me that the depression was responsible for a lot of my admiration for Eliot and his followers ... I had loved the world ... I had felt rejected by the world ... and wanted to get my own back.' It was not long, however, before he reverted to his old fondness for romantic and optimistic literature. In discussions with Bottrall he came to see that Eliot's 'is not a poetry of love but of dislike, not of attraction but of repulsion, not of the country but of the town.' Later he was to say, by way of advice to his student Leonard Cohen: 'Eliot should soon be embalmed. After all he has been turning himself into a stuffed shirt for years, has believed his own build-up and has sold a considerable part of his integrity to the vested interest of academic poetasters who find him satisfactory to teach since they share his distaste for life. [His poems are like] an equation enclosed in a cryptogram.'[30]

None the less, he and Bottrall spent a good deal of time comparing poems and arguing about the relative merits of romantic and modern poetry. Along with a few other Princeton men, they met once or twice a week at a tavern just outside the town, to discuss left-wing politics but more often to play a game, invented by Bottrall, called 'Poetic Consequences.' Each player had to supply a rhyming line to what came before and supply a second line for the next player. The poems tended to be bawdy, but Charles Gifford, a Scottish Wykehamist who later became a financier and millionaire, could be relied on to be the 'straight man,': when, for example, MacLennan supplied the line 'She threw the hairy legs from out her bed,' Gifford replied 'And introduced a halibut instead.'[31] It was against Bottrall that MacLennan worked out his own theories of writing; he also showed him bits of the novel he was working on and consulted with him about how to improve his style. For years afterward they remained correspondents, though they were to see little of one another.

Besides Bottrall, MacLennan's main friends at Princeton were the house boys and other staff who did the menial tasks around the institution. As Stacey remembered it, this too marked him as an odd figure. While other students were gathering for casual discussions over coffee or drinks, MacLennan was off on long hikes with these boys, deep in conversation; his peers concluded that he had been unable to make friends with more suitable men. There were, however, good reasons for his choice. These boys were mainly German immigrants – especially his closest friend, a tall, handsome, fair-haired young fellow. Just as he had earlier hated the pretensions of the wealthy and cultured élite who came to St Moritz in season, he now rebelled against the snobbish cliques of Princeton. To him, the ordinary men who worked around such establishments were infinitely more interesting than the clientele.

In the first place, these boys gave him a chance to practise speaking German, but he had in common with them also a knowledge of Germany itself. He had shared, to some extent, their experience of turbulent history in the making, the drastic effects of the Depression in their homeland, the rise of the Nazis under Hitler. These were the very reasons they had emigrated, and many of them were sympathetic to the communist alternative; hence his new interest in Marxism formed no small part of their discussions. Through these friends, it was not long before he became a frequent customer at the rathskeller of the German-American Athletic Club at 190 Third Avenue in New York. It was here, in the company of his German friends, and of Dorothy when she managed to come in by train from Chicago to meet him,[32] that he learned a great deal more about the events that were increasingly commanding the attention of the whole world. Leaving the ivory tower of Princeton behind, he drank beer and talked at the rathskeller until the early hours of many mornings.

As at Oxford, he threw himself whole-heartedly into the sports program. Again he took up rugger as well as running, handball, and a little tennis, making a considerable mark for himself as the university handball champion; his coach on the rugger team was James Sinclair. But sports alone could do little to alleviate his frustrations.

Keeping in close touch with Dorothy by letter, he sent her poems as well as sections from the novel he had begun at Oxford. Its genesis had been his conviction that he had been in Europe during a critical period. As he saw recent history, the world, coherent in the nineteenth century, had been deteriorating from about the beginning of the twentieth century. His own life seemed inextricably tied up with this transition: with his conscious memory originating at the beginning of the First World War, he had become acutely aware that the secure and solid world he had been taught to expect was vulnerable. In 1928, as he had moved far outwards from the secure, home-centred life he had known until then, he had felt inside himself a reflection of the increasing complexity of the outer world. Especially in his experience of other cultures he had come to feel the breakdown of the absolute values he had brought to Oxford; even his classical studies seemed to provide an example of an old order that was no longer suited to meet contemporary needs. Now, his inner depression, he felt, mirrored perfectly the condition of the Western world.

This strong sense of disillusionment and confusion, both personal and in the larger world, was reflected in the works of Ernest Hemingway, whose novels MacLennan read and idolized in his first year at

Princeton.[33] As he was to observe some years later: 'The greatest and most influential novelist of the 'twenties was, of course, Ernest Hemingway. Here [was] an American Byron with a miraculous style and a flawless sense of art. His work was the expression of a unique personality, gentle, yet fascinated by violence ... On surveying the literature of the 'twenties one cannot avoid a startling conclusion. Hardly an important writer of that period saw any value in existing society or even in ordinary human beings unless they served to prove a thesis (in the case of the naturalists), or to provide a background of conventionality against which the adventures, passions and despairs of romantic heroes could stand in relief.'[34]

It seems likely that Hemingway's work triggered MacLennan's imagination largely because it combined a number of things already present in his mind. His novels provided just the right combination of *Boys' Own Paper* adventure, Byronic lyricism, romantic heroes, observed violence, and the quest to find man's place and values in a war-torn society. Besides, to a young man who longed for fame as a writer, Hemingway's success seemed awe-inspiring.

MacLennan thus began his own first novel, 'So All Their Praises,' with Hemingway as his chief model. His title arose from Shakespeare's Sonnet 106:

> So all their praises are but prophecies
> Of this our time, all you prefiguring;
> And, for they look'd but with divining eyes,
> They had not skill enough your worth to sing;
> For we, which now behold these present days,
> Have eyes to wonder, but lack tongues to praise.

The novel covered the years between 1929 and 1933; the setting, taken from his experiences on holiday from Oxford, was Germany, with side-trips to New York and Nova Scotia. Three main characters form a love triangle. Michael Carmichael, an English expatriate, is a sensitive writer who, somewhat like Jake in Hemingway's *The Sun Also Rises*, cannot bring himself to act or believe with much conviction. Although his drinking bouts dull his pain, they also create the conditions in which he can see into the heart of darkness which is modern life. 'Oh God,' he cries out on one occasion, 'make me feel something. I'm dry.' His best friend is a strong-minded German student named Adolf Fabricius who struggles in rebellion against his dictatorial Victorian father at a time when the nation as a whole is falling under Hitler's power; in one brief scene Hitler appears in an open car in 'a pageant of Caesarism.' In contrast to Michael, Adolf is a man of action who can find no cause in which he can invest his energies. 'I'm betwixt and between the 19th and 20th centuries,' he complains; 'I'm too young for the old men and too old for the Nazis.' Alienated from both eras, he attempts to commit suicide but is saved from drowning by Michael and a Freiburg prostitute. Between these two men – Michael, the observer, Adolf, the man of action – stands Sarah Macrae, a dark-haired Nova Scotian girl who has failed to become a pianist. Michael meets her first on a trip to Nova Scotia, which he and Adolf have taken aboard the *Martin Swicker* from Germany – a ship they later discover is engaged in nefarious smuggling operations between Halifax and New York. (The section of the book set in Nova Scotia affords MacLennan the opportunity to give long rhapsodic descriptions of the landscapes and seascapes there.) Although Michael falls in love with Sarah, he worships her from a distance, while she turns to Adolf who, unlike Michael, has no difficulty pursuing her. This love triangle – the passive, artistic man, the man of action, and the dark-haired woman – prefigures the plot of every MacLennan novel to come. While Adolf and Sarah eventually marry and find happiness together, the story really centres on Michael, who is left at the end of the novel in painful isolation searching for spiritual meaning aboard a ship bound for England. Seduced neither by the easy path of established religion nor by the even easier path women offer him, he moves out into the world alone. 'His isolation loomed at him in the full profundity of its significance, and for a second it seemed that he had really grasped what it meant.'[35]

Throughout the novel MacLennan emphasizes that the whole age is caught, like his three main characters, in tremendous upheaval. In a storm at sea aboard the *Martin Swicker* (a similar storm appears much later in *Return of the Sphinx*), Michael contemplates the role of the individual caught in history:

> The forces of history of which he had become conscious seemed for a second to take tangible form, heaving on the mass as the moon heaves the tides about, and he saw himself in the mass and the mass like the ocean he was on; himself, the individual, subject to accident, but the movements of the mass predetermined.
>
> In everything we see and hear something is struggling to be born. The world is tense with the tenseness of a steel cable and ultimately as static. There is a tide in the affairs of men in the affairs of the mass, not myself struggling out of the mass, no flood tide yet, only pregnancy. Until the birth comes the non-creative individual can do nothing of objective importance.

Grow inwardly. A man's greatness is proportionate to his potential energy, to the potential energy of his spirit.

'When the transition is all over,' he speculates elsewhere, 'maybe we'll be old enough to call the transition a depression.' In these passages, which so strongly anticipate theories of history and character he would demonstrate more clearly in *The Watch That Ends the Night*, MacLennan wrestled with the notion that man is a pawn of forces too great to be measured and too inevitable to be diverted. If he is to have any significance, he must look inward to his own spiritual growth rather than to 'any outward success' in order to invest life with meaning. The empty cathedral in which Michael imagines that he hears the voices of those who make the forces of contemporary history – the Pope, Hitler, Mussolini, Baldwin, Hoover, MacDonald, and an American magnate, as well as the masses of unemployed – offers no solution through established religion.

In terms both of content and style, 'So All Their Praises' reveals a young author in search of his own kind of novel. Sections concerning the 'adventure story' of Adolf and Michael aboard the *Martin Swicker* vie for centrality in the novel with the love triangle theme, the revolt of Adolf against his overbearing father, and a social study of the Depression in Germany and North America. Although some of these strands are interrelated, the novel as a whole is not one clear unity: it is a mélange of MacLennan's interests which have not yet been integrated. Of special interest, given his later writing, are the scenes depicting men and women intimately. Here, more than in any of his later work, such relationships are portrayed frankly and lyrically. Sarah's inner thoughts when Adolf first makes love to her in a mossy cave are probably the best example:

He is coming to me under a tor of the Great Glacier, it is no longer Adolf coming to me, I cannot see him under the rock, spreading a rug over the moss for me to lie, it is no longer he I am looking at for I am staring into my own mind and it is a well, people I knew speaking to me at a distance and their voices coming to me out of the well. Now it is being offered that I may myself be offered.

She was conscious of fear and at the same time of nobility, aware of these concepts as though they were concrete and living and meaningful, and soon she ceased thinking altogether and lay against him, he feeling that he was coming home, feeling her back arching her body inward against his own. There was power in them both and each was conscious of the power. She waited in what seemed to her a numbness of exaltation, and was not dominant.[36]

As this passage also demonstrates, MacLennan was experimenting with the 'stream of consciousness' technique which had recently become popular in the fiction of James Joyce. But his use of this technique, randomly assigned to his central characters, is juxtaposed with sections of dramatic dialogue and descriptive narrative by an omniscient author in the third person. Here, as with his content, there is no unity. It is as if he were trying out different perspectives in his material and different 'voices' for his story.

'So All Their Praises' most strongly echoes Hemingway's novels of what Gertrude Stein so aptly called 'the lost generation.' Like Frederic Henry in *A Farewell to Arms*, his hero Michael questions the validity of belief in any absolutes at such a time. In details of style and dialogue, too, the novel is strongly influenced: tough dialogue, the use of foreign terms like *Stube* and *Wirt*, colourful European street scenes involving prostitutes and young expatriates, even the short declarative sentences for which Hemingway had by this time become infamous. Like many of Hemingway's characters, Michael claims that 'bawdiness and art were inseparable' – a philosophy he has some trouble living down to.

The view MacLennan actually took in his novel is best stated by Adolf when he says: 'These times are such a forcing house that there is always danger of slipping into sexual mysticism, and I am so afraid of that. When every door is locked against us we tend to think that if only the simplest part of ourselves were satisfied we should live well. And surely that is not so.' MacLennan simply could not agree with the premise that there was no value in society or in ordinary people. Although he toyed with Hemingway's stance, he found it too cynical. Ultimately, Michael's search for life emphasizes not despair but eternal hope. Somewhere at the centre of this quest was the search to understand a vague sort of mysticism. Although MacLennan had noted at Oxford, somewhat to his surprise, that his poems tended to be 'mystical,' it was in 'So All Their Praises' that he really began to probe the meaning of this mood. On one occasion, Adolf feels a 'movement of forces wandering everywhere and evolving in himself, himself and phenomena being in flux out of a great formal cause. These could not be translated into thought, much less into language, but as he sat and looked out over millions of people towards the smoulder of sun above the North River, he seemed to feel a catharsis working through his body and finally into his mind.'[37]

This mystic vision is surprisingly similar to the 'apparition' MacLennan was to claim he had experienced as a sixteen-year-old boy looking out over the dark sea near Halifax: in his daydreams, like his character Adolf, he had sensed 'millions of other worlds' both in the outer world and inside himself; to understand such visions through art had been his calling, and here for the first time he created characters who were also trying to understand that mystery. He tended to assess society in terms of the extent to which it allowed the individual to fulfil himself; thus, if 'So All Their Praises' seems a dark novel, it is because world events between 1929 and 1933 increasingly limited the scope of such a quest, not because of any cynicism about human nature.

At odds in this fundamental way with the model he had chosen, MacLennan's novel was flawed. It lacked coherence. When he completed 'So All Their Praises' in the fall of 1934, he took it around to publishers without success. Only one, Robert Ballou and Company in New York, was willing to accept the manuscript, provided revisions were made. Under financial strain because of the Depression, the company folded before the novel could be published.[38]

Coming so close to realizing his ambition to become a published writer put enormous stress on MacLennan, whose studies were beginning to suffer as a result of the energy he had transferred to his novel. Not surprisingly, he had failed to obtain a teaching fellowship for his second year. To ease his despair, Dorothy used the free train pass she had because of her father's connection with Union Pacific to come to New York for a week that Christmas. Her description of this occasion shows how deeply sympathetic she had become: 'things were getting rapidly bleaker for him. The novel had been finished during his second winter in the United States, but no one wanted to publish it – good stuff they said, but the subject was too hot. A Ph.D. to add to his name was practically in the bag, but there were no academic openings of any nature for a young man whose subject was classical history. Only science was paying off in the United States in the early thirties. If he thought merely being with me, and being able to talk out the burdens of his mind, was a help, that seemed to me ample reason for being wherever his work kept him.'

Going to the theatre and visiting friends in New York helped to distract him from his sense of failure. And Dorothy noticed that he had, to some extent at least, adjusted to the American way of life he had reacted so strongly against when they had first gone to New York together nine months earlier: 'Crowds had ceased to be thousands of individual faces for him by that time. Instead of feeling the impingement of countless strange personalities upon his own, he had learned how to lose himself in city streets, noticing only now and then a particular human being whom he found of interest – the waiter who always served us in the rathskeller on Third Avenue, the haunting eyes of Alfred Stieglitz as he showed us behind the scenes at An American Place, an English poet [Bottrall] who was training for the Foreign Service by way of a Commonwealth Fellowship, a girl demonstrating hair curlers in a five-and-ten ... But he was still a Nova Scotian with a Highland lilt in his voice, a belief in the essential worth of human life, and an insatiable sense of wonderment.'

Since that pledging of vows in the spring of 1933, according to Dorothy, they had agreed to marry, although they both realized that it would be some time before they could. At least that seems to be the meaning of the convoluted and evasive statement with which she concluded her account of that Christmas week in 1934: 'Unable to control the future, he was unwilling to tempt its possibilities by borrowing on the unknown; so our friendship kept the seeds of its ripening within itself.'[39] With no prospect of a job in Classics, having failed to publish his novel as he had earlier failed to publish his poems, MacLennan tended to view the Depression in the egocentric way of many intelligent young people at the time, as a jest of God arranged at his expense. With a persistence worthy of the MacQuarries and the MacLennans, he began a second novel in the New Year when he returned to Princeton.

Mainly because his heart had not been in his studies from the beginning, MacLennan did not perform well at Princeton. In fact, at the end of his second year in the spring of 1934, when he took the comprehensive examinations – the last hurdle to be cleared aside from a thesis – he almost failed. His contempt for Princeton was so great that he had moved out to a neighbouring farm in the fall of 1933 rather than spend any more time in the Graduate College. At Boxwood Farm he took breakfast and dinner and during the day went in to the library to work on his thesis. 'It was the happiest place I knew in my Princeton days,'[40] he later recalled. The reason for his happiness is clear: whenever circumstances allowed Dorothy travelled from Chicago to stay with him there. As she recalled in a book published several years later: 'A few miles outside of Princeton there is an old renovated cottage on the Van Cleve farm [Boxwood] with an immense open fireplace, which we felt compensated amply for the distance we had to travel in the winters to the campus and to shops. Ever since we lived and loved it there, we have felt it imperative to have a hearth capable of burning great logs, around which we could centre our life.'[41] Dr Sam would not have been amused, but for MacLennan, in his rebellious frame of mind, this was his means of keeping a sense of balance.

His thesis adviser was the man who had brought him out to Princeton in the first place, A.C. Johnson – a scholar under whom he had already studied and who, according to Charles Stacey, did not have a particularly good opinion of his work. Considering that he had not wanted to go there in the first place; that every day at Princeton made marriage to Dorothy further away; that he really wanted to write and was spending a lot of time on his novels; that classical scholarship there was far from his taste; that he really believed, as one of his minor characters had put it in 'So All Their Praises,' that 'the [Ph.D.] degree was lousy and ... working for it in times like these was like burying your head in the sand so as not to see the sandstorm,'[42] it is no wonder he was a poor student. None the less, mainly because he really had no other choice, he proceeded to his thesis in the summer of 1934.

His topic was more or less thrust upon him. Johnson assigned those of the Oxyrhynchus papyri that had so far been published (approximately twenty large volumes), which were documents recording the accounts of life in the Egyptian town of Oxyrhynchus during the Roman and Byzantine periods. From these, his task was to trace the economic and social changes that had occurred between the late Ptolemaic period and the servile state of Byzantine Egypt, the purpose being the possibility of making more general statements about the actual local causes of the decline of the Roman Empire. As MacLennan himself scathingly described his thesis work during that 'winter of considerable discontent': 'the papyri disclosed a jumbled record of uninteresting human activity prolonged over the period of nearly seven hundred years ... If an African scholar fifteen hundred years from now were to do a similar job on the waste-baskets of Regina, his would be an effort comparable to mine, and he would probably discover neither more nor less.' According to him, 'I discovered nothing from all this research that I had not known since high school.'[43] His hours of translation and reconstruction simply verified the generally held view that the town had shared the well-known fate of the Roman Empire: that it had steadily declined and fallen and that its people had become more and more barbaric during this period.

In fact, his thesis echoed the work of the major scholar in this field at the time, Mikhail Ivanovich Rostovtzeff, whose *Social and Economic History of the Roman Empire*[44] he duly acknowledged in his introduction. At a time when most students of papyrology, especially those at Princeton, were concentrating on difficulties in individual texts, MacLennan followed the Russian scholar's lead in attempting a broad sweep through the documents. As a 'progressive' historian, Rostovtzeff had concluded that the decline of the empire was inextricably linked with the decline of the urban upper classes; MacLennan based his own remarks firmly on this view: 'The rapacity of the early Roman capitalists had led to the capture of more provinces than the empire could control without a top-heavy military establishment ... The civil wars produced by the troops steadily destroyed the confidence on which a commercial civilization depends. So, Oxyrhynchus, once a thriving town ... decayed to the ghost capital of a country where nearly everyone was a serf to a family of absentee landlords.' Rostovtzeff's influence strengthened his Marxist leanings; as he was later to comment: 'In the pink thirties, this was just the sort of thing that might have turned a promising young man into a communist.'[45] And in a way it did. While Marxist scholars may dispute his application of the term 'capitalist' to ancient Rome, the source of his inspiration is clear: in passages that mount to a crescendo of moral outrage, he outdid Rostovtzeff himself in the vehemence with which he denounced the erosion of integrity among the land-holding class of Romans. His interest in writing this social and economic study consisted not in experiencing the delights of scholarship but in implying a relationship between the pattern of decline in ancient Rome and the events that had resulted in economic crisis in his own time. He had successfully resisted three years of pressure to conform to the Germanic tradition of scholarship his professors at Princeton had tried to force him to imitate; his thesis was sweeping and general in the style of his Greats tutorial papers at Oxford.

The thesis was finally finished in April 1935, and at last, he thought, his formal education was virtually completed and his days at Princeton were almost at an end. Professor Johnson had told him that in his opinion the thesis was *summa cum laude*. All that remained was confirmation by a second reader – a mere formality, he had been told, for it had been over a decade since a second reader had challenged the opinion of the first one. His former professor, Kelley Prentice, with whom he had had many a run-in over Thucydides, had been chosen to give his opinion. MacLennan was in for a rude shock. As he remembered it, Prentice 'called me into his office and said, "Well, I think maybe if you work at this a few years longer maybe you'll have something of a thesis here."' The impact of this statement was almost more than he could bear. It was, he later confessed, 'one of the traumatic experiences of my earlier life.' Prentice's main objection could not have been more humiliating for a man who had ambitions to become a writer: he claimed that it was written in 'unsatisfactory English.' 'It was my distinct impression,' MacLennan observed, 'that he intended to do all he could to prevent me from obtaining a degree.' Johnson's advice was to 'stand up to him.' So he did. 'As this was the depression, and I was sick of graduate schools anyway,' he recalled, 'I wanted to have done with it. Prentice threw me out of his office as a trouble-maker.'[46]

Caught between what he later called 'the upper and nether mill-stones of an academic fight,'[47] between Johnson and Prentice, MacLennan, distraught, was turned over to the chairman of the department, Professor D.R. Stuart, who proceeded to rewrite most of the first chapter himself. 'Prentice did not seem to be aware of this,' MacLennan remembered, 'or perhaps he was, and returned it with the message that this was worse than the original.'

Stuart was very angry with Prentice over this and told me he had been acting 'very strangely lately.' I replied that this might well be so, but that I saw no reason why this should keep me from a degree. Stuart may have had a row with Prentice behind the scenes. He was very discreet, and did not say so. But suddenly Prentice changed. He came out to the farm where I was staying and asked the farmer whether I was getting sufficient food, whether I acted normally etc. Then he became full of melancholy kindness to me and Stuart told me I could get a degree if I re-worked the text with Prentice ...

At the end of my time in Princeton nobody could have been kinder to me than Kelley was. I went along with all of his alterations.

MacLennan revised his thesis as he was forced to do under these circumstances, but he stubbornly held on to the original version he preferred. When the thesis was published by Princeton University Press later that year, it was his own version, and not Prentice's, that he used. Ironically, Prentice missed the substitution entirely: 'He did not seem to notice, for he wrote me a very nice letter of congratulation on it.'[48] Unlike the vast majority of doctoral theses, *Oxyrhynchus: An Economic and Social Study*[49] enjoyed a modest but continuous success; in 1968 a Dutch publishing house, A.M. Hakkert, asked to reprint it as the original had gone out of stock.

The difficulties of surmounting this last devastating academic hurdle affected him profoundly. As he summed up the experience later: 'I was certainly immature in getting along with academics then. Doubtless the Graduate School was dead right about me: I never was fitted by temperament or talent for Germanic scholarship.'[50] So deeply disillusioned was he by the events that had so nearly blocked him from the degree, that he would never, under any circumstances, from then on use the title 'Doctor MacLennan,' which was his by right. With saturnine humour he referred to the Ph.D. he had come so close to missing as his 'academic union card.' Inside, he knew that his best efforts had been going into the fiction he really wanted to write. The disdain with which he had come to view academics and universities in general by this time, combined with his poor performance in the type of scholarship Princeton specialized in, ensured that he could not rely with any conviction on recommendations from the professors who had taught him. He thus forfeited the only possible avenue to an academic position during the Depression. Not even the honour Princeton eventually extended to him in 1953, when he was asked to participate in a major conference of alumni there, changed his views.[51]

When the thesis was finally completed in March 1935, he immediately published a related article in the *Dalhousie Review*. In 'Roman History and Today' (1935-6), he gave a thorough and somewhat emotional justification for the kind of history he believed worthwhile and contrasted it to the type of history his professors at Princeton had tried to make him write. As he expressed it, there are two types of history: a 'Spenglerian' type, which utilizes facts as Spengler had done in *The Decline of the West* to explain the present times and predict the future; and a 'scientific' type, which addresses itself to the close examination of specific data. Although he conceded that history must clearly employ 'scientific methods in collecting and weighing material,' he asserted that 'it is no special science, and as now treated it is inadequate.' Of these two streams of history, represented, as he saw it, by two nineteenth-century German historians, Karl Marx (the 'Spenglerian') and Theodor Mommsen (the 'scientific'), he predictably endorsed Marx.[52]

By adapting Rostovtzeff's interpretation of the decline of the Roman Empire, he concentrated, as he had done in the thesis, on social and economic speculation that would be relevant to his time. He attempted to classify whole periods of history in a broad, expansive view, emphasizing the class antagonisms in the Roman provinces and the private enterprise system as causes for change. Over all, his view was moderately deterministic. The article revealed that he was aware of and sympathetic to a reform movement in the discipline of history that included Marxist views, though he was by no means a Marxist. His concern with social and economic history and his fondness for a broad generalizing approach, which tried to make use of the scientific scholar's data in contemporary terms, illustrated his conviction that the study of history demanded scope, conscience, and a purpose other than the purely descriptive. Ironically, had he heard of the New History which was currently coming to the fore through the work of such American historians as Charles A. Beard,[53] James H. Robinson, and Carl Becker, he would have seen his own views confirmed; but he did not know about it at the time and therefore did not realize there was much support for such theories.

'Roman History and Today' indicates that MacLennan's sympathies on graduating from Princeton were much closer to the leftism of the intelligentsia of the day than to the principles of rigorous scholarship in the Classics. The dawning awareness of socialism that had characterized his last year at Oxford had, after three years at Princeton, developed into a strong belief in the potential of the left to remedy the economic crisis that gripped the Western world during the 'hungry thirties.' Like Edmund Wilson (whose *To the Finland Station* he would later read and admire) and many other intellectuals of the period, he lost faith in the capitalist system and in the efficacy of gradual and peaceful methods of change. The conservatism of his father with which he had voyaged out to Oxford in 1928 now seemed to him, as it did to many, a political philosophy that had been in large part responsible for the present grim state of affairs. The conservative notion of an élite with rights and privileges, no matter how responsibly such an élite might treat those less fortunate than itself, effectively blocked the radical measures that many of his generation thought were needed to remedy present ills.

Paradoxically, since he now saw himself as flying in the face of his father's traditional political views, it had been some of Dr Sam's attitudes which had prepared the way for his new sympathies. At base it was the Christian ethics instilled in him by his father that he now transferred from any formal religious expression into the political and social arena. Dr Sam had persistently held up the American business community as the prime example of excessive individualism and self-seeking and, hence, as an example of a deplorable indifference to 'the golden rule.' This opinion of big business merged easily with the theories of the proponents of the New History and with the leftist theories of social change which had come to the fore. To MacLennan it now seemed that if the increasingly large number of the poor were indeed to be cared for, it must be through some kind of revolutionary change in the political system.

Later he would qualify the enthusiasm for Marxism that had informed this article, declaring that even when he was at Princeton he had had reservations about the degree to which the views of Marx could be applied to the present. 'Time as we know it now,' he observed in an article called 'History – What Is It?' (1956), 'is not the same as the time known to the Oxyrhynchites or even to our fathers ... If modern time is radically different from Roman time, then it is obvious that an entirely new factor has entered the historical equation.' 'The Marxists,' he concluded, 'were hopelessly off the beam when they claimed that they could discover from past history a pattern of laws which enabled them to predict and control the future of the twentieth century.'

In 1935, however, MacLennan's personal predicament, an educated man with no real prospect of a job in his field, led to bitterness and attempts to find larger excuses and explanations. The Ph.D., he claimed in 'Roman History and Today,' was nothing more than 'the apotheosis of the scientific' or Germanic approach to history. 'The austere circumstances in which we find ourselves to-day are also our teachers ... All people but the young have been discredited,' he complained, 'and if the young have escaped thus far, the main reason is that the world has no longer room to give them a vantage place from which they can be vocal; in other words, a good job.' Considering his situation, it was not surprising that he should have been drawn to a moderately determinist interpretation of history.

> The *time* at which an event takes place most certainly hinges on human decision; the *manner* in which the event takes place more or less hinges on human decision. But, notwithstanding, there are tides in the affairs of men that no individual can possibly stem. There are times when the process of events is seen, with pitiless clarity, to be issuing from formal causes far remote, when individuals are like flies on a torrent, when almost everyone seems to want something not to happen, and yet later ages, looking back, see that it had to happen. Such times are vital crises, like the Roman Empire, like the 1790's. In fact, like events of our own day ...
>
> It concerns us, in the twentieth century, to know what is underneath our times. Obviously a great social idea, at least in its application, is very nearly played out.[54]

MacLennan was crying out against a world situation that had him trapped. His father had not only convinced him that if one persisted and worked hard no obstacle was too great to overcome, but he had also held up his own success in medicine as an example. Now, after having slaved with the fixed purpose of becoming a classical scholar for thirteen long years – from age fifteen to twenty-eight – he had to face the fact that no amount of labour could change the nature of reality in 1935.

Fed up by this prospect, disillusioned by his failure to publish so far, he commenced work on his second novel, fittingly titled 'A Man Should Rejoice.' The novel's biblical epigraph (Ecclesiastes 3:22), from which this title is taken, clearly explains his conviction that he *must* continue to write: 'Wherefore I perceive that there is nothing better, than that a man should rejoice in his own works; for that is his portion: for who shall bring him to see what shall be after him?'

'A Man Should Rejoice' was originally conceived as a story about a young American artist David Culver, whose alienation from life is a result of social and economic upheaval. In full rebellion against his capitalist father, Culver ultimately joins a revolution in Austria against fascism, with tragic consequences. A much more autobiographical character than Michael Carmichael in 'So All Their Praises,' Culver sets out, as MacLennan himself was doing, 'to create, in a book, something of the form and rhythm of the most rapid transition from one era to another that mankind has ever known.'[55]

The earlier portion of this novel summed up in mood, if not in precise fact, those three years at Princeton he much later called his 'barren' time.[56] Although Culver later becomes a writer, he is at first a painter. Like MacLennan, he has an artistic mother and an aggressive, overbearing father. At Princeton, where he goes to study chemistry, he finds no one to nurture his hopes and talents. MacLennan's presentation of his experiences there very closely parallel his own:

> During the middle and late twenties I went to Princeton, for there seemed nothing else I could do ... [His father, whom he calls Culver] knew nothing about colleges, but he wanted me to go to Princeton for some personal prejudice of his own. I think his first boss had been a Princeton man.
>
> ... 'You'd better study chemistry ... I don't mean you just to be a chemist of course ... I guess at Princeton you ought to make some connections that will be useful to us later on.'
>
> So I went to Princeton and majored in chemistry, which I found I liked fairly well. I learned something about it, though not very much. Other things interested me more. I became fascinated by history and read volume after volume. I learned some German and Latin because I liked the languages and a little French because it might be useful to me if I ever got to Paris to paint. The connections I made were, from Culver's standpoint, the worst possible, being all poorer boys and all Socialists. So I read Marx at Princeton also. I used to take long runs by myself along the shores of Carnegie Lake and on Sundays used to go off on ten hour walks on the small roads behind the Trenton Pike in the direction of Hopewell and Huntington. I painted whenever possible. And finally I managed to graduate.

About Princeton and the time I spent there it might be possible to select several patterns and develop them, but apart from the work I did by myself these were four deadly uninteresting years. Any pattern I might make of them would be uninteresting too. After I left college I met Princeton men who seemed to love the place with an incredible intensity. They were business men and bond salesmen and brokers and bankers.

I grew older in Princeton, and that is about all I can say. Certainly I learned nothing there to improve my painting or increase my joy in existence. Such men as I met there and the values of the college woke me up to what Culver's real values were with an electric shock. But although I hated Princeton then, I soon came to laugh at it.

... I do not think Culver used Princeton as a means of breaking me in; I doubt if he even thought about me that way, and though he knew I liked painting better than anything else, he knew so little about it that he never took me seriously. Yet Princeton scared me and I began to lose confidence. I suppose waking up to things scares anybody. I felt I was about to be projected into a machine from which no one who ever entered ever escaped ... No one I met who had authority in the university seemed to question the belief that man was made for the furtherance of efficiency, and this simple fact, that no one in America should ever dream of sacrificing power for happiness, was so appalling that I felt more and more isolated every month. There were months when no painting at all was possible. The making of pictures seemed ridiculous when you thought of the towns that lay between Princeton and New York: New Brunswick, Rahway, Elizabeth, Newark, Jersey City, factory after factory, slum after slum, and grey faces. Half of a man is what people take him to be. Half of myself was this Princeton-Industrial background. I was the son of Culver and it was at Princeton that I came to realize what that meant.

After commencement I went off by myself, intending a sketching trip to Maine. I did not get further than Boston. A revulsion against what Culver was intending for me made me leave the train and spend a night walking through the poorer districts of Boston, hearing Italians and Bohunks talk, wanting to get the feel of people who sweated at manual work, wanting above everything else, simply to feel their humanity.[57]

So serious was the shock of recognition MacLennan experienced at Princeton that he occasionally wondered whether it was himself, not the time, that was out of joint. In Halifax the summer after coming down from Oxford he had met an Englishman called George Barrett, who had taken a teaching post at Dalhousie; the two men had become friends and carried on a desultory correspondence. Now, as his time at

Princeton drew to an end, with his novel only just begun, MacLennan wrote to him an intense letter in which he tried to explain what his novel was about: 'Whether the new world comes violently or not makes no difference to the set-up ... We belong to the transition, and to me that's all there is to it ... Frankly I don't think there is as much sterility as there is insanity ... The criticism my new book (it's not done yet) has met is not that it is sterile, but in places mad. Frankly, I don't often feel mad, but if most of my neighbours are taken as a quantitative ratio of sanity, then I am completely mad. If, after the result of much training and association with trained minds in a variety of countries, if, again, one has rid oneself of early Christianity and grew up as a child after the war – after all this, if one can hardly keep up with the pace of the world, what is to be expected of the masses?'[58]

Although MacLennan had lived with Dorothy at Princeton when he could and had kept up a flow of correspondence with her for three years on the subjects of the horrors of Princeton, his novel, the appalling state of the world, Marxism, and all the other things close to his heart, his family had not yet met her. Now, with his work completed at Princeton in the spring of 1935, the time had come to face both families. First, in June, MacLennan went to the Duncans. It was not a particularly auspicious occasion. In the summer of 1934 he had bought an old Ford in a Trenton junkyard for sixty dollars to take him back and forth between Boxwood Farm and Princeton. With canny business sense, he had traded in the Ford and paid seven dollars for a 1919 Studebaker a year later.[59] After numerous mechanical breakdowns the car finally got them to Chicago. Inordinately proud of his achievement in getting there at all, MacLennan received nothing better than disapproval from 'the Colonel' for his efforts. As Dorothy remembered it: 'When my father reached home several hours later and saw the rakish, disreputable old hag of a car standing before our doorstep he ordered it around to a garage at once, insensible of the pride a Nova Scotian can feel in having made such a good thing out of nothing.' To avoid the mountains which had been more than a match for the car on the way out, MacLennan drove back alone through Detroit and Windsor, Ontario; this was his first glimpse of any part of Canada other than the Maritimes.

In July, a week after he arrived back at Princeton, Dorothy joined him by train. They packed his books and belongings into the Studebaker and set out for Halifax. Even under the best of conditions, taking Dorothy to meet the MacLennans was a risky business; Dr Sam could not have been expected to approve in any way. And the conditions could not have been worse. In the tremendous heat wave that rolled over the east coast as they proceeded north, the tires blew out on the average of once every hundred miles. By the time they reached Bangor in Maine, Dorothy had come down with a high temperature; MacLennan, thinking only that she must be subjected to as little stress as possible, put her on the next train to Halifax, while he stayed overnight to see to the car, which had, once again, broken down. Dorothy's thoughts as she headed for the first time into Nova Scotia were just as bad as MacLennan's had been on first visiting her country. 'I began to realize,' she recalled, 'why the words *hell* and *Halifax* are so often considered synonymous in the United States. The journey to both localities is a murderous one.' Instead of going directly to South Park Street on her arrival at midnight, she checked into a hotel overnight to brace herself. The next morning, alone and apprehensive, she arrived on the MacLennans' doorstep. She later recorded this first encounter with her future parents-in-law:

the door behind me opened and one of the most naturally gracious women I have ever met stood there smiling as I turned around, waiting for me to announce my business ... My solitary presence frightened her anyway; she had never seen a picture of me, but I must have looked unmistakably American. One hand went to the region of her heart and she spoke his name, as though all her life she had been waiting and dreading bad news of him ...

It took only a moment to explain where he was and how I happened to be alone, and then another figure appeared from behind the blue hangings at the library door. His was the sandy hair paling to white, the long upper lip, and the high complexion of the pure Scot; but all I could see as he emerged was the glittering head mirror, still attached to his forehead, which he had been using in examination of a patient's throat, forgotten as acute ears heard his wife's outcry. He had no idea that he was scaring me as much as I was upsetting him; he never dreamed that I was quite as shy as he, though I showed it in a different way. He stood there looking at me steadily; muttered 'God bless my soul!' as his wife explained there was no need for worry; and then disappeared into the shadows again by a far door, taking the glittering thing on his head with him.

Simply by acting according to her American upbringing, Dorothy alienated many Haligonians:

I began to say the wrong things in public and in private because I uttered the first idea that came into my head, and it wasn't done; I wore the wrong things because my tastes were sharply defined on individualistic lines; I did the wrong things because my training was of the business world, not a town-and-gown society. Had I spoken a foreign language it would have been far easier for me to accept the outward differences in our manners, even as it would have been easier for them to accept me. But we're all so foolish that way – both Britishers and Americans ... The Britisher is proud and shy; the American is aggressive and unconstrained ... I was a trial and a third to my family-in-law [to be] that summer, in spite of the fact that I was admiring them tremendously every minute. The mistakes I made were apparent to me only after years of learning to be ashamed of myself, and my errors in judgement were corrected after tears and fury on my part and endless patience on the part of the young Nova Scotian I married.

The fever that had precipitated her into the MacLennan household in advance of their son was not without its redeeming side. By the time Hugh arrived a day later, Dr Sam informed him that he had just removed Dorothy's tonsils. According to her, it was the infection that saved the day: 'To the Doctor I was transformed almost immediately from the representative of an idea which he had no wish to pursue into a patient whose needs he understood completely, and over whom for the time being he could exercise absolute authority.' By the time she recovered, there was less than a week remaining before she set sail on the *Britannic* from Halifax to New York. Whether the MacLennans liked it or not, the die had been cast. Looking down once again from the upper deck of a ship on the man she loved, she recalled that night three years before when she had first glimpsed him: 'I found myself remembering the night in Southampton ... never dreaming then that I should be leaning over a ship's rail looking at him so again.'[60]

Chapter four

Becalmed: Lower Canada College

In the summer of 1935 the prospects for many were bleak; by MacLennan's calculations, only about five per cent of students like himself emerging from graduate school were able to find jobs. At home in Halifax because he had nowhere else to go, he resigned himself to the humiliation of accepting support from his father into his twenty-eighth year. Searching the want ads was futile; employers didn't even bother to advertise any more. The best he could do with his Oxford and Princeton degrees was to register his name with every teachers' agency in Canada and a few in the United States. September came and went; then, in mid-October, when there seemed no hope of a post that year, he was offered a job teaching Classics at Lower Canada College, a private boys' school in a west-end suburb of Montreal. In almost every mention of this job he was later to make, his despair at having to take it is apparent. Given his qualifications and the tremendous effort that had been necessary to acquire them, to teach in such a school was far beneath him. Furthermore, he had already expressed his abhorrence of boys' schools when his father had suggested he try to teach in one in England after he graduated from Oxford. In fact, he could have taken such a post in Canada without ever having gone to Oxford at all: his Dalhousie BA would have been qualification enough. However, any job was better than staying at home with no job, and MacLennan accepted at once.

Lower Canada College was, and still is, an institution to which some English Montrealers sent their sons to be educated in the British man-

Dorothy Duncan in her wedding dress, Wilmette, June 1936

ner and to make the proper contacts to ensure future success. In 1935 it was what MacLennan was later to call 'a ramshackle institution'[1] fossilized in time by the forces of colonialism. Its head was Dr C.S. Fosbery, 'the Boss,' an eccentric Englishman who came for the months school was in session, then literally took the next ship 'home' when term ended. That same year in which MacLennan began, there also arrived from England a young French teacher called Stephen Penton with whom he shared a common living room; though neither of them could have known it, in Penton lay the seeds of the future for the college, for eventually under his leadership it was to raise itself from the erratic and outdated methods MacLennan found there into solidity and success. This year 'the Boss' had discovered, once term began, that he needed an extra staff member; since it was too late to import another Englishman, he had offered the job to the young Oxford graduate from Halifax.

In essays written much later, MacLennan recorded his impressions on arriving in Montreal. In the first place, he had come with a number of preconceptions: 'I came to Montreal in the mid-thirties with the usual freight of misinformation outlanders still have about the place. It was gay and it was wicked. On the sophisticated level of André Siegfried it was an English garrison enclosed in an overgrown French village.'[2] Just as he had done abroad, he viewed Montreal through the literature he had read. In 'The Best-Loved Street in Canada' (1953) he described his first day in the city:

I had arrived in the old Bonaventure Station in Montreal and from there had been driven by devious ways to Lower Canada College in Notre Dame de Grâce, but the drive had told me no more about Montreal than I thought I knew anyway, namely, that its people spoke French and English, that there were toboggan slides on Mount Royal, the Canadiens and Maroons in the Forum and financiers in St. James Street who were indirectly responsible for the fact that Nova Scotia had been voting Liberal ever since 1900.

When I reached the school it was almost empty, for it was a Saturday morning. This was in the middle of the depression and there were few boarders around. But there was breakfast ready and I ate it alone in a dining-hall such as I have never seen before or since. A gallery of stuffed animal heads – buffalo, moose, deer, caribou, wolves, foxes and Kootenay rams – overhung prints of dead British politicians that stretched all the way round the walls.

After breakfast the housemaster showed me to my cell-like room and told me there was nothing I had to do until Monday morning.

He spent the rest of the day walking around Montreal, liking what he saw. Even the obvious signs of the Depression – the general tawdriness everywhere and the 'For Sale' signs on the regal homes of the Square Mile – seemed less melancholy than the results the economic slump had elsewhere. 'In spite of the depression,' he recalled, 'it seemed good-natured. The unemployed ... looked a little less wretched here than in New York and Berlin and London.' Since it was a Saturday, he indulged that night in a 'pub-crawl,' talking to the Montrealers who frequented the town's taverns. 'In Europe,' he explained, 'I had discovered that the best way to get a sense of a city is to make a long pub-crawl, drifting with the current and taking the city as it comes.' What he found out that first day was that many of his preconceptions had been wrong:

> Most of what I had heard of Montreal was at best half-true and ... the sum of it had missed the whole character of the city. Montreal did not seem to me gay. I saw no people cavorting or laughing in the streets ... Nor did the city remind me of any habitation I had seen in France. Even west of Bleury Street I kept being reminded of London and Southampton, and it occurred to me that both these English cities had grown out of a mixed population of Saxons and Norman Frenchmen.
>
> V.S. Pritchett, writing of London in *Holiday* and comparing it to Rome, said that while Rome reminded him of violence with murder lurking in a thousand doorways, London made him think of experience. That is what Montreal has always made me think of.[3]

From the beginning he responded favourably to the new cosmopolitan environment of the city in which he would settle. Aside from his brief drive through southwestern Ontario on his return to Princeton from Chicago earlier the same year, this was his first real experience of a landscape and social setting in what he would have called 'Canada.' As a Nova Scotian and an outsider, he was able to view the city afresh. But his European travels and his years at Princeton near New York also afforded him a perspective within which he could compare it with many of the major cities of the world. In this comparison, Montreal seemed to him an excellent place, in which some of the flavour and experience of London and the European cities he had liked combined with a North American character.

Once his duties began under the obsessively energetic regime set up by 'the Boss,' he must have wondered how he would ever find time to pursue his writing. Fosbery had run Lower Canada College since 1909 when St John's School had been moved west to Notre-Dame-de-Grâce from St James Street in downtown Montreal and given its new name. Stephen Penton later wrote a history of the school filled with anecdotes that reveal Fosbery as an extraordinary and peculiar man: 'His personality dominated the whole School. He was his own accountant, bookkeeper, secretary and banker. He kept the records and, sometimes, on week ends stoked the fires. He was here, there and everywhere, and wherever he was, that place was a centre of activity. His voice was usually a roar in which protest was mingled with exhortation whether he was delivering a homily at morning prayers or expounding Latin in a classroom. As the classrooms were anything but soundproof, his presence was always felt everywhere.' With his stooped and skinny body, topped with a tuft of white hair, Fosbery resembled an ancient crane or heron who 'loped with a springy gait which caused his knees and shoulders to sink a bit.' In repose, according to Penton, he seemed never to know what to do with his long legs and feet, swinging them awkwardly over the backs of chairs or crossing them atop his desk.[4] Under his regime, which resembled nothing so much as that of a military camp in wartime, MacLennan was to labour hard and long for the $25 a week salary he was paid there in addition to his room and board. Thirty hours a week, he recalled, were the teaching hours alone; add to that the preparation of classes and marking, another eight or so hours a week. Two nights a week each teacher had duties supervising the boarders. Then there were noon-hour duties on a rotation system.[5]

A fairly accurate picture of MacLennan's life at Lower Canada College, and more than a hint of his distaste for his first job, can be seen in his lengthy satire of Waterloo School and its head Dr Lionel Bigbee in *The Watch That Ends the Night*. For George Stewart, as for MacLennan, the business of being a schoolmaster was at times a dreary matter. As George puts it: 'There is no man ... I pity more than the man not born to [schoolmastering] who falls into its trap and stays till the chalk dust passes through his pores into his bloodstream and soul.' His time at the school is really 'five years of servitude.' 'I liked the boys and got on with them,' he states, 'and I was thankful to have a job of any kind, but I was nervously exhausted most of the time, for Waterloo was as wild a jumble of improvisations as a British army in the first year of a war, with life a constant emergency.'[6] Although one of MacLennan's contemporaries at Lower Canada College claims that he 'exaggerated in retrospect what was a horrid situation for him,' another comments that 'MacLennan caricatured the school, but not by much.'[7]

Like George Stewart, MacLennan found the whole business of teaching exhausting. In 'The Thankless Profession' (1949), an article written after he had left the school – on behalf of 'the most exploited, neglected and underprivileged class in Canada,' the nation's schoolteachers – he was to generalize from his own experience: 'So far from being easy, good teaching is one of the most arduous, exacting and difficult tasks a human being can perform. To teach well requires an unending expense of a man or woman's spirit ... To teach well means more than the transference of knowledge; it means the transference of some of one's own energy to the pupil ... It is this necessity of outgiving which makes good teaching so racking to the nervous system, just as it also makes being a teacher something of a reward in itself.' Teaching drained him of the energy he wanted to use in his writing, partly because the students themselves were unruly: 'Under the best of circumstances the teacher deals with humanity in the raw, with a clamorous humanity which in these days feels no reverence for elders and is quick to exploit every weakness of anyone in authority. By the constant exercise of wit, personality and such spiritual force as he possesses, the teacher must canalize the diffuse energies of growing children into tasks which few of them have an instinct to perform.'[8]

Not only by spiritual force were the masters of Lower Canada College expected to 'canalize' their students' energies, but by physical force as well. MacLennan's method was the cane. At the beginning of each year in every class he carefully placed on his desk a yard-long relic of dowling – only half of which had retained its purple paint – grinned, and issued fair warning.[9] Though by training he could have expected never to have students young enough for such treatment, he did not shrink from using it. Although discipline seemed impossible for some other masters to keep, MacLennan had learned too much from Dr Sam to be controlled by his students. None the less, the imposition of force on the boys he taught was never to his taste. In one of the annual articles he wrote during his years there for the *Lower Canada College Magazine* (February 1936), he counselled the boys to 'Beware of Your Elders.' Seeing the film *Mutiny on the Bounty* had stimulated him to think about the relationship between authority and servility. In the contrast between the childlike society of the South Sea islanders and the stern English values by which Captain Bligh ruled the *Bounty*, he saw a moral lesson he had himself taken to heart somewhat late in life. Wanting to tip off his students at an age when it might help them, he advised them to be sceptical of their fathers' values. 'Men can learn just as much from boys as boys can learn from men,' he asserted. With the Pacific islanders in mind he added: 'A child can sometimes grow in harmony with nature, but the mature life of civilized man loses this idyllic quality very quickly.' His lifelong fascination with the *Bounty*'s story originated from this date; here, as elsewhere, that mutiny stood symbolically for the revolt in himself against a regimentation too strictly enforced in his own childhood. Since his discontent at Princeton, his father had appeared to him like an unfair Captain Bligh; now, trapped once more in a British school system, he did not want to perpetuate its harsher aspects any more than was necessary.

According to some of his former students and colleagues alike, MacLennan was an excellent teacher for the top group in his classes.[10] Classics was far from being a favourite subject, but the brighter students found his classes exciting and stimulating – more for his digressions on his travels and on current events than for the translations that were required.

Despite the fact that he hated the place, felt the job was beneath his dignity, and resented the long hours of work required of him for so little money, he did not do a bare minimum of work as he might have. He became friends with some of the staff, involved himself in committees at the school, and put much extra time into both the school's athletic program and its drama productions. In a letter in 1942 to Victor Block, an immigrant from Germany and a friend who came to the college as a French and history teacher in 1945 (and later became his colleague at McGill), he revealed his inner thoughts on the matter: 'The whole world is marking time. Essentially it's the problem, the psychic problem, of every constructive mind now alive, to school himself to wait until the world can use his activities.'[11] 'To school himself to wait' was his personal challenge. In part he was able to 'mark time' at Lower Canada College by joining in the life of the school.

The tide of his despair slowly began to turn, however. His first taste of financial independence, even though it was far from what he had hoped for, gradually encouraged his inner confidence, and he began to develop along lines no one else had chosen for him. For the first time he was free to sort things out for himself.

No one could accuse him of taking time from his duties to devote to his novel, yet he managed to continue to write. Stephen Penton recalled being kept awake night after night as MacLennan typed furiously above him in the tiny room that had once been part of the infirmary.[12] Although Penton believed that the novel he was working on was *Barometer Rising*, for the first three years at Lower Canada

College he was in fact completing and revising the novel he had begun in January 1934 at Princeton, 'A Man Should Rejoice.'

Just about the time he had finished his thesis, when he was about one year into his novel, he had written to his Halifax friend George Barrett in March 1935 to sound out his thoughts on contemporary fiction. If Hemingway had been his model for the novel that had already failed, 'So All Their Praises,' he certainly was no longer to be. 'Inside a few years,' he wrote, 'the Hemingway school will be a back number. It is now in process of apotheosis, which is evidence for my statement. The apotheosis of Shaw took place around 1928, and now he is a joke. I believe that by the time we are fifty the Hemingway crowd will be studied as examples of stupidity and derangement just as nowadays we consider Carlyle. He will likely not even rate as high as Carlyle.' The problem with the Hemingway school, as he now saw it, was that 'as affairs are rotten, most [American] writers are swimming up and down sewers saying how tough they are. Presumably this is a reaction against their early years of manhood when they believed that the States was a land of opportunities.'

His rejection of Hemingway as a model for his fiction in no way signalled an admiration of British writers. On the contrary, in the same letter to Barrett he maintained: 'If one wants to write one must turn one's back on England altogether. Sterility is certainly the leitmotif over there and Spender, Bottrall and Auden, the latter two with their talk about "intelligence" until you go bats listening to them, are good examples and are already ending nowhere.' The choice between the British and the American schools of current literature, as he saw it, was one 'between the dusty dry sterility of an attic, which is England; and the succulence of mortified flesh, which may be America.' He really wanted to pick up where D.H. Lawrence had left off. 'I agree with you,' he wrote to Barrett, 'that Lawrence is the greatest of the lot of them, but in his final period he got deranged too, and escaped into a mysticism which had little else to recommend it but good writing. Eliot and Co. would abnegate all feeling; Lawrence all thinking, and one is as absurd as the other. You can't feel with your mind and you can't think with your thighs. They all seem to me to fall victims of the lust this age has for specialization. It seems to me that whereas a painter can present only one picture of one subject and have it good, a novelist will be making a false statement by implication unless he does more. I see it as my job to start in where Lawrence left off, though I admit that is at once a tall order and a partial statement. The upshot is, in practice, that you have to know a hell of a lot about a variety of things, and that you have to be more than an ordinary craftsman, for the complexity of everything is almost beyond one's grasp. One must write, not of mechanical causation, but of organic causation, and the difference is primarily a difference in mental process.'[13]

In these remarks he reveals himself to be evolving a theory of literature which was defined against British writers on the one hand and American writers on the other. Although he identified more closely with the American stream, he objected strenuously to a moral slant there that appeared to him to dwell too much on the material, ignoring the spiritual. His argument was for wholeness, for spiritual health, although he did not in any way put such thoughts in Christian terms. Although he did not anywhere suggest that he was interested in starting to write from a 'Canadian' angle of vision, as opposed to British and American, his statement of a theory of writing, which followed neither of the trends currently popular in the English-speaking world, both expressed his growing sense of independence and paved the way for his later theories. 'To know a hell of a lot about a variety of things' and 'to be more than an ordinary craftsman' were the means by which he thought the 'organic causation' he wanted to capture in fiction could be accomplished.

'A Man Should Rejoice' was to incorporate both MacLennan's new literary theories as well as his developing political views. With neither the decadence he thought typically American nor the cold intellectualism he found representative of the English, he presented a situation very close to the vortex of world events of the time. His hero, David Culver, is a communist who first attempts, within the limits of his personal background, to better the lot of the working class, and later joins an armed revolution of the left in Austria against the fascist dictators there. David is the son of the 'robot-like' American capitalist Bernard Culver, who owns two mills in Pittsburgh, controls two banks, and later becomes president of an oil company. (MacLennan's presentation of this character owes much to Sinclair Lewis' novel *Babbitt*, which was to remain for him for some time the prime example of 'social realism'; through Bernard Culver and his neglected, artistic Russian wife Arina, he tried to portray what he called 'the Babbitt age.') Like MacLennan, David Culver completes his formal education at Princeton reluctantly under the thumb of his father; there he obtains the degree in chemistry which will enable him to join his father's capitalist operations. His heart, however, is not in his studies; nor does he share his father's aims for him. Resembling much more that 'woman of art,' his mother, he wants to paint. After a year in

Paris studying under a socialist artist, and a holiday in Lorbeerstein in Austria where he passes his time in the company of young socialist intellectuals (and meets Anne Lovelace who is to become his wife), he returns to America in 1929 to work for his father in one of his mills. Fired both by a natural antipathy to his father's inhumane exploitation of himself and the other workers and by the new left-wing ideas he has encountered abroad, he performs his duties in the mill unfeelingly, 'like a machine.' At night, however, he pours his emotions of 'fear, guilt and hatred' onto his canvasses.

David's father has introduced him to his industrial empire from the bottom up; so, after a brief stint in the mill among the workers, he is transferred to the laboratory of an oil refinery near New York, which is under the control of a Machiavellian scientist called Horace Pigou, who coldly believes that science is the sum total of reality. David introduces to the lab an old childhood friend, Nicholas Eisenhardt, who is living with a girl named Jean whom he has persuaded to have a traumatic abortion. Both Nicholas and David become members of the Communist party, attending cell meetings and working towards the establishment of a union in Culver's refinery. A meeting of the workers, arranged by Nicholas for the purpose of discussing the possibility of establishing the union, is infiltrated by a gang hired by Pigou to create the impression of a Communist-organized strike. Pigou's plans are successful; the riot squad he has notified raid the meeting; Nicholas and David are both apprehended as Communist agitators.

After a long court scene, in which even Jean's abortion comes to light, both men are imprisoned. In a section reminiscent of Arthur Koestler's *Darkness at Noon* (a novel MacLennan was to praise later), David fends off a nervous breakdown. After his jail term, he rejoins his wife Anne and they travel back to Lorbeerstein, as do Nicholas and Jean, to take part in a disorganized, sporadic socialist revolution. Like 'rats in a trap,' they realize the revolt is a lost cause. In a final passage filled with vivid description of the horrors of war, Anne, now pregnant, has a miscarriage in shock and is later killed in a terrifying bomb attack by the fascists. As his wife dies, David's thoughts flash back over his life:

And then I seemed to be thinking clearly again, seeing it as though it were a map of the world. I saw my father bending over his desk and the ticker-tapes pouring past under the eyes of the brokers, the dictators shouting and the armies forming; all abstractions, because it was abstractions in which most of them dealt. I saw all I had been a part of in the past, the joy and the trying and the discovering of new worlds, the misery and then the unspeakable delight she and I had found in each other; I saw the frustrations that made men incapable of understanding anything but the fact that they were unhappy and that every man's hand was against his neighbor, knowing that nothing they did brought the reaping of the fruit, that nothing they could hope for became theirs in their lifetime, but passed into the hands of the bloodless men who reaped what the poor had been driven to sow, I saw all these ideas as distinct images or groups of images that revolved slowly as in a ritual around the dying figure of Anne alone in that room. In her solitude, did she see this too?

The novel ends, as did 'So All Their Praises,' with the hero alone, attempting to make some sense out of his isolation. That order David Culver, unlike Michael Carmichael, derives from Christianity. As a priest counsels him in his grief:

'"I am the resurrection and the life" ... I think this is true, but you don't have to believe it. You don't have to believe in any miracles at all. You only have to believe that there are more good people in the world than evil and know that they will always be your friends.'

'Yes,' I said, and my eyes turned to the hills. 'Yes ...'

The novel's Preface reveals that after this tragedy David has become a recluse in Nova Scotia, where his mother had moved when he was in his teens. After such shattering events, he feels compelled 'to set down what happened to my friends and myself' in order to keep sane. 'A few years ago I could not accept this knowledge,' he confesses, 'but now I know that what happens to us can be greater than ourselves.' 'Whether I can freeze a durable form out of a state of flux,' he speculates, 'I don't know. At least I shall write something of the life of my friends and myself, not because we were important personages, but because the chaos of our lives and ideas seem to me now to have been a pattern of our time.'

In keeping with the mode of 'social realism,' MacLennan had deliberately assigned to his characters the specific roles that would reveal this 'pattern of our time.' As David describes them on one occasion: 'I consider people as though they were physical forces, I thought. I see the wood but apparently I am never able to see the trees. Nicholas? He is the positive force, the force of communism, of the future. Jean? She is the balancer of Nicholas, the force of present vitality. Culver? I can see in him only the force of destruction, the force of competition driving the world to wars. And [Paula] is sensation, a woman my Russian grandfather would have bankrupted his state to possess, a woman whose physical motions are a drug for the present.'[14]

Throughout the novel MacLennan's sympathies with the left are clear. Although a sprawling and jagged affair, the novel reveals a much more consistent point of view and a better integration of themes than his previous attempt.

Some of the credit for this new assurance and advance in skill belongs to Dorothy Duncan: throughout the manuscript of 'A Man Should Rejoice' are the comments, questions, and revisions she made. MacLennan at Lower Canada College would type out sections of his manuscript; then off it would go by mail to Chicago where Dorothy would read it, comment on it, and return it. Her suggestions took many forms. Mainly she edited his original into a more concise style: sentences, words, sometimes whole paragraphs and sections are crossed out. She also had an eye for accuracy: one long comment, for example, explains the details of the American legal system for the court scene – details she took the trouble to glean from her father by telephone. Careful not to offend, she noted on another occasion: 'My change was made not because you are writing for an American audience (you're not) but because David is an American.'[15] Weeding out irrelevancies, making technical terms accurate, improving dialogue, paring down wordiness, and even typing – in all these ways Dorothy was of real assistance in his writing. The back and forth dialogue of his manuscript and her comments were almost like love letters, so deeply were they sharing in this novel. '*The End*,' Dorothy wrote on the last page as she finished her revisions, 'And my love to you, Darling.'

By March 1936 MacLennan had, with difficulty, finished his first draft of 'A Man Should Rejoice.' His main anxiety about its success was that events in Europe might prove the failed revolution in Austria, with which he had concluded his book, to be an historical inaccuracy. At the end of March, in a letter to George Barrett, he described what the last stretch of writing had been like:

> My own book is finished and feels finished. Dorothy is typing the last section now ... Its main enemy from the publishing point of view will be the newspapers and to tell the truth the papers seem so bad these days that escape literature has something to be said for it. However I feel that the book is a unity and that it is logical and inevitable and fairly well written ... I believe it will be published but I also believed that the first book would be published too ... I was nearly always short of sleep, for I teach thirty hours a week and

the duties are long and arduous and the task of writing 500 pages of typescript in addition to my regular work was pretty hectic, for I had to be patient and had to select constantly. I found the best method was to think a chapter entirely through seeing it all around before I tried to write it. I spent most of last winter in my spare time writing scenarios of various parts and testing them against each other. The actual mechanics of writing I found a heavy emotional strain but only a fraction of the actual work of writing the book. The last section had to be entirely created this winter and although it is only 150 pages and although the characters were almost formed and certainly familiar by that time I found it emotionally more exhausting to accomplish than all the rest of the book put together. Towards the end it became almost intolerable and I was sleepless and unfit to live with and on the verge of jitters for the past month. Finally I wrote the last page and spent a week of revision – almost the hardest of all when you see for the first time what you have perpetrated ... I have felt like a free man ever since. Somehow I feel as though I had done what I had set out to do. The last book ['So All Their Praises'] always seemed incohate [*sic*] and parts kept recurring that I wanted to finish long after the m.s.s. had left my hands.[16]

After a year of teaching at Lower Canada College, MacLennan was at last secure enough financially to support a wife. On 22 June 1936 he married Dorothy at the small Presbyterian church near her home in Wilmette. For their wedding trip they spent a leisurely week driving from Chicago to Boston where they boarded the *Evangeline* for Nova Scotia. Fittingly enough, it was Dominion Day when Dorothy disembarked at Yarmouth and filled out the papers which officially made her a subject of the British Empire without taking away her American citizenship, although its significance was lost on her at the time. 'I omitted to tell Hugh,' she later recalled, 'I had never heard of Dominion Day.'[17] From Yarmouth, where they watched 'on that pink and blue ... morning' while their old car was once more transferred to solid ground, they drove on to Halifax for a summer with the MacLennans.

At last in Montreal, they took an apartment near Lower Canada College at 5265 Côte St-Luc Road in Notre-Dame-de-Grâce. There, by her own account, Dorothy concentrated on 'the business of maintaining the kind of routine that suits his temperament.' Together they consolidated a partnership in writing in which they envisaged future fame for both: while MacLennan continued with revisions on 'A Man Should Rejoice,' Dorothy wrote a practical do-it-yourself book called *You Can Live in an Apartment*, based on a combination of her own and her husband's experiences of living arrangements around the world (it was eventually published by Farrar & Rinehart in 1939). Judging from this book, Dorothy had remarkable skills of organization, cooking, and decorating. Doubtless she provided order as well as pleasant surroundings in which they could work productively. In the evenings they entertained friends with whom they could discuss intellectual issues and politics. Alone, they listened to their favourite music: for Dorothy this meant the popular songs of Irving Berlin, the instrumental jazz of Bix Beiderbecke, and the 'big band' sound of Benny Goodman; Hugh preferred classical music, especially the religious oratorios from which his mother had sung selections – the *Missa Solemnis* of Beethoven, for example, and Handel's *Messiah*. For MacLennan, popular music and jazz would remain the expression of an urban life and they lacked the sense of mystery and wonder to be found in the classical music he enjoyed.[18]

In December 1936 they returned to Halifax to spend the first Christmas after their marriage with the MacLennans. While Hugh found everything quite normal, Dorothy was in for a shock: she simply could not have imagined a Christmas so dull. To her, Christmas had always been a time of gaiety and late night parties, extravagant gifts, lavish decorations. Unluckily, Christmas that year fell on a Sunday, which meant that what modest festivities were in store had to be put off until the following day. Having retired to bed early on Christmas Eve, they were all up early the next day. Dorothy was deeply disappointed: 'It was the first time I had gone to bed before midnight on Christmas Eve since I had attained the stature of being allowed to stay up and participate in family rituals – candlelight, carol singing, fruit cake, and wine ... The Doctor looked at his watch, wound it, remarked that it was ten o'clock, and went upstairs to bed. Within ten minutes everyone had followed.' Breakfast the next morning was even worse. Without so much as a 'Merry Christmas,' the whole household was off early to St Matthew's Church where Dr Sam followed the lesson in his Greek testament. No Christmas dinner appeared; only the usual Sunday joint of beef. Games, radio programs, and knitting were out of the question; the only acceptable entertainment for the day was reading. At teatime some family friend paid a call for an hour or so, and at six Hugh at the piano played some hymns, concluding with the family favourite suitably titled *Martyrdom*. Then back to church at seven for the evening service, and by ten-thirty everyone was in bed again. Not surprisingly, Dorothy concluded: 'Halifax in winter is enormously ugly ... It is monstrously impressive and forever unforgettable in its dreariness.' Eventually she came to realize that the MacLennans 'don't want that kind of fun; it would be inimical to their natures. They behave as they do because they *like* it that way.'[19] The adjustments that had to be made between Dorothy and the MacLennan family were by no means complete.

Sometime during the winter term in early 1937 at Lower Canada College, after their return from Halifax, Hugh and Dorothy met Frank R. Scott and his wife Marian. In 1923-4 Scott had himself taught at the college; he was now in the faculty of law at McGill University. Poet, scholar, social reformer, civil rights champion, he was one of the pillars of the socialist movement in Canada. In 1932, the year MacLennan moved from Oxford to Princeton, he had helped to organize the League for Social Reconstruction; the following year he was one of the founding members of the Co-operative Commonwealth Federation. About the time MacLennan arrived at the college, the league's publication, *Social Planning for Canada*, to which Scott had contributed no small part, had appeared; the next year, 1935-6, Scott had been president of the league. Meeting him brought MacLennan face to face with the Canadian left.

The democratic socialism of the CCF appealed to him much more than the policies of either the Liberals or the Conservatives; he admired also the men involved – F.R. Scott, J.S. Woodsworth, Stanley Knowles, Frank Underhill – who with great integrity committed themselves to the ideals of their party. But he did not join them, perhaps because his interests at the time were elsewhere. 'They were not Marxists,' he later commented, 'but were really small "l" Liberals. And they had no solid base in the east, since the party consisted mainly of a number of farmer and labour groups in the west.' Cautious about what they stood for, he also instinctively was not a party joiner. As Frank Scott recalled: 'MacLennan shied away from socialism like a horse shying away from a dark object in a field.'[20]

He continued to be interested in communism. Although never a party member, he did attend meetings of the United Front and even, on one occasion, delivered an anti-fascist speech with his friend George Barrett at one of their meetings in the chemistry theatre of Dalhousie University. At a later meeting he met Stanley Ryerson, the Marxist historian and activist, after hearing him lecture in Montreal on 'The Radical Tradition in Canada' for the League against Fascism. His response to this lecture, as expressed in a letter to Barrett, indicates that, while looking to the Communist party for some alternative to the traditional parties and the CCF, and being well-disposed towards Tim Buck, the leader of the party in Canada (whom he had not met), he found Ryerson's interpretation of Canadian history too simplified and biased to be acceptable: 'I met Stanley Ryerson, the Montreal secty. of the League vs. Fascism, and heard him lecture ... It was all right, but I came away more than ever convinced that the orthodox Communist approach is hopeless for this country. There is too much sour-grapes about it and it does not win converts to a better world to tell them that Lord Strathcona was a hypocrite. Workers' advocates must somehow get over their defense-mechanisms, for people want confidence and pride in a speaker. I believe Tim Buck has both, though I have never heard him. Strathcona collared the major holdings of the Hudson's Bay Co. by a manipulation, but he also had a lot to do with building the C.P.R. and it is utterly inadequate to say that the only thing he was interested in was money. We die of this academicism.'

Much later MacLennan recalled that his interest in the Communist party during the mid-1930s was naïve. Partly because so many remarkable intellectuals were drawn to the left, and partly because it seemed to offer a humanitarian resolution to the economic and political crises that were convulsing the entire Western world at the time, he gave it serious consideration. Looking at his letters from the period, it is obvious that he was keeping up to date with events as the world gradually shifted from a post-war to a pre-war state. The truth seems to be that he did not know what to believe in. On the one hand, he had lost confidence in the England he had been taught to admire in childhood. 'The diabolic intriguing of the British,' he wrote in disgust to Barrett, 'who have successively helped out Mussolini and now have made France so helpless that she will shortly be forced to give over the Russian alliance has absolutely killed in myself the last remnant of pro-English feeling I used to possess.' Looking at developments in Italy he saw an analogy with the ancient Egyptian town he had studied in such detail: 'Oxyrhynchus ended up by becoming the property of a single man. Why can't Italy become the property of a single man too? It just about is anyway.' These were events which Marxism, in his mind, simply could not explain or remedy: 'Marxism is wrong in asserting the inevitability of a proletarian rising, for it has never been inevitable in the past and it is quite a different thing to see ignorant workers and raw peasants who have never been civilized rise against a despotism from seeing people whose brains have become petrified by machines and radios and cinemas and regimentation rise against their masters.'[21] On the other hand, he felt deeply about the conditions of workers and about the brutal inhumanity of fascism. What, then, was the answer?

Confused by theories, bombarded daily by facts in the press, MacLennan decided to go to Russia, as so many intellectuals of the time were doing, to see for himself what a Communist government could provide. Dorothy had spotted an advertisement in the *Saturday Review* which offered a free trip to any German speaker who would conduct a tour to the Soviet Union, Germany, and Scandinavia for five weeks in the summer of 1937. The German he had acquired at the Holtzmann household in Freiburg proved to be more than adequate. So, after the term at Lower Canada College had ended, he set off in July with his sister Frances, one of Dorothy's cousins, and another girl, leaving Dorothy behind because she had fallen sick.[22]

MacLennan arrived in Russia expecting to find a brave new world; what he saw provoked profound disillusionment. In this second year of Stalin's purges, commercial painters in Leningrad were busy painting out the faces of former leaders in the murals that decorated the walls of the Finland Station. As far as he could determine, the Russian Revolution had not brought greater freedom, but more stringent censorship. 'The Bolsheviks,' he observed, 'do not dare let any but the more educated Russians see pictures of a city like New York.' Not only were Marxist theories, as he understood them, inadequate to account for what had happened in Russia, he also believed that the revolution had done far more damage than good: 'The idea of communism, as defined by Marx, leaves in my opinion much to be desired. Russia shows – although neither Marx nor Lenin, but the war and the incompetence of the Czar produced the revolution – that class war aiming at armed revolution is fallacious in a western country.' If capitalism could be decadent and corrupt, so too could communism, according to the evidence he considered. 'There is no communism in Russia,' he exclaimed in a letter to Barrett; 'and if people say there is, they are liars. I cannot put it any lighter than that. If hundreds of men can afford champagne frequently – I saw the same faces on several nights drinking it – and millions are what we would call in destitution, I submit there is no communism. Things are getting better. Yes, but 1937 has disclosed what 1929 did not know, that to put a nation of coolies – and I believe the average Russian lacks the diligence of the average coolie – to work on western principles requires rewards and punishments on a scale the Jesuits never dreamed of. I would say that 90% of what I understood to be communist theories to have been scrapped, at least for the time being.'[23]

He grounded his analysis on a fairly thorough inspection of the Soviet system. He recorded wages and prices in a wide variety of areas; looked into education and talked with all sorts of people; examined the legal and judicial system and visited a collective farm; and looked at the armed forces and the current rearmament program. Only in the specific areas of education (state-controlled, though élitist), hospitals, factories, utilities, railroads, shipping, and most of the farms, as well as state-run day-care centres, did he find communist principles, as he understood them, in action. Although some visitors to the Soviet Union at the time, Malcolm Muggeridge for instance, reacted similarly to MacLennan, some looked at Russia more with a sense of her future. Dr Norman Bethune, for example, had converted to communism only three years earlier partly as a result of a trip to the Soviet Union which seemed to him a civilization on the upgrade. J.S. Woodsworth, co-founder of the CCF, though he never thought of becoming a communist, saw Russia as a nation emerging from feudalism and felt that the Communist party appeared to be handling its evolution into an industrial state well enough. But MacLennan's response was totally negative. Like his character George Stewart in *The Watch That Ends the Night*, who also travels to Russia in 1937, he concluded that many workers under communism had just as bad a deal as the serfs had had on the feudal estates. As a cynical American tourist tells George: 'See Russia, and let your theories die.'[24] George was to agree.

Any tendency MacLennan had to entertain communist theories did die on seeing the Soviet Union for himself, and so did the ability to believe in any political theories from then on. Having seen what revolution had done in Russia, fearing what the rise of dictatorship in Germany and Italy might eventually mean, he became, more than anything else, anti-war – and, in common with many North Americans, isolationist. As he wrote to Barrett: 'I admit that the U.S.S.R. is doing all it thinks it dare do to avert war, but I think any attempt to foster class war in the traditional manner in other countries is disastrous. It will only breed Fascism; in other words it will only breed war. And no war, regardless of its causes, will be relevant in Europe now, because the causes become irrelevant just as soon as the first soldiers move. I can see one purpose and one purpose only in America now: to keep us out of any war whatever, to be opportunist and concessive if necessary and to use as much common sense as possible, but at all costs to increase the confidence of this continent in its own resources, abilities and its own good fortune.'

Although Russia loomed largest in importance among the countries he visited that summer, he also went to Germany and Scandinavia. It was in Sweden, Norway, and Denmark that he found the kind of political, economic, and social life he liked best; in the notes he took on his trip he jotted down: 'The best course is to evolve, as Scandinavia has done, towards Socialism, but a country like England is too inferior in its masses and petit [*sic*] bourgeoisie to do this. A better country like France might; a still better country like the U.S.A. might, if Americans were not such egotists; a really good country like Canada has a good chance.' Or, as he explained to George Barrett shortly after his return: 'I admit that the Social democrats in England were a washout. But the social democrats in Scandinavia have produced three demi-paradises. In Sweden, too, capital was as strongly entrenched as it is here in Canada. I know that here, in England and America, it is not so simple. But I also know that doctrinaire methods are not according to our genius. I hate to say all this, but if any Canadian can return from Russia *today* and feel absolutely confident of the infallibility of "communism" for our purposes, I can only say he is a religionist. England is now so decadent that this religionism of men like Spender and Auden is excusable .... Personally, I believe our salvation lies through some method on the analogy of Scandinavia.'

Having discovered the merits of democratic socialism, and being so firmly opposed to war, he might well have joined the CCF, whose prominent members he already knew and admired. But so great was his sense of betrayal after what he had seen in Russia that he wanted to steer clear of all political parties. Even directly on his return to Montreal he had written wearily to Barrett: 'I should say this much after seeing Europe in 1937, a man should have great respect for ideas, but no confidence in them.' By late September he emphatically declared: 'No absolute is ever right and if we can realize this we may save ourselves ... I can't see any clear way out.'[25] He was in no frame of mind to join any party, even one which had in mind long-term goals for society similar to his own. Bitterly, he refrained from playing any active role in the political life of the nation, from this point on refusing to jeopardize his freedom of thought and choice by getting locked into any single political stance. 'I think I grew up in that fortnight in the U.S.S.R.,' he announced to Barrett a few months later. Certainly, the youthful idealism with which he had set off to view the Soviet Union had been replaced by a strong determination to keep himself detached from politics; it felt, at least, like maturity.

Nor did he want to return: 'though I would not have missed Russia for worlds,' he declared in February 1938, 'I would not look at another Russian [tour].' He never did travel again to Russia. In fact his 1937 tour was the last Canadian study group to get through. 'Two others,' he told Barrett, 'were turned back on the border by terrified comrades who were afraid of the responsibility of letting in a crowd of eager school teachers and brethren who would see a factory as modern as ours were in 1860. Stalin's Russia, if it were not so tragic, is the biggest and most ridiculous bluff since Noah's flood.'[26]

During 1938 his main concern was to get his second novel published. In December he had been almost certain that 'A Man Should Rejoice' would at last go into print. Of the twenty-eight publishers to whom he claims he took the manuscript, a reader's report from only one of them remains today. The comments that reader made give a good assessment of his strengths and weaknesses as a writer; fault was found chiefly with some of the characters and with the dialogue. Bernard Culver, David's father, is 'no more than a symbol of industrialization'; many of the other characters speak in an unconvincing fashion. 'I don't believe in such loquacious people, and such articulate people ... All the talking the characters do about themselves and each other frequently serves to obscure them, rather than clarify them.' On the other hand, the reader praised the novel itself strongly: 'It is not a proletarian novel just for the sake of being a proletarian novel, though there is no doubt where the author's sympathies lie, but his purpose mainly is to show the effect of these things on one sensitive young man ... There is some extraordinarily good writing here ... I am not in favour of taking the book now, but if the author could be persuaded to rework it I'd like to see it again.'[27]

Longmans, Green and Company had as good as made a commitment to publish, after extensive revisions directed by the editor Whit Burnett; finally, however, he wrote to say that the novel too closely resembled two others they had published. MacLennan, unconvinced by this explanation, suggested to Barrett that they were really more worried about associating themselves with left-wing politics. 'My agent,' he wrote, 'seems to think they were afraid of getting a leftist label. This may be true; I'm inclined to think it is, for Burnett did not pull his punches any when he dealt with the first draft. I'm rather pessimistic at the moment. Truly, when I was told by the agent that it was just a matter of a few details being fixed up before the contract would be signed, and then heard it was dropped, it was like a good heavy sock in the balls.'

As usual, he found an outlet for his frustration in athletics, playing hockey three times a week in addition to his busy sports schedule at Lower Canada College. And, he was falling in love with Montreal, 'the grandest place I have ever seen in winter barring Switzerland ... We have skating parties on the weekends in the nights, cold days always a little below zero and dry, with much sunshine.'[28] The city to which he had so randomly come was taking hold of his imagination.

He now took the novel to Duell, Sloan and Pearce, who seriously considered publishing it until the Munich agreement in September 1938 caused them to worry that the subject matter might soon be made irrelevant. They did not, however, reject it outright, but held onto the manuscript until such time as events in Europe either confirmed or proved false the prophecy of revolution with which the novel ended.

Suddenly, on 17 February 1939, MacLennan received a cable from his mother: 'FATHER ILL. COME IMMEDIATELY.'[29] Dr Sam had been suffering for some time from high blood pressure; indeed, he had gone into semi-retirement in Windsor, Nova Scotia, as a result of advice he had obtained from specialists at Johns Hopkins University during Hugh's last year at Princeton. Called out to perform only those operations no one else could handle, he had led for two years a much less busy life than he had in Halifax. One of his specialties was the 'labyrinth,' a technique for operating on the labyrinth of the ear, especially difficult in the days before antibiotics, which he had learned in Vienna in 1935 from the famous Jewish physician Dr Neuman (he had refused to operate on Hitler, lest his people be blamed if something went wrong). That stormy 15th of February, as MacLennan remembered it, a local doctor had asked Dr Sam to perform this operation on a young girl; to get to his patient it was necessary to travel by sleigh over the hills and through the backwoods in a fierce snowstorm. Although he saved the girl's life, the strain was too much for him. A day or two later he woke up very early and turned to his wife.

'Would you go downstairs and get my cheque-book.'
'What do you want that for?' Katie replied, her voice thick with sleep.
'Do what I ask.' he ordered.

Cheque-book in hand, feeling already some kind of nameless fear, she re-entered the bedroom and watched while he wrote a cheque for four or five thousand dollars.

'Get that to the bank when it opens at 10 o'clock,' he said calmly. 'You'll probably have to cash some securities, but this will authorize you to do it.'

Katie had not been a doctor's wife so many years for nothing. She knew.

'Get the doctor,' he now went on. 'And, after that, call Frances and Hugh. I will be unconscious by midnight probably.'

MacLennan took the night train to Saint John, then caught the ferry to Windsor. Rushing to the house, he ran up the stairs. Entering that room where the man whose concern he prized above all things lay dying, he heard distinctly the Cheyne-Stokes breathing that heralded the end. Minutes after he got there, his father died.

A few days later, on a raw day, bitter with the cold of a swirling snowstorm, Dr Sam was buried in the Camp Hill cemetery in Halifax. On the gravestone in the shape of the Celtic cross was inscribed 'Peace, Perfect Peace.' This simple phrase was no mere cliché. While the storm clouds of a war he would have hated gathered as thickly as those of the blizzard that struck that February day, having led a life in which he himself had been driven like one of the snowflakes that scudded round his gravestone, Dr Sam did at last know peace. In tribute to the help he had given, often without payment, about two hundred men and women put aside their chores for the day to follow him to his grave.

Hugh felt an enormous sense of loss. During the previous year he and his father had at last struck up a friendship which had been a profound delight to the younger man. Talking over the state of the world man to man, the father had come closer to accepting his son and his views, even though they differed from his own. He must have been more reconciled also to Dorothy, about whom he had had so many reservations at first. In reading the two manuscripts on which he was staking his future career, Dr Sam had finally come to see the importance of his son's ambitions and the talent he had.

So great a force had his father exerted on him for so long, it was hard to believe that he was really gone. He had treated him as an extension of himself, had managed his life to a remarkable degree. It seemed to Hugh that if he were alive, then his father must be too. So, peculiar as it may seem, he continued to write letters to his father for seven months after his death. In these six letters can be seen the real warmth that had developed between them and his longing to continue talking with his father.

Dear Dadden:

It was just a month ago yesterday. It seems to have been such a long time. You are as much alive to me now as you ever were. It is a strange thing, yet very true. Not yourself, not the you that could perform operations, but the you that has always stood in a part – perhaps in the central part – of my mind ... I am largely what you made me.

The letters continued throughout that summer from South Laguna, California, where Hugh and Dorothy spent a month with her parents who had moved there after the Colonel's retirement.

Most of the comments in these posthumous letters concern the events in Europe that were leading up to the Second World War. They are clearly a continuation of discussions well under way between the two men, and MacLennan, with great detail and logical reasoning, predicted the outbreak of war with surprising accuracy; he wrote consistently that war would start in mid- to late September; it was declared on 3 September 1939.

The main perspective he and his father had taken on the possibility of war was a moral one. How would war affect society in general? How would values be changed it there were a war? What, in the meantime, was happening to society as Hitler, step by step, confirmed the world's worst fears about him? 'As I believe that for the next ten years at least Europe can produce no cultural advance and almost certainly will move backwards, the issue which this summer and autumn should clarify will be this: is the world to move forwards or backwards? A war will ruin us all. If there is no war, it will be tough on millions of people but ultimately civilization, now that the social sciences have wakened up, will be sustained by the technological advances which continue to occur. The settlement of middle Europe on a workable economic basis, however, is essential to that improvement, and Germany is manifestly the only nation capable of making that settlement. It is their real destiny. If they can see it and are not blinded by their habitual megalomania, next year and those following will be somewhat more worth living.'[30]

The power of technology turned to constructive purposes, instead of to the destructive ends of war – this is what MacLennan anticipates here. As he had concluded after visiting Russia two years before, no good purpose is ever achieved by war. That his father encouraged and shared these views is certain; his own experience during the First World War in the medical corps at Folkestone had shown them both what war does to men, as had the Halifax explosion once he got back. The incredible loss of life and human potential in the Great War had demonstrated that war is never worthwhile. The war had been, as MacLennan always maintained, 'an incredible stupidity.'[31]

By now, he was beginning to relate the gloomy world situation to the decline in Christianity. A few years before he had deplored Christianity, as he had eschewed any organized religion; but now he was not so sure:

Since Napoleon's time the history of the world has never looked more doubtful, but now there is a difference, because everything is darker. The contempt for mankind, the logical result of fifty years of technical and scientific education, has grown to unbelievable dimensions in every land except France, England and North America, and even here it is dangerously strong. For Christianity – how cunningly did Stalin and Hitler exploit Marx's old-fashioned theory of the opium of the people – has practically perished. It has gone down in the theory that the state must replace it in reverence, which by a dextrous use of chicanery and propaganda, has in turn been developed into the belief that reverence for the tyrant, the murderer, the exploiter should take its place. This is a reversion to a primitive theology which perished from the west more than three thousand years ago. To worship the hand that kills your children, to offer the youth of the nation in a giant hecatomb to a tyrant-god! Can fifty years of scientific education alone have accomplished this and rendered this belief possible? I believe so. Because scientific education ... never was really an education at all, because it neglected all the coordinating principles which the Greeks and the Chinese developed over the centuries ... In advance graduate schools it produced great physicists and chemists and medical scientists, most of them so over-specialized that their opinion in other fields were worthless. It is significant that Bertrand Russel [*sic*] was almost unique among them, and although he seems to have attacked the old-fashioned brand of education ... he still was for years unable to demonstrate that scientific education must be coordinated.

Although MacLennan here decried the lack of what he calls 'a coordinating principle' to interrelate scientific specialties, he was really objecting to the headlong advancement of technology devoid of moral responsibility as the social sciences advanced at the expense of the Classics. To use technology for destructive purposes, for war above all, was a step backward for civilization. Only when moral responsibility and knowledge went hand in hand would social progress occur. That these opinions would have found ready sympathy in his father is indisputable. For MacLennan, his father had come to represent, perhaps even to personify, the positive aspects of scientific advance. If war was the ultimate horror in the use of science, then the doctor, especially the army doctor, who used his scientific knowledge to cure the wounded, was the epitome of scientific advancement.

The two men must also have discussed what MacLennan's role might be should war break out. Would he join the armed forces if Canada entered the war? Given their views, so strongly anti-war, so convinced of its futility no matter what the cause, his decision is not surprising. As he expressed it in one of these letters to his father: 'Somehow I feel I can face this future with more courage now than I previously could. I, like yourself, am one of those who have apparently been predestined to have the task of clearing up the messes of other people. If conscripted, I shall use every influence to avoid the fighting forces. The prospect of losing my own life does not affect me so much as does the degradation of being put in the position where it would be my "duty" to take that of another man. That prospect frankly does appal me. So, possibly a job in the Army Service Corps or the Medical might be arranged – more probably the former.'

Although MacLennan's father never did get to see the success that lay in store for his son, he died confident that he had the stuff of a writer in him. He could see at least the possibilities Hugh had before him. Today MacLennan maintains his father might not even have liked the novels that eventually did get published; he would, however, have been proud of the acclaim they brought his son. As for MacLennan, the possibilities before him were severely circumscribed by international events; his letters to his dead father were filled with self-doubt: 'In a society at peace – even in a society in the throes of a great struggle towards a better world – I would be able to take my place. I would be able to have fulfilled your best hopes of your son. Now, with Caesar within and without, there is only a small place for the individual. It seems to me, therefore, that ambition is largely an illusion. To do a small job such as I have, to do any job at all, as well as I can, is about enough.' The death of his father and the outbreak of war marked the end of an era. 'The old world you knew will be changed forever,' he wrote; 'I am glad, Dadden, for your sake, that you are not here to witness the *dénouement*. The rest of us must bear it as best we may. At least, we can have no choice in the matter.'[32]

Fortunately, MacLennan was spared the agony of making any military decision. The perforation in his left ear that had troubled him since his youth developed an infection; without antibiotics, such an infection was impossible to cure permanently and in time caused almost complete deafness on one side. His doctor, who happened to be the local recruiting doctor, told him not even to bother volunteering as he would be turned down for active service on account of his ear.[33]

Both circumstances and his own personal beliefs kept him out of the Second World War. His disillusionment with political theories had also made it clear that he was not to serve his country, as Frank Scott had done, by throwing his energies into a political party. His job at Lower

Canada College could not provide the challenge of a satisfying career. How was he to contribute?

It seemed to him that now, more than ever, the times were in need of a chronicler. Convinced, as he had been for some time, that this was an important, unusual period of transition, he channelled his thoughts and energies towards becoming one of those who would record it. Not entirely without guilt, he would become 'a man of art,' not a 'man of action.'

While his novel's fate lay in the hands of Longmans, Green and Company, he tried his hand at a short radio drama, *Augustus*. Augustus had been a figure of special interest to him during his classical studies, and his reign had come to stand for the epitome of civilization: 'He had made order out of chaos; he had relieved the provinces; he had created a salaried civil service; he had made the provinces prosperous and even happy, so that it was with real feeling that they worshipped him after his death as a god. But the decay in stock was already beginning in the capital. A new avenue for self-expression was needed and was not found.'[34] He used the figure of Augustus in his play to allegorize some of the historical events he had observed. Its central theme was the nature of political power.

The play takes place between the time of Julius Caesar's death and the old age of his successor, Octavius Caesar (Augustus). The career of the hero is traced through the political cycle from naïve idealism to pragmatic compromise to abdication. His resignation, which forms the play's climax, is unacceptable to the populace who instead reinstate him and rename him 'Augustus.' Among the many prices paid for peace is the death of the senator Cicero, whose initial advice to Octavius is responsible for his success (MacLennan here is exploring what might be reasonable alternatives to fascism). To his mother's accusation that he must be mad to try to take over after Caesar's death, the young Octavius replies: 'No, Mother. I'm so sane I merely appear to be mad in a world where insanity has become normal. I happen to have discovered the secret of how to govern Rome, that's all. Rome must have two things ... freedom and organization. Up to the present, when she's had freedom, there's been chaos. When she's had organization, there's been tyranny. I intend to marry freedom to organization.' Octavius defeats the decadent 'fascist' Marc Anthony, partly through the political compromises which involve the death of Cicero. Having gained power and brought organization to his people, he decides to give them freedom too by resigning his dictatorship. What he discovers in so doing is that few people, if any, really want freedom: 'How few people in this world really want to be free! Give them work, give them food, give them security! Is comfort the only purpose of life in our new system? Agrippa, I intend to get rid of that name "dictator."'

After accepting the responsibility thrust on him by his people, 'Augustus' pledges to be worthy of their trust. Yet at the same time he recognizes that he is one of those rare people who understand the nature of power and can be trusted: 'Power is a disease – a kind of necessary disease that a man like me deliberately takes into his veins and vitals. Not one man in a hundred million can take the volume of the disease that I have taken and remain sane. If the Roman people knew as much about power as I do, they would hate me and tremble for their children. Will my successor be one man in a hundred million too?'[35] MacLennan left no doubt about the answer to that question; he portrays Octavius' grandson already intoxicated with the prospect of the power he will inherit.

From this play we can see that MacLennan believed absolutely that dictatorship and the circumscription of freedom it entailed was an unacceptable form of government. Although it might be that one man in a hundred million could handle personal power responsibly, all the rest would not; and, even so, accession to that power would inevitably involve moral decisions that were painful to a responsible man.

Never performed, this radio play was mediocre, especially in its dialogue – a fatal flaw in drama – and through writing it MacLennan must have concluded that if Shakespeare was to be a model for him it must be in ways other than the dramatic form. But the play's subject is fascinating. Through classical history MacLennan examined the world of 1939. What could be done about dictatorships? What were the consequences? Was it possible that a 'benevolent dictator' could exist? Was even the accession to power of a 'benevolent dictator' a suspect thing in and of itself? In *Augustus* he revealed that for him organization and freedom are the two essentials of political life; if either is missing, he suggested, war is more than likely. Above all, he was a pacifist.

Not just because he was objectively interested but also because the fate of his novel depended on political affairs, he was keeping a close watch on events in Europe. In March 1939, a month after his father's death, he wrote to him: 'Last week I got a letter from my agent in New York, completely unexpected, saying that *Longmans', Green* were thinking of publishing my book. They considered me, to use their own words, "a find." I could have wished that you might at least have seen that letter. In my heart I do not expect that book to be published at all. Last week, when the prospects for peace this year seemed better, I had some hopes, but this last move of Hitler's has dashed them.' By September, when war had broken out, he concluded that there was still hope for publication, since he now saw many of his prophecies fulfilled:

In 'Man Should Rejoice' I seem to have built a little better than I knew. The book is still unpublished; if the war is lost by mankind it never will be published. But some time, if the war is won, it yet may take its place at full stature, and be understood, although at the time it was originally offered for sale its real meaning was misunderstood even by publishers. Its main view of life, understood intuitively by me during those hectic years after I left Oxford, has now been corroborated by the things which have happened.

For even in 1934, when the book was conceived, I understood that the evils of the time were occasioned by unbridled science. I knew that the indifference of scientists to anything except objective success in a limited field had permitted quasi-scientists to have dreams of magalomania [*sic*]. André Malraux half-realized this, but did not entirely. His great title *Days of Contempt* is only my own title in reverse. Hitler, Stalin, Mussolini and the rest – Pigou is the picture of these men's minds seen in miniature, with the difference that Pigou has no nerve and too much imagination of what may happen to himself. Well, when the war is over, science will either become the tool of mankind or the slave of tyrants.[36]

His hopes for 'A Man Should Rejoice' proved futile. Shortly after the outbreak of war, Duell, Sloan and Pearce decided not to publish; in their opinion, the novel's subject matter was now irrelevant. What he learned about writing from this failure was, as he explained much later, that 'there is no short cut to universality.' Imitating Hemingway or Sinclair Lewis or any other successful writer from outside one's own country was bound to result in a lack of 'the drive and compulsion of genuine native work.' Such work could not be done in a new country until the time was ripe. Looking back, he saw that he had been impatient, that he had not sufficiently realized that 'time is the essence of his and his country's problem.'[37] He was not crushed by his failure to publish his second novel; despite his occasional self-doubts he still firmly believed in his personal ambition to become a writer.

The tide had now shifted almost completely from the low point of despair at which he began to teach four years earlier at Lower Canada College. Having his own job and income, no matter how meagre, had flooded him with a sense of inner worth resulting in greater self-confidence. His marriage in 1936 had increased this confidence and had lent his life emotional and physical stability. The death of his father had freed him to write without fearing his censure. His trip to Russia in 1937 had developed an independence that affected more than his politics; as an artist, too, he was asserting his detachment from both English and American traditions of writing. The crisis of conscience about his own personal role in the war had strengthened his political detachment into a stronger sense of vocation than he had yet known. He would stand aside, observe and record. Now the failure of his second novel had shown him that to be successful one cannot simply ape the themes and methods of those who are. As all these issues clarified themselves in the late thirties, he himself felt that something must soon happen. Both he and Dorothy aimed steadily at the success they wanted. 'Dorothy is well,' he wrote his deceased father from Montreal on 7 April 1939. 'We are both on the threshold of the careers for which we planned and trained. An inch more and we will be over it.'

TEL :

Chapter five

The Breakthrough: *Barometer Rising*

In 'A Man Should Rejoice' MacLennan's hero, the young painter David Culver, goes to Paris to study technique: 'Even then I had ideas about how to paint North American scenes which were authentic, but I lacked the technique to bring them to life. And so I went to Paris to learn how.' His painting master tells him that he thinks he is good, but adds: 'I say you cannot paint a French landscape. I cannot paint an American one. The light there is different. What American painters there might have been, if they did not try to copy us all the time. There was Whistler. He was only a talented amateur. And why? He would look at America through French eyes and paint something of France there. There was Morrice, the Canadian. Now he was a painter. He could paint France and America too, but do you in America know Morrice?' Culver takes these remarks very much to heart; they confirm his first instincts to paint the land and people he knows best. Looking around him in France he observes: 'Every corner and little shop was gracious, like the wrinkles in the face of an old man painted in the seventeenth century, and in this scene the compositions that occurred to me and that I could paint were as crude as an American suburb. But still I felt old, not in history but in the future as all Americans, and I had a longing to paint men as they worked on the American plan, not because they were beautiful or because they possessed the blood-vitality of the Europeans, but because somehow or other they were the future.'

The time has come for Culver to pack his bags and return to America. Once there, he visits Nova Scotia where he responds with pro-

In the Laurentians north of Montreal

found feeling and artistry to the landscape – a response MacLennan renders in one of the novel's finest lyrical passages:

> The floor of the ocean swung against the continent, thousands of miles of water heavy with salt, and there were no people. Here on the rocks a man could find peace. The Great Glacier had scraped them and they stood bare and enormous on the edge of North America. I looked at them and felt my mind being cleansed, for the heat went out of it and instead of wanting to defend myself by hating people I felt suddenly humble. These ancient bones of the earth had not altered since man lifted his forearms and learned to walk. I looked at them and ceased to feel mean. Six thousand years of history and we had conquered this heavy immobility!
>
> No one could identify these formations with his personal emotions or sense a human analogy in the ponderous fluid forms that pressed against them. Smooth forms of water bulged against the granite, their color that of grey daylight, and with sinuous intricate balance they swung inward, and among them the granites stood like antediluvian monsters. Some, where the water washed, were sleek and smaller, like sea-dwelling mammals, but the quartz [that] glittered in the more massive forms and the backs of these had the hard, scaly gloss of a dry snake. Usually the colors were grey and nordic, but while the sun was setting the whole coast began to glow, not with flame but with a luminous shade of red, like the color in resin wine.
>
> Today there was no color at all, only form and the process of water. Dulce and algae were sucked to and fro at the water's edge, and the water washing them looked strong and tannic; but always the ebb swung back to the shifting fog-veils – formless and mysterious and active, like life itself.

Although MacLennan neglects Culver's artistic development because he emphasizes instead his political involvements as a leftist sympathizer, he makes it clear that his young artist wants to paint scenes from his place of birth, despite the fact that the traditions of art lie elsewhere. Beyond this, he shows that his artistic attempts differ in a particular way from those of other artists; while in Nova Scotia, Culver meets Paula 'Paul' Alvarez, a Venezuelan dancer, who stage-manages his first sexual experience and shows great interest in his paintings of the Nova Scotian landscape: 'There aren't many painters who are even trying to get what your're [*sic*] after ... You're trying to paint the world as though no one had seen it ever, as though no people existed in it and as though rocks had a life of their own. You're trying to forget about human time and understand geologic time.'[1]

MacLennan's 'portrait of the artist' in 'A Man Should Rejoice' was prophetic. Like Culver, he himself was to turn in his third novel to a portrayal of his homeland, Nova Scotia. By a mere shift of emphasis he centred his action in Halifax, showing the effect a European war has on Canada rather than locating his main action in Europe with side-trips to Canada, as he had done previously. And he took the sense of 'geologic time' Culver tries to capture in his paintings and located it at his novel's centre instead of leaving it a peripheral insight as he had in 'A Man Should Rejoice.'

According to MacLennan, it was Dorothy who first convinced him to abandon the idea of trying a third novel set abroad and suggested instead that he write about Canada; in his essay 'How We Differ from Americans' (1946), he wrote: 'It was she who showed me why the first two novels I had written were failures. I had set the scene and characters of one book in Europe, of the second in the United States ... It was my wife who persuaded me to see Canada as it was and to write of it as I saw it.' Dorothy's own earlier recollection of a conversation during a car trip they took in the late 1930s bears out his statement:

'If I tried to tell anyone at home what this part of Nova Scotia looks like they wouldn't believe me ...'

'Why wouldn't they?' he said. 'It's not so different along here from parts of the Maine coast.'

'But they've heard a lot about Maine ... They'd never believe anything so beautiful as this could exist without being publicized ... Why don't you put all this part of Nova Scotia in your next book, so they can really see it? ...'

'I'm going to write about something I know better than anything else next time,' he said finally. 'One of the most important places in the Western hemisphere ... a combination of fogs, ringing bells, ships' horns, foreign tongues, ancient bitches, glorious —'

'Men?' I interrupted ... 'Halifax? ... Don't forget the odor of lime trees in summer. They're magnificent ... I long to see that book get written. Nobody's ever going to understand Canada until she evolves a literature of her own, and you're the fellow to start bringing Canadian novels up to date.'[2]

Elsewhere, MacLennan was also to record the moment when Halifax first struck his imagination as having possibilities for fiction; in 'Canada for Canadians' (1947), he recalled looking out from the Citadel over the harbour one morning some years earlier:

In 1940 I was in Halifax, right after France surrendered ... I talked to a man on Citadel Hill who was also watching the ships go out.

'Look at that,' he said. 'England's going to hold on, all right.' After a pause, he added: 'But she'll never again be what she was. We might as well face it. The time has come when we've got to stand on our own feet.'

> I looked out over the roofs of the city to the harbour, and beyond to the rugged, untamed land around it. I thought of this town in which I had grown up, an ancient clearing in a wilderness of spruce and granite, shabby, inarticulate, staunch, neither British nor American ... By 1940, she had become the funnel through which the life-giving supplies of the western hemisphere were flowing ... That morning Halifax was the most vital city in North America, and she was completely unconscious of the fact. Almost, one might say she was unconscious of herself.
>
> At that instant the whole movement, drama, pathos, and unwitting loneliness of Halifax and of the country behind it surged through my mind. I decided, not knowing how it could be done, to put something of the essence of this city into a book. The result was my first published novel, *Barometer Rising*.[3]

That year, 1940, Hugh and Dorothy spent the summer at Baddeck, a tranquil holiday community of rambling houses on the shore of Bras d'Or Lake; they had no money to go elsewhere. There, in the MacLennans' summer home, 'Three Chimneys,' set back from the road, overlooking the lake, they worked daily. Upstairs, Dorothy was preparing a guide-book of Canada for American tourists; downstairs on the front verandah, Hugh worked on his novel.

When he had returned to Canada in 1935 after eight years of studying outside the country, the circumstances for a writer were unique. As in the *Titanic*'s sadder history, there was on the one hand the individual launching a will of his own, with a particular destination in mind, and on the other hand an environment alive with a force of its own in which that voyage took place. The environment in Canada to which he returned consisted in part of a literary, or more accurately a fictional, vacuum, as compelling as that which draws down lifeboats in the wake of a sinking ship. As Claude Bissell, Canadian literary critic, later described this phenomenon: 'during the first three decades of this century, fiction was in Canada a minor literary activity to be mentioned casually and with some embarrassment by the critics before they hastened on to pay their respects to the poets.'[4]

At first MacLennan did not perceive this vacuum. From 1935 to 1937 he was deeply engrossed in his duties at Lower Canada College, his first year of marriage with Dorothy, and the completion of 'A Man Should Rejoice.' That book, which he had begun at Princeton, was essentially a political novel with an international setting; although it is the brief episodes in Nova Scotia that ring most true, it did not suit his purpose at the time to shift the major North American scenes away from the United States. The voyage he had in mind for himself was one which would bring international acclaim for his literary efforts, and as far as he could see, to reach international stature a writer would have to choose international themes and settings.

One of his own compatriots, Morley Callaghan, had already accomplished this aim. Lucky enough to have met Ernest Hemingway in 1923 when both were, for a time, young reporters for the *Toronto Daily Star*, Callaghan had made the most of this entrée to the international scene by spending 'that summer in Paris,' 1929, on the fringe of the group of literary expatriates who had gathered there.[5] His fiction in the thirties was affected by the influence of these writers whom he so much admired. By avoiding specific references to his Canadian settings and by depicting ethical dilemmas of a universal nature, he had successfully launched his novels into international markets.

The Canadian environment MacLennan at first failed to notice was one of resurgent nationalism. The turning point had been the First World War: many believed that Canada had 'come of age' on the battlefields of Flanders and France, and, from being a somewhat insignificant British colony before the war, she had emerged, because of her considerable war effort, as a nation in her own right. On the political stage, this independence was acted out in the gradual whittling away of the last remnants of colonial status; a series of imperial conferences in the 1920s led to the declaration of 'dominion status' within the Commonwealth, and in 1931, at the very time MacLennan at Oxford was first turning his mind seriously to becoming a writer, the Statute of Westminster formalized the autonomy Canada had won by her increasingly prominent role on the world stage.

This new sense of national pride was unlike earlier manifestations of national sentiment. The men of the 'Canada First' movement, for example, who had grouped together in the years immediately following Confederation with the express purpose of cultivating a Canadian national identity, believed that Canada's colonial relationship to Britain would ultimately be transformed into an 'alliance of nations,'[6] with Canada playing a leading role; they had asserted, as did imperialists such as George Grant, Stephen Leacock, and Andrew Macphail a little later, that Canada should cherish her ties with Britain if she wished to realize her unique identity. Cultural expressions of such theories understandably relied heavily on the traditions of the old world. Aspects of Canadian life were typically cast in romantic forms by the 'Confederation Poets' – Roberts, Carman, and Lampman; popular historical romances characteristically emphasized the link with a tradition abroad.

But the national spirit that welled up after the Great War was based on different assumptions. As Donald Creighton later described it, in a manner that reflected his indignation that such a shift of gravity should ever have occurred: 'Canadian historians and social scientists, like the Canadian journalists and politicians [in the 1920s and 1930s], sought instinctively to depress the importance of Europe as the source of Western civilization and to exalt the creative power of North America ... North America had become a faith; and what was needed was a cultural Book of Genesis which could serve as a first chapter in the new religion's Holy Writ.'[7] As Brooke Claxton, a young nationalist at the time who would one day become a Liberal cabinet minister, later enthusiastically described this spirit in Canada: 'every kind of organization, national and local, cultural and religious, political and commercial, was at a peak of activity hardly equalled since ... All these were manifestations of the growth of national feeling – it was nation-wide, spontaneous, inevitable. It cut across political, racial and social lines; indeed, it was curiously a-political.'[8]

In art and in poetry this nationalism had already found expression by the mid-1930s. As MacLennan's reference to J.W. Morrice in 'A Man Should Rejoice' indicates, he was aware of the stirrings of a new Canadian vision in landscape painting, though he nowhere mentions the more important, seminal work of the Toronto-based Group of Seven, which had come together about the time of the First World War and had opened the doors to their first public show in 1920. As Claude Bissell noted, Canadian poets, too, had struck new, modern forms of poetry to give a voice to the times. Not only E.J. Pratt in Newfoundland, who like the Group of Seven had taken the war itself as one of his themes, but also right in Montreal A.M. Klein, Leo Kennedy, A.J.M. Smith, and MacLennan's friend F.R. Scott had rebelled outright against the romantic modes of the 'Confederation Poets' in favour of a harsher, more realistic style of writing and subjects that reflected the issues of the day.

But in Canadian fiction no comparable work was being done. Callaghan had effectively shifted fiction into the realistic mode, but he had done so in a way that side-stepped nationalism. The only other writer in Canada of sufficient stature to compare with Callaghan was Frederick Philip Grove. Foremost among the group of prairie writers (along with Robert Stead and Martha Ostenso), who had also begun writing realistic fiction in the twenties, Grove did not fill the vacuum in Canadian fiction: although the literary naturalism of his work was a remarkable contribution to Canadian letters, it was off-centre for reasons the opposite of those that made Callaghan's work unsuitable for the purpose; whereas Callaghan had, as it were, bypassed the nation altogether, Grove's work was too 'western,' too regional, to express Canadian sentiments at large.

Considering that Dorothy was an American, it is deeply ironic that she was the one to focus MacLennan's attention on Canadian nationalism. On the other hand, it may have been because she was an outsider, eager to become a part of her husband's world and curious about the specific differences between her birthplace and her new home, that she perceived what at first he did not notice. Whatever the cause, she acted in character as the 'organizer' and 'pragmatist' of the two; she not only prompted him 'to start bringing Canadian novels up to date,' but she avidly researched tourist information about each province and incorporated the information into her practical guide-book almost too enthusiastically called *Here's to Canada!*

Judging from her introduction to this book, she had quickly observed the national mood which had once more intensified as the beginning of the Second World War in 1939 touched off memories of Canada's achievements in the earlier war. In her first chapter, significantly called 'Canada in Motion,' she opened with Sir Wilfrid Laurier's somewhat apocryphal remark that, although the nineteenth century had belonged to the United States, the twentieth century would belong to Canada, and then proceeded to describe Canada as 'the coming nation of the World': 'Overnight, eyes have become focused in her direction and the exciting fact is now taking root in our consciousness that here, just over the border, a young cousin is involved in drama ... So the inrush of new strength, vitality and purpose which has come about as a result of her war effort is sufficient to hearten us all ... Canada's star is unquestioningly ascending in a world that is ready for maturity and wisdom. It will be an exciting thing to watch for those of us who live next door.'[9]

At what exact point Dorothy's urgings at his elbow and his own intuitions conspired to move him into the vacuum that existed in Canadian fiction is uncertain, but by 1938 MacLennan had published a short autobiographical sketch called 'Concussion' for *Lower Canada College Magazine* (June 1938), which described the Halifax explosion. This sketch represents the transition he was making from the great international themes he really longed to body forth, to the Canadian concerns his wife had pointed out he should be writing about.

The common denominator in this transition was war. So great was his horror at what war could do to human beings that he had confessed to having had great difficulty in writing the last chapters of 'A Man Should Rejoice' in which David Culver sees his pregnant wife Anne destroyed by a bomb. To get at such scenes, as far as he could see, meant setting them in Europe where another war seemed imminent. By describing his own reminiscences of the Halifax explosion from the First World War, however, he was to single out the one instance in twentieth-century history when, for one blinding moment, Canada was at the centre of international action.

From his political perspective in 1938, he drew a clear analogy between that moment and the present: 'This Halifax explosion, and what resulted from it, showed in miniature plenty of those relapses towards crude instinct which menace civilization now.' Capitalist manufacturers of munitions, he pointed out, had become rich because of the war in 1917, as they were becoming rich in 1938. And, as was happening in the late thirties, the proletariat was suffering the most. 'Down where I lived [in a better section of town] we had got the easy end of it,' he recalled, 'why, one wonders, does even an accident in war give the workers the worst of it?' He also drew a connection between these Halifax workers and the victims in the Spanish civil war: 'What happened to the people in the north end, however, was not spectacular and was not pretty. It was very much what happens to people in Spain today, except that, in this case, it was an accident and the munitions makers had not expected their products to be detonated so prematurely.' As he concluded, with savage humour: 'It was believed, in those times, a natural thing to blow up a man if he wore a uniform, but barbarous to blow up a person in civies, and particularly barbarous to blow up women and children ... During the next two decades of the twentieth century the military mind has escaped this illogicallity and now considers it desirable to blow up everyone except the generals of the opposite side.'

Even the nature of the two ships 'represents in miniature' the tragedy of events as he saw them in the late 1930s. On the one hand, the *S.S. Imo*, a Norwegian liner, was docked in Halifax to pick up coal on the way to New York where she would collect relief supplies for war-torn Belgium; on the other hand, the *S.S. Mont Blanc*, a French vessel also picking up coal, was carelessly loaded with munitions for the war.[10] To MacLennan in 1938, the contrast between these two ships must have appeared symbolic: they represented in their diametrically opposed missions the constructive and destructive uses to which mankind could put technology. The relief vessel from a Scandinavian country, whose co-operation and practical socialism he had admired, illustrated how man could turn science to good ends; the French munitions vessel, in carrying out the work of a 'belligerent nation,' showed in its 'clumsy' loading, the decks covered 'with canisters of benzol, loose,' the irresponsible drive to power which technology, hand-in-hand with man's destructive impulses, had unleashed in war. The fight for 'right of way' that resulted in their collision and the explosion of the *Mont Blanc*, symbolized a struggle at the heart of twentieth-century life. 'One could go on talking about this for many pages and still be at the beginning of a fairly typical story of the twentieth century,' he exclaimed in 'Concussion.'

Writing this sketch as a personal political commentary in 1938 paved the way for the insight he had upon Citadel Hill in the summer of 1940. With the Second World War under way, Halifax had once again become 'the funnel through which the life-giving supplies of the western hemisphere were flowing.' To MacLennan it seemed 'the most vital city in North America,' though 'unconscious of the fact.' By great fortune, it was the Canadian city he knew best; to give it and the 'untamed land around it' conscious literary expression became his challenge.

As he had in 'Concussion,' he now set out in his novel to use the First World War as a commentary on the present one. This shift from dealing directly with contemporary events, as he had done in 'A Man Should Rejoice,' was entirely logical; by dealing with the earlier war he would be able to treat the same themes without running any risk of having publishers say, as they had before, that political developments made his subject matter seem dated.

Barometer Rising is an eloquent protest against war. In it, MacLennan vividly depicts a city disrupted by war, filled with maimed men and fractured families. He clearly demonstrates how war changes the quality of human life for the worse: mass-production replaces fine craftsmanship; bureaucracy replaces the intelligent and sympathetic co-operation of working people; relationships between men and women are confused as women are thrust into male jobs and ambiguous social positions. The next generation, Roddie and his friends, are being conditioned by what they see and hear to adopt the wrong values; they are quickly learning to be callous, ruthless, devious. MacLennan's villain in the novel is the capitalist Colonel Geoffrey Wain (whom he later described as a 'fascist'[11]); for Wain, the war is 'the greatest power-bonanza in the history of mankind,' and he does not want it to end. Throughout the novel the wrong men seize and hold power, using it for graft and corruption. War-profiteering and personal immorality characterize the men thrown into prominence by the war. Engineers, who 'play' with technology like 'precocious child[ren] ... with a set of meccano,' are the tools of capitalists and fascists alike. Ironically, all these power-mongers keep safe, far from the front where their pawns, the ordinary men, are being gassed and killed by the thousands. It is to these ordinary workers and soldiers that MacLennan is sympathetic: men who are farmers, longshoremen, waiters, fishermen, and ship-builders, the victims of the lust for power of the few men who control their fates. Although he never uses the term 'proletariat' he does have Wain suspect that Neil Macrae, the novel's hero, is a socialist.[12] As if the risk of life itself were not enough, the very occupations in which these men find human dignity and a sense of accomplishment are being outmoded by the technological 'advances' of the war. Throughout the novel his own political sympathies are clear.

Barometer Rising is dedicated 'To the Memory of My Father' – a fitting dedication since in its anti-war aspects it is like a continuation of those strange letters MacLennan addressed to Dr Sam after he died in 1939. Almost predictably, one of the novel's main characters, Angus Murray, is a doctor. Like MacLennan's father, he returns from the front with an arm wound just prior to the catastrophic blow-up. Like Dr Sam, too, Murray is profoundly disillusioned at what he has seen overseas: the unremitting stream of stretcher cases he has treated in France has in no way enhanced his medical knowledge; it has shown him only that war is a sickening, futile business – an opinion he expresses more than once in the novel. Like Dr Sam, Murray is concerned with moral issues: among the books listed as his favourite reading are some that moulded MacLennan's father's and his own sense of right and wrong – Plato's *Republic*, Aristotle's *Nicomachean Ethics*, Rashdall's *The Theory of Good and Evil*, Horace and Catullus, Thucydides, Shakespeare, and Milton.[13]

In one scene MacLennan pits two opinions directly against each other. The humanitarian Dr Murray argues: 'If the generals had any sense, the war would be over now. At least they could reduce casualties. All they need do is sit tight and wait for the Germans to have a revolution.'[14] But Colonel Wain, the megalomaniac capitalist, has too much to lose: 'So you think that would solve it, eh? No, an outright military victory is essential and it's going to take a long time. Three years, perhaps.' Wain, it turns out, believes that the war is merely a stepping-stone to a world revolution after which he and other military men will control the world. Murray, on the other hand, thinks that the generals should call the war off or that the men should refuse to fight. MacLennan's alignment of the two sides in a debate about war, of which this conversation is only one small example, sets the stage for the climactic collision of the two ships. On one side are the capitalists, fascists, engineers; on the other the workers, the common soldiers, and the doctor. Technology used for egoistic self-aggrandisement in war or technology used for constructive co-operation among men: which is the real 'advance'? The munitions ship, carelessly loaded, or the relief vessel: which has the 'right of way'? These were the issues for MacLennan at the time he was writing *Barometer Rising*. As he wrote to George Barrett on 24 May 1940: 'this [war] is a form of world-revolution caused by technology and ... the issue is whether or not machines are to be used for man's benefit or his ultimate enslavement.' His moral stand, clearly voiced in this novel, is perhaps best expressed by the waiter in a small café from whom Neil buys his first meal on returning: 'I was in it myself for a while but I didn't get very far. I got to Quebec. My wife thinks that's funny. She says, when you got in the army you started moving backwards before you even began.'

If war is madness, as MacLennan attempted to portray it in *Barometer Rising*, then it is doubly mad from a colonial perspective: to support another country's war from such a distance simply because of ill-understood 'ties' is absurd. Dr Murray speculates: 'And Halifax, more than most towns, seemed governed by a fate she neither made nor understood, for it was her birthright to serve the English in time of war and to sleep neglected when there was peace. It was a bondage Halifax had no thought of escaping because it was the only life she had ever known; but to Murray this seemed a pity, for the town figured more largely in the calamities of the British Empire than in its prosperities, and never seemed able to become truly North American.'

In the character of Neil Macrae, MacLennan explores a move away from what he perceived as blind colonialism to a new stage of self-consciousness. Like David Culver in 'A Man Should Rejoice,' and MacLennan himself, Neil returns to Canada after some years abroad, and in some sense really sees the country for the first time. He responds, like Culver, to the long stretch of geologic time evident in the land's formations: 'the contours were clear and he had forgotten how good they were. The Great Glacier had once packed, scraped and riven this whole land; it had gouged out the harbor and left as a legacy three drumlins ... the hill on which he stood and two islands in the harbor itself.' After dwelling much longer and lyrically on the specific features of the scene before him, he concludes: 'Merely to have been born on the western side of the ocean gave a man something for which the traditions of the Old World could never compensate. This western land was his own country. He had forgotten how it was, but now he was back, and to be able to remain was worth risking everything.'[15]

MacLennan shows that it was men like Wain *within* Canada who are the real colonizers; they believe everything in Canada is second-rate. It is the ordinary people, both workers and the middle class, who feel, as Neil does, that 'no matter what the Canadians did over there, they were not living out the sociological results of their own lives when they crawled through the trenches of France. The war might be Canada's catastrophe, but it was not her tragedy; just as this explosion in Halifax was catastrophic but not tragic. And maybe when the wars and revolutions were ended, Canada would begin to live; maybe instead of being pulled eastward by Britain she would herself pull Britain clear of decay and give her a new birth.'

Neil, finally, looks ahead with faith to a time when his country will become 'the keystone to hold the world together.' To accomplish this future greatness, MacLennan demonstrates through his character Neil, Canada must remain 'non-committal'; as Neil has, she must maintain a balance between extremes 'intellectually gripped by the new [the United States] and emotionally held by the old [Europe], too restless to remain at peace on the land and too contemptuous of bourgeois values to feel at ease in any city.' Only if the country does remain 'non-committal' can she become what Neil also calls 'the central arch which united the new order.'[16]

These views, fairly common in Canada at the time, had been publicly expressed by MacLennan a year and a half before the publication of *Barometer Rising*; in a letter to the editors of *Life* magazine on 22 January 1940 he declared: 'it is Canada's national function to stand half-way between the Old Country and the United States, and to be a hostage for their mutual friendship. Unfortunately, however, there are still professional imperialists among us who fail to understand that Canada is American because it is on this continent, British because it is part of the Empire, and yet manages to remain itself. There is no reason why we cannot be loyal to all three aspects of our destiny. Most of us are.' Despite the fact that at the heart of such views lay more than a smattering of the older, post-Confederation style of nationalism,[17] the emphasis MacLennan placed on the loosening of colonial ties mirrored the contemporary national spirit.

At Dorothy's prompting, MacLennan gave the book to an agent to place for him. Since literary agents were a species unknown in Canada at the time, this meant locating one in the United States: he chose Blanche Gregory in New York. As might be expected, she began with New York publishers and readily negotiated a contract with Duell, Sloan and Pearce. Wm. Collins Sons and Co. Ltd. in Toronto were, at the time, their Canadian agents, and arrangements were made with them to print and issue a Canadian edition of the book. But all North American rights remained in the hands of the American publisher, which meant that the Canadian market for the novel would be treated as foreign.

On 2 October 1941, Duell, Sloan and Pearce published *Barometer Rising*. The book's cover depicted the *Imo* and the *Mont Blanc* silhouetted against the huge and fiery catastrophe their collision had caused. 'As exciting a novel as may safely be published,' ran the tantalizing slogan under which it was advertised. The reviews were generally ecstatic. The *New York Times* commented: 'you could not have known this to be a first novel ... the book is distinguished by maturity of thought ... Both in conception and workmanship it is first class ... Mr. MacLennan, in fact, has scored a bull's-eye first shot.' American reviewers, on the whole, overlooked the novel's 'Canadianness'; the *New York Herald Tribune*, for example, a little bewildered by MacLennan's theories of Canada's future role, stated categorically that 'It does not appear quite to sum up to any dramatic statement or philosophical whole.'[18]

For Canadian reviewers, however, the main point about *Barometer Rising* was the fact that it was 'as Canadian as maple sugar.' Hugo McPherson, reviewing it for the *Windsor Daily Star*, commented typically: 'It has been a long time coming, but 1941 finally has produced a great Canadian novel – a story of Halifax in wartime. It is not THE great one we hear about, because that presumably is the reach that always exceeds our grasp ... He writes as a Canadian, scorning to slant his story to catch the American reader's eye.' Robertson Davies in *Saturday Night* went even further: 'This novel is an important addition to our Canadian literature and, unless something unforeseen happens, Mr. MacLennan will give us more books and better ones. Will they be on Canadian themes? That is entirely up to us. We are apt, in this country, to neglect our artists until they go to countries where they are appreciated, and it is high time that we overcame this unlovely national trait. By reading *Barometer Rising* now you will be doing something which will not only give you great satisfaction but you will also be helping to cherish the tender sapling which is Canadian literature.' And W.A. Deacon wrote for the *Globe and Mail*: 'The appearance of a new Canadian novelist is always a matter of interest, and of keen interest when it is a case of welcoming a talent as pronounced as that of Hugh MacLennan ... In stimulating scrutiny of our opinions and attitudes and aims, the author has performed one of the greatest services a novelist can.' Critical of this excessive concentration by Canadian critics on the 'Canadianness' of *Barometer Rising*, MacLennan was to state candidly a year later: 'Most Canadian reviewers have to unlearn so many misconceptions of the Canadian novel they are apt to miss the point entirely.'[19]

Nothing could have been more calculated to strike a sympathetic response in Canadian readers than Neil Macrae's highly nationalistic musings modelled on John of Gaunt's patriotic speech from *Richard II* ('This royal throne of kings, this sceptred isle'): 'this anomalous land, this sprawling waste of timber and rock and water where the only living sounds were the footfalls of animals or the fantastic laughter of a loon, this empty tract of primordial silences and winds and erosions and shifting colors, this bead-like string of crude towns and cities tied by nothing but railway tracks, this nation undiscovered by the rest of the world and unknown to itself, these people neither American nor English, nor even sure what they wanted to be, this unborn mightiness, this question-mark, this future for himself, and for God knew how many millions of mankind!'[20] This description, and others like it elsewhere in the book, caught for Canadians their sense of place. Like the description of the Nova Scotian coast in 'A Man Should Rejoice,' it put into words the same view of the land itself – rough, nordic, intense – which the Group of Seven had caught in their paintings and E.J. Pratt and Frank Scott had been incorporating into their poetry. This sense of place, which suggested strong moral character, self-denial, and physical toughness, gave back to the nation the very qualities the First World War had crystallized into a self-image. As literary critic Frank Watt later argued, this sense of the land played a key role in the development of Canadian literary nationalism; in his article on the subject he cites Hugh Kenner who wryly observed: 'The surest way to the hearts of a Canadian audience is to inform them that their souls are to be identified with rock, rapids, wilderness, and virgin (but exploitable) forest.'[21]

That Neil Macrae's fervent statement of literary nationalism should be created by a man whose views and attitudes for eight years had been formed not in Canada but at Oxford and Princeton (and latterly by his American wife), and who, furthermore, had been fierce in his outrage that Nova Scotia had ever joined Confederation, remains deeply ironic. In the larger groundswell of Canadian cultural assertion that accompanied increasing parliamentary autonomy, fed by the lesser tributaries of an increasing curiosity from the United States and Britain, such mere details were as paper boats. Critics responded to the appearance of *Barometer Rising* not simply as a first novel by a native son but as *the* novel which at last would ensure a place for Canada on the world's literary map. They responded, in short, to the whole situation. MacLennan had filled, at least temporarily, the vacuum in Canadian fiction.

Although these same reviewers did occasionally mention what they saw as weaknesses in the novel, their criticisms were lost in the spirited congratulations for its themes. Davies, for example, found MacLennan's prose style too 'rigid' and 'monotonous'; this he wrongly attributed to the 'fact' that his previous writing had been academic and was, consequently, 'scholarly' and 'dry.' Two later reviews found the plot unconvincing; some reviewers felt that his characters were overshadowed by description. In fact, in terms of the novel's artistry, reviews were divided: some consisted of undiluted praise for his craftsmanship; others concentrated on the novel's flaws.[22] In the rising tidal wave of Canadian nationalism that was stirring Canadians to assert themselves culturally, these comments on artistic pros and cons seemed unimportant. *Barometer Rising* was taken up as 'Holy Writ' in the new nationalism; to look at it as fiction only was beside the point.

All over the Allied world, soldiers in barracks and hospitals wrote to MacLennan in gratitude for voicing their feelings about their native land. Letters flocked in from Rhodesia, India, New Zealand, Italy, as well as from points nearer home. Among these was a letter from Captain Gordon Mackinnon, who as a boy in Halifax had been MacLennan's friend and would later be the model for his story 'The Lost Love of Tommy Waterfield' (1955). Mackinnon wrote from a hospital in England, where he was serving in the Medical Corps:

> I have just finished your book 'Rising Barometer' [*sic*] ... and I would like to congratulate you.
>
> The story is very well told ... it was with difficulty that my brother officer could get the book away from me and turn off the light at two thirty a.m. I ignored him and finished the book the following night.

Your description of the explosion was very good; it took my mind back the many years ... your further description of the evacuation on account [of] the fire in Wellington Barracks brings it all back. I even remember the rumors.

I have been trying to place the different people, certainly old Mr. Mitchell, the treasurer of St. Matthew's cannot be mistaken. The Colonel must be a composite character because he certainly makes me think of a number of people. His end recalls certain undisclosed facts about the Queen Hotel Fire in '38.[23]

Mackinnon's remarks about the Queen Hotel fire upset MacLennan deeply. As he later confided to one of his students, the future novelist Marian Engel: 'the story came close to being literally true, as I discovered later with cold chills, and feared the possibility of legal repercussions.' Guessing games about the models for the various characters was a favourite topic of discussion in Halifax for some years to come after *Barometer Rising* appeared. Only in one detail is MacLennan willing to admit that there was a single model in his story: the source for the Wain house was the old Odell House, which stood at the top of Ked Street next to Fort Massey Church (later it became the Ajax Club and has since been torn down); it, too, was turned into a makeshift hospital during the aftermath of the explosion, in much the same way as the curmudgeonly Aunt Maria commandeers and transforms the Wain's house.[24]

Servicemen who did not know MacLennan or even Halifax itself were equally impressed. An excerpt from Collins' journal, *Book News*, ran as follows:

Lieut. W.T. Purkis, 3rd Anti-Tank Reg't., R.C.A., writes: 'In his parcels from time to time Dad usually includes a couple of books, usually Collins' books. After I finish reading them I pass them on to other chaps in the regiment, just as everyone else does with books received. Thus each book enjoys a fair circulation. *Barometer Rising* by Hugh MacLennan, however, was in a class by itself. I started reading it at Christmas and made the mistake of telling others how interesting it was: then every other officer in the Battery started on it too and I had considerable difficulty in getting it away from them in order to finish it. That was just the beginning. From the officers' mess it went to my Battery. You will understand its popularity there when I explain that 95% of our chaps come from down East. Even now I still occasionally run across some gunner curled up in a corner with all his thoughts back in Halifax. That copy of *Barometer Rising* is now a dirty, dog-eared relic of a book but it has done a good job.'[25]

Although the majority of reviewers, concentrating their attention on Canadian identity, overlooked the central significance of the war theme in *Barometer Rising*, even though the dust-jacket clearly announced that it presented 'a picture of that almost incredibly tense activity which is being reenacted today,' some critics did notice. The *Toronto Star* observed, for example: 'while the scene is set during the first world war, there is a certain timeliness to this narrative, coming as it does during another great war ... one cannot help but picture the same scenes occurring on other troopships in this later war.'[26] Had the themes of 'So All Their Praises' and 'A Man Should Rejoice' been matters of public knowledge at this time, a fuller understanding of the novel would have been possible. As it was, Duell, Sloan and Pearce were careful to conceal MacLennan's earlier failures by cleverly wording the book's dust-jacket as follows: '*Barometer Rising* is a first published novel. As the sure skill and the narrative pace reveal, it is the work of no untrained writer. Hugh MacLennan, a Nova Scotian, made certain of his craft before he began to write this story of Canada in wartime.' Although more than one reviewer expressed surprise that this was his first book, no one appears to have suspected that it was in fact a third novel by a writer who had been wrestling with techniques of fiction and contemporary themes and theories of art for over ten years. At the time *Barometer Rising* came out in 1941, MacLennan was presented to the public as a brilliant young Canadian novelist who had just struck off his first book; partly as a consequence of this, the book's major theme was overlooked in favour of its national message.

In 1952, looking back in an article called 'My First Book,' MacLennan described his problems and difficulties in writing *Barometer Rising*:

> When I first thought of writing this novel, Canada was virtually an unknown country. It seemed to me then that if our literature was to be anything but purely regional in character, it must be directed to at least two audiences. One was the Canadian public, which took the Canadian scene for granted but had never defined its particular essence. The other was the international public, which had never thought about Canada at all, and knew nothing whatever about us.
>
> As drama depends on the familiar, and as the social and psychological novel depends on the capacity of the public to recognize allusions, to distinguish the abnormal from the normal, to grasp instantly when a character is motivated by the pressures of his environment and when by his own idiosyncrasies, it seemed to me that for some years to come the Canadian novelist

would have to pay a great deal of attention to the background in which he set his stories. He must describe, and if necessary, define the social values which dominate the Canadian scene, and do so in such a way as to make them appear interesting and important to foreigners. Whether he liked it or not, he must for a time be something of a geographer, an historian and a sociologist ... He could not, as the British and American writers do, take his background values for granted ... He must therefore do more than write dramas; he must also design and equip the stage on which they were to be played.

... In *Barometer Rising* the background is the most essential part of the book. The plot is melodramatic and some readers have said it is improbable, but the catastrophe which struck Halifax – more improbable than any novelist's plot – was at least an historical event. The book is more a *tour de force* than a novel, and when I wrote it I regarded it as an experiment.[27]

MacLennan's critics have often quoted from this passage with a surprising naïvety, taking his remarks at face value without considering their context. Although he presents here an image of himself not unlike that of James Joyce in *Portrait of the Artist as a Young Man* dynamically 'forging the uncreated conscience of the race,' the key phrase is 'whether he liked it or not.' 'Whether he liked it or not,' the means to fulfilling his ambition to become a writer was not of his first choosing; he had clearly made a virtue of necessity. An 'experiment' *Barometer Rising* certainly was, but not in exactly the way MacLennan in this article would have it appear. It was, in fact, a fourth experiment by a man who had tried one book of poetry and two international novels and was still determined to become a writer, a man who hoped that by trying a national theme (his emphasis being on the 'historical'), he might attain the position and acclaim he was after. 'My First Book,' along with many other public statements given by MacLennan as 'spokesman' for Canada, are themselves part of a public image that has always overshadowed the literary merits of his work.

Nor was he blind to his own predicament after a time. As he wrote in 1950 to his editor at Macmillan's, John Gray, two years before he published 'My First Book': 'It is the [Canadian Authors' Association] which limited me by calling me a "nationalist" when all I was trying to do was to define the background out of which any Canadian writer has to work. This build-up backfired, as I knew it was bound to, among the critics later on, and one of the most necessary things in marketing my work in the future, I believe, will be to undo some of these labels which have been pinned around my neck.'[28] It is odd that, realizing the state of things so clearly, he continued to publish material and to give addresses and to make other public appearances which tended to confirm the 'nationalist' image he wished to be rid of. It may be that he feared the consequences of shedding his public image, that dissociation from his 'Canadian spokesman' role might mean literary obscurity. Be that as it may, he did little to unpin the labels which so chafed him.

Perhaps even his openness at the time about his three false starts would not have dissipated the aura of success that surrounded him. The October 1941 issue of the Book of the Month Club *News* listed *Barometer Rising* as one of the 'Other Books Recommended This Month.' MacLennan was written up in the 8 November issue of *Publishers' Weekly* with several quotations, among them the wry comment 'that he hopes that he may become known to his fellow Canadians for something besides tennis.' On the same day this article appeared, he was giving the opening speech on 'Canadianism' for the annual book show of the Canadian Authors' Association to a capacity crowd at 99 Yonge Street, Toronto. By the 11th of November, *Barometer Rising*, after three printings, was sold out; the *Globe and Mail* published an 'Apology' that no more copies were available, promising more soon. In the same week, Burton's Bookstore in Montreal featured an entire window display of the book, including photographs, news clippings of the famous explosion, and a huge poster depicting the cover illustration. By the end of November, *Barometer Rising* was the ninth most popular novel on the Toronto Library List; Hemingway's *For Whom the Bell Tolls* was seventh. Published in England by George Harrap Limited, it was a Book Society Choice in July 1942 and was soon high on reading lists in English newspapers. By August 1942 it had gone into a fifth printing in North America; by 1945 it had sold over 100,000 copies all told. Even in translation the novel did well, between 1963 and 1969 selling over 100,000 copies in German; it was also translated into French in 1966 and into Romanian in 1971.

In the winter of 1941-2 MacLennan was off to New York to discuss the possibility of turning *Barometer Rising* into a movie. His discussion with Richard Mealand, story editor of Paramount Pictures, one of the two Hollywood studios interested in his book, was recounted with saturnine humour in his essay 'A Boy Meets a Girl in Winnipeg and Who Cares?' (1959):

> I saw dollar signs all over the Windsor Station the night I boarded my train for New York, and there were still more of them on the pavement of Madison Avenue when I rode in a taxi to the old Ritz Carlton to meet the representa-

tive of the studio which was the more interested of the two. He was a knowing man exceedingly affable, though somewhat boiled looking about the eyelids. Before ordering a fabulous lunch, he gave me two cocktails; he also told me the deal was off.

'It's like this,' the man explained. 'This book of yours, it's about this town Halifax and who's ever heard of Halifax down here except as a word nicely brought up kids say when what really they mean is Hell? "Go to Halifax," is what nicely brought up kids down here say. Well, of course, this wouldn't make any difference if this was an ordinary book. We could work a switcheroo. But the trouble is in this book of yours Halifax gets itself blown up in the climax of the story. We fooled around with a switcheroo even on that. We thought of the Johnstown Flood, but that happened so long ago that who cares, so we canned the whole idea.' He looked at me in sincere friendship and said: 'It's tough, but that's how it is. All you got to do is next time set the scene in the United States and *then* we'll be really interested.'

Being naïve in those days, I asked what difference the locale of a story makes so long as the story is good.

'Well, take Paris,' he said, 'that's okay for one kind of story. Take London – that's okay for another kind. But take Canada – that's not okay because what do Americans think when they hear that word "Canada" except cold weather and Mounties, or maybe when they hear it they don't know what to think. Now this is not the way it ought to be and it's tough, but look at it like this. A boy meets a girl in Paris, one thing leads to another and they – well, it's interesting. But a boy meets a girl in Winnipeg and they swing into the same routine and who cares? I'm not saying it's not just as good in Winnipeg as it is in Paris. Maybe it's even better because in Winnipeg what else is there to do? But for the American public you've got to see it's a fact that Winnipeg kind of kills the whole thing.'

I protested (I was *very* naive in those days) that my books tended to be serious, what you might call social novels. 'That's exactly what I've been trying to say,' he explained. 'The way you write, if you want a big market down here, you just haven't got much of a choice. The way you write you've got to make it American ...'

'The thing for you to do,' he said, 'being a Canadian, is make the best of both your worlds. Mix up the English and Americans in the same package, and fix it so somehow this Englishman in this book comes over to the States with certain ideas and he changes them, understand, when he finds out about American women and democracy.' He shook my hand warmly as we left the Ritz. 'Now just one more little thing and it shouldn't be too hard to do. Try to work Lincoln into the story somehow. Work Lincoln in, you a Canadian work Lincoln into it with this Englishman, and something very wonderful ought to come out.' He paused as we passed through the revolving door. 'And one more thing – sex. Let yourself go on that. The American public is growing up. It likes to have its sex spelled right out for it.'[29]

So there were limits on his success after all; an American audience for films, at any rate, did not want Canadian content. As for the subject of sex in the novel, he was caught in a double bind. On the one hand, American readers like Mealand thought there was too little; on the other, many Canadian readers protested that there was too much. It was common during the war for soldiers and their girls to say 'farewell' with more than just a kiss; in some cases, illegitimate children were the inevitable result. MacLennan's frank treatment of this theme offended many, as did his forthright language.

His contact with Richard Mealand, however, had an unexpected result; through him he was to encounter the novelist Ayn Rand. As one of Paramount's readers in 1941, she had been assigned *Barometer Rising* and had been deeply impressed by the novel, counting it among the only two during the course of her work she actually wanted to buy. 'I didn't ... write Hugh MacLennan a fan letter at the time, because of the Paramount rule that readers mustn't communicate with authors,' she regretted. Later, in 1944, learning that MacLennan particularly liked her novels, she sent off a belated fan letter to him, recalling her reactions when she had first read *Barometer Rising*:

> I stayed up all night, to do the best synopsis I ever did for them [Paramount]. I certainly tried my best to have them buy it for the screen – but you know that readers have very little influence on a studio's decision.
>
> Since you read 'The Fountainhead,' you must know that I admire nothing in people – except the quality of genuine originality, the ability to do one's work in an unborrowed way of one's own ... That is the quality which 'Barometer Rising' had – and that's why I loved it and why I'm very interested in you as an author and a person.
>
> The two things I liked above all in 'Barometer Rising' were: beautiful writing, completely *un-trite*, and a brilliant plot structure ... the only modern novel I've read in years that showed a beautiful skill of plot integration was 'Barometer Rising.'
>
> If you want to know what particular sequences stand out in my mind, for sheer beauty of writing and treatment, it's the scene between Penelope and the doctor on the train, the scene when Neal [*sic*] returns and meets her again, the description of the explosion ... I loved the *strength* of your characters.

Predictably, given Ayn Rand's personal philosophy of individualism and her hatred of altruism, Christian or otherwise, she objected to MacLennan's conclusion:

The thing that did not seem to fit with the rest of 'Barometer Rising' was the final sequence where you reverted to the 'and so he solved his personal problems by losing himself in unselfish service' pattern. That didn't ring true. It never does, anyway, but it seemed particularly out of place in your book because all your characters were too strong and too good for that.

When I finished your book, my guess about the author was: here's a brilliant writer, with the natural talent and instincts of an individualist, who felt that he had to apologize for himself by sticking in some 'social significance' at the end of his book.[30]

Ayn Rand was not the only contemporary writer to object to MacLennan's ending, while praising the novel in many other ways. The month after it was published F.P. Grove, now in his seventies, sent him a letter:

I have not been so impressed with a Canadian book for many years. From the start I liked its tone and the quiet sureness of touch in the characterisation. Penny, I think, is a triumph; and so is Angus Murray.

Another triumph is the description of the effect of the explosion and the general way in which you make the old town come to life.

And yet I have my criticisms to offer; and I hope you will forgive me for voicing them ruthlessly. Believe me, my purpose is not a destructive one.

Grove then went on to describe a conversation between himself and his wife:

... last night, while I was drying the dishes which she was washing, I asked, 'Just what was your objection to the end?' She replied, 'The end evades the issue. Up to the explosion we witness the unfolding of a problem, between the two men, McCrae [*sic*] and Wain. That looks like the theme of the book. It raises certain expectations. The explosion comes; and, magnificent as that part of the book is, it disappoints us in what we were led to expect.' Again I agreed. 'One of two explanations,' I said. 'Either the author did not know how to solve his problem; or he was so carried away with the calamity that he considered his original problem unimportant as compared with it. Too bad. It spoils the book for me.'

Now that is not entirely true; for, as I found today, there are certain things in it, to which I want to return; f[or] i[nstance] the scene between Penny and Angus in which she tells him that Jean is her daughter; it is a very true and very beautiful scene; and perhaps I should be satisfied that the book contains even one such scene ... I could not pay you a greater compliment than by saying that, while the torso of the Venus de Milo, let me say, is very beautiful and makes me dream, the fact that the arms are lost remains a pity.[31]

Grove's criticism of the novel's ending was echoed by the poet Ronald Bottrall, who wrote at once to congratulate his former colleague from Princeton. As he succinctly put it, unfortunately the ending is a '*deus ex machina*.'

Although reviewers were almost unanimous in their praise of the novel's conclusion, being swept away by the magnificent description of the explosion, fellow writers who read it with a more discriminating eye to technique were critical. MacLennan himself agreed. In a letter to George Barrett shortly after the first reviews started coming out, he admitted: 'what you say of *Barometer Rising* – a consciously limited book with a definite defect of structure inevitable in any novel which takes a catastrophe as its high point – is entirely true.'[32] There was only one notable exception to this response from other writers. C. Day Lewis, reviewing the book as the Book Society (London) selection for July 1942, claimed that the ending did not artificially resolve conflicts; it simply served 'to precipitate the crisis in the lives of his characters, and to symbolize the destructive forces latent in them.'[33]

MacLennan's ending must be seen in light of his own natural tendency to be optimistic. There are a number of correspondences between himself and Neil Macrae, as we have seen, especially in the sense of discovery with which Neil views his homeland after some years away. MacLennan unconsciously related this 'discovery' on returning home to that of Odysseus coming back after ten years to his Penelope and his country. Like Odysseus before him, and like his creator, Neil comes back from abroad to establish a nation, or at least to see a coherent vision of its future greatness.[34] The attention that has been paid to this aspect of Neil's return home, notably by George Woodcock and Kathleen O'Donnell,[35] has overshadowed another allusion deliberately introduced into the story. Angus Murray, in the scene in which he is drunk with a local prostitute, blurts out with the same kind of clarity Michael displayed in 'So All Their Praises': 'Everyone comes and goes around here, eh? So, like the wanderer, the sun gone down, darkness be over me, my rest a stone – that's your Nova Scotian, if you've the eye to see it. Wanderers. Looking all over the continent for a future. But they always come back. That's the point to remember, they always come back to the roots, like you and me.'[36]

The lines 'So, like the wanderer, the sun gone down, darkness be over me, my rest a stone,' come from the second stanza of *Nearer, My God, to Thee*, one of the earliest memories in MacLennan's mind. This was the hymn he had heard the ship's orchestra play when, as a six-year-old, he first travelled to England. That this commemoration of the sinking of the *Titanic* should surface in relation to the other major tragedy at sea in his living memory is not surprising. And it was from the pattern that recurs in the hymns from his childhood that he took the optimism that invariably was to mould his stories' endings. In *Nearer, My God, to Thee* the message, typical of so many hymns, is that no matter what grief and despair may occur to man, it serves to bring him closer to God in the end: 'Out of my stony griefs Bethel I'll raise, so by my woes to be nearer, my God, to thee.' Or, as the first stanza declares: 'Even though it be a cross that raiseth me, still all my song would be Nearer, my God to thee.' Thus, the *pattern* of the hymn in general, and of the second stanza in particular, gave him the structural resolution for his novel:

> Though, like the wanderer,
> The sun gone down,
> Darkness be over me,
> My rest a stone,
> Yet in my dreams I'd be
> Nearer, my God, to thee,
> Nearer to thee.[37]

'In my dreams' could not better describe the way the novel's wanderer, Neil, moves at its conclusion from the depths of sorrow and despair to the vision of a glorious future for the nation. Like the rainbow that indicates hope for Noah after the flood sent by God to remind mankind to keep his laws, the 'arch' Neil visualizes signifies hope for Canada after the lesson learned by the explosion of the *Mont Blanc* and the *Imo* – that man must employ his knowledge for humanitarian purposes, not for destruction. *Barometer Rising*'s conclusion, like its title, is infused with an optimism drawn from Christian principles in which virtue is rewarded and evil punished by 'an act of God.'

For MacLennan, the publication of *Barometer Rising* was a trial balloon; it was one aspect of his attempt to work out the problem that had, so far, prevented him from becoming a successful writer. He had abandoned a plan for larger themes and an international setting for his third novel, and undertaken 'a subject more modest, as well as distinctly modern Canadian.'[38]

The novel may have been a sort of 'Book of Genesis' in the rise of Canadian cultural nationalism, but for MacLennan himself it was an experiment in point of view. Although the letter he wrote to George Barrett on 20 October 1941, after the first reviews were in, makes it clear that it had been a successful experiment, MacLennan was still wrestling with the theoretical problems that were influencing his career; he was still feeling his way into a role:

Your statement that what I have written seems 'a mixture of English and American ... because it is not a synthesis,' seems to me to be aiming straight at the roots of my problem ...

Do you mean that I appear to recognize, *intellectually*, the gist of my problems, but do not realize them emotionally? If so, that may be a grievous fault. Again, it may be caused by my preoccupation in that first novel [*Barometer Rising*] with the fact that I had to write about Canada for an American public. If the latter, I do not feel it is a fatal weakness, for in the next book I would have a sufficient background of confidence to go right ahead. But – and this is important – *Canadians* themselves *take their own notions* about themselves from English and Americans. The enthusiasm with which this job – with all its faults and limitations – has been received in Montreal and Toronto have given me the certain knowledge that Canadians are hungry for a spokesman ...

Is your point that to be 100% Canadian is impossible? Even 100% Nova Scotian? By which I mean, in the artist's ability to achieve a universality out of a native background.

If that is your point I agree with you, almost entirely. But with a certain reservation. For the whole world is ... now in a state of becoming. God only knows what is 'becoming' but we know something collossal [*sic*] is. I wonder if my own problem, therefore, is any more hopeless than anyone else's, except from the immediate standpoint of marketing? What basic novels have come out of any place since the war began? What novels of the past two decades – except for a very few – have managed to keep their point of view in face of the war and Hitler and the gyrations of the U.S.S.R.? Why did Virginia Woolf commit suicide?

I see Canada as a bridge – a bridge with the ends unjoined. I don't believe there can be a synthesis until the ends are joined. I am trying to go ahead on the assumption that the failure of our people even to understand the necessity of joining the ends of the bridge is responsible not only for our own national schizophrenia, but to a greater extent causal and symptomatic of the international breakdown as well. In that state of 'becoming' I seem to detect the possibility of a universality for a writer who attempts to write out of the Canadian scene.

> I am sure of this: no artist can possibly write of any society – as a base – than his own. What happens to an artist when he is young is what conditions his perceptions.
>
> I feel that I pretty well have to sink or swim as a Canadian writer. The book before this ['A Man Should Rejoice'] was international in scope and in point of view, with a slightly American bias ... A Canadian can't write authentically about the American scene. Nor is Canada important enough – yet – for a Canadian's point of view on Europe to be important. The Americans would not care, the English would not be able to distinguish it from American.
>
> Therefore, without benefit of any background or tradition beyond what I succeed in making for myself, I seem doomed to continue.

In this letter MacLennan, like a sailor out of sight of the shore, brought the full force of his mind to bear on an assessment of his position. His aim was to make a living by writing. How could he ensure a continuation of the success he had had with *Barometer Rising*? As he concluded here, the nation was 'hungry for a spokesman'; why not himself? Since, by his own logic, he had no hope of striking universality unless he grounded his stories in his native land, he was 'doomed to continue' to do so; he would have to 'sink or swim' as a Canadian writer. Although he tried to rationalize that this might be worth doing in the long run, that Canada might become a great nation, indeed might even symbolize in her national 'schizophrenia' the international breakdown that was resulting from the rapid transition of the modern world into something 'colossal,' the general tone of his remarks here is gloomy. He really concluded that he had better make the best of a pretty bad situation if he were going to succeed as a writer. It was clearly going to take more thought and great determination.

Swept into the role that awaited him, he neglected his craft. He did not stop to consider that there might have been reasons other than an interest in things 'Canadian' which accounted for the success of *Barometer Rising*. What had happened, in fact, was that the Canadian point of view had given him a *focus* which threw the many aspects of his earlier two novels into a meaningful relationship to each other. They had been, by his own admission, 'bulging at the seams'[39] with the many interests he pursued. Fixing on any kind of focus was exactly what he needed to discipline his subject into a structured whole. Choosing a Canadian point of view, he himself said, had involved dropping the plan for 'larger themes' and undertaking 'a subject more modest.'[40] And, with Aristotelian simplicity, he had imposed the three unities of time, place, and action on his story. *Barometer Rising* consequently was the most carefully planned of all his novels; it was written with a specific conclusion in mind, somewhat like a detective or mystery novel. As he maintained much later: 'Since *Barometer Rising*, which was contrived as regards its story, I have never known how a novel was going to end until it ended. I have felt that the books wrote me, and not *vice versa*.'[41] Instead of concerning himself with questions of craft, of why certain techniques had worked better than others in the first two attempts, he deliberately courted the role of 'spokesman for Canada' which he perceived as soon as *Barometer Rising* drew such encouraging reviews.

Less than half a year after its publication, in March 1942, he appeared in print in New York's *Saturday Review of Literature* analysing Canada's cultural scene in an article called 'Culture, Canadian Style.' Shortly afterwards, he was asked to write an article on the occasion of Canada's seventy-fifth Dominion Day for the *Montreal Standard* entitled 'Anniversary of an Idea.' These are but two of the many public statements in which he made the most of his new image as one of the voices of the rising generation. In several speeches and radio appearances he was also busy reinforcing the role the Canadian public expected of him once *Barometer Rising* was launched. In these two articles his concerns were transparent; both focused on questions in which he was suddenly intensely interested, the same sort of questions he had already posed in letters to his friend George Barrett: 'What is a Canadian? How do we, as a people, rate among other nations? What do we want our country to become? What sort of a future have we a right to expect, considering our own past as well as the present of the world in which we live? ... Can we blame Americans if they think only of the [Dionne] Quintuplets when Ontario is mentioned?' 'Why has the gift of tongues passed Canadians by? Why is it more difficult – and personal experience has taught me that it is infinitely more difficult – for a Canadian to write a good and honest book about his own society than for an American or an Englishman to do the same about his? ... Will the Canadian buying public be sufficiently large to sustain a literature of its own? ... From what deep remembrance of things past, from what sources in our various racial memories, do these [Canadian] values spring?'[42]

His main purpose in posing these questions was specific: he was clearly trying to understand Canada as fully as possible so that he could proceed in his next novel to a second success. Not fully comprehending why *Barometer Rising* should have been so well received when his earlier novels could not even find a publisher, he doggedly tried to be more certain of his market for next time. As far as a knowledge of Canada was concerned, he was at a great disadvantage. He had known only Nova Scotia until the age of twenty-seven and, as a Nova Scotian, he had had a pronounced antipathy to 'Canada.' Although he had been interested in politics, he had concentrated on the international scene, not the local one. Furthermore, he had married an American who was even less familiar with Canadian history and politics than himself. If he was, as he had written to Barrett, 'doomed to continue' as a Canadian writer, he had better understand what Canada was; how the rest of the world, especially the United States, viewed her; and what was the essence of that Canadian character. It was pure coincidence, perhaps, that these highly personal musings, and the questions he posed for himself as he mulled over what his next book would be about, happened to correspond to the national questions uppermost in the minds of Canadians in general. As he raised the issues that must form the basis of his future success, as he saw it, he gave the impression of considering more general questions of national identity and culture.

The extent to which he really meant 'I' when he wrote 'we' in these two articles can be deduced from a critical rejoinder to 'Culture, Canadian Style,' which appeared in the *Ottawa Journal* a month after his article appeared. P.D.R. Ross, president and editor of the *Journal* which he had founded in 1886, objected to the fact that MacLennan used the word 'culture' to refer chiefly to literature and art.[43] In fact, he pointed out, he nowhere even defined culture, but simply assumed that it meant the single aspect of the term in which he was most interested. Ross provided strong evidence to show that there was no reason why Canada should, a mere seventy-five years after Confederation, show much in the way of literature and art at all. More time, he argued, must pass; MacLennan was rushing things.

MacLennan's own answers to some of the questions he raised were equally personal. He deplored the state of ignorance in which such questions must be asked in the first place; for him personally, it meant that no writer from Canada was likely to appear interesting to the rest of the world. 'If every individual in Canada perished tomorrow,' he lamented, 'we should be of less interest to future historians than the people who lived in the old Graeco-Egyptian colonies of the Upper Nile are to us today ... Canadians ... are in the unique position of having no essential point of view germane to themselves as a geographical or political unit.' Nor could a writer in Canada in 1942 draw on a common cultural heritage or a 'bank' of racial memories that were firmly established. Given the fact that he was by now convinced that a writer must write out of his own national setting, and that he must also do his best to avoid provincialism at the same time, this fact constituted a devastating obstacle for him. He thus went to some lengths to figure out why such ignorance existed in Canada. First, he argued, Canada had no national literature. That this was his first point indicated his extreme frustration in having no heritage in which to write:

> Although we have produced a few poets who have written beautiful individual poems, and a few novelists whose work has sold into the hundreds of thousands, no Canadian writer has thus far succeeded in achieving a body of work upon which the rest of us can build a philosophy which satisfies us. Indeed, no Canadian novelist has even been able to provoke a controversy. So far there has been no Canadian Dickens or Thackeray, no Thoreau or Emerson. We haven't even been able to settle for a Canadian Hemingway.
>
> This is the real reason why Englishmen and Americans do not know us. Far more important, it is why we don't know ourselves. The day has yet to come when one of us, deriving his philosophy from his own native society, will be able through the medium of the novel to give it back to his society as a living force, distilled by his own personality and informed by his own intuitions.[44]

MacLennan himself, of course, was to attempt to live up to this vision of the future. He had failed to become 'a Canadian Hemingway,' but *Barometer Rising*'s success gave him hope that he could 'give back' to his country a 'philosophy' of its own. Second, he stated that Canada's cultural backwardness could be attributed to the nation's 'provincialism'; generalizing from his own experience, he declared that Canadians were loyal to the *province* before the nation. This phenomenon he attributed in part to a political and educational framework which came under provincial, rather than national, jurisdiction. Finally, he claimed, 'the most important reason why we are ignorant of ourselves is that we have forgotten how our historical origins condition the way we think about ourselves today.' By this, he meant specifically that Canadians were loyal to the groups from which they came rather than to the nation as a whole. He went on in 'Anniversary of an Idea' to articulate a theory about Canada he was to hold for a lifetime, and for which he would eventually become well known: 'The United States is what she is because Americans are a people who have rebelled all through their history ... But our ancestors were always on the losing side. They lost several causes two centuries ago, but they never lost their dignity or their sense of themselves. They acquired the innate caution of men who know the meaning of defeat in their youth ... Not for nothing is the motto of Quebec *Je Me Souviens* ... That same loyalty to the group, blindly and narrowly followed, keeps Canada from achieving a full nationhood.' Two other groups of ancestors on the 'losing side,' in addition to the French, were specified by MacLennan: the Loyalists, who came to Canada because 'they refused to rebel,' and the Scottish Highlanders who had lost the Battle of Culloden. 'Our country,' he concluded, 'has never been a melting pot, and it has never had a uniform school system. It has staked its future on union arising out of diversity, on union arising out of three main groups which in the past have all fought against each other.'

In this theory was the first inkling of the subject his next novel was to treat. He divided Canada's founding fathers into three groups: French, Loyalist, and Scottish. But he also defined a simpler division between French and English: 'Too easily we say that Canada is half-French and half-English, and let it go at that. Too many French-Canadians believe that their English-speaking compatriots are mere colonists of England, with a colonial point of view; too many English-speaking Canadians fail to realize that the French-Canadian's loyalty to his own race is, in his own eyes, loyalty to Canada.'[45] After eight years in Montreal, MacLennan was able to perceive this more general split with greater clarity; he had come to see it as symbolic of the 'group loyalty' he thought was holding back Canada's development as a nation.

His glances south of the border were envious ones. Americans, if they gave Canada a thought at all, were likely to think of nothing but the Mounties, the Quintuplets, cheap raw materials, and wildlife waiting to be shot. 'The rivers of ideas,' he sadly recognized, 'have consistently flowed from south to north, from the United States into Canada. Week after week the flood continues: magazines, books, radio programs, movies, newspapers, advertisements, and comic strips.' Furthermore, the United States had a well-developed literature, a thriving market for books, and, consequently, a strong sense of identity. He contemptuously defined this 'Yankee tradition' of literature as 'a realistic literature of escape, of dissenters from authority turning the tables or moving on elsewhere, of the clever fox.'[46] With this tradition, he self-righteously maintained, Canadians have nothing in common.

His articles at this time were only one example of the way in which he was working hard to forecast the climate for his next novel so that it would be successful. In his public speeches and on radio programs at the time he was also wrestling with identical issues, trying out his ideas on a public that was at last listening to him, hoping that objections would be raised in a context in which he could further adjust his thinking about his next book. 'Culture, Canadian Style' was broadcast by the Canadian Broadcasting Corporation from coast to coast in early May.

He was also at this time trying to get rid of Blanche Gregory, the American woman who was his agent. At the end of June 1942, shortly after 'Culture, Canadian Style' appeared, and just before he began writing 'Anniversary of an Idea,' he wrote a letter to Charles Duell asking him for advice about this matter: 'I have nothing whatever against Miss Gregory personally. I believe that according to her lights she has represented me as well as she can. But I have always found it hard to get clear answers from her, and frankly have never yet been helped by her advice.'[47] He had written to her earlier, releasing her from his service, only to find to his dismay that a clause in the contract bound him to continue with her for his next two books, something he had not realized at the time he had signed. The Canadian Authors' Association had advised him that he was not bound to her for anything other than future sales of *Barometer Rising*, but the contract was binding and Blanche Gregory continued as his agent.

This incident made him much more aware of the business angles involved in being a successful writer. He increasingly realized that an American agent suggesting vaguely that he write articles for *Reader's Digest* was not what he needed. Blanche Gregory had no knowledge of the Canadian critical scene or even of the major serial publications in Canada. She nowhere demonstrated an understanding of the surge of Canadian cultural nationalism at the time, and of MacLennan's emerging role as one of its spokesmen. He was correct in trying to get rid of her: there was no reason for him to continue paying her ten per cent of his profits. Because of the war, these profits were already meagre. Furthermore, as he was to protest in public addresses, Canadian taxation laws were crippling; royalties, he claimed, were taxed three times over: fifteen per cent at source for Canadians publishing in the States, then again at the border as imports, and yet again as personal income for the author. A $2.50 book published by an American netted about twenty-five cents a copy; the same book would net only four cents for a Canadian.[48] And his own personal living costs, he claimed, were up forty per cent over 1937. Thus, despite its popularity and high sales in Canada, the United States, and Britain, *Barometer Rising* could not earn him sufficient income to leave Lower Canada College as he desperately wanted to do.

The full resolution of the questions raised by *Barometer Rising* had to be put aside for the moment. Looking outward in 1942 at the world, which was to provide the context for whatever happened at home, he was again struck by the rapid transition that was taking place everywhere: 'History, which used to be a slow force moving on wagon wheels along Roman roads, sleeping in monasteries through the Middle Ages, rolling uncertainly westward in square-rigged galleons, has now become a terrible rushing force which every man and nation must ride or be swept aside. Within the lifetime of Canada, history has taken to the railroad, the motor car and finally to the airplane. It has created science and embodied itself within its own creation. This mysterious force, which is nothing more than the collective life of mankind, the product and master of human beings, permits no nation a constructive share in her processes which that nation has not itself appropriated.'

Here was the challenge. Just as he had hinted to George Barrett that 'In that state of "becoming" I seem to detect the possibility of a universality for a writer who attempts to write out of the Canadian scene,' so now he stated that 'we [Canadians] may well be offered an opportunity unique in history': 'In the revolutionary process which has covered the earth in our time, a nation must grasp the moment or be crushed by it ... There is no place for "little Canadianism" or for Canadian provincial politics. Mr. Churchill has already called our country the "lynch-pin" between Great Britain and the United States. But we can be more than that. We can become, if we will, the keystone of the central arch ... Canada must first stand as a nation united in fact. She must know what she is and what she wishes to become. She must state to the world what kind of a future she wants for her children.'[49]

Somewhat like Pirandello's *Six Characters in Search of an Author*, MacLennan's career had been set in place by the force of a role that needed to be played. His ambition to write a grand international novel had been deflected to fill a vacuum in Canadian letters. *Barometer Rising* had been a successful first step, but if he were to continue in the nationalist vein much remained to be done. Some clear sense of national identity above and beyond narrow 'group loyalties,' a public in Canada sufficiently aware of itself and its values, general recognition of the relatively few filaments of distinctly 'Canadian' culture – in short, a market for more novels such as *Barometer Rising*: these were the conditions he now hoped would come to pass. Only then would he be able to realize his dreams of becoming a famous writer. Perhaps he would have to forge such conditions himself.

Meanwhile, Dorothy's efforts too were bearing fruit. In a *tour de force* of non-fiction called *Bluenose: A Portrait of Nova Scotia,* which had been commissioned by Harper's, she expanded the chapter on Nova Scotia from *Here's to Canada!* into a full-length book. Writing much more quickly than Hugh, she had completed the manuscript in a mere five months, adapting many of the techniques of fiction such as dialogue, anecdote, and description to her non-fiction work. As a result, her book was colourful, dramatic, but, of necessity, distorted. Nova Scotians generally did not like being described so vividly through the eyes of an outsider. Many are the errors of fact and attitude they eagerly point out to this day, and yet all insist that her skill in writing is consummate. Certainly, the critical reception was excellent. A whole page was devoted to *Bluenose* in the *New York Times* magazine section; it was also treated by all the major Canadian papers and highly recommended. Within months it went into a second printing. In MacLennan's opinion, it was 'the best thing of its kind on any part of Canada.'[50] At this point they thought of themselves as a team. Both *Barometer Rising* and *Bluenose* were deliberately aimed at the vacuum in Canadian letters they had perceived. Spurred on by their respective achievements, more certain of the direction in which success now must lie, each commenced books that would eventually win the coveted Governor-General's Award.

Chapter six

On Solid Ground: *Two Solitudes*

Canadians who tuned their radios to the national network at five p.m. on Sunday, 29 November 1942, heard a roundtable discussion called 'Canadian Unity and Quebec.' In a flat, somewhat nasal voice, coloured by the remnants of an Oxford accent, Hugh MacLennan aired his views on what was popularly called 'the French problem' with John P. Humphrey, a professor of international law from McGill University, and the French-Canadian author and lecturer Emile Vaillancourt. As the discussion got under way, he found himself more or less in the middle, sympathetic to both the English and French points of view: like Humphrey, he was obviously part of the English-speaking élite in Quebec, but because of his loyalty to his Nova Scotian background he also identified with the underdog position expressed by Vaillancourt.

In this broadcast MacLennan continued to explore the national issues he had raised a few months earlier in 'Culture, Canadian Style' and 'Anniversary of an Idea.' There, he had come to the conclusion that if Canada were to have a national literature at all, she had first better become a real nation; at the moment, loyalty to the individual group or province superseded allegiance to the nation. Caution, he had argued, was understandably the most typical Canadian trait: a caution born of the experience of failure that each of the three founding groups – French, United Empire Loyalist, and Scottish – had known in the past. Now, in discussion with Vaillancourt and Humphrey, each apparently representing one of these founding peoples, he reiterated his notion that Canada must pull together towards some

At North Hatley in the Eastern Townships of Quebec

greater destiny than that of the combined purposes of her individual elements. For him at this point, 'Canada's national purpose after this war has got to be ... to provide proper social security for our people' – in other words, policies similar to those he had learned to admire in Scandinavia.

But he was not only expressing his own ideas in this broadcast, ideas on a subject he had already chosen for his next novel; he was listening as well to the opinions of the other two men, each of whom could elucidate certain points about sentiments in Canada at the time. Especially from Vaillancourt he gleaned a good deal of information, picking up a number of ideas he could incorporate into his writing. Describing ways in which French-speaking people were being hurt and exploited by the English-speaking majority, Vaillancourt documented the extent of Quebec's battered pride; like most of his people, he lamented the fact that there was no Canadian flag and that the nation was still referred to as a 'Dominion'; these shortcomings were like a 'slap in the face' to French Canadians. As for the current war in Europe and the threat of conscription, he was specific: 'it is neither fair nor sensible for anyone to expect French-speaking Canadians to feel it necessary to fight merely because Great Britain happens to be at war. There will never be a Canadian national understanding until that fact is accepted and repsected. But – let no one forget this – Quebec fights now because she believes that England's cause is her own cause and the cause of humanity.' He made it clear that the voices of a small group of trouble-makers who wanted to resist the war altogether did not represent the true spirit of Quebec. But if Canada could only define 'a clear vision of what she wishes to become,' he concluded, 'a flood of energy would be released from all nine provinces.' From Humphrey, to a lesser extent, MacLennan also learned something about Quebec; he described 'a great evolution' presently taking place: 'The old, established spokesmen of Quebec have always been professional men. But now we see a great change beginning ... Engineers, business men, technicians and industrial workers are beginning to make their voices heard. There is a lot of new energy to be tapped in Quebec.'[1]

That same month MacLennan wrote to George Barrett: 'The novel I am working on now will have far more weight to it [than *Barometer Rising*] if it comes off, and I think will at last solve the dilemma of how to handle a Canadian novel.' Presumably he was attempting to realize in the novel now under way the theory he had earlier expressed that Canada's 'national schizophrenia' might well symbolize the 'international breakdown' in the world at large.[2] When he had spoken of 'national schizophrenia' before, of course, he had been referring to the division between 'British' and 'American' that characterized the English-Canadian consciousness. Now, after living in Montreal for several years, he was coming to see that 'what was wrong here [in the city] was what was wrong with the nation itself.' It struck him forcibly that 'the crucible of Canada's future was Montreal.'[3] Thus, to write of the French-English split, so evident around him, was to strike at the heart of the nation's deepest problem. And, a forceful analysis of the impediments to national unity within Canada, it seemed to him, might appeal to an audience beyond Canada's borders: the barriers between the two 'races' might turn out to resemble those that kept the great nations of the world from peaceful coexistence.

As for the novel's proposed 'weightiness,' a great deal of his purpose can be understood by looking at a brief article he published almost a year after *Two Solitudes* appeared. In 'How Do I Write?' (1945) he discussed in considerable detail the process by which he had written this novel. 'The writer must be closer to mystery than to answering questions,' he maintained. 'He must be himself, and find his own harmony. This is absolutely all he has to offer.' Intuition, not intellect, must determine creative writing – a philosophy in sharp contrast to the method by which he had written *Barometer Rising*. 'The best way [to learn about technique],' he asserted, 'is to study one's own mistakes.' The chief 'mistake' he saw in his earlier book had been its disciplined *planning*, which had resulted in a facile conclusion and the exclusion of many of the 'great themes.' As he had written to Barrett: 'what bothered me about [*Barometer Rising*] was the unavoidable necessity of making the explosion a deus ex machina. Also, the deliberate limitations I imposed on myself for the sake of the market.' *Barometer Rising* remained for him, always, too superficial, too lightweight for his liking. Thus, the next novel would not be arranged 'deliberately' by using the intellect; it would be intuitive, or, as he stressed in his article, *organic*: 'as life grows organically, it can't be subordinated to a plan. At the same time, a novel without any plan at all is a shambles. Every novelist must somehow solve this dilemma, and generally he must solve it in his own way ... Somehow, the novelist must turn his mind into a seminary where organic growth may occur; then he must distinguish the tendencies of the growth and ultimately provide a proper form to hold it. He must therefore be prepared to throw aside any of his preconceived ideas of plot, character and general views of life if the growth of his book runs contrary to them.'[4]

After considering how other writers had solved this dilemma, he fixed on John Galsworthy's *The Forsyte Saga* as his model. He proceeded to enumerate what he considered to be Galsworthy's many shortcomings as a writer: his narrative limps in comparison to Joyce; beside Forster, the flatness of his characters; his lack of Hemingway's drive; his inferior knowledge compared to Wells; his craftsmanship less satisfactory than Maugham's. None the less, *The Forsyte Saga* had lived on in vivid clarity in his mind for a number of years. Why? Because Galsworthy had handled time brilliantly, and because his work was so *readable*. From him, he took instruction in how to make time pass smoothly and naturally, how to advance the story through dialogue, and how to pace the parts in relation to the whole. Galsworthy's 'mastery of time,' he wrote in 'How Do I Write?' 'has added time itself to our experience when reading him. It is such a mighty asset that it balances all his other lacks.' Because of this, he argued, although it might not have beauty and great thoughts, *The Forsyte Saga* was always a pleasure to read. *Two Solitudes*, then, as MacLennan conceived it, was to be a Canadian version of *The Forsyte Saga*, in which he aimed for a convincing handling of time and readability above all – it might well have been entitled 'The Tallard Saga.' This type of chronicle of generations in which Galsworthy specialized, moreover, could incorporate the Canadian material he felt to be essential in a Canadian novel at the time. Using Aristotle's dictum that drama proceeds from the known, he reiterated his own statement that 'in Canada, [the novelist] must build his stage along with his drama.'[5]

Another source of inspiration was the writing of Jakob Wassermann. 'I was much moved [in writing *Two Solitudes*],' MacLennan wrote much later to Marian Engel, 'by ... *The World's Illusion* [1917], which set out to create a kind of double-world (rich and poor in that case) of German society on the eve of the first war.'[6] From Wassermann's novel he derived the notion of a 'double-world' in Canada, one half of which was the French Canadian community of Quebec. To portray this community presented a formidable challenge: his notion that the French-English split characterized Canada, and that he should be writing about it, flew in the face of his conclusion on completing *Barometer Rising* that a writer must create out of his own background in order to be authentic and universal. He was not French Canadian; he did not speak French fluently; nor was he a Roman Catholic. How was he to go about portraying French Canadians with even the slightest degree of credibility?

This problem was especially perplexing for MacLennan, who, like the majority of the English-speaking Montreal community he had joined comparatively recently, lived a life that was almost hermetically sealed in the English-speaking sections of the city, with virtually no interaction with the attitudes, customs, and aspirations of the majority culture. He was still teaching in Lower Canada College, which was possibly more English than the English schools themselves, and spending his spare time almost exclusively with other English-speaking people, mainly from McGill University, discussing current events at informal gatherings or playing tennis at the Montreal Indoor Tennis Club on Atwater Street.

It is true that he did cultivate the friendship of the only French Canadian then teaching at Lower Canada College, S.E.H. Péron; other teachers from the time remember how they used to spend long hours discussing hotly many subjects, especially Péron's beloved French Canada. But Péron was hardly typical: not only did he work in an Anglo-Canadian environment, but his religion, in the tradition of his Huguenot ancestors, was Protestant. Aside from Péron and Vaillancourt, with whom he had appeared on CBC Radio, he knew only one other French Canadian, an ex-farmer from the Eastern Townships who helped him to cut down trees and do other odd jobs around his cottage in North Hatley.

MacLennan's knowledge of French Canada, on which *Two Solitudes* was based, came primarily from Ringuet's classic *Trente Arpents*. Written by the French-Canadian oculist Dr Philippe Panneton, who at first disguised his identity by using his mother's maiden name as a pseudonym, this novel had set all Quebec astir in 1938, the year it was published. It marked the first major realistic portrayal of French Canadians since the First World War, depicting the shift of the agrarian society of the habitant into the industrial and urbanized life of the twentieth century. The flurry of prizes and awards that followed its publication – especially the Prix du Gouverneur général du Canada – attracted wide attention. MacLennan read the French version that year and then he read it again two years later when an English translation appeared. 'Had I not read *Trente Arpents*,' he asserted, 'I could never have written *Two Solitudes*.'

When the two men met in Montreal after the publication of *Two Solitudes*, Dr Panneton acknowledged with surprising generosity Mac-

Lennan's reliance on his novel for the details and atmosphere of daily life in French Canada. When MacLennan thanked him for all his novel had contributed to his understanding, he replied: 'You have brought to *Two Solitudes* an international perspective I never could have possessed, caught as I am in the narrow milieu of my own people. You have rendered my people a great service.'[7]

Since Dr Panneton had based his novel on the meticulous notes he took on his patients at Trois-Rivières and on his chats with local farmers in the smoking car of the train to Joliette where he kept another office, MacLennan could hardly have found a better literary source for his own portrayal of French Canada. But in the absence of the first-hand experience he now believed to be essential to the novelist, he was uneasy. In a talk he gave much later on the origins of *Two Solitudes*, in which, incidentally, he judged it expedient not to mention *Trente Arpents*, he opened with the remark: 'Fools rush in where angels fear to tread ... This is a perfect description of myself when I began writing *Two Solitudes*.'[8]

MacLennan began to write *Two Solitudes* in a way quite unlike the one in which he had begun *Barometer Rising*. In that novel, with Canada his main concept, he had taken the Halifax explosion as the end of the novel and then worked out a plot that led up to it. Now, with no particular story in mind, he had simply started drafting scenes around certain characters who represented some of the ideas floating around in his head with no fixed sense of how they would ultimately fit into a total picture. His earliest scenes had been written about Paul Tallard, a young French-Canadian student in a seminary in Montreal.

It took an extraordinary dream to throw these random scenes and characters and ideas into a significant relationship to each other. Early in 1943 his unconscious brought to the surface an image so striking that in it he would recognize his novel's thesis. Indeed, to him this dream would remain its 'genesis'; as he later described it: 'I saw a tall, angular blonde man arguing with a stocky, darker man. They were shouting at one another more in frustration than in anger and a voice in the dream said to me, "Don't you see it? They're both deaf."'[9] At first, the dream seemed to him to be about his own deafness in one ear and its association with his father whom he had thought had caused it; the two men shouting at each other reminded him of the shouting matches between his father and himself that had taken place over the Classics during his childhood. But he became even more convinced in time that the dream was about his novel. At some unconscious level he recognized that Lord Durham's description of the country over a hundred years earlier as 'two nations warring in the bosom of a single state' still applied: French and English in Canada remained very much at odds with each other and deaf to one another's needs. Just as the small, dark son had at times been unable to get through to his powerful, fair-haired father, so the minority of French Canadians within Canada was finding it impossible to make the dominant Anglo-Saxon majority understand its difficulties. Through this dream his theories about French and English, and the few scenes he had already drafted, jelled into the concept of 'two solitudes' that would be his concern – though the title itself had not yet occurred to him.

According to MacLennan himself, *Two Solitudes* took shape much as he described it in 'How Do I Write?' – that is to say, it grew organically. A note attached to the manuscript in the McGill University Library confirms what he had already said at the time he was writing, that Athanase Tallard was originally intended to play a minor role: 'I had planned that Paul Tallard be the chief character in the book, and began with him as a seminary student. Then, in order to account for Paul, I began thinking of his father and writing scenes about him, and from that moment on, old Athanase Tallard took over the novel and held command of it until his death.' So effectively did the old man dominate the novel that the section of the book that follows his death seemed redundant to Claude Bissell who dispensed with it altogether in his later school edition.[10] The novel's later section, however, is essential; in it are found all the scenes about Paul with which MacLennan began his book.

Paul Tallard was intended to be the central character of *Two Solitudes* in exactly the same way as was Stephen Dedalus in James Joyce's *Portrait of the Artist as a Young Man*. Just as Joyce used Stephen to dramatize his own emergence as a distinctly Irish writer, MacLennan presented Paul to record his own struggles in writing the first self-consciously Canadian novel, *Barometer Rising*.

Like MacLennan, Paul is ambitious to become a writer; like him, too, his first attempts at fiction concern the 'great themes' whose focus is Europe. His novel, 'Young Man of 1933,' like MacLennan's earlier unpublished novels, concentrates on 'The year of Hitler's rise, a young man caught between the old war that was history and the new one whose coming was so certain it made the present look like the past even before it had been lived through.' The businessman, Huntly McQueen, suspects that anything Paul writes will be 'modernistic nonsense about socialism and sex that no decent publisher will touch,' a comment reminiscent of criticisms MacLennan had received from publishers and critics. In a later scene, in a conversation that echoes Dorothy's remarks regarding the need for 'Canadian' writers, his girlfriend Heather asks: 'Why didn't you set the scene in Canada?' Paul replies in words that had already come from MacLennan himself:

> Because no world trends begin here. I thought of it, but – everything that makes the world what it is – fascism, communism, big business and depressions – they're all products of other people's philosophies and ways of doing things ... Canada was imitative in everything. Yes, but perhaps only on the surface. What about underneath? No one had dug underneath so far, that was the trouble. Proust wrote only of France, Dickens laid nearly all his scenes in London, Tolstoi was pure Russian. Hemingway let his heroes roam the world, but everything he wrote smelled of the United States. Hemingway could put an American into an Italian Army and get away with it because by now everyone in the English-speaking world knew what an American was. But Canada was a country that no one knew. It was a large red splash on the map. It produced Mounted Policemen, Quintuplets and raw materials. But because it used the English and French languages, a Canadian book would have to take its place in the English and French traditions. Both traditions were so mature they had become almost decadent, while Canada herself was still raw ... The background would have to be created from scratch if his story was to become intelligible.

In a frenzy of excitement at having discovered that 'an artist has to take life as he finds it' and that his job will be to record Canada for the world, Paul hurls his other manuscript into the fire and watches triumphantly as the pages burn.[11]

The dramatic discovery of his task as potential spokesman for the nation he has just discovered constitutes the novel's high-point:

> out of his own life, out of the feeling he had in his bones for his own province and the others surrounding it, the theme of his new book began to emerge. Its outlines grew so clear that his pencil kept moving steadily until three in the morning. He was not formulating sentences; he was drafting the design of a full novel. He had never before been able to see so far into any work he had attempted. Its material and symbols lay ready in his subconscious: the dilemma that had nearly strangled him all his life and which at last he had managed to escape. He could view it now as though it belonged to another person; with pity, with some tenderness, but clearly and at a distance. Outlines of scenes he would later create followed each other inevitably, one by one out of his subconscious. He picked up ten pages covered with

scrawled notes, and as he reread them he found that each scene had retained in his mind the transparent clarity of still water.

In this self-conscious 'epiphany' reminiscent of Joyce's portrait of the artist as a young man can be seen similarities to MacLennan's own experience in writing his first 'Canadian' novel. There, too, the novel's whole shape came to him at once. Although there are other themes in *Two Solitudes*, its central concern is to render the forces that go into the making of an artist. Every aspect of the novel from its beginning to its conclusion bears upon this theme: it traces all the influences – international, national, and personal – on the individual who will be the one to create the first novel in the nation's cultural history. The story begins in 1917 at exactly the same time that Paul, a boy of seven, becomes conscious of the larger world of human affairs; it ends in the fall of 1939 with Paul halfway through the novel that will record Canada's 'first irrevocable steps toward becoming herself, knowing against her will that she was not unique but like all the others, alone with history, with science, with the future.'[12]

As the retired Nova Scotian sea captain John Yardley observes on one occasion: 'The obscure conflict within the Tallard family would certainly centre on this youngest member. Beyond that, the constant tug of war between the races and creeds in the country itself would hardly miss him ...' Paul knows that his father Athanase, a stubborn Norman from Quebec, is a member of Parliament in Ottawa, where he comes in for a good deal of criticism from both French and English. He is also aware that his mother is English while his father's first wife, mother of his half-brother Marius, was French. Early on, he sees Ontario business interests, in the person of Huntly McQueen, moving in on his father's property. In contrast, the old French servants in his father's seigneury in the parish of Saint Marc encourage his love for the land, helping him with his own garden; this loyalty to French Canada is furthered by his half-brother, who wakes him in the middle of the night asking for his help in avoiding conscription. His father eventually disrupts this allegiance by sending him to an English school where he will study science. After Athanase has quarrelled violently with the local priest, Beaubien, who finds his ideas revolutionary, Paul is dragged off on the train from Saint Marc to Montreal where he accompanies his father to a Presbyterian church to be converted to Protestantism. At the age of eight, as a schoolboy, he is taken to watch the parade of soldiers returning from the war, and later he sees the decadence of their behaviour on the streets of Montreal. At the bedside of his dying father, he witnesses Athanase's instinctive relapse into Catholicism for the last rites, after which his English mother and his French nationalist half-brother fight bitterly over the direction his education should now take. Athanase's will reveals that the business risks he took on behalf of McQueen have ruined him financially, a state experienced directly by Paul who must now live in greatly reduced circumstances. He consequently becomes a victim of the Depression as well as being isolated from both English and French cultures. As he tells Heather later: 'It's a tribal custom in Canada to be either English or French. But I'm neither one nor the other.'[13] Now, like Stephen Dedalus at the conclusion of *Portrait of the Artist as a Young Man*, he is sufficiently detached to observe the nation as a whole.

But in trying to account for Paul, as he admittedly tried to do once he had fixed on him as his central character, MacLennan felt compelled to demonstrate the enormous extent to which Paul's father had made him what he was. This digression was understandable: if he were to explain how he himself had arrived at the place in national cultural history he had occupied since the publication of *Barometer Rising*, he would have had to explain the inflexible perfectionism with which Dr Sam had driven him in his youth; the grip Athanase Tallard exercised on MacLennan's imagination testifies to the intensity he responded to for so long in his own father. Only when the old man is dead is the son able to direct his own energies towards writing. Like Dr Sam, Athanase fixes on education as the key in his son's development away from a primitive, provincial setting towards a larger stage.

Athanase is torn between two forces: the emotional bond to his group, the French Canadians in Quebec, who cautiously cling to the values of the past, and his rational understanding of English industrial society and the promise it holds for a better future. MacLennan had commented in 'Canadian Unity and Quebec': 'at the present moment, Canada is like a woman with two men courting her. Both those men think their future wife should be just like themselves. But the two men happen to belong to different races, they have different values in life, and they go to different churches. And because they're so different – well, the lady hasn't made up her mind yet, and the marriage hasn't yet taken place.' With his character Athanase, MacLennan simply reversed this situation: he has two wives consecutively, one French Catholic, the other English Protestant. His central place in the novel has much to do with the fact that in him is symbolized the conflict MacLennan perceived at the heart of the nation. Athanase *sees* what can and should be done for Quebec, but he is paralysed by his traditional attachments. All he can do is place his son in a school that will ensure that Paul will not be emotionally bound to French Canada to the same extent. As he tells his eight-year-old son: 'We'll choose an English School. You'll learn science. You'll find out what makes the world go around.' Paul replies: 'Isn't it because God wants it to?' To which his father responds: 'Yes, yes, I know ... Next year you will go to a fine English school. You'll still be a Canadian, mind you. Don't forget that.' Later, Athanase explains to the priest in defence of his decision: 'I want him to learn to mix naturally with English boys. I've never believed in this artificial separation. I want our people to feel that the whole of Canada is their land – not to grow up with the impression that the Province of Quebec is a reservation for them.'[14]

In his radio roundtable talk with Vaillancourt and Humphrey, MacLennan had pointed a finger directly at the educational system as 'the greatest weakness in the province of Quebec.' 'Quebec educators,' he explained in support of this argument, 'encourage their pupils to dwell too much on the past. I don't mean by that merely an excessive study of history. History can be a modern study ... if you use it for guidance in your own affairs ... In Quebec, provincialism is mainly the result of a traditional point of view.' These strong opinions can be traced not only to the emphasis on education in his own childhood but also to a job his wife had taken on as secretary to Arnold Heeney on the Hepburn Commission, a group investigating Protestant education in Quebec during the late 1930s and early 1940s. Dorothy had been hired to help assemble statistics and to write a report on the current state of education; her awareness of such matters, and consequently her husband's, was heightened at just the time MacLennan was working on his novel. So, in *Two Solitudes*, a change in education was fixed on as the key to any development away from group loyalty towards true nationhood. Paul will know French and French Canada, but he will also be on an equal footing with English Canadians who are up-to-date in the study of science; as an artist, his point of view will be 'Canadian,' not just French Canadian or English Canadian.

The dream Paul has on the night his fugitive half-brother sneaks into his bedroom reveals a good many of these elements within him and foreshadows the role as artist he will eventually play: 'Paul began to dream that Christ hung from a cross in the sky and that light poured down from Him holy to the earth. But underneath the holy light there was darkness, and terror moved through it with a droning sound. The drone ceased, the darkness rolled up like a curtain, and soldiers staggered out of an underbrush that covered the ground, lurching forward with weapons to kill each other. There were soundless explosions that remained motionless in the scene as they did in pictures. Paul saw himself crouching behind a rock witnessing what was happening, both hands gripping the top of the rock and his mouth opening and closing as he begged them to stop it, but no sound issuing from his lips. Then he saw two soldiers stabbing each other and they were his father and Marius. He looked up and the eyes of Christ on the cross rolled ...'

The dream that had been the novel's 'genesis,' two men shouting at each other, each stone deaf, is here transformed into the substance of the novel. The significance of MacLennan's own dream becomes clear: he was not only the son in conflict with his father, the French-Canadian sympathizer in the face of English domination; more importantly, he was the *observer*. In the dream 'a voice' had said to him: 'Don't you see it? They're both deaf.' It was with this 'voice' that he identified most fully. Like Paul, who in his dream sees 'himself crouching behind a rock witnessing what was happening ... as he begged them to stop it ... no sound issuing from his lips,' MacLennan had felt the conflict between the two men in his dream primarily as one who is looking on, detached. It was his calling to be a chronicler in *Two Solitudes*, just as it will be Paul's vocation to speak for the nation in the book he begins at the novel's close.

Paul's development towards a pan-Canadian point of view suggests that the title *Two Solitudes* ultimately meant something different from the commonly held view; it has usually been taken to mean the irreparable isolation of English and French Canada from each other. Only at the novel's beginning is this meaning of the phrase applicable; as Athanase Tallard puts it: 'The trouble with this whole country is that it's divided up into little puddles with big fish in each one of them ... The French are Frencher than France and the English are more British than England ever dared to be.' By the end of the novel, however, once Paul has experienced the insight that binds him to his vocation as a writer, the phrase has come to mean something else: it has come to mean precisely what it originally meant.

In the fall of 1943 MacLennan had set off for New York on a John Simon Guggenheim Fellowship; this prestigious American award had been made on the basis of his argument in his application that he wished to pursue Canadian subjects but had insufficient time to do so properly because of his long hours of work at Lower Canada College. It was sometime during that winter, spent with Dorothy in New York, that he first came across the phrase 'two solitudes.' He was reading a review in the *New York Times* of a relatively insignificant novel, which concluded by saying: 'This writer might accomplish something if he could begin to understand the truth of Rilke's statement that "love consists in this, [that two solitudes protect, and touch, and greet each other]."'[15] He was two-thirds of the way through his novel at the moment he read this, and at once seized on the phrase for his title. Once back in Montreal, in the summer of 1944, he had written to a vacationing colleague from McGill, an expert in German literature, who tracked down the source with considerable difficulty; the sentence, eventually located by Professor W.L. Graff, had occurred in a letter from Rainer Maria Rilke to his friend Franz Xaver Kappus on 14 May 1904. Graff reported to MacLennan that the ideas expressed in the quotation preoccupied Rilke at a time when his marriage was in difficulty: 'love cannot exist in mutual assimilation or in the subordination of one party to another, but that it ought to consist in a mutual respect and protection of each other's inalienable identity and solitude.'[16] Hardly ever considered now in its full context, the phrase 'two solitudes,' as Rilke meant it and as MacLennan understood it, was not simply a definition of two isolated entities; it was a definition of *love*. As such, the phrase captured perfectly what MacLennan had shown in Canada's evolution by the novel's end: English and French Canada are no longer envisaged as the 'separate puddles' Athanase knew, but as 'oil and alcohol in the same bottle.'[17] This somewhat cold and clumsy image reveals MacLennan's view that respect and love must characterize the relationship between English and French in Canada. To cut off the last third of the novel, as Claude Bissell later did, distorted the novel so that the real meaning of its title could not be comprehended.

It is one of MacLennan's great technical accomplishments that Paul's development as an artist, like his own, is intricately linked to Canada's development as a nation. The same years that traced Paul's growth from boyhood awareness in 1917 to the full realization of his literary vocation in 1939 are exactly the years in which profound changes in the nation make a pan-Canadian novel possible at all. Using *The Forsyte Saga* as an example of how to manipulate time over a long period and relate historical events to individual lives, MacLennan structured his book around the four stages he saw as most crucial in Canada's development to nationhood: 1917-18, the last years of the First World War; 1919-21, the post-war years and reconstruction; 1934, the middle of the Great Depression; and 1939, the eve of the Second World War. He controlled the passage of time as Galsworthy had done by alternating sweeping scenes of world events with detailed scenes that illustrate the effect of these events on the individual lives of his characters.

In treating a span of time that began in 1917, the year of the Halifax explosion, he was able to take up in *Two Solitudes* where *Barometer Rising* left off; in doing so, he was also able to return to some of those 'great themes' that had concerned him in the two unpublished novels. *Two Solitudes* included treatments of the horrors of war and the psychic shock individual soldiers experienced in it drawn from his father's recollections. Again, he was emphatically opposed to war. He showed how the Great War had been but one reflection of a technological age which was insidiously accelerating. Through the war, capitalism and scientific 'advancements' had reached new heights; at the same time human moral development had taken a large step backwards. As he had consistently maintained in his speeches, letters, and essays, the age was one of transition, a transition that had thrown many individual lives into tragic relief. As Athanase Tallard, somewhat too self-consciously, comments: 'Every man has to act according to some principle. He – he must make his life aim at something. He must live in accordance with the times. That's going to be the tragedy of so many people we know – they'll have to pass through a long period of transition from their present way of life to the way science compels us to live.'

The thing to be feared above all was the disintegration of civilized, human values in a time characterized by primitive reversion to destructive brute force. This is something only Captain Yardley, among the novel's characters, has glimpsed while moored once in the tropics, a state of mind he calls 'the ultimate solitude': 'Leaning over the taffrail he had watched the fish gliding through ten fathoms of sunlit water below. Sharks and barracuda moved in their three-dimensional element, self-centred, beautiful, dangerous and completely aimless, coming out from a water-filled cavern hidden beneath the promontory and slipping under the ship's keel, fanning themselves for seconds under the rudder, then circling back into the cavern again ... the memory of the hour had never left him. Self-centred, beautiful, dangerous and aimless: that was how they had been, and he could never forget it.'[18] In this passage, MacLennan juxtaposed the 'aimless' killer fish and the 'rudder' that will steer the ship back on course. His values could not be clearer. A cosmos separates 'the ultimate solitude' of a Darwinian world from the love composed of 'two solitudes' reaching out to protect each other. This essentially Christian morality underlies the whole novel. Man, as individual or as nation, has the choice: he can hate and destroy, aimlessly, or he can love and create, with purpose. War is but one example of man's wrong-headedness in applying science to destructive ends; capitalism is another.

In MacLennan's portrait of Huntly McQueen can be seen a human 'barracuda' in action. Named 'Huntly' to suggest his predatory nature and 'McQueen' to suggest his colonialism, this industrialist from central Canada has megalomaniac dreams, not unlike Colonel Wain's in *Barometer Rising*, to 'impose his will' on the nation:

> He wanted to produce. He wanted to make himself an integral part of what he considered a world trend. He was no longer interested solely in profit. Organization was the new order of the day.
>
> To organize Canada seemed a colossal task; impossible, most of his contemporaries would say. Economic lines ran north and south across the American border, not east and west through the country. But it could be done. If a man owned and controlled sufficient means of production, twenty years from now he might impose his will to an extent undreamed of as yet. McQueen wanted some metal mines, lumber mills, textile factories, a packing house, construction companies, engineering works ... there was no limit to what he wanted to complete his picture. Further, he wanted his enterprises so well spaced over the country that his influence would touch every part of it.

Canada's provincialism, her 'group loyalties,' work to McQueen's advantage. As MacLennan had commented in the radio roundtable in November 1942: 'privileged men of [the] ... Anglo-Saxon race have actually acquired a vested interest in the lower wage rates of Quebec.' After considering McQueen's scheme for a new factory in his parish, Athanase observes: 'Science was sucking prestige from the old age of faith and the soil. And prestige was a matter of power. One by one other nations had surrendered to science. In time, Quebec must surrender, too, learn to master science or be crushed by others who understood how to manipulate the apparatus she neglected. But how could Quebec surrender to the future and still remain herself? How could she merge into the American world of machinery without also becoming American? How could she become scientific and yet save her legend?'[19] Athanase is split between the two views: that of keeping abreast of science to protect his province from 'English' exploitation, and that of remaining loyal to the creed of French-Canadian people everywhere by loving the land and believing that from it God would provide. MacLennan uses McQueen to dramatize the vulnerability of minority groups in a country where no national allegiance commands widespread loyalty; the absence of 'love,' of the instinct 'to protect, and touch, and greet' the other sections of the country, not only isolates him personally but more seriously it also prevents the country as a whole from achieving true nationhood.

MacLennan was hopeful that men like McQueen would ultimately fail. As he saw it, the left-wing point of view now had more chance to succeed against such capitalists than ever before. In a letter to his friend Barrett on 16 November 1942 he analysed the situation:

> I definitely know first-hand that the capitalists have lost most of their confidence. Two things help a lot in Canada. One is that beloved England is going Socialist. The other is that most capitalists in Canada, being old, have enough religious conditioning to feel uncomfortable unless their consciences are clear ... Now it's harder for them to rationalize ... A careful propaganda addressed *to them* [Canadians], with plenty of quotes from Roosevelt, Churchill and the Bible, with emphasis on the friendliness between Churchill and Stalin, with something of an offer of co-operation with labour, will do a lot right now to weaken them into those initial back-steps which is just what labour needs at the moment ...
>
> You probably feel as I do that now above all is the time for kicking out the pegs. Labour has had to yield a lot in the war, but I do feel it has achieved more real solidarity and sense of its own power and dignity than it had before ...
>
> However, there's no doubt we're in for one hell of a five years when this war ends. Personally I believe it will turn out better than many of us hope. The men over forty and under fifty lack both the conviction and ability of their fathers – the Tories, I mean. The old men like [Herbert] Holt and [Sir Charles Blair] Gordon are dying off. The younger men are all to the left. And those who are on the right seem to me to lack the ability to win, though they actually have enough power to mess things up a lot. It will all turn on how the returned soldiers feel.

MacLennan's ideal of a society modelled on Scandinavia's three 'demi-paradises' was clearly in his mind at the time he was writing *Two Solitudes*. If only Canada could overcome her divisive provincialism and define a national purpose that concentrated on 'proper regional development' rather than on mutual exploitation, the country could be truly noble.

As many readers at once recognized, McQueen was a caricature of William Lyon Mackenzie King, then prime minister of Canada; his name is an amalgam of elements from King's, with 'King' changed to 'Queen' and the 'Mac' transposed. Both are bachelors who work in their upper floor studies at night; both men revere their dead mothers and 'commune' with portraits of them for advice. Each wears and adjusts his pince-nez and speaks in a ponderous style; each actively dislikes air-conditioned railway cars and airplanes. Certainly these superficial resemblances were intentional. Beyond that, MacLennan associated King, like McQueen, with Canadian industrial development: 'without [King] we should never have developed into the ranking industrial nation we are today.' In his view, too, the mainspring of King's lonely life was the thirst for power. But as he remarked in a letter to his friend Dorothy Dumbrille, a novelist he had met through the Canadian Authors' Association, who had served in the Department of Defence in Ottawa during the First World War, 'McQueen in a sense does bear a few outward resemblances to the P.M., but otherwise not. The P.M. is a genius and a great statesman. Without the genius he might have been like McQueen, but there's quite a difference.' In fact, in a later article for *New Liberty* magazine (1949), he selected King as one of the ten greatest Canadians, claiming he was 'a master workman in the trade of politics,' endowed with exceptional 'insights,' whose main achievement was his ability to keep the nation together during the conscription crisis in 1944: 'Out of that maelstrom of emotion I am certain he produced beneficial and lasting results ... a nation which once and for all saw itself as larger than its separate parts.'[20]

Though he did not know it at the time, the letter MacLennan had written to George Barrett in November 1942 would be his last. Shortly afterwards, his friend was killed in an utterly senseless accident in Halifax, when a truck, wildly out of control, smashed into the side of a bus where he was sitting. This loss, deeply felt, was eventually compensated for, in terms of discussion of his work and ideas, by a new correspondence with William Arthur Deacon, literary editor for the Toronto *Globe and Mail*. The affable Deacon was already well-established as an author whose several books on Canada argued strongly in favour of cultural nationalism; his weekly column, 'The Fly Leaf,' continued to draw attention to achievements in the arts of which Canadians might be proud. Although they did not meet him until Christmas 1945, Hugh and Dorothy began corresponding with Deacon eight months or so beforehand on literary subjects of mutual interest.

While MacLennan had been busy mulling over the theories of fiction, themes, and characters that would eventually come together to form *Two Solitudes*, Dorothy had been hard at work writing *Partner in Three Worlds*. In the fall of 1941, through some mutual friends in

Shingletown, California, they had met a man who was to become her subject in this biography. Roger Ritter, a private soldier in the Canadian army, was a handsome, fair-haired European who had been born in Prague. Something about his presence and his personal history gripped both the MacLennans for the year or so that he waited in Montreal for his orders to go overseas. This 'saintly Bacchus,' as Dorothy called him, was a man of such intensity and with such 'mysterious sources of strength' that they were spellbound by his long tales from his past. As a result of these conversations, she took on the difficult task of rendering his biography. Using the technique of fiction, she cast his life in the first person as if it were an autobiography, changed his name to Jan Rieger, and tried to capture the spirit of his life using the principle that 'Facts can become fairly well what we make them.' For her, the essence of his life consisted in the fact that he had experienced what amounted to three separate lives: one as a child in the Austro-Hungarian empire, one as a soldier during the First World War, and a third as a farmer in the United States – thus the title *Partner in Three Worlds*. The book was a rave success in Canada when it was published in 1944 by Harper's. Triumphant, Dorothy was awarded the Governor-General's Award for non-fiction. In the United States, however, mainly because of Harper's poor distribution and advertising, the book sold poorly.

What did all this mean to MacLennan? People who knew them both at the time, and to whom they introduced Roger Ritter, simply could not see why they were courting his friendship. Their fascination was not shared by others. In fact, some of what Ritter told them of his personal history turned out to have been more than a little exaggerated. In many ways, MacLennan's friendship with him seems to have been a continuation of the kind of acquaintance he had formerly struck up at Princeton with the European kitchen boys. Certainly the two of them shared anti-fascist sentiments: MacLennan from an intellectual perspective, Ritter from the accidents of history which had involved him directly. They also shared a sympathy for socialist principles, like the boys at Princeton. MacLennan's way of demonstrating his faith in these principles, as we have seen, was speculative: he could write about the 'great themes,' but he abhorred the whole idea of war. Ritter, on the other hand, was a man of action who couldn't wait to get back into combat. 'I have never seen,' Dorothy remarked, 'a man try harder ... to get a German in the sights of a Bren gun or within range of a grenade.'[21] To MacLennan, Ritter must have seemed like an 'alter ego': in his fiction he had portrayed exactly this type of man – Adolf in 'So All Their Praises,' Nicholas in 'A Man Should Rejoice' – and he would continue to do so, most notably his later character Jerome Martell in *The Watch That Ends the Night*. These men were in contrast to the speculative protagonists, who were closer to MacLennan himself. The two men complemented each other strongly, each admiring in the other traits he would never possess.

Nothing could have been more gratifying to MacLennan than the public reception of *Two Solitudes* when it was finally published on 17 January 1945. By noon of that day, on which many rave reviews appeared, the entire first printing of 4500 copies was sold out. In the *New York Times*, Orville Prescott declared: 'MacLennan is a creative artist using the novel as a medium for the novel's best and fundamental purpose – the telling of a story about people whose concerns are made emotionally important, whose affairs can illuminate a general situation ... His story is also one of the twentieth century as it has been and is everywhere – a century of war and social strife, of unemployment and the blind onward march of science and industrialization ... "Two Solitudes" is superbly vital.' MacLennan apparently had succeeded in touching the 'great themes' through a local situation; his novel, at least by the *New York Times*, the most influential paper of the day, was considered to be not merely 'regional.'

Actually, he had not entertained high hopes about the kind of reviews he would receive for the book. 'When I finished *Two Solitudes*,' he had written to Bill Deacon a year later, 'I knew that no reviewer in the United States would begin to understand it. I knew that nearly all of them in Canada wouldn't know what to make of it, and would talk about the politics of the book with one eye over their shoulder to see what the boss would say.'[22] This premonition proved right in some respects, although he need not have had any fears about the novel's universality, as can be seen by Prescott's review.

Unfortunately, however, a good many critics in the United States read the novel in relation to another successful Canadian book, published the previous year and enjoying enormous sales there, *Earth and High Heaven* by the Montreal novelist Gwethalyn Graham. In her novel Graham had depicted a love story between a Jewish boy and a Christian girl; partly because it was set in Montreal, and also because it concerned an 'interracial marriage,' the two novels appeared to be closely related to some American reviewers. Hugh and Dorothy knew 'Gwen' Graham well; they had met her at the Canadian Authors' Association meetings in Montreal and Toronto and shared with her the common purpose of Canadian writers in difficult times. But

MacLennan thought that his novel was entirely different from *Earth and High Heaven*; 'her book is not really Canadian,' he observed to Dorothy Dumbrille.[23] As he saw it, she was following a track similar to that of Morley Callaghan who, by setting his stories in Toronto but with no details that would emphasize the fact, was attempting to give an impression of any large urban centre in the modern world. Like Callaghan, she was not concerned with 'explaining' Canada to her readers, using rather a setting and style that would make her story recognizable to anyone in the English-speaking world. MacLennan, on the other hand, had decided that there was 'no short cut to universality' and that he would 'sink or swim'[24] as a Canadian writer. Already he had suffered the consequences of his choice in that no film company would purchase the rights for *Barometer Rising* simply because the Halifax explosion could not readily be transposed to the United States. Graham's novel, predictably, sold over a million and a half copies eventually and was bought by Goldwyn films. The problems of intermarriage between Jews and Christians were universally acknowledged; racial tensions between the French and English in Canada were not. So it was that many American reviewers, with *Earth and High Heaven* fresh in their minds, drew a comparison that led them to misread the novel; *Two Solitudes*, to them, was simply another mixed marriage story.

The novel was even more flagrantly misread by the majority of American reviewers who concentrated on the mutual isolation of the two separate cultures in Canada rather than on their potential reconciliation as the novel's main message. The review titles themselves give an excellent indication of this trend: 'Cleavage in Canada between French and English Theme of Novel,' 'Hugh MacLennan's "Two Solitudes" Pictures the Struggle of Two Races,' 'Novel of Conflicts between English and French Citizens of Canada,' 'Novel Explains Canada's Racial Conflict,' 'Where Two Civilizations Meet,' 'Clashing Worlds North of the Border,' and so on. One reviewer maintained that 'the maple leaf and the fleur-de-lis have never attained the harmony of a garland.' To most American reviewers, MacLennan was explaining, for their benefit, the political and social realities in eastern Canada. One reviewer commented on 23 January, for example: '[*Two Solitudes*] concerns some of the interbellum developments in Canada, that interesting "foreign" country across Lake Erie ... The background of the conscription fracas, which exploded again over the week-end, could be better understood by reading MacLennan's book. The current political experiments and unrest in the dominion, also find their reason for existence in the picture painted in this novel ... Since some of us know more about China and South Africa than we do about our next-door neighbor, I heartily recommend this novel as a pleasant way of correcting the fault.' Another remarked that '*Two Solitudes* is tremendously revealing to the American reader.' Still another extravagantly claimed: 'it opens the door for us to know our geographical and political Siamese twin much more intimately than we have before.' Over a year later, J. Donald Adams attempted to put an end to this naïvety by arguing as follows in the *New York Times*: 'Nothing could be sillier ... than for an American reader to imagine that he had arrived at a real understanding of Canada's most acute problem from a reading of Hugh MacLennan's excellent novel, "Two Solitudes" ... The novelist's first concern ... is to enlist your sympathies, not to provide you with bases for judgment. For that, you must have more unadulterated fact than the novelist can comfortably provide.'[25]

Canadian reviewers acclaimed *Two Solitudes* as a leap forward in the by now feverish race to assert a cultural identity. Leo Kennedy, the Canadian poet, reviewing the book for the *Chicago Sun*, called it unreservedly 'the GREAT Canadian Novel.' Merrill Denison, a Canadian playwright (*Brothers in Arms*) who was later to write the history of such industries as Massey-Harris, CCM, and Molson's (and was in turn reviewed by MacLennan), claimed that the subject of this novel 'is at the very core of Canada's future.' Mason Wade, a Guggenheim Fellow in Canadian history at the time who would publish the first comprehensive history in English of the French Canadians a decade later, insisted that the novel was 'required reading for every Canadian who is concerned with the fundamental problem of his national life.' *Two Solitudes* sent Canadian critics scurrying for superlatives on all sides. The *Canadian Forum* was extravagant in its summing up: 'Canada should stage a coming-of-age party this year. We have produced two novels of the full stature of manhood [Grove's *Master of the Mill* and *Two Solitudes*] ... The latter will probably have the more popular appeal. Here is the substance of Canada, her countryside, her cities, her conflicting cultures, and, above all, her people. We move comfortably among them, knowing them for our own, yet, if it were translated into, say Russian, it could be read over there with something of the pleasure we have in reading *War and Peace*.' In a review for the Toronto *Globe and Mail*, which MacLennan himself particularly liked, Bill Deacon labelled him 'a social novelist' whose new novel relegates 'the excellence of *Barometer Rising* ... to the level of an apprentice piece. The promise of the first book is justified abundantly in the second. Considering style, theme, characters, craftsmanship, significance and integrity, *Two Solitudes* may well be considered the best and most important Canadian novel ever published.'[26]

And how was it received in Montreal, the story's main locale? There, too, the reception was generally favourable. The English-language newspapers praised the novel, the *Star* labelling the book's publication 'one of the biggest literary events in Canada since the twentieth century dawned.' The *Gazette*'s reviewer claimed *Two Solitudes* was 'the outstanding Canadian novel of this or any other year.' As Dorothy commented in a letter to Bill Deacon: 'Have you seen the reaction of the French press to T.S.? They're going over the deep end. *La Presse* is crazy about it, it's been reviewed on the air in French, and the most unlikely nationalists think it's terrific.' *La Presse* was indeed enthusiastic, praising in particular MacLennan's 'don de sympathie': 'C'est le grand livre de l'heure ... Il parle d'unité nationale, et cela est logique.' But Dorothy's boast preceded *Le Devoir*'s review by a week: in a devastating review, it was claimed that MacLennan's thesis in the novel (that English and French could get along) was too long and quite weak; what is more, it gave a thoroughly inaccurate picture of French Canada: 'Le grand malheur, c'est qu'un tel livre donnera une très fausse ideé du Canada français et catholique à des lecteurs de langue anglaise et non catholiques au Canada et aux États-Unis.' This review, however, was the exception, not the rule. French critics in general followed the line of thought expressed a few months later in the *Montreal Star* by Abbé Arthur Maheux, in a bilingual review called 'A Masterpiece: Un Chef d'oeuvre': 'Truly it is impossible, in this chronicle on National Unity, not to note the generous and intelligent effort and the marvellous success achieved by a Canadian writer, to help in solving our national problems.' In short, most French-Canadian critics saw in *Two Solitudes* what MacLennan maintained to his friends was assuredly there: 'a deep respect and affection for French-Canada.'[27] Siding with the underdog was easy for a Nova Scotian of Scottish background.

The main grounds on which he was criticized in Canada was for his inclusion of too many sexual scenes. The trend in American fiction had increasingly taken the direction of much freer use of language and incident, as one of the most popular novels of the day, Kathleen Winsor's *Forever Amber*, showed. MacLennan himself did not like this novel, and felt that his treatment of sex was not merely sensational, as Winsor's had been, but strongly framed by a moral code. Critics disagreed. As the reviewer for *Saturday Night* put it, somewhat awkwardly: 'In subjection to a modern slant of reader-fashion, he has the habit of stripping his women characters to the skin, one after another, and seating them to contemplate, not without approval, their ripening charms. Like the figures of Peter Paul Rubens, his women don't seem in the least degree susceptible to drafts. The difference between a nude and a naked is considerable. One is artistic, the other sensational.' Or, as *Queen's Quarterly* claimed: 'Puritanism has been completely outgrown, or authoritatively silenced. *Two Solitudes* might be said, almost, to have made clear the way for a Canadian *Forever Amber*.' Even Dr W.D. Woodhead, chairman of Classics at McGill, voiced strong objections: 'What must trouble many readers, both of this book and of *Barometer Rising*, is the generally quite unnecessary intrusion of sex. Is no book really complete without this? Does some power stand over writers waving a magic wand and proclaiming "Let there be Sex"? ... Although sex has undoubtedly a place in literature, it is difficult to justify its intrusion when it is quite irrelevant.'[28]

In an article about her husband written that summer for *Maclean's* magazine, Dorothy, somewhat tongue-in-cheek, defended him from this type of accusation. She attributed his use of sex to his classical education: 'It is his classical training, of course, which has given him his straightforward, honest approach to human behaviour.' None the less, these attacks probably confirmed a feeling he already had, that Canada had in large part, as he had expressed it in *Two Solitudes*, 'the mind of the maiden aunt.'[29] Puritanism became one of his bugbears. If people couldn't see the difference between his use of sex and Kathleen Winsor's, there was some educating to be done.

There was also some criticism of his craft, but objections to characterization, style, and plot were submerged in the general paean of praise that greeted the author of the 'great Canadian novel.' Here, in fact, the tendency to schizophrenia that had characterized reviews of *Barometer Rising* was confirmed. MacLennan was praised unreservedly for his *themes*, for what he was doing; the reservations expressed at *how* he presented those themes, at the flaws in his craftsmanship, were consequently overlooked. To look at his novels *as fiction only* was beside the point; he was clearly doing his national duty, and so must the public by supporting him.

However, one astute reviewer, Diana Trilling, reviewing the novel for the *Nation*, touched on a serious problem: '"Two Solitudes" has little true drama, however; nor is it by virtue of narrative, characterization, prose manner, or any other of the expected skills of fiction that it makes its way; on any of these counts Mr. MacLennan's novel is more workmanlike than gifted. I suspect, then, that what we have in this case is one of those rare instances in which an author's seriousness and decency do a very good job as proxy for art.' Bill Deacon also noticed the same kind of thing when he pointed out: 'Two Solitudes does not contribute anything new in ideas. It merely arranges the pieces with deadly logic to prove the depth and ramifications of the rift that exists; and by personalizing these he has brought the impact and reality of art to an otherwise academic debate.' *Saturday Night* called it 'a tale of cunning tailoring with no gaps at the seams'; another review referred to his 'newspaper knowledge.'[30] This 'workmanlike' quality was in fact a serious drawback in *Two Solitudes*. Despite MacLennan's statement that he had been attempting an 'organic' approach to this novel, 'deadly logic' lurked too close between its pages. As so many critics noted, it was a 'thesis' novel, and because of this character inevitably suffered. To most readers the novel's central theme was the history of French-English relations in Canada between the wars, not Paul's development into an artist, as MacLennan had intended. So it was that he himself did not like the American reviews, which he thought dealt with the novel in 'too sensational' a way. In other words, he thought they had played up far too much the English-French split; 'it was not so much the Quebec problem, as a Canadian novel,' he protested to Bill Deacon. 'For me personally,' he went on, 'there was no sense of controversy at all; merely a prolonged and often mind-breaking effort to bring the various pieces into focus.' Bringing the various pieces into focus meant sacrificing character, unfortunately. 'I wrote of a legend,' he confided to Dorothy Dumbrille; 'this was not easy, and required endless re-writing, as the characters, once I had made my choice, had frequently to be rejected if their own lives interfered with the design I had felt at the beginning was true.'[31]

Although MacLennan may have been trying to let the book develop organically, these statements indicate that he let logic, not intuition, dictate a good deal of the story. As a result, he came in for some detailed criticism from sections of the reading public with a vested interest of one kind or another. Reading the book as an historical or political document, not as a work of art, these critics objected on factual grounds. Marxists in the New York *Daily Worker*, for example, complained that there was 'no character to represent the living thought of the peasants or city workers'; Catholic critics protested that he erred in presenting several details of Roman Catholic ritual and failed 'to portray the full strength of Catholicism.' And a few French Canadians, such as the reviewer for *Le Devoir*, picked up on the fact that he did not really know much at all about their culture.[32]

The most serious misreading of the book came simply from concentrating, as almost every reviewer did, on the portrayal of the French-English split itself. It was because of the novel's title, more than anything else, that this occurred. The editors at Duell, Sloan and Pearce had tried to get him to change his title at the time they had requested many minor revisions, but he had categorically refused to do so. The catchy phrase 'two solitudes' stuck in the minds of all readers and drew attention away from 'the fusion of this Canadian dichotomy,' which he was really writing about, towards the more stark reality of the two isolated cultures. The fact that the title has passed into the vocabulary of all Canadians to express the quintessence of opposition between the two founding nations, is testimony in itself that it did not convey what he intended. Even René Lévesque, in his argument for Quebec independence, used the phrase to indicate the impossibility of achieving unity within federation.[33] Instead of expressing the best kind of love, it has come to mean just the opposite.

The most obvious flaw in the novel, and one noticed immediately by many reviewers, was the fact that the last third of the book was considerably weaker than the rest. The *New York Herald Tribune*'s review was typical in saying: '"Two Solitudes" is uneven: that is, parts of it – the first two-thirds, say – are considerably more interesting, more vigorous, fresher than the rest of it.' After the death of Athanase Tallard, the 'canvas narrows,' as one critic put it, and the level of drama falls off. The blurb on the novel's dust-jacket asserted categorically that Paul is the novel's protagonist: 'it is Paul Tallard who dominates the book. With his mixed education and background, his story becomes essentially a struggle to establish a balance within himself, to integrate the various forces which have worked upon him since he was born, out of the welter of transition to find a home for his mind.' There is no doubt that to MacLennan this was so, but for at least half the novel's reviewers, regardless of whether they were American, Canadian, or, later, British, Paul's father, Athanase Tallard, was the hero of *Two Solitudes*. The last third of the novel, important in MacLennan's mind because it contained the 'epiphany' based on his own breakthrough with *Barometer Rising*, towards which the whole early part of the story moved, was a disappointment. As the *Commonweal* observed: 'All this first half of "Two Solitudes" is well thought out and soundly depicts a society in profound transition. Once Tallard is dead, however, the quality of the performance deteriorates. His half-Irish son now dominates the narrative, and we are presented with a long study of almost purely individual development. Where the canvas had been broad, it becomes narrow. It would have been far better had Mr. MacLennan gone on to tell us about Saint Marc, which he drops utterly the moment the Tallards move away, rather than about the evolution of Paul and his beloved Heather. For Saint Marc is the real drama, not the struggle of an aspiring young novelist who happens to come of a French father and an English mother. Novelists within a novel – that is dubious matter at best.' The New York *Daily Worker* voiced a similar objection: 'Well educated, sensitive, athletically constructed, and interestingly mated, Paul nevertheless does not live up to the task the author has set for him. He simply avoids carrying on where Athanase left off – thus wasting much of MacLennan's groundwork ... he becomes a fairly irresponsible little man with a Literary Future. Fine, even plausible, but hardly relevant!' Although one reviewer perceived that 'in the way a wheel revolves around the hub, Two Solitudes revolves around Paul Tallard,' he criticized more than anything else MacLennan's failure to make the character of Paul real: 'The cast of characters, from top to bottom, is dramatically conceived and brilliantly executed – with a single exception. Curiously but understandably, this is the character of Paul Tallard himself ... Unfortunately, the adult and mature Paul is not with us long enough to solidify into a person. It was Mr. MacLennan's only serious error to assume that an adequate portrayal of Paul, the boy, would permit him to skimp on the character of Paul, the man.'[34] Most reviewers concluded something along the same lines as the *Canadian Forum*: 'When the book is closed, with Paul enlisted for the war of 1939, Athanase Tallard returns to memory and dominates the whole. Imagined intensively and drawn with surety, this figure will live in Canadian literature.'

MacLennan himself did not recognize this problem with his character Paul until after the reviews started coming in. In a letter to Bill Deacon in September he confessed: 'I had not realized the full weight of Athanase Tallard, and the effect his death would have on the subsequent chapters.' However, he had suspected that the whole novel may have needed a final rewriting. As it stood already, it had taken a colossal amount of time and effort. In his article in December 'How Do I Write?' as well as in letters, he described the incredible difficulty with which he had written the book: 'I have been criticized, I think rightly, for not having polished Two Solitudes with greater care, and for not having developed certain characters more than I did. It was a book of about one hundred and sixty thousand words. I used up more than six thousand sheets of typewriter paper in the composition of it. In retrospect, I think I should have used more.' Why didn't he revise then? 'If I had done that I would not have been able to finish it until next Christmas owing to school work, and would still be back at school this fall,' he told Deacon. Otherwise, he saw in retrospect, '[*Two Solitudes*] would have been better had I been able to cast it off when I had finished it, and taken a complete vacation for about six weeks, then spent another three months work on it.'[35] Too impatient to get free of his duties at Lower Canada College so that he could write full-time, MacLennan had submitted his novel too soon.

What *Two Solitudes* really lacked was a focus that would emphasize Paul's development and throw everything else in the novel into a suitable relationship to this concern. As MacLennan confessed in an interview a year and a half after it was published: 'Writing's an endless business ... because I seem to see too many angles all the time. I'd like to present things simply, the way, for example, Maupassant ... does.'[36] Joyce's *Portrait of the Artist as a Young Man* does this successfully by centring on Stephen's point of view at each stage of his growth. Much later, in *The Watch That Ends the Night* and in *Voices in Time*, MacLennan found the angle of vision that might have given *Two Solitudes* the focal point it so badly needed. He came to see that the drama of spiritual growth, such as Paul experiences, is best illuminated from *within*. Had he centred his story on Paul's consciousness, either in the third person as Joyce had done with Stephen Dedalus, or in the first person as he himself was to do with George Stewart in *The Watch That Ends the Night* and John Wellfleet in *Voices in Time*, the fascination of Paul's inner growth could have been felt by the reader. Like George Stewart, Paul is not externally interesting: he is neither dramatic nor eccentric. Only from the *inside* is he an exciting individual. However, his development, his struggles, the insight which prompts him to become a writer, were matters of the greatest personal interest to MacLennan since they so closely resembled his own personal struggles, and, had he shown Paul from within, that excitement could have been communicated to readers – even to readers who felt *a priori* that 'Novelists within a novel' were 'a dubious matter at best.' Readers could have seen Paul as MacLennan was beginning to view himself, not as a 'little man with a Literary Future' but as a spokesman for a noble nation.

Subjugating all his episodes to one central concept had worked in *Barometer Rising*, but to MacLennan this had meant intolerable 'limitations.' Enthusiasm for 'Canadianness' in that novel had distracted him from seeing that the focus itself had been just what he needed as an artist. He knew that his earlier novels had been 'bulging at the seams'; *Two Solitudes* was too. Had he used Paul's point of view as a focal point, it would have meant that all the scenes that were irrelevant to his growth towards his vocation would have had to be cut; only those scenes in which he directly participated, or those which he could reasonably be expected to hear about through the people he knew, could remain. That this would not have truncated the novel's content too severely can be seen in his later novels where he managed to include not only the 'great themes' he longed to wrestle with but also several minor ones as well. 'I have never been able to know in advance whether to enter into a chronological narrative or to plunge in medias res and then explain the background through flashbacks,' he complained in 'How Do I Write?' With *Two Solitudes* he chose the former method and the omniscient point of view he so admired in *The Forsyte Saga*: within him, a battle waged between Galsworthy and Joyce, and Galsworthy won. Since Dorothy had just used the first person for such an unusual purpose as a biography in *Partner in Three Worlds* with such striking success, it is surprising that he did not try to same device. It may be that he was not prepared to sacrifice the fairness of mind and the cooler tone which he wanted his novel to convey.

Although it was admired for the wrong reasons, and misread by the majority of readers, *Two Solitudes* was an undisputed success. By mid-February 1945, a month after its publication, it appeared on the *New York Times* bestseller list; by the end of February it had climbed to eleventh place among such distinguished company as John Steinbeck's *Cannery Row* (4th), Edna Ferber's *Great Son* (6th), Lloyd C. Douglas's *The Robe* (9th), Aldous Huxley's *Time Must Have a Stop* (12th), Ayn Rand's *The Fountainhead* (14th), and Somerset Maugham's *The Razor's Edge* (15th). A.J. Cronin's *The Green Years* was first; Kathleen Winsor's controversial *Forever Amber* was second; Gwethalyn Graham's *Earth and High Heaven* was third. For the rest of the year *Two Solitudes* maintained a position on bestseller lists in the United States, and rated high on library lists in Canada, topping the Toronto list for the month of April. By March 1945 the novel was chosen as the Book of the Month Club selection; that same month it was abridged in *Omnibook* magazine. In the first week of April, Hugh and Dorothy were off to New York for a series of interviews, cocktail parties, luncheons, and dinners; there, he went on the air twice: once with Mary Margaret McBride and later on University of the Air. Meanwhile, he received hundreds of fan letters, among them one addressed simply to 'Hugh MacLennan, writer, author of "Two Solitudes" – Somewhere near the slums in Montreal.'[37] Eventually the Book of the Month Club sales alone reached 30,000 copies; by MacLennan's account, total sales in Canada and the United States skyrocketed to over 50,000 copies. Income from these and other sales, plus the *Omnibook* fee of $150, plus CBC Radio fees for a radio adaptation by Hugh Kemp of $50, netted him $3354.21 by March 1946; the $12,000 the novel eventually brought in after taxes enabled him to support himself for the next three years.[38] Negotiations were under way almost at once for a Spanish translation, and by April 1946 a Dutch translation was arranged. Despite the fact that French reviewers urged a French translation, and several translators contacted him personally offering to carry this out, no such translation appeared until 1963. This delay, which seriously affected his potential French-speaking public, was partly due to the collapse of Pariseau et Cie. who held the translation rights for three years – arrangements that had been handled by the agent he had tried to get rid of after *Barometer Rising*, Blanche Gregory. Ultimately, the novel also appeared in Swedish, Czech, Estonian, Japanese, Korean, German, and Norwegian. In March 1946, he heard rumours, confirmed shortly thereafter, that his novel was to win the laurel wreath of Canadian literature, the Governor-General's Award for fiction. In 1957 the 'Festival du Montréal' featured a stage production; in 1977 an unsuccessful film version was produced by Harry Gulkin and James Shavik and directed by Lionel Chetwynd.

In the flurry of activity that followed the publication of *Two Solitudes*, MacLennan became a public figure. As Dorothy wrote in a letter to Bill Deacon: 'neither of us manage to make a connection in our minds between the persons we know ourselves to be and the individuals who appear to have become more or less public characters.' At last, a decade later, the ambitions with which they had bravely set out together in 1936 had been realized. Both were now successful writers – Dorothy in non-fiction, Hugh in fiction. The high sales of *Two Solitudes* meant that MacLennan could resign in the spring of 1945 from Lower Canada College where, in Dorothy's opinion at least, he had always given too much of himself to his classes. 'Lord, but I'm glad to see him through with teaching,' she wrote to Deacon. 'The trouble has been that he's too good a teacher; he gives everything he's got to it, and it leaves him deflated and enervated and limp.'[39]

More money meant, too, that the MacLennans could buy a cottage in North Hatley, a small summer resort community in the Eastern

Townships of Quebec. Stone Hedge, as it was called, was situated high on the hillside overlooking the small lake, Massawippi. They had been renting each summer there since 1942, when MacLennan's former friend from Dalhousie, Hugh Turnbull, had introduced him to this charming spot. North Hatley was, and still is, a lively community, in the summer made up partly of Americans who did not like American resorts, some of whom travelled long distances by train each year to get there; in its earlier days, vacationers from the South actually pulled their blinds to avoid having to look out on Yankee territory as they passed through (today, one can still see the barrack-like building that housed their black slaves).

The summer community was a yeasty mixture of professional and creative people from Westmount, Boston, Philadelphia, as well as the South. Conversation was stimulating when people of such diverse backgrounds assembled – people such as Frank and Marian Scott; Raleigh Parkin, historian; George Homans, Harvard sociologist; Craig Wylie, editor, later editor-in-chief of Houghton Mifflin Press; Eloise Bergland, poet; Isabel Dobell, author, later curator of the McCord Museum in Montreal; Frank Keppel of *Time* magazine; William Bender, dean of admissions, Harvard University; the Ogilvys of Montreal; Mason Wade; Bernard de Voto, Dorothy's former English professor at Northwestern; Gregory Armstrong, editor of *Foreign Affairs*; Ogden Nash, president of Bishop's University in Lennoxville. These people, with their chintz-and-wicker summer style, provided the best and most exciting social conversation the MacLennans had known. Night after night, at informal dinner parties, cocktail parties, and at the local beach club, they engaged in discussions about art, politics, history, publishing, social happenings, and sports. MacLennan's essay 'Everyone Knows the Rules' (1951) captures the gaiety of these social sparring matches.[40] Coming to North Hatley was in many ways a 'homecoming' for MacLennan, for there he came closest to his good times at the Waegwoltic Club in Halifax while a student at Dalhousie. He could relax, and find listeners for the theories he wanted to sound out – listeners that were worth impressing if he could do so.

As in Halifax, he became deeply involved in the tennis matches run by the local club. The matches he played there are still recalled with glee by local residents. His main opponent was John Bassett, a younger, taller man, who was to inherit the Toronto *Telegram* from his father and become an enormously successful businessman in Toronto. So heated was the competition between these two men – one who had to win, the other who could not bear to lose, as one observer described it – that whenever they played children ran up and down the streets calling people to come and watch. Although MacLennan never lost a singles game to Bassett, he did lose many a doubles match playing alongside Page Dane, a Philadelphia lawyer, against Bassett and his partner Jim Barclay. When he did lose, his reactions could be spectacular: throwing his racket away, he would fall down on the grass and tear it up with his bare hands, or pitch himself in fury onto the wire fence that surrounded the court, such was his frustration at losing. Dorothy meanwhile, was so involved as a spectator, holding distilled water, salt pills, and wrist bandages for her husband, and calling out advice, that she seemed to control him as if he were an extension of her strategies. MacLennan fought as persistently for success on the tennis court as he did in the literary arena.

It was at North Hatley, too, and under Dorothy's influence, that he took up a hobby that was to afford him great satisfaction – gardening. 'Three years ago,' Dorothy recalled in April 1945, 'he laughed at me for wasting time putting seeds in the ground. Never expected to see them grow, and begrudged every minute he spent helping me to spade and hoe. It really wasn't much of a garden that first year, but you'll never be able to tell him so. It was a terrific miracle to him, and now he spares no labor ... some day, when his tomatoes cease to be a great wonder to him, he's going in for roses. He's listening to their siren-call this spring.' MacLennan eventually did respond to the siren call of roses, as his charming essay 'The Secret and Voluptuous Life of a Rose-Grower' (1954) eloquently attests.

Now that they had bought Stone Hedge, they stayed much longer each year in North Hatley – from May to October. For the first time, MacLennan started to turn down public speaking engagements and radio broadcasts. 'Up here,' Dorothy wrote, like the business manager and public relations agent she had become, 'the book can speak for itself. Ministers are preaching laudatory sermons on it in Montreal already, and the French-Canadian reaction is extremely good, to put it mildly. It doesn't need any further comment from the author.'[41] Instead, he turned his spare time into learning French, signing up for conversation courses in the hope that he could eventually become as fluent in French as in English and so, like his character Paul, more authoritatively represent Canada. He also looked to the possibilities of film. Gwethalyn Graham's sale of *Earth and High Heaven* to Sam Goldwyn rankled. In a script that still exists he wrote the scenario for a story to be set in Halifax after the Second World War. 'Background for Original Story on Halifax' did not, however, outline any plot; it simply explored the scenic and social possibilities offered by post-war Halifax for such a story. He displayed a good filmic sense, linking character closely with environment, especially with the sea. Paramount Pictures turned it down, but he kept his eye on the market for film, as therein lay the single most lucrative aspect of writing at the time.[42]

He also took up again the injustices of the Canadian tax laws in regard to writers. At the twenty-fifth anniversary convention of the Canadian Authors' Association, at the end of June 1946, he joined Gwethalyn Graham in attempting to work out an argument against the government for a fairer system. Graham in particular had an axe to grind: the enormous sales of *Earth and High Heaven* and the sale of the movie rights combined to earn her a spectacular amount of money for the year 1945. As far as the tax office was concerned, earnings such as these were taxed without regard to the fact that this was a once-in-a-lifetime deal. This meant that a writer could not pro-rate any windfall, such as the one Graham – and MacLennan, too, with *Two Solitudes* – had experienced, over more than one year. Taxes were consequently devastating, and seriously affected the writer's ability to be self-supporting.

None the less, MacLennan at last was happy and free to write. For him, this was the real 'beginning' of what he hoped would become a full-fledged career as a novelist. His next novel started to take form from a basis more solid, more secure, than any previous one. Looking back on the novel just completed, he hoped his next would not 'swell into anything as long and difficult as *Two Solitudes*. At present it seems simpler, which may well not be the case later on.' Looking ahead, he felt enormous confidence. As he had written to Bill Deacon in early April 1945: 'I had to write that book [*Two Solitudes*] to orientate myself toward any future work I might do. It is my complete conviction that no writer can function in a vacuum. As his point of view, his method of regarding phenomena, derives from his childhood environment, he can't help writing out of the society in which he was produced. It gradually dawned on me – very gradually, I'm afraid – that so far as I was concerned my own society was obscure, not clear-cut, a queer congeries of various subtle inner and outer relationships which in my own time were gradually coming into focus. Unless it were possible for me somehow to effect something of a fusion of this Canadian dichotomy, I felt myself stymied. *Two Solitudes* was the result of that, and now that it is finished, I feel greatly released. Whatever the book may have done for others, for me it has put something like solid ground under my feet.'[43]

At work in 'Stone Hedge,' North Hatley

Chapter seven

Charting a Course: *The Precipice*

The tremendous public success of *Two Solitudes* posed questions of the utmost seriousness. In 1946, at the age of thirty-nine, MacLennan stood poised on the brink of a future he could only guess at. What he wanted to achieve is made amply clear by his statements in letters, articles, and speeches: he wished to maintain himself financially as a writer, and he preferred to stay in Canada rather than move to the United States, even though success there appeared to lie down easier paths. To fulfil these ambitions he engaged in a struggle to understand the forces at work in his surroundings. Attempting to gauge market trends, public tastes, Canada's probable cultural future, the combination of factors that had spelled success for other writers, and to assess publishers' agreements along with their financial implications, he applied the full force of his mind towards the consolidation of his career. *Barometer Rising* had been a promising and successful novel; *Two Solitudes* had widened considerably his reputation well beyond national borders. What should he write about now to make the most of this momentum?

Looking carefully at the success of writers currently in fashion, he came to a conclusion, with Dorothy's help as usual, that dramatically affected his theories of literature from this point on. As he wrote to his friend Bill Deacon in May: 'Writers like Proust, Gide, Isherwood and Waugh, who probably have the greatest prestige of any now practicing (Proust, though dead, still lives in influence) have bothered me all the past year. Suddenly, thanks to Dorothy, I realized not only that I had nothing basic to learn from them, but why their influence is so bad – both for writing and for society. The whole damn lot are homosexuals. The ultimate in decadence, that the interpreters of society should see life through a homo-sexual's eye, and that the intellectuals of society should accept such a view. Waugh, of course, is not strictly that; certainly not in the literal sense. But his point of view is. I admire these men vastly for their skill, but I think their influence is corrosive.'

The 'mind of the maiden aunt,' towards which MacLennan had been so condescending in *Two Solitudes*, lurked closer than he thought. His own puritanical upbringing blinded him here to the high order of human perception and artistic achievement these writers had attained. They were hardly the 'ultimate in decadence,' and no doubt it was reckless of him to abandon such potential models so inflexibly. Certainly this view resulted in a decidedly *moral* base for his theories of art. In the same letter he revealed a second blind spot: he thought that his talents lay in fiction alone and that he had no particular flair for the essay form. 'I often envy a man like yourself,' he confessed to Deacon, 'who can write articles and non-fiction so well. I'm hopelessly inept at both, and fundamentally have little to say in both. My sole talent consists in fusing thought with emotion within a certain symbolic form.'

Having settled it that fiction was his genre, and also that his writing must uphold sound moral principles despite the current trend towards so-called 'decadence,' he turned his attention to the particular type of novel that might now be appropriate in the evolving national literature in which he had already played so great a part. Regionalism was his bête noire. 'I think Canadian literature has been done harm,' he had written to Deacon in March, 'by the indiscriminate praise bestowed in the past on costume novels and third rate stuff. That is beside the point. The whole issue, to my mind, rests now on whether it will be possible for us to join the mainstream of world literature or whether we are doomed to be considered regional.'[1]

His examination of this problem forms the whole theme of an article that appeared in September in the *Saturday Review of Literature*, 'Canada between Covers.' If Canadians are to reach international audiences, he argued, 'how are we to bridge the vast gap that lies between our own social evolution and that of older nations of the world?' After showing how the contemporary literary era was an exhausted 'decadence' (Proust, Joyce, Thomas Mann, Aldous Huxley, Evelyn Waugh were his examples) – the literary cycle begun during the

Renaissance giving one last dying gasp – he theorized that in the United States there had arisen 'a branch cycle' of literature that dealt mainly with the 'peculiar fringes of American life, and not with its heart.' He then asked whether Canadian writers ought to follow 'the decaying Renaissance culture of Europe' or consider themselves part of 'the American branch cycle.' He chose the latter: 'Canadians must write for the American market because it is the cultural pattern to which they naturally belong. It is their only avenue to a world audience.'

He was extremely careful to delineate exactly how Canadian writers were to accomplish this aim. Above all, they must *not* move to the United States and become American: 'Canada is in search of herself today. She is desperately in need of interpretation, not only to herself by one of her own, but to the rest of the world as well.' 'A Canadian writer, like any other artist,' he continued, 'must write out of his own background.'[2] But if he were to avoid the narrowly regional novels MacLennan deplored, he must also choose, within these familiar settings, themes that were truly 'universal.'

On more than one occasion he used Canadian novels other than his own as examples of the type of universality he felt could be achieved in Canada. In particular, he cited Gwethalyn Graham's *Earth and High Heaven*, not only because of its indisputable success but also because it had begun a whole trend, in his opinion, of 'race relations' stories. He also referred to Gabrielle Roy's *Bonheur d'Occasion* (1945), a novel, based on the author's observations of Montreal's St Henri district after she had moved east from Manitoba in 1939, which showed universal conditions in a Canadian wartime setting. MacLennan had just met Gabrielle Roy in April 1946, an occasion he cherished: 'We finally made her acquaintance, and she spent three hours over tea with us. Her personality confirms, and more than confirms, the opinion I had formed of her from her book. She's a first-class human being, and probably the best natural novelist this country has ever had. I think she'll go on beyond *Bonheur d'Occasion* and keep on developing.'[3] In his own writing, he clearly aimed to go on developing as well.

In his personal life, the need for more money prevailed. In a grim letter to his publisher in New York, Charles Duell, in March 1947, he confided why his next novel was not yet ready: 'I had hoped to finish at least by now, but I have had to interrupt work on it to write articles and give lectures because I needed the money. And during the past month Dorothy has been seriously ill and I have had to be nurse, cook and housekeeper. She is on the mend now, thank God. And I anticipate no further interruptions, except for a couple of weeks in Banff in August – again to make a little extra from two weeks of lectures.' This letter is important in understanding the extent to which he was by now aggressively crafting his own career. Essentially, he had written to ask Duell to reconsider the terms of his contract for the new novel. He argued that he must have a separate Canadian contract. He had already persuaded Duell to raise the royalty rate on his next book; now, he argued, if that increased rate were to be added to the costs of Collins in Canada, they might well decide not to print a Canadian edition of the book at all, especially since paper, cloth, and bindings were in short supply in Canada as they were in the United States immediately after the war. Furthermore, a single contract would force him to make his subsequent dealings for reprintings, radio broadcasts, and anthologies through Duell, Sloan and Pearce instead of directly with Collins. As he explained to Duell: 'The past few years have shown me that such a situation is intolerable for me as one of the leading Canadian writers, and should it continue I can have no confidence whatever in my future as a Canadian writer *in Canada* ... This whole situation ... will have to be resolved before the novel is finished. The position I have assumed in Canada is the result almost entirely of my own efforts, aside from my published books. Over a period of five years I have written carefully considered articles, given considered addresses, and refused to make ten times as many more which would not have accumulated to my benefit. At the moment, the Canadian market is the one thing on which I feel I can rely entirely. I am forty years old. I don't write easily and I don't write glibly. I have yet to repeat myself. I have plenty more books in me, but none of them will come out quickly, and I have got to make certain plans for my future ... At the moment of writing, deep in the labour of it, I need the sustaining force of knowing that I can at least rely on something definite, and not be haunted, as I now am, by the knowledge that during the best years of my life my years of working in the Canadian market – and indeed in partially creating its present dimensions – are profiting almost everyone concerned [but] myself.' His arguments won the day. With this, his third published novel, he successfully negotiated his first separate Canadian contract with Collins.

By the time this letter was sent, in March 1947, MacLennan had actually written two-thirds of the novel. 'But I still cannot hurry the last third,' he told Duell, 'for the book is such a tightly knit organism, is in my belief such a great advance over *Two Solitudes* both in scope and depth, and even in construction, that every attempt to hurry it has been a failure.'[4] Later he was to feel that, even as it was, he had submitted the manuscript too soon: 'I think I would have done better to have waited ... longer than I did, but at that time I couldn't write non-fiction and thought fiction was all I could do.' But he was impatient to get it into print. This was a novel for which he had great expectations and for which he forecast not only great success in Canada but also 'a far wider appeal in the United States,' even to the point of a possible movie version.[5]

Meanwhile, Dorothy's health continued to decline dramatically. On New Year's Day 1948, she suffered a severe embolism which almost took her life. An invalid for the three months following, she was not at all well by the autumn, and was ordered by her doctor to seek out a warmer climate for the winter. Thus they left the day after MacLennan, feeling 'like an empty pail,' finished the final revisions on his novel, and drove across the United States in mid-December 1948, 'with winter nipping at our heels all the way to the Gulf of Mexico.' They stayed with Dorothy's retired parents until April at South Laguna, California – a setting MacLennan enjoyed thoroughly, though he missed his friends at home.[6] Dorothy's health during this winter sojourn marked yet another relapse; but had they not sought out the warm climate, she might have died.

MacLennan's third novel, *The Precipice*, was inspired by Anthony Tudor's ballet *Pillar of Fire*, an American Ballet Theatre production which he and Dorothy had seen in New York in the spring of 1946.[7] In its first performance on 8 April 1942, *Pillar of Fire* had signalled the emergence of an erotic and modern mode of ballet: both Anthony Tudor, choreographer and male lead, and Nora Kaye, the spectacular prima ballerina, soared into instant popularity to an ovation of twenty-six curtain calls. This enthusiasm – especially for the dramatic abilities of Miss Kaye in her role as Hagar – continued well beyond the year in which MacLennan saw the production.

Why Nora Kaye should have gripped his imagination is not difficult to understand. Her public appeal was based on her flamboyance in dramatic roles: she was, above all, a *character* dancer. With his great interest in drama, perhaps above all other art forms, MacLennan was, like the audience in general, entranced. Nora Kaye brought emotion and sensuality into an art form previously thought to be 'cool' in tone. She was vital – and sexy. Beyond that, dark and statuesque, she so resembled Dorothy that she might have passed for her twin. She was unmistakably the 'type' of woman who would have appealed to MacLennan.

Pillar of Fire caught his attention for other reasons. Before seeing the ballet he had been mulling over two ideas in relation to his next novel. At the suggestion of his friend, the Ottawa journalist Blair Fraser, he was considering setting a novel in 'darkest Ontario' – not Toronto, but those small towns scattered throughout the province which still embodied what he had called 'the mind of the maiden aunt.' Puritanism had long since gone sour in the United States, Fraser pointed out, and showed signs of being about to do the same in Canada. This sociological transition, he surmised, might prove to be an interesting subject for a writer. Receptive to the idea, MacLennan had spent a week or so in the three Ontario lakeshore towns of Port Hope, Cobourg, and Belleville, chatting with the people and getting a feel for the countryside. At Port Hope he had seen a huge sanitary company that had degenerated into mass-producing second-rate items because it had recently been taken over by an American company. Listening, as he must have done, to the outrage of some of the townspeople at this takeover of their interests, gave him the idea for Grenville's similar economic shift, in the novel, to American production methods and the chain of consequences both personal and national that took place.

At the same time as he considered his setting, he was toying with the idea that he would like to try to make his central character a woman; the challenge would be to present convincingly the female point of view. This idea had come from Dorothy. At this time she was herself working on a novel that was never published about sorority life in Chicago, based on her experiences as an undergraduate at Northwestern University.[8] MacLennan was reading her manuscript with an eye to improvement, just as she had always read his, and it was probably their discussions of the several female personalities in Dorothy's book that suggested to him the possibility of trying something along similar lines.

Be that as it may, seeing *Pillar of Fire* in 1946 produced in him 'an immediate strong creative feeling.' Here, with surprising suddenness, was an electrifying story which drew together the themes uppermost in his mind. Hagar, the middle one of three sisters, undergoes a sexual awakening in a small puritan community which transports her from a narrow upbringing and potential spinsterhood into the full blossoming of womanhood. As Dorothy commented after the ballet: 'There, Hugh, is the plot for your novel, right there.'[9] MacLennan returned to see this 'remarkable ballet' a second time, confirming his first impression. After six months of thinking and drafting his plot, in the fall of 1946 he began to write. By the time he wrote to Charles Duell on 5 March 1947, he had still not named his work, unless, as he wrote on that occasion, 'we can call it *Pillar of Fire*.'

This was by no means the first transposition of *Pillar of Fire* from one art form into another. Originally, the story had appeared in a poem sequence called *Weib und die Welt* (*Woman and the World*) by the nineteenth-century German romantic poet Richard Dehmel. As a student at Oxford, MacLennan had read some of the poems in *The Oxford Book of German Verse*. The sequence in its entirety describes with great passion an altercation between two lovers in which the woman confesses that she is pregnant through a casual relationship with a worthless man. This experience, she says, has taught her how superficial the relationship has been, and how true is the love she now knows. As they walk through the moonlit woods, the man forgives her, accepts her, and maintains that their love is so great that it will overcome their difficulties in the same way that the moon transfigures the night. This poem sequence, in time, was to inspire Arnold Schönberg's modern musical composition *Verklärte Nacht* (*Transfigured Night*). And it was this music, in turn, which suggested the ballet to its choreographer Anthony Tudor.[10]

As George Balanchine explained in his *New Complete Stories of the Great Ballets*, Tudor 'takes this story and presents it dramatically, introducing additional characters, giving us a picture of the community in which such an event can take place, motivating the characters as completely as possible.'[11] In keeping with the biblical title he had chosen, Tudor named his main character 'Hagar' to suggest the Egyptian bondswoman of Abraham who is sent by Sarah, his wife, to conceive a child by him; having done so, she becomes an outcast, wandering in the desert until God gives her direction. This name, Tudor recalled, suggested to him the original 'lost woman'; the biblical context he added also suggested a night transfigured not so much by moonlight and love as by divine revelation.

Hagar, in *Pillar of Fire*, has two sisters: the 'Eldest Sister' is a rigid, church-going spinster who dominates the household; the 'Youngest Sister' is a pretty, insubstantial flirt. The two men who correspond to the true lover and the casual lover in *Weib und die Welt* appear in the ballet as the 'Friend' and the 'Young Man from the House Opposite.' The community in which Tudor sets these characters is Victorian, in keeping with the date of *Verklärte Nacht* (1899), and is puritanical in order to set up a moral framework in which Dehmel's tale can most fully express dramatic conflict.

This, then, is the history that lay behind the ballet MacLennan saw, a history of which he was at least partially aware through his reading of Dehmel. He took the central story and its characters wholesale for his own novel *The Precipice*. Like Hagar, Lucy Cameron is the middle sister of three and the story concerns her sexual awakening to womanhood through her affair with Stephen Lassiter, a young American industrialist who is roughly parallel to the casual lover in *Pillar of Fire*. Certainly her affair with him scandalizes the puritanical Victorian town of Grenville, much as did Hagar's with the 'Young Man from the House Opposite.' The 'Friend' from the ballet becomes, in MacLennan's novel, Bruce Fraser, Lucy's next-door neighbour.

In a number of ways *The Precipice* betrays its origin. Lucy is in appearance and essence exactly like Nora Kaye in her role as Hagar: 'She moved with the quiet grace of a shy animal, yet in all her movements there was an air of conscious control, as though she hoped whatever she did would escape notice. This same characteristic was even more marked in her face. It was an intelligent face ... essentially a proud face. Her chin and the upper part of her head could have modelled a cameo, clean-cut and distant. But in the eyes and mouth unknown qualities brooded. Her large eyes were brown and widely spaced, with curving brows. Her lips were soft, warm, and sensuous. These features, together with her air of dignified solitude, combined to give her the prevailing expression of a woman who has never been recognized by others for what she knows herself to be.' In his descriptions of the five principal characters taken from *Pillar of Fire*, MacLennan habitually emphasizes movement, as if the physical stage presence of the dancers were still before his eyes: Lucy, here, 'moved' with 'quiet grace'; elsewhere, Stephen 'moved on the [tennis] court with feline precision'; Jane, the eldest sister, is 'brisk'; Nina, the youngest sister, has a 'short neat body that was never still' and 'gambols.' Even the setting for the turning point in Lucy's transformation occurs at a dance to which Stephen takes her, after which she 'never felt herself a spectator again.'[12] This scene is strongly reminiscent of the section of *Pillar of Fire* in which Hagar dances with the 'Young Man from the House Opposite' before they enter his house where her sexual initiation takes place. During this scene in the ballet the 'Youngest Sister' has danced off-stage with the 'Friend,' a situation roughly paralleled by Nina's taking Bruce Fraser as her partner at the same dance in *The Precipice*.

Although the basic theme of a woman's transformation through natural physical love to the full awareness of womanhood is essentially unchanged from ballet to novel, the alterations MacLennan did make are worth noting. These changes mainly concern the roles of the two men. Both in Dehmel's poem sequence and in Tudor's biblical story line, there is one man, a casual lover, with whom the woman conceives a child out of wedlock, and another man representing a more permanent type who, knowing her predicament, can forgive and love her. MacLennan alters this situation considerably. Lucy Cameron does not become pregnant out of wedlock, although she is seduced; she marries the divorced Lassiter and remains with him, despite his later betrayal of her. Bruce Fraser, on the other hand, unlike Dehmel's true lover and Tudor's 'Friend,' never has an affair with Lucy at all, though he realizes after she has married Lassiter that he has been in love with her for some time. He marries nobody. MacLennan thus censors the original story. Lucy can, in the reader's eyes, be excused from Grenville's charges of 'adulteress' at the time she falls in love with Stephen, since she does not know of his former marriage and his divorce is imminent; more important, she is faithful to him throughout. Stephen's brief affair long after he has married Lucy remains the only categorical infringement of established social and moral codes.

Why did MacLennan clean up the original story like this? First of all, he was, as we have seen, in direct opposition to what he considered the 'decadence' of current fiction, especially the 'cynicism' of Hemingway. His aim, in part, was to avoid the kind of sensationalism that was likely to encourage immoral behaviour – or at least to show immoral behaviour as unsuccessful in the context of his story. Consequently, he allowed Lucy to compromise her reputation only in so far as it served his purpose of exposing the too rigid puritanism of Grenville. The fact that he thereby betrayed his own puritanism seems to have escaped him. As well, a certain gallantry on his part can be detected here: hard though he is on Stephen's lapses from morality, he seems to have wished to protect Lucy from too great a fall from grace. Above all, though, his motives were practical: he wished to avoid the kind of criticism his two previous novels had unjustly received for their 'loose morality.'

As for his characterization of Bruce Fraser, he made him the kind of stoical friend who lets his love for Lucy go untold like the proverbial 'worm in the bud.' He thus sacrificed the tension and irony in the ballet that results from the 'Youngest Sister's' attraction to the two men interested in Hagar. With Bruce, he provided instead a male parallel to

Lucy, his life contrasting with hers. Lucy's true nature is seen and nurtured by Stephen; Bruce is not lucky enough to meet anyone to do the same for him. Like Nick Carraway in Fitzgerald's *The Great Gatsby*, Bruce is the observer who merely looks on and records the lives of those more passionate than himself. Had MacLennan allowed him to narrate the story, as he was later to do with similar characters in *The Watch That Ends the Night* and *Voices in Time*, the novel would have been a stronger and more ironic one. With Bruce occurs the first appearance of the 'Everyman' theme, which would be brought to full fruition in *The Watch That Ends the Night*. It must have been Hagar's anguished isolation at the beginning of *Pillar of Fire* which most struck him as emblematic of the human condition for men as well as for women. He seems not only to have recognized in Hagar a type of the Canadian woman in small towns throughout the nation but also to have identified himself with her role. Through *Pillar of Fire* and the recasting of its themes in *The Precipice*, MacLennan was to strike the motherlode that was not fully mined until *The Watch That Ends the Night* almost a decade later.

Although *Pillar of Fire* provided the genesis of *The Precipice*, any reader will recognize at once that MacLennan did not let this framework stand on its own. He fleshed it out with themes, characters, and concerns that overwhelm the 'Cinderella' plot of Lucy's story. Even the novel's title testifies to the centrality of another theme suggested by the Port Hope sanitary company – that of the puritanical drive for material success that motivates the American industrialist Stephen Lassiter.

MacLennan, as we have seen, at this point hoped to join 'the American branch cycle' of current literature; in 'Canada between Covers' he had expressed his belief that Canadians had to write for the American market because it was to that culture that they naturally belonged, and one through which they had a chance to reach international markets. He also needed money, and beyond that he wanted success and fame. *Two Solitudes* had proved that his main market and reputation were located in the United States. His wife, herself ambitious to publish a novel to cap her success as a non-fiction writer, was American and intended to remain so. There is every reason to believe that they shared an image of themselves as a lively literary couple launched on internationally famous careers. It was absolutely logical, therefore, for MacLennan to aim *The Precipice* at an American audience. It would not be enough to settle for the story of Lucy Cameron in Grenville, Ontario. Her lover must be American, her life with him after marriage must move to two of the American cities MacLennan knew best, New York and Princeton. To take the story out of Grenville would also increase its chances for universality. Fearful that his work would be considered merely 'regional,' he tried, by crossing the border in his fiction, to ensure that critics would not attach that label to his work. Thus he hoped to march along that 'avenue to a world audience' he longed to reach. As he wrote in March 1947 in an article called 'Do We Gag Our Writers?': 'It is [the] opportunity [for Canadian writers] to hammer out a literary pattern for Canadian life. They must capture the flavour of the varying shades of Canadian speech, bring the landscape to life as our painters have done, make visible the small towns of the provinces and the changes wrought when small-town people move into larger cities. And they can't afford to stop there. Somehow they must go on, and link up the pattern in Canada with the patterns of older nations.'[13]

This article is but one of three that appeared during the time he was writing *The Precipice* in which we can see him formulating his own theories of fiction. Uppermost in his mind was the concept of nationality. What did it mean to be 'Canadian,' especially as defined against 'American'? In 'How We Differ from Americans' and in 'Canada for Canadians' as well, published respectively in December 1946 and May 1947, he speculated that current problems for Canadian writers could be explained largely by Canada's proximity to the United States. He observed, as was commonly believed, that there was a noticeable 'time lag' in Canada, which put her, as a nation, forty or fifty years behind her southern neighbour.[14] For a writer, this meant that the Canadian background must be explained to readers in much the same way American writers half a century before had described the characteristics of each region. While American writers were now able to write within a nationalistic frame of reference, Canadians still thought provincially. In a wider sense, proximity to the United States presented a painful contrast for those who wished to write, as MacLennan did, of national themes. The United States was a large, powerful nation much like the Roman Empire, with a dramatic history of wars fought and won; thus world interest was focused on her writers. By contrast, Canada was a small country in which evolution, not revolution, had been the guiding political and social principle; consequently, she was of little interest to the world at large. Here MacLennan cast Canada as an Oxyrhynchus to the United States' Rome.

This situation, he argued in 'Do We Gag Our Writers?' posed real problems for a writer like himself, who perceived that he must write in what he took to be the main current of contemporary literature – the sociological novel. Citing Sinclair Lewis' *Babbitt* and Arthur Koestler's *Darkness at Noon*, as well as works by Fitzgerald, Hemingway, John Dos Passos, Eugene O'Neill, and Sherwood Anderson, he observed that 'The serious novel of modern times has usually concentrated on what I have called social symbolism – on man in his relation with organized society, with politics, war, economic conditions, with the local morals of a specific group.' Although he personally did not believe that this was the highest form of literature, preferring instead the 'heroic' literature of the Greeks and of Shakespeare which embodied more universal themes, he resigned himself to writing in this 'social' tradition: 'At the present it is not practical for any writer, in Canada or anywhere else, to leave out of his work the effect of his own society on his characters.' By 'not practical' he meant that a writer could not hope to make money enough to live on if he did not follow the route then currently in fashion. Though he admitted that he would prefer to write more 'heroic' and more 'universal' novels, and felt as well that 'the sociological novel has already neared the saturation point in human interest,' he did not choose to follow his own instincts as an artist. Instead he left that for writers of the next generation: 'At this moment – somewhere in the Maritime provinces, somewhere in Ontario or the West, perhaps in Montreal itself – there may be an unknown young man who has within him the genius to discover an entirely new form of writing.'

If he was to write in the sociological tradition in order to be 'practical,' and if he was to 'link up' the pattern in Canada with that of 'older nations' (that is, the United States in particular), he must analyse and understand the sociological trends both in Canada and in those nations. He was struggling to define 'Canadian' and 'American.' Well, how did they differ?[15] The main difference, as he saw it, could be traced to that forty-year time-lag, which had seen a revolution against puritanism in the United States but had left Canada's original puritanism intact. 'Darkest Ontario,' as Blair Fraser had pointed out, was a striking example of a type of puritanism that contrasted dramatically with American mores: Canadians were conservative, cautious, restrained; Americans, as a result of this revolt against puritanism, were more optimistic and outgoing, unafraid to make mistakes, franker about sex, concerned with accomplishing whatever would increase their wealth and pride as a nation.

Although MacLennan was jealous of the freedom with which American writers could ignore background description, he did not envy a good many of the results of this revolution against puritanism. While he deplored the puritanical severity of some Canadians, mainly when it was expressed in censorship of books like his own in which writers used sex not for sensationalism but to portray life honestly, he saw worse problems in the United States where the rebellion had, in effect, thrown out the baby with the bathwater. As far as literature was concerned, a whole stream of fiction based on sex had arisen for the sake of sensationalism alone; his example remained Kathleen Winsor's best-selling *Forever Amber*, which he deplored. The divorce rate was rising at an alarming pace as the social fabric weakened. Concentration on achievements had resulted in a kind of 'hardness' of mind: Americans, as a group, he wrote, are 'as coldly impersonal as steel'; their emphasis on technology had accelerated life's pace to an inhuman degree. Canadians, with their slower pace of evolution, might, he speculated, have a better deal in the end: 'At the present time of transition, our small size of population makes the strains easier. In facing the future, we are less the prisoners of our own past. For it seems that nothing but catastrophe can check the furious progress of Americans into a still more bleak and dangerous desert of technology than they have reached now. The very vastness of the apparatus their genius has created stands over them now like a strange and terrible master ... Canadians have as yet fallen in love with no such Frankenstein.'

These theories of literature and society go a long way towards explaining the tone of *The Precipice*. The novel's title, arising as it did from the biblical parable of the Gadarene swine rushing blindly off a cliff to their own destruction, was a symbol at the heart of the novel reflecting MacLennan's views on American technology. It stood as a lesson to Canadians and Americans alike that rapid social change was likely to come to no good, and that technology was apt to prove a Frankenstein's monster if moral considerations did not govern its development and application. By fixing on the general theme of puritanism, he was able to link patterns in Canadian life with those in the United States, thus widening both the scope of his novel and its potential audience. To show the differences between the two societies in regard to puritanism, he brought into play the effect of the American efficiency expert Stephen Lassiter on the Canadian girl Lucy Cameron. In this way he showed how an aggressive society affected a more passive and weak one whose economy was closely intertwined with its own. The impact of urban life with its extensive industrial environment on those who move from rural communities is demonstrated in Lucy's elopement with Stephen to New York. The immorality in

American life he abhorred is shown in Stephen's affairs, but also in the many divorces in the novel. To themes already complex he added his personal indictment of American advertising through the villain Carl Bratian, whose Romanian name he had gleaned from his immigrant barber in Montreal; Bratian stood for the awful manipulation of Western civilization through the techniques of advertising MacLennan had read about in Frederic Wakeman's *The Hucksters*.[16] 'Social symbolism': this was MacLennan's mode in *The Precipice* as he wove with considerable skill the many influences on him and the many considerations he had gauged to chart the novel's success.

In 'Do We Gag Our Writers?' he stated: 'It is one thing to recognize a need, and an entirely different thing to fulfill it. Art can't be organized by the government or created like an automobile factory by an act of will. It is a mysterious activity.' And yet, in a letter several months later to Bill Deacon, on 12 January 1948, he seemed to contradict this statement. 'What is a genius?' he speculated. 'Surely it is nothing but a peculiar combination of will-power, tenacity, and the ability to make one's subconscious work for one.' Although he suggests that the perfect novel for a time and place cannot be *willed* into existence, there is reason to believe that in his attempts to craft his career at this point he was trying to do exactly that. He had deliberately chosen a type of fiction he believed would be popular, rather than the type he personally preferred. He had done a masterful job in analysing the current situation in writing throughout the English-speaking world. He had been particularly careful to assess precisely the political, social, and cultural relationship of Canada to the United States. He had anticipated contract difficulties with his publisher to ensure a fair deal for himself. There is something unusual about the phrase 'hammer out' that he had applied to Canadian writers in their present situation; his own sheer will-power and determination are almost tangible in the term. We can imagine with what physical and mental force he was himself 'hammering out' the novel he believed *must*, by joining the 'branch cycle' of American literature, advance Canadian literature and his own career.[17] As with *Barometer Rising*, he made the decision here to follow logic and the advice of his wife and friends rather than risk failure through following his own instincts. How his career might have been different, had he not done so, is impossible to say, but it's probable that he would have developed more essentially as a *writer*.

Just before *The Precipice* was launched in June 1948, MacLennan felt uneasy: 'When I finished *The Precipice* and mailed it to Toronto and New York, I had a vague presentiment, which grew over the months, that the hopes I had once had that the book would mean a good deal financially were going to be dashed. The presentiment grew in spite of the fact that Duell, Sloan and Pearce felt it was the best book they had ever received and were confident of a [Book of the Month Club] selection.'[18] These fears, as it turned out, were justified; the novel sold only about one quarter the number *Two Solitudes* had during the first sales period (about 11,000 in the trade edition as compared to 42,000). He placed the blame for his novel's failure, as he came to see it, squarely on the shoulders of his publishers, forgetting that he did nothing to alter their plans as he could have done. Both in the timing of publication and in the advertising press, Duell, Sloan and Pearce in the United States and Collins in Canada let him down. The book appeared in Canada on 17 June 1948, but was not released in the United States until three months later, on 8 September. As a consequence, the Canadian reviews preceded the more favourable American ones, and the inevitable influence of American reviewers on the Canadian public and critics was lost. Furthermore, the low-key press releases at the time of publication did not present the book as he wanted it presented. This, at any rate, is how he interpreted events, and he never changed his mind.

That he was experiencing difficulties with his publishers long before publication is evident. In his letter to Charles Duell in March 1947 he had complained of receiving unsympathetic treatment; in fact, he had thought it necessary to be unusually aggressive in demanding fair rights in relation to his prospective Canadian publisher, Collins, by insisting on a separate Canadian contract. His correspondent at Collins had been Frank Appleton, a man with whom he felt *en rapport*. Appleton, however, had left the company by the beginning of 1948, a fact MacLennan noted with regret in a letter to Bill Deacon, because it meant his manuscript was caught mid-stream: 'Since delivering the mss. six weeks ago, I've received only the barest note from them, a contrast to my N.Y. publisher, who has maintained a steady flow of correspondence. Not that I require anything of Collins, or they of me, but I do miss the idea of Frank being around. With all his limitations – and mainly they seem to have been limitations in organizing the bureaucracy of the office – he was in many respects a great publisher. I hope the new order will continue to consult him, for he had an irreplaceable instinct for his work and for his particular market.' In the same letter he commented that 'it seems definite that Collins will publish in the late Spring while they [Duell, Sloan and Pearce] will publish in the autumn.' At this point, he seems to have had no particular objection to this plan. Six months later he even sounded eager to have the earlier Canadian publication since it would mean the book would start earning money a little sooner. 'In the States,' he wrote Deacon, '[the new book will] probably not [appear] until September, but there's a good chance of a Canadian publication in May or June.'[19]

Collins had also irritated him by selling permission for the inclusion of the Halifax explosion section from *Barometer Rising* in an anthology edited by John D. Robins, *A Pocketful of Canada,* which they were publishing, without either notifying him or sending him promptly his share of the sale.[20] Now, their blurb for *The Precipice* upset him greatly. Reading that blurb today, there seems little to object to, but MacLennan may have taken exception to the fact that it emphasized the grandeur of *Two Solitudes,* and then went on to describe the life portrayed in *The Precipice* as 'an existence of monotony'; furthermore, it centred attention on the contrast between the 'deadness' of small-town life and the 'artificiality' of New York, rather than the themes he thought he had handled so well.

Interest in MacLennan's new novel had reached a high pitch by the time it appeared in Canada. The majority of reviewers confessed their eager anticipation of the book that would follow the success of *Barometer Rising* and *Two Solitudes*. What they hoped to see, however, was not the novel MacLennan provided. Looking back at the reviews that greeted the Canadian publication of *The Precipice,* compared to the later American reviews, it is apparent that they do fall far short of the unanimous praise he desired. Perhaps *no* novel could have lived up to expectations of this order. Some reviewers felt downright betrayed. Jack Scott, in a review for the Vancouver *Sun* on 23 June 1948 entitled 'Novelist Denies His Canadianism,' gave the most extreme version of a reaction that infected a number of reviews:

> It is my guess that we can kiss Hugh MacLennan good-bye as a distinctly Canadian novelist ... [*The Precipice*] obviously has been written with a careful eye on sales south of the border. The result is somewhat disappointing for the Canadian reader ...
>
> 'Two Solitudes' ... was ... a promise of a potentially great Canadian novelist. 'The Precipice' reduces the promise to a whisper.
>
> I suppose it couldn't have worked out any other way. A purely Canadian scene is faint recommendation for a novel in the United States. The Canadian market, alone, is hardly enough to keep an author in typewriter ribbons ... The book may well be a best-seller in America. It seems tailor-made for Hollywood ... It seems to me no more than a token gesture that the earlier

> scenes of this novel are laid in 'Grenville,' Ontario. They might just as well have been set in any small town of America ...
>
> We are confronted with a fabricated contrast between Canada – dull, cautious, small-thinking, inhibited – and the United States – dangerous, aggressive, exhilarating.
>
> I want to be among the first Canadians to call this nonsense.
>
> I think MacLennan must necessarily choose between being a pride to Canada, with precious little financial reward, or a highly successful novelist in the United States. I do not think it is possible to be both.

When MacLennan himself read this diatribe, he laughed at its absurdity, but it rankled sufficiently for him to send a copy in a letter to Bill Deacon, explaining that it may have resulted from 'the stupidity of Collins blurb.' Deacon himself, like many reviewers, thoroughly liked the new novel: '*Barometer* was a one-bagger,' he wrote to bolster MacLennan's spirits after reading it; '*Two Solitudes* a brilliant two base hit; *The Precipice* is a home run.' It would go faster though, he added, '[if] Collins put advertising weight behind it as Frank Appleton would have done.' Deacon's optimism is reflected in his own review for the *Globe and Mail*, which MacLennan liked greatly; in it he emphasized MacLennan's 'better command of his medium' and the handling of character.[21] Most reviews, however, fell between these two extremes. The majority of Canadian reviewers, while praising many aspects of the book, concluded that it was not as good as *Two Solitudes*.

When the book finally appeared three months later in the United States, reviewers there saw it in a quite different light. Indifferent to MacLennan's Canadianness, they were much more hearty in their praise. Two of the first reviews to appear, in the influential *New York Herald Tribune* and the *New York Times*, were unstinting in their admiration. In the former John K. Hutchens began: 'The admirable aspects of Hugh MacLennan's new novel would make a fair list'; and then he proceeded to dwell on some of them – the 'solid story,' the themes, the characters. In the latter Orville Prescott called MacLennan 'a mature and technically accomplished craftsman in fiction,' and concluded by saying that modern writers in general had much to learn from his 'healthy outlook on men and life.'[22]

A good deal of praise revolved around *what* MacLennan had done in the novel. Many critics pointed to the pioneering efforts apparent here. The Canadian poet Leo Kennedy, who had himself taken a job as vice-president in an advertising firm in Chicago, wrote: '[MacLennan is] the only one who has successfully tackled the Canadian Anglo-

Canadian problem [in *Two Solitudes*]. Certainly he's the first to tangle with the Canadian-United States cultural imbroglio.' Although one or two critics took mild issue with factual errors in the book (that one could not see a taxi descend into Grand Central Station from Park Avenue, for example) or with the weakness of the American section as opposed to the Canadian, they were better disposed towards the novel than their Canadian counterparts. 'Many-Sided International Romance,' 'Americans Learn in This Novel What Canadians Think of Them,' 'Dashing N.Y. Boy Marries Canadian Girl – Sparks Fly,' 'Surmounting the Border,' and 'Theme: Two Countries' – these review titles give a good impression of the way in which critics in the United States perceived the novel, welcomed it, and commended it.[23]

Whether or not MacLennan was right in concluding that these favourable American reviews might have modified the Canadian reaction to the novel, it is difficult to say. Certainly no one can deny that the *New York Times* and other leading American publications were immensely influential in setting cultural trends. Canadian reviewers might indeed have been swept up in the American enthusiasm for the novel, but the same American enthusiasm might have made Canadian critics even more irate than they already were that MacLennan had abandoned the nation as his whole concern. MacLennan was especially sensitive to the effects of book promotion because of the treatment Dorothy's award-winning book had received three years before at Harper's. '*Partner* [*in Three Worlds*] was a first-class flop below the border,' she had written to Bill Deacon in explanation of her lack of interest in writing another book, 'for the reason that Harper's appear never to have cared whether it lived or died. They have had too many best-sellers and Books-of-the-Month this winter to "waste" any paper on my book, which would have required a certain amount of honest promotion and advertising to awaken public interest.' MacLennan took a similar line of complaint on *The Precipice*: 'The poor Canadian reviews caused Duell, apparently, to boggle at any kind of promotion, and when the good U.S. reviews came along, he wasn't ready to cash in on them. That's when I decided to leave both Duell and Collins.'[24]

Although it was certainly not the 'home run' Bill Deacon claimed, *The Precipice* did not do badly once it was released. Within the first week after its publication in Canada, by 23 June, it had climbed from twelfth to ninth place on the Toronto Library List; by the end of July it had topped the list. Simultaneously it headed the Montreal bestseller list in the fiction category. By September it headed the list of Most Popular Books (Fiction) in the Oshawa newspaper and was in second place on the Toronto list. By November it stood first again on the Toronto list, and in that same month it was dramatized for CBC Radio by Hugh Kemp, with Budd Knapp as Lassiter and Alice Hill as Lucy, for *Sunday Stage 49*. In the United States it was Book of the Month Club selection for October, ranked fourth on the bestseller list in the *New York Times* for the same month, and topped the bestseller list simultaneously in Minneapolis. In May 1949 it was selected for the Governor-General's Award as the best fiction written in Canada during 1948. Even as late as 1968 it was selling well – 15,000 paperback copies in that year in the United States alone.[25] Eventually the hard cover edition netted MacLennan about $12,000 after taxes – the same amount *Two Solitudes* brought him.

In fact, by most standards, *The Precipice* was a success, though not as great a success as *Two Solitudes* had been. Perhaps MacLennan's expectations were simply too high. As he maintained in 1956: 'I like *The Precipice* best of the books I have published because, while its form is not in any way original, it is directly observed throughout and uses time to pretty good advantage.' And in 1979 he continued to claim: 'there was nothing the matter with that book.'[26]

Probably a number of factors contributed to its relatively slow initial sales. First of all, the book trade in general was undergoing significant changes. Paperback versions of world classics and the previous year's bestsellers were flooding the market at prices so low that hard cover first editions were bound to suffer. Publishers, especially in Canada, were suddenly finding the practical aspects of publishing, especially the locating of paper, bindings, and so forth, difficult. Not only did this mean that their attention was temporarily diverted from advertising and other aspects of their work, but it meant also that financially they were worse off than they had been for some time. Lavish book launchings were no longer taken for granted, a fact that affected the presentation of *The Precipice* as it did other books at the time. These were all external factors over which neither MacLennan nor any other writer, nor their publishers, could have any control.

The reviews of *The Precipice* also help to explain the situation. A good many Canadian readers did feel a litle betrayed that their national spokesman had turned his attention from Canada to the United States. Beyond that, however, MacLennan had also turned his attention away from one of the aspects of his earlier work that had most captured his readers' admiration and interest. He had not, in *The Precipice*, treated a theme involving war. Readers who had thrilled to the dramatic descriptions of the Halifax explosion and the crisis surrounding conscription apparently felt that something was missing. Although the reviewers did not pin-point this missing element, there were a number of vague remarks suggesting that this was the case. Typical is an excerpt from the *Ottawa Journal*: 'In contrast to "Two Solitudes," essentially a dramatic and sensational book, this may seem a little dull.' Or, as Bill Deacon expressed it more positively in his review: 'Improvement in technique is striking in this third novel. But this improvement is not obvious, since it consists of a display of controlled power, of restraint in dramatic situations and of finer work in description and explanation ... Smashingly brilliant passages in the earlier books were interspersed among writing of poorer craftsmanship, with the result that everybody admired the powerful writing ... The more consistent excellencies of The Precipice avoid these contrasts. Consequently, a first reading may not bring to the reader immediate awareness of the author's better command of his medium. The classic merits of the new novel will only be admitted generally after its continued popularity over the years has proved its superiority.'[27]

The disappointment many readers felt in not finding the gripping action, the high-flown passages, they had learned to expect, led to the overlooking of his technical advances, much as Deacon feared. That he was gaining control of his medium, was now better able to blend character, action, theme, and symbol into a coherent whole, was lost on an audience who could forgive unevenness in his writing provided they were titillated by his brilliant action passages. In charting his course for the future, MacLennan could only have concluded that craftsmanship *per se* did not much matter.

Another reason for the novel's somewhat reduced appeal can be deduced from an odd theory MacLennan included in an essay he wrote during the year following its publication. In 'Changing Values in Fiction' (1949) he argued that 'a good woman is an enemy to a good plot': 'The tighter is your fiction pattern, the more difficult it is to find any role which a truly feminine personality can play ... The truth is that nothing is harder to deal with in a rapid-action novel than a good woman, and even Shakespeare has paid tribute to this difficulty by having a surprisingly small number of genuinely good females in his novels. For it is the nature of the good woman to absorb conflict rather than create it, and if the conflict is violent, it is generally an accident that she finds her place in it.'[28] That Shakespeare did not write 'novels,' that MacLennan's theory here raises other commonsense objections, are clues that, on this occasion, his views were deeply idiosyncratic. Could it be that focusing on a 'good woman' as his central character in *The Precipice* had somehow toned the whole book down? Had Lucy Cameron, in fact, 'absorbed' instead of heightened the story's conflicts? It is notoriously difficult for any writer to present with authenticity the point of view of the opposite sex; indeed it is seldom attempted. But critics did not seize on Lucy Cameron as an unconvincing female, a mute tribute to MacLennan's success in presenting her. His fears may have been justified to some extent, however. That Lucy is a 'good woman' no one can dispute; perhaps her central position in the story did lessen the effects of some scenes that, from a male point of view, might have been told with the 'drama' and 'brilliance' many readers found lacking in the novel. It is most likely in this sense above all that MacLennan considered *The Precipice* 'a failed experiment.' In choosing the woman's point of view for his story he was true to the ballet from which it had come, but he would have been more comfortable and freer to strike brilliant passages had he told the story either from Stephen Lassiter's or from Bruce Fraser's point of view. Later, in *The Watch That Ends the Night*, he was to take a similar trio – the aggressive, primitive man, the good woman, and the quiet, speculative man – and centre his point of view on George Stewart, the quiet, speculative one. From writing *The Precipice*, he actually learned a great deal about his craft. From now on, for one thing, he would choose to write from the perspective of a man.

The recognition he gained as a commentator on the American scene in *The Precipice* involved him briefly in some further reportage south of the border. He was interviewed for American journals and by American radio stations, and was invited to address the Canadian Society of New York in May 1949. A year or so earlier he had gone to Philadelphia to cover the Republican Convention held there and wrote two articles recording his impressions, 'The Elephant on Parade' and 'What Does Uncle Sam Want?' (1948).[29]

With Dorothy still recovering from the after-effects of her first embolism, which had struck with such suddenness on 1 January 1948, MacLennan produced what articles and essays he could to defray medical expenses. Collins temporarily saved the day by agreeing to publish *Cross-Country*, a collection of his best short pieces to date, in the fall of 1949. This collection included the American reportage and several essays on the Canadian identity, making the most of the international reputation he had acquired by the publication of *The Precipice*. In addition, though, there were several essays on another subject, religion, heralding significant developments in his choice of themes. In 'Are We a Godless People?' which first appeared in *Maclean's* on 15

March 1949, he explored those questions concerning the decline of religion in contemporary society that had been raised in *The Precipice*: was the power of the state rapidly replacing a sense of the divine; was guilt, sadly, the only legacy of puritanism in a world where spiritual values were disappearing?

In September 1948, at the same time as *The Precipice* began to appear in American bookstores, 'The Future Trend in the Novel' was published in the *Canadian Author and Bookman*. In describing new directions for the novel in general, MacLennan outlined the course his own aesthetic theories were taking as he mapped out his next book. At the time he was writing *The Precipice* he had only reluctantly thrown in his lot with the currently popular stream of fiction he had described as 'social symbolism' – where man was depicted 'in his relation with organized society, with politics, war, economic conditions, with the local morals of a specific group'; he had all along, he stated, preferred a more 'heroic' mode of literature. Now terming this trend not 'social symbolism' but rather 'naturalism' or 'naturalistic realism,' he stated that he felt it was time for a different approach to fiction. His main argument, aside from a sense that change was in the air, was that 'Modern psychology has scuppered the old, easy theory that personality is the product of economic conditions.' For a redefinition of the direction fiction should now take, he returned to one of the writers he had dismissed earlier as holding no lessons for him: 'Evelyn Waugh is wise when he says, "The artist's only function in the disintegrated society of today is to create independent systems of order of his own ..." It looks like a long overdue return to the principle which should guide all artists, which is to seek for value and beauty, pity and terror, humour and love in the scenes around him and in the thoughts and images which emerge naturally out of his own personality.' In other words, MacLennan felt that the time was now ripe for the type of literature he had always preferred, the 'heroic' or the 'universal.'

His readmission of Waugh into the ranks of the acceptable is misleading. He had not changed his mind at all about the decadence of modern fiction; if anything, he was even more certain than he had been prior to writing *The Precipice* that literature had a moral role to play. 'The period we are now entering,' he wrote in 'The Future Trend in the Novel,' 'will be a period of reconstruction, both in society and in the arts. Such periods are always hard for the artist, for it is incumbent upon him, not on the statesman, to discover new values. This he can do only by the process of creating potential values into real symbols.' As illustration for his theory he divided the writers who were currently popular into two types: those who presented the dark side of life alone, of whom he disapproved, and those who showed that despite life's times of despair affirmation is possible, of whom he approved. In 'Changing Values in Fiction,' which appeared in the fall of 1949, he considered, for example, that Hemingway had ultimately failed to meet these standards, because of his 'total, his almost nihilistic pessimism'; John Dos Passos he termed a 'bleak' writer, whose ruthless depiction of the United States represented a 'dead-end' for art. Norman Mailer's *The Naked and the Dead* had come to represent the essence of the moral stance he could not tolerate, a book he described as consisting of 'the most appalling destructive intensity.' On the other hand, he praised Evelyn Waugh's *Brideshead Revisited* as 'affirmative of life because it is pregnant with beauty, and is written by a man who – at least for a while – preferred love to contempt.' He also praised Graham Greene and Joyce Cary because they value life 'for its own sake.' And, because it came from a colonial country yet stood universally acclaimed, he held up Alan Paton's *Cry, The Beloved Country* as one of the finest contemporary examples of the type of book he wanted to see written because it was 'a work of tremendous affirmation': 'Which of these two trends – the one exemplified by Mailer or the one exemplified by Paton – will ultimately prevail. I have no means of saying. Perhaps neither will. There is no reason why either should. But Paton's work has at least made clear the spiritual bankruptcy into which a successful North America is in danger of falling.'[30]

With these theories of religion and art stirring him to action, he absorbed the disappointments of *The Precipice* without changing his private assessment of the book in any way. He was truly pleased when he heard about the Governor-General's Award it had won. 'Yes,' he wrote to Bill Deacon on 7 June 1949, 'I am gratified by this award, more so by a lot than by the one for *Two Solitudes*, for in my own mind there isn't the slightest comparison between the worth of the two books as novels. *The Precipice* is felt emotion all the way through as the other two books never were. However, in retrospect I'm grateful I was jumped [on] so heavily in Canada as I was. I had it coming to me, and it released me. I feel able to do much better work now than I could before ... I'm working hard on what will far and away be the best book I've ever done if I can hold onto it. I only hope it won't take too long, but the best prospect I have is finishing it next spring, and it will probably be longer.'

Chapter eight

New Departures: *Each Man's Son*

On New Year's Eve, 31 December 1948, MacLennan surveyed the events of the past year, as all Scotsmen must, and was not pleased. Although he thought it his best novel so far, *The Precipice* had plainly not constituted a significant building block in his career: it had not sold nearly as many copies in Canada as *Two Solitudes*, in part because reviews had been poor. Choosing an American theme had likely been a mistake, he thought. He had counted on the success of this novel as his passport to greater fame and fortune in the United States. Despite his protestations to the contrary, he had contemplated staying on in California where he and Dorothy were spending the winter with her parents; there, the climate suited Dorothy's precarious health, her own writing was more likely to flourish, and he might command a potentially larger market for his own writing. But *The Precipice* had not been a huge success in the United States either. From his perspective there, he now felt a subtle bond with the country that had rapped his knuckles for straying away from home in his fiction. Just three weeks earlier, he had confided to Bill Deacon: 'after travelling across the United States this time – the last time was before the war – I've been more than ever struck by the potential richness of Canadian society for a novelist as compared to the scene here. Superficially, the United States offers a much easier environment, but this apparent ease is deceptive. More than ever before, Americans seem to be growing outward rather than inward. What they do is infinitely more important than what they think, feel or are; and what they do which is interest-

Dr Sam in his 'surgery'

ing is more conditioned by scientific and engineering techniques than by the characters of the doers. Also I feel that they are much more committed to history than we are. Their course has been to a large extent determined ... I don't believe any serious American writer today can feel the same kinship with the public, or get the same response from the public, that a writer can experience in Canada.'[1]

His attempt in *The Precipice* to join what he called 'a branch cycle' of American literature had backfired; as he would later maintain: '*The Precipice* was a gamble on which ... I lost.'[2] It was not only that sales had been disappointing, he now realized that he had forged for himself a unique relationship with his Canadian public which felt like 'kinship' and which he did not want to abandon. But the hard facts were clear; as Dorothy's medical bills mounted he knew that if he did not make a popular success of his next novel, he could no longer support the two of them by writing alone. Either the next one made it or he would have to get a job. This was the cold truth he faced that New Year's Eve.

The time had come for some new departures. That very evening he sat down to take the 'painful step'[3] of announcing to Charles Duell that he had decided to find another publisher. Feeling deeply betrayed by what he believed to have been Duell, Sloan and Pearce's cavalier mismanagement of the release and publicity of his novel, he wrote in sadness and anger:

> You know to a penny how much I have been paid during the past year by Duell, Sloan and Pearce, and you can make a better than fair estimate of what I have earned through Wm. Collins Sons & Co. In all, it has turned out insufficient to enable me to continue writing novels to the exclusion of other means of support, inasmuch as I have no private income whatever to fall back upon.
>
> Therefore, I shall be forced to take a job some time in 1949, probably a university post of some sort; I hope either at Harvard or McGill. I am sorry, because I should prefer to give all my time to writing, as I do now. Until the job materializes, I shall finish as much as possible of the current novel on which I am working, which has at least started a little faster than the others.
>
> But in order that there should be no misunderstanding between us, it is proper that I tell you now that I feel myself obliged to sign a contract for my next novel with another publishing house. At the moment I have made no decision in this respect, but my choice is reasonably wide. The reasons for such a decision must be obvious to us both.

Charles Duell replied hastily, begging him to stay with Duell, Sloan and Pearce, even suggesting that he accept from them a monthly stipend; but MacLennan remained adamant, spelling out his position very clearly:

I am not leaving you because of a 'set-back' over *The Precipice*. I have finally written a novel which, coming as a culminating improvement on the previous two, has been given in the United States top critical reception – all a writer could ask. I do not, however, believe that its low sales figure to date is entirely due to the state of the book market ...

There is only one reason for my decision, Charles. Your conception of promoting and selling a book is incompatible with my own. If I have not discussed this matter before, it was because I realized it would have been merely a futile complaint on my part. Publishing is your business, not mine. It is traditional for a writer to gripe, and the answers he receives are also traditional.[4]

MacLennan had no difficulty locating a new publisher: in fact, two American firms, Little, Brown and Company and Houghton Mifflin, quickly rose to the bait. He decided on Little, Brown because he sensed, in the discussions he and his agent Blanche Gregory conducted with them, a keen interest in his work that would provide the kind of moral support he felt he needed from an editor: 'Experience with my previous three books, both in the United States and in Canada, had made me realize that my self-confidence required a publisher who completely sensed the peculiar difficulties under which I had been working and who agreed that I was at least on the right track in working them out.'[5] Little, Brown was jubliant at this coup. Almost immediately he was contacted by Angus Cameron, who was to become one of the great American editors of the future despite the persecution he endured in the McCarthy period. His warm words must have been a welcome balm to MacLennan's troubled mind. Having set up his American publisher, he now arranged for Macmillan's of Canada to handle the book at home; since Frank Appleton had left Collins, there was no particular reason, he felt, to return to them with his next book. His New Year's resolution to find new publishers had been accomplished.

As soon as *The Precipice* had been released in Canada in June 1948, MacLennan had begun thinking about the topic of his next novel. Early in July he had written to Bill Deacon: 'About my next book I'm not sure. There are several subjects I want to tackle, and I seem unable to decide which until *The Precipice* has been read a little more widely and I get a more accurate feeling of how I stand with the public.'[6] Once he did sense his Canadian public's disapproval of his sortie into New York and Princeton, some of those 'several subjects' were undoubtedly shelved. He still wanted both to pursue the nationalist themes to which he owed his present fame and to compete successfully in the international popular fiction trade. Were these two aims incompatible in 1948?

Many reviewers had praised the early section of *The Precipice* set in Canada, claiming that it was the American part of the book which seemed false. He had himself, as early as 1947, suspected that 'the sociological novel had already neared the saturation point in human interest.'[7] Once he absorbed the information, distressing as it was, that *The Precipice* had not done as well as he hoped it would, he seized the opportunity to take a new tack. By mid-July 1948 he emerged from a brief hospitalization for a severe reaction to penicillin with the general thrust of his new novel clear. 'I feel now that my period of "definition-making" is over,' he announced to Deacon; 'I feel finally released to delve directly into story and human nature.'[8] He at last felt free to write in the mode of the 'heroic' or 'universal' literature he had always wanted to imitate. In doing so he could have it both ways: he could return to the exclusively Canadian situations his public at home demanded of him, but he could do so in a way that raised such situations to a universal level.

His decision to turn to new publishers was to be a new departure in more ways than one. Working with Macmillan's in Toronto, instead of Collins, put him in the hands of an editor he already knew and respected. John Gray had first heard of MacLennan in May 1945 in Holland, where he was stationed in Intelligence Headquarters with the Canadian army. Just after the war had ended, a friend from Montreal had recommended that he read *Two Solitudes*. 'It's the real stuff,' he was told, 'it has the real flavour of Canada.' Gray, who was not only the same age as MacLennan but also actually looked remarkably like him, had taken the book out of the army library and sat up all night reading, finding himself 'breathless' with excitement that such a fine and true novel had come out of his homeland.[9] On his return to Canada, where he took up the job of managing editor at Macmillan's, he had sought out MacLennan at the June 1946 meeting of the Canadian Authors' Association in Toronto. Their meeting had been an auspicious one, mainly because the two men shared a common sense of outrage at the injustice of current publishing contracts. Now, four years later, having seen Gray on and off at CAA meetings, MacLennan wrote on 27 May 1950: 'I'm sure you will understand how much I look forward to working with you. I have always admired your candour with writers and your understanding of the position of writing here in Canada. We can each help the other by talking things over in regard to a mutual venture.'

Gray quickly replaced Bill Deacon as MacLennan's main correspondent, and set up eventually the best contract he had yet had. But, as always, MacLennan's eye was on the venture itself, this time a 'mutual' venture, for here, more than with any of his novels, he was open to advice and discussion in the hope that the novel's success would be ensured. Not secure enough financially to gamble as he had with *The Precipice*, almost broke, he moved cautiously. Just as he had found in Duell, Sloan and Pearce a scapegoat for the wider circumstances that had resulted in a cool reception for *The Precipice*, he now blamed the Canadian Authors' Association for what were really the intangibles of his time and place. 'It is the C.A.A. which limited me by calling me a "nationalist,"' he complained to Gray, 'when all I was trying to do was to define the background out of which any Canadian writer has to work. This build-up backfired, as I knew it was bound to, among the critics later on, and one of the most necessary things in marketing my work in the future, I believe, will be to undo some of these labels which have been pinned around my neck.'

With his next novel, as he saw it, he had three things to accomplish: he must follow his own literary taste for the 'heroic,' he must ground his situation in Canada, but he must also do so in such a way that did not use the obvious 'stage setting' he had needed for *Two Solitudes*. He must choose a subject at once 'universal' and 'Canadian,' but not heavy-handed. He decided to go right back to his own roots, to the life he had known as a child in Cape Breton: Glace Bay, he imagined, had been as primitive as anything in Greek tragedy.

As the medical bills he could not pay mounted up over the winter of 1949-50, he pushed himself hard to complete his manuscript. 'I managed the writing this winter,' he confessed to Gray in May, 'solely by cutting out every other single activity. We went nowhere and saw practically no person.' That same month he had almost finished his first draft. As he described it to John Gray: 'It is the first novel I have written with a theme absolutely universal, in the sense that it could exist anywhere on earth and at any time on earth. The whole action occurs in Cape Breton, and though the date is the year before the first World War, my reason for setting the date then is merely because it liberated the theme from niggling details. The date is mentioned once only in the whole book and I believe the reader is quite unconscious of it. The speech, the colour – all of that is Cape Breton. But these things are secondary. The book moves almost as fast as does *Barometer Ris-*

ing, but it certainly has a great deal more depth and works itself out in terms of character. As I said to Little, Brown (because the chief character is a doctor) it is a book not about a doctor, but about a man who happens to be a doctor, a book not about Canada, but by a man who happens to be a Canadian. And of course, it is about a good deal more than a single man.'[10]

He would not choose a woman to be his central character this time, as he had in *The Precipice*. Instead, he would select a man, Dr Daniel Ainslie, whose experiences could be modelled on his father's as a colliery doctor in the mining community of Glace Bay. To portray him, MacLennan drew on his own childhood memories of the brook-encircled house outside the town where he and Frances had grown up with the consciousness that Dr Sam was an important man in the community. Dr Ainslie, the self-driven doctor with a passion for translating the Classics, who badly wants a son, is based to a great extent on Dr MacLennan. The novel's sub-plot, which revolves around the coal miner Archie MacNeil, who has gone off to the States as a successful prize-fighter, leaving his wife Mollie and their eight-year-old boy Alan to fend for themselves, reflects the barbaric underside of life in Glace Bay. The two plots merge with tragic inevitability when Dr Ainslie and his wife Margaret adopt Alan after Archie returns home, finds Mollie in the arms of her French lover Camire, and kills them both in a violent rage.

MacLennan himself stood somewhere between these two plots. On the one hand, he could go back to his early admiration of coal miners and boxers (he himself had managed once to elude his father's disapproving eye to slip in to see the Glace Bay fighter Roddie Macdonald, who won the light heavy-weight championship in his time) to explore 'primitive' heroics; on the other hand, now that he himself was about the same age his father had been in Glace Bay, he could try to understand what had made Dr Sam the tyrannical and dogmatic man he had been. He projected himself as fully as possible and with great sympathy into his father's point of view. It was as if he were tossing a grappling hook into the mind his father had so seldom shared in order to draw him closer.

The key to his father's character, he decided, was Calvinism. For the first time he gave serious thought to the nature of the ethics by which Dr Sam had lived. Friends at North Hatley recall that during the summer of 1950 Calvin became an obsession: MacLennan talked of little else, maintaining that he had been one of the most evil men, if not the most evil man, in history. By the end of that summer, however, he had clarified his own views on the matter considerably. As he wrote in August to Gray, 'Calvinism is not as absurd a theology as it appears to be':

I can't believe, as the old Calvinists did, that God takes such an intense personal interest in me that his foot is poised constantly above my neck. But when one leaves out the egoism of the theology, I suggest that it comes closer to the truth of man's personal fate than any other. When I think back over the past seventy-five years, I see no evidence that society is being forgiven its trespasses during that period. When I look around me at some of the intellectuals of the 1920s, unhappy, broken-down, bewildered and miserable in their early fifties, their marriages on the rocks, their ideals locked up in the Kremlin, the easy prestige they once enjoyed become a mockery, I see little difference between their position and that of the sinners who (according to the old Presbyterian minister) had insisted there was no hell until they found themselves there. 'And there they were, cryin' oot to Jehovah that they never knew it wad be as bad as this. And Jehovah turned and said, "weel, ye know noo."' As this book developed, I felt I was working within human truths. Not with all human truths of course, and only on a small scale with a few human beings; but I did feel, and still do, that those human beings were reproduced within the range of experience, and I respected them as I dealt with them because none of them ever denied his experience as it came, or invented new phrases or jargons to pretend it was other than it was. Calvinism, as opposed to neo-puritanism, did that, and in the Cape Breton I knew God was more important and formidable than all the Mrs. Grundys of Toronto, even when they denied his existence. My mortal quarrel with Calvinism was not that it denied realities, but that it inculcated into children the idea that God was each man's personal enemy, and that a man committed a sin merely by existing. Theoretically, the Anglicans also believe this, and so do the Catholics, but the Catholics presume to be able to forgive this sin and the Anglicans (once they had rid themselves of the puritans) treated God much as they treated parliament. While parliament possesses the right to boil an Englishman in oil at its pleasure, the individual Englishman seems able to live with confidence that it won't do so.

From this you gather that in spite of my outward seeming, I'm rather an archaic personality.[11]

Something of the hold Calvinism continued to exercise on his imagination can be seen in a dream he later recorded in 1960: 'Around three A.M. I woke after a long trance-like dream in which I had had him [Calvin] in my power along with other modern victims of him, in Geneva in his heyday. Though amply armed with all the TV weapons, we found ourselves too Christian to shoot the bastard and he licked us even in dream, for when we proposed to live there with a modicum of pleasure, and told him we would protect any others who chose to do the same, he looked right through us and said that none would. And none did. And then I awoke with a post-fever sweat. But one of these days I'll settle that bastard somehow or other.'[12]

In his novel, he would attempt to demonstrate the terrible effect Calvinism could have on a man and illustrate that those who tried to live by such ethics were as much victims as torturers. Ironically, the foundations of the house that once supported Dr Sam and his religious household later supported many a Christian congregation in the building that replaced it – the Newsom United Church.

To attempt a psychological study such as this was a new departure for MacLennan. Forgetting for the moment some of the work of Grove and Callaghan, he even considered that it was a type of fiction unheard of in Canada before. At any rate, coming to grips with such intimate truths of character as he was now dealing with was difficult: 'I find myself still more faced with Freud's statement that in psychology courage is almost everything.' Apparently he felt that he had found the courage to come to grips with his characters. On 5 July 1950 he sent off the manuscript of *Each Man's Son* to Angus Cameron in New York and to John Gray in Toronto with a confident flourish: 'Nobody ever wrote a book even vaguely like this in Canada before.'[13]

It was a great relief to feel at last that he need not be 'a geographer, an historian and a sociologist'[14] as well as a novelist. It would no longer be necessary, he was convinced, to set the stage in addition to providing the plot and characters, as he had done in *Two Solitudes*. He thought Canadian writers, like those in Britain and the United States, could now take their background for granted. With this novel, for the first time, he felt free to concentrate on whatever he wanted. To him, it looked like the real point of departure for Canadian literature.

For models he had turned to the real giants: the classical Greek tragedies he had studied and the Shakespearean plays he revered. This was the literature he thought of when he used the terms 'universal' and 'heroic.' These models also especially suited his own tendency to begin a novel by drafting 'scenes,' not necessarily in any logical order. Both the Greeks and Shakespeare emphasized a well-structured plot and the three unities of time, place, and action. He would follow suit. His subject lent itself well to heroic treatment: both the heroism of his Calvinist protagonist, who must transcend his loss of faith and overcome his guilt in order to break through to an acceptance of human error in himself and others, and the more down-to-earth heroism of his prize-fighter Archie. Shakespeare had shown how local rustics with their bawdy jokes could be used for comic relief in a tragedy: why not cast the pawky people of Cape Breton in the same role? He could take Glace Bay for granted, adapt tried and true techniques from his models, and concentrate on the intrinsic story alone. In June, a month before he sent the manuscript off, he had written to Gray: 'Inwardly I have known beyond doubt that this novel had a deeper reality than any others I have written ... I knew the time had come for bold strokes and a minimum of social explanation.' But once Cameron and Gray read the manuscript, they thought otherwise. In their opinion, this new departure was premature. The market was not ready to understand the novel as it was; he would have to provide at least a few remarks in a preface, explaining Calvinism and Cape Breton.

MacLennan was disappointed: 'It was my aim to pare this novel right down to the bones, because in the past I have done more explanation than I now care to do or feel is necessary.' But his editors insisted on more background, and reluctantly he co-operated: 'The necessity of writing such introductory stuff galls me hard, but I see no way of avoiding it, for nothing I have heard either from Angus or yourself confutes my original discovery that drama proceeds from the known, and never from the unknown. No matter how I have been inhibited by the sneers of Canadian reviewers from indulging in explanations of various actions and states of mind, the lack of definition in the Canadian scene continues to make some explanation necessary.'[15]

The situation would have been tolerable had the addition of background material been the only change demanded, but this was not to be the case. The financial pressures that were accumulating at home spurred him to hope for early publication. Dorothy, despite the ups and downs of her health, remained in his opinion 'a superlative editor,'[16] going over every chapter with great care. When he had submitted the manuscript he had been confident that it would not be long before it appeared and began bringing in the money he needed. But it was to be the best part of a year before *Each Man's Son* was published. Cameron and Gray raised other questions of such importance that he had no choice but to embark on major revisions. That he hastened to implement every editorial suggestion without resistance indicates the lengths to which he was prepared to go in order to ensure this novel's success. He had arranged for himself an editorial context which he was convinced was a vast improvement over his relationship with his previous publishers; so firm was his conviction that his two new editors held the knowledge necessary to make this novel a popular success, that he put himself entirely in their hands.

Unfortunately, no copy of the original manuscript of *Each Man's Son* survives. But from what Angus Cameron called the 'round robin correspondence'[17] of the three men who shaped its final version, a good deal can be reconstructed. Both editors thought the novel's ending in particular needed considerable change. Cameron felt that it must be more explicit especially in suggesting the conflicts that would inevitably ensue after such a tragedy. He suggested that Dr Ainslie's 'life and his relationship with [his wife] Margaret would be injured as well as improved by the tragedy in Alan's family.' He also suggested that Alan should witness all or part of the devastating episode in which his father returns and kills his mother; thus, he reasoned, 'Ainslie would be inheriting a great charge and a great problem.' In addition, he believed that the irony would be heightened if Alan turned not to Ainslie but to his wife in this crisis. Gray wrote in support of this criticism that he and three other Macmillan readers found 'some difficulty in defining a lack of complete satisfaction in the ending.' In the original version, Archie MacNeil was imprisoned, not killed. A short final chapter, comical in tone, featured a magistrate and a Montreal reporter discussing the crime and ended with a humorous Cape Breton anecdote. 'As it stands it is over-packed and ... races too fast.' It needed, Gray added, 'shaping-out and clarification.'[18]

Other aspects of the book, in the opinion of both editors, needed more than the minor revisions MacLennan had hoped for. Cameron felt that Alan would certainly have found out what his father did for a living, and that he would realize that it was his mother who needed to keep it a secret. Gray confirmed this view and added that he thought that Dr Ainslie's sense of personal guilt should be more explicit. He raised a few other points: Alan should be older than five; many of the scenes concerning Mollie should be removed; the Cape Breton stories should be made more organic; and the period of the story should be defined more clearly. MacLennan, it would seem, had 'pared the novel down' too much.

Both editors, however, accustomed 'to dealing with unsure people who bruise easily,' as Gray put it, were careful to couch their substantial criticisms in the context of sincere praise. Cameron's comment that he, though American, found the people quite familiar – 'the older ones reminding me of my grandfather's farmer friends in Indiana' – confirmed MacLennan's belief that the novel was 'universal' in its appeal.

Gray admired the 'wonderful group of characters' and 'certain stills' in the ending, 'the breaking down of the door, for instance, and the doctor's entry.' 'We will not only be proud to sell it, but confident of doing well with it,' he reassured the nervous author. Later, MacLennan was to thank both men by saying 'you, in your own criticisms of *Each Man's Son*, made me feel that you were sitting right inside my mind, perceiving my intentions better than I could perceive them myself.'[19]

If anything, MacLennan may have been a little too co-operative in attempting to implement almost all of these suggestions. Nevertheless, he was in for a heavy blow. Sometime in the fall of 1950, after the manuscript had been thoroughly revised, John Gray showed it to his friend L.A.A. Harding, then a graduate student in English literature at the University of Toronto (and later professor of English at the Collège Militaire Royal de St Jean in Quebec). Harding had some serious criticisms to offer. As is clear from a letter to Cameron on 26 September, Gray had a premonition that he ought not to show these remarks to MacLennan. None the less, misjudging his mood the following Thursday evening at a gathering at his home that included the Toronto *Telegram* literary critic Jim Scott, Gray introduced Harding's critique for discussion. MacLennan, already shaken by the reception of *The Precipice*, his back to the wall financially, having laboriously completed what he believed to be final revisions to a manuscript he had hoped would need only minor changes, was not receptive to further criticism.

Since some of Harding's objections – that MacLennan's women seemed shadowy, his conclusions weak, his writing devoid of emotion – were those that have plagued him generally throughout his career, they are worth reproducing here at some length:

I think it misses being a very good novel for various reasons. It has considerable emotional depth, but not as much as a tragedy of this magnitude should have. I am not as moved by the ruined Archie, the dead Mollie and the probably ruined Alan as I should be. There is a vague suggestion of impartiality – such as I feel in a newspaper report of the deaths of people unknown – rather than an intimate sympathy – such as I should feel from the death of people I knew well. In fact I do not know Mollie well enough. I find it hard to picture her now, so she will not live in my memory as a tragic figure (which she was). She should have more blood in her and quite a bit more flesh. Her temptations (were they real?), her loneliness, her thoughts, should be written much more fully to make her less of a shadow, more of a woman. With Mollie fully alive, which she is not, the emotional power of this novel would be terrific. (I imagine the pointlessness of, say, 'Tess of the D'Urbervilles' if Tess were not Tess).

In the same way Archie fails to move me as much as he should. There is something pathetic about any broken down fighter yet Mr. MacLennan unfortunately limits him, dispassionately, to mere loutishness ...

The effect of the third character, Alan, is also minimised by this same inadequacy of Mollie ...

This action does not misfire, but it is fired with half a charge. There is tremendous power in the tragedy and it is not ever let loose; Mollie's lack of vitality is, I think, the main reason and it affects both Archie and his son, and therefore the whole book, which is a pity.

The doctor, with his Calvinistic Cape Breton hound of heaven snapping at his heels is excellently drawn, and I have no criticism of him. If, however, Mollie were to be rewritten the doctor's annexation of Alan would have to be rewritten too, if only slightly.

One final criticism must be made and that is against the last chapter. It disrupts the unity of the book. It is written in a different tone and in an entirely different mood. It clashes with the whole of the rest of the novel, and it could not be more different from the quiet feeling of the opening. It is inartistic ... Mr. MacLennan appears to have forgotten that he has just written a tragedy; or he has forgotten the mood of it ... I should have liked (with all deference) a bitter lunatic commentary from Mrs. McCuish [a minor character used for local colour].[20]

MacLennan's virulent reaction to Harding's remarks fairly lights up the pages of the long diatribe he immediately sent off to Angus Cameron:

The Ph.D.'s report was clever, intelligent and not much more irrelevant than such academic judgments usually are; the bulk of the criticism developed from the man's own premises, which managed to blind him to the nature of the book I have written.

You will remember that he said I had mounted a powerful charge in *Each Man's Son*, but had fired only half of it. He felt no particular emotion at the end of the book because the final scenes were 'reported' instead of 'realized.' He also complained about the character of Mollie. He felt that the book failed because Mollie was not developed in her own right. It made *Each Man's Son* like *Tess of the D'Urbervilles* without Tess.

None of these specific criticisms had you or John made to me after your first readings of *Each Man's Son*, though you may have implied them. After your long and wonderfully provocative letter about the changes you would like to see in *Each Man's Son*, added to John's reaction, I felt I knew exactly the faults I had made, and I also felt I could correct them. Whether or not I did correct them, they are still not the points on which the Ph.D. got hung.

To begin with, *Each Man's Son* is not a story of a single woman, like *Tess of the D'Urbervilles*. It is the story of a middle-aged man in search of a son, whom he would equate with a God, a faith – and a purpose in life. It tells what happens to the people who are unwittingly involved in that search. In it is also the story of a child who sees his mother struck down by his own father. *Each Man's Son* happens to be laid in Cape Breton in 1913. It could have been laid in any country of the world at any time within the last two thousand years.

To go on with the criticism about Mollie as a character: I didn't just happen to play her down. I wrote many more scenes focusing on Mollie, I wrote much more about why Mollie was as she is and what Alan thought about her, and what other people thought and felt about her. But I chose in the end to let her remain as nebulous as she is because a) that is how she would have seemed to Alan, for one thing, and b) to make her a clear-cut, three-dimensional character would have turned the book into her story, not Ainslie's. Forgive the comparison, but I've already used it on John: if Shakespeare had made Ophelia a more clear-cut character, what would have happened to Hamlet?

Finally, the English Ph.D. says he obtains no emotion from the final sections of *Each Man's Son*. I'm sorry about that, but I think that's because he was looking for something I never intended him or anyone else to find. By the end of the book, when a small boy is wakened in the middle of the night and comes downstairs to face pristine violence, and a reader feels he is not involved in that child's emotions – after the manner in which I have built up the four characters involved – then there is nothing I can do to help him feel it more deeply. Perhaps it is the last scene between Ainslie, Margaret and the boy that he can't feel. If you, or John, know what he means specifically, and you agree with him, I'll listen to you and see what I can do. At the moment, I'm inclined to believe that John's friend finds that I lack the tendency to self-pity which would make my characters easier to understand. By which I mean that if my characters displayed more self-pity it would make identification with them easier for my readers.

And now to the Ph.D.'s last point, on which he spent an entire page of a three-page letter and levelled his main attack. I give him his way with the last two pages – the reporter and the magistrate – because it would be a pity to find that other reviewers were giving one-third of their space to showing why those two pages do not belong in the book. John wants that final scene out of the book. Very well. If you agree, out it goes. If you and John do not agree, I suppose the Canadian edition could omit it. But I stand by your decision, whatever it may be.[21]

After hearing of MacLennan's angry response, Harding, taken aback, defended his position:

I may be entirely wrong (and probably am) but I do think the author's memo fails entirely to explain the weakness I think I see in the book. If it is written as 'a product of emotion' why does the reader feel so little? How much emotion is there in the creation of Archie? How can one sympathise very deeply with him? If he is not very fond (apparently) of Mollie, and hardly thinks of his small son at all, how pathetic can he be? One's reaction is likely to be ... 'poor oaf.' Mollie killed, by one she loves, and who loves her even slightly, would be far more moving than Mollie killed by, well ... Archie as he is now. How much emotion is there in the creation of Mollie when she cannot evidently feel much beyond a dutiful and rather bloodless regard for Archie which forsakes him at the nadir of his career for a not very sympathy-producing reason – Camire?

I haven't time to finish this but I do think that Mr. MacL[ennan] is unable to view his book *from the reader's point of view*. Every book is an imperfect transference of the writer's 'six-month's world' to paper. That world is complete, understandable and emotion-charged to him but the reader depends upon his words to feel it. The author is perhaps the worst judge. *Macbeth* and *Hamlet* are *plays*. Hardly comparable with a novel.[22]

The upshot of these pyrotechnics was that MacLennan, while refusing to touch the novel further, did agree to drop the final short chapter. On Angus Cameron's advice the book concluded instead with Dr MacKenzie's remark to his colleague Dr Ainslie: 'Yes, Dan. Now I think you do [love the boy].'[23]

Almost immediately, MacLennan regretted his outburst, though he continued to maintain to John Gray, more coolly, that Harding had failed to understand the meaning of the novel. Seeing his view as yet one more strand in a sort of critical network against which he must fight, MacLennan connected what he had written to a recent radio review by 'another professor' who, 'after saying that I had become a national issue ... then proceeded to spend most of the time saying what was wrong with me, and in line with the comments of Jim Scott and [Robert] Weaver [literary critic at CBC Radio], it reduces itself to a pattern. I lack "emotion." I explain too much. I am over intellectual.'[24]

The entire correspondence that preceded the publication of *Each Man's Son* greatly illuminates MacLennan as an artist. He continually complained of the loneliness of the arduous task of writing. To a very great extent, this solitude was alleviated by the closeness he felt to his editors, Gray in particular. Early on in their correspondence, the two men, so alike physically, so sympathetic intellectually and emotionally, became close friends. The 'Dear John' of the days when their acquaintanceship revolved around their common aims in the Canadian Authors' Association became 'My dear John' in May. By October the relationship had deepened into close friendship and MacLennan wrote to thank Gray 'for a wonderfully enjoyable and stimulating time in Toronto. It was the best talk I've ever had with a publisher, ever. It made me eager to go on working and lifted a considerable feeling of solitude and working in the dark.'[25]

MacLennan relied heavily on the advice, as well as the encouragement, of his editors. Confident that they were working towards a common end, engaged in 'a mutual venture,' he rarely contradicted the observations of Gray or Cameron. 'When a book is created and one lives alone with it,' he wrote to Gray, 'it takes on a much intenser reality when a discriminating reader has seen it, and it gives the writer enormous confidence to know that the thing exists in its own right ... to be sure, in other words, that the word-and-structure medium has been in any sense adequate.' Consequently, he acted on their suggestions at once, without resistance, accepting their judgement as superior to his own at the time he had written the words. That he was unusually malleable in this way is suggested by Gray's observation: 'I much appreciated your careful discussion of my letter but shouldn't like you to feel that it is necessary unless you're in the mood to talk a question out. I think a publisher's vantage point should permit him, and his job occasionally require him, to tell an author what course the publisher thinks he is making in relation to his public – never (or almost never) in relation to his art.' When Harding criticized his book, however, MacLennan was outraged. Why was he so receptive to his editors, yet so hostile to a critic who probably meant him equally well? First, the critic was a 'Ph.D.' – an honour he had considered dubious ever since his Princeton days. He had by now also developed a low opinion of professional literary criticism in general. In 1946, for example, he had complained bitterly to Bill Deacon about the academic critics: 'The darkest corner of [the academic grove] ... is labelled "English literature." [It] should never be studied in a vacuum ... Their complaint about affairs in Canada is so naïve it is pitiful. They feel a grievance we have no writers who can produce sufficiently abstruse books to warrant endless academic articles written by them!' This attitude, he explained to Gray in October, was in large part responsible for his reaction:

You did quite right to show me the letter, and in retrospect I think a great deal came out of it, however indirectly. I'm sorry if I seemed angry at the time I read it, but for all its honesty, its point of view stemmed directly from an attitude towards criticism which first got under my skin as long ago as 1934 and has been burrowing there ever since. Sometimes those people are right. They are seldom wrong in the general details of what they say. But seldom, also, does their critical faculty allow them to approach a book in the spirit of a man at the theatre – to approach it willingly and without reserve. They do this, I think, only in the case of a man whom they are strongly predisposed to like ... *After* that first approach is the time for the detailed criticism. That's how it worked with you and Angus, and that's why I was able to use your criticism. I may be wrong about Harding, and I hope I don't sound querulous, but for once in my life I felt impelled to talk back strongly about my own work. Not so much Harding, but the general attitude of the letter, seemed to me to sell *Each Man's Son* short.[26]

With Harding there had been no basis of friendship; more important, he had not balanced his criticism with praise. Whereas Cameron and Gray had the experience of dealing with senior writers, and so were constantly tactful in their criticism, Harding naïvely stated in his report: 'I do not make any comment upon the good points of the book as with an author of the stature of Mr. MacLennan those things are understood.'

Furthermore, it is likely that MacLennan, resenting his critics in general, and the fairly extensive criticisms of Gray and Cameron in particular, yet unwilling to risk giving vent to his frustrations at having to revise, found in Harding a ready, anonymous scapegoat for his anger. Something of this he vaguely realized later for he apologized to Harding and explained to Gray: 'I was probably tired that night in Toronto, and Mr. Harding certainly merited better than to be the recipient ... of feelings which probably had nothing to do with his letter at all.' Elsewhere he accounted for his extreme sensitivity by revealing the intense emotional involvement that accompanied the gestation and birth of each creative work: 'How peculiar a profession writing is, how strange are the areas of silence between a writer and his audience, and how impossible it often is to bridge these voids. The writer ... demands intuitively that the public accept his own private world in its own terms – worse still, that the public accept the private world of this or that particular book. While writing, he must write with this feeling. But he would do well to get over the feeling once the book is over. It may be of psychological interest to note that I didn't mind in the slightest anything Jim Scott said of my previous books. Why? Because I'm finished with them. They're out of me. They no longer belong to me. I'm now nearing the point where I will feel the same about *Each Man's Son*. So from now on you need not worry about me being so touchy about it.'[27] His response to Harding was indicative of his strong sense that a 'pattern' of hostile criticism (Jim Scott and Robert Weaver in particular) was emerging in Toronto.

Trying with this novel not to intellectualize his themes and characters, he demonstrated clearly that he did understand the difference between thinking and feeling in the creative process: 'If a book or play can reach the subconscious it has little to worry about. I'm trying to make this book do just that wherever possible ... Having faced it [the problem of Dr Ainslie's sense of guilt] intellectually, it will now be necessary for me to feel into it once more.' Elsewhere he maintained: 'Any psychoanalytical handling here would be out of place. The book is from the inside out, not from the outside in.' On more than one occasion he asserted that this book, more than any of his previous works, was a product of the 'total personality.' Work of that nature,' he explained, 'doesn't come easily, but once you've done it, everything else in fiction – at least anything else one does one's self – seems on another level entirely. One has to engage one's total personality in order to make a created character anywhere near total.' He believed, on completing *Each Man's Son*, that he would refute those critics who claimed that his characters were mere mouthpieces, weakly conceived and portrayed; critics, he warned Gray, 'expect a different kind of novel from the one they'll get.'[28]

Despite all the quibbling over revision that preceded the publication of *Each Man's Son*, MacLennan's great achievement in his novel was understood. In Dr Ainslie he had created an extraordinary character. Even Harding had agreed that 'the doctor, with his Calvinistic Cape Breton hound of heaven snapping at his heels is excellently drawn.' The character matched exactly his author's conception of him; as he later wrote to Marian Engel: 'There is no doubt in my mind that Ainslie is a true doctor, a very able one, [but] twisted and quite impossible to live with.' Certainly, he knew that his character was 'unsympathetic' and he feared that he would be considered 'an unsuccessful character if only for that reason.' Because he had used Ainslie both as the protagonist and as the structural pivot on which the resolution of both the main plot and the sub-plot depended, he was never really satisfied with the novel. '*Each Man's Son* is pretty personal, and I'm afraid rather muddy for that reason,' he admitted.[29]

A good indication of the way in which his own personal memories clouded his judgement about doctors can be seen in two articles written within a year after the publication of *Each Man's Son*. In 'Power and Love' (1951) and 'A Layman Looks at Medical Men' (1952), he expounded theories that made heroes of them. For him, 'medicine is the only profession in modern times in which men have fairly met the challenge peculiar to this century.' By this he meant that doctors used their power responsibly, with love, in their work: 'in medicine alone ... modern man has been entirely worthy of himself. Here power has been totally beneficent.' Not only did he believe that doctors are engaged in 'the finest human activity of modern times,' but he extravagantly claimed that the doctor had virtually replaced God as the object of worship and the dispenser of grace. He described the doctor as a lonely, isolated figure, set apart from his fellow citizens.[30] Such idealization was bound to provoke contradiction; and it did. Outraged at his misrepresentation of their profession, doctors responded hotly in letters to the editor of *Canadian Doctor* saying that they were neither isolated nor godlike, but merely hard-working. MacLennan's view of doctors was a highly idiosyncratic one. Although Dr Sam himself had, much more characteristically, said gruffly that he believed 'medicine kept a lot of people alive who would be much better off dead,'[31] MacLennan still looked up to doctors with a residue of the admiration he had had as a boy for his father.

Although such a personal view was unrealistic in everyday life, it did not really 'muddy' the novel; in fact, it served his artistic purposes well. With Dr Ainslie he returned to the theme that lay at the centre of *Barometer Rising*: the use and misuse of power. Just as Dr Murray in the earlier novel represents the beneficent uses to which scientific knowledge might be put, so too does Ainslie, who departs with his wife and newly adopted son at the novel's close for an international career as a specialist. In contrast to Ainslie, the boxer Archie illustrates the destructive uses to which power can be put.

As the publication date for *Each Man's Son*, 9 April 1951, drew close, Angus Cameron and John Gray carefully prepared their publicity campaign, knowing that MacLennan had been highly critical of the way in which Duell, Sloan and Pearce had launched *The Precipice*. As early as October 1950 he had started making suggestions himself. Irritated and perhaps a little frightened by the 'pattern' of persecution he thought was emerging among some critics in Toronto, he wanted to promote *Each Man's Son* by throwing 'the whole lot of them off balance.' As an advertising angle he suggested: 'Hugh MacLennan has confuted his critics in this book, etc., etc.' Calmly showing better judgement in this matter, Gray, by now his steadfast personal friend as well as his editor, quietly suggested coming at the critics 'obliquely in appealing positively to the general reader: "This is the warm and moving book that Mr. MacLennan's admirers have been waiting for." That is not elegant but I think it suggests the feeling we want; "a book for every man or woman who has had a son – or merely wanted one," etc.' Neither MacLennan nor his editors wished to highlight the novel's main theme, Calvinism, despite Cameron's initial enthusiasm for the slogan 'the first real Calvinistic novel in years.'[32]

Gray, especially, worked hard on a publicity campaign: an excerpt from the novel would appear in *Saturday Night*; CBC Radio would run a series of five half-hour programs dramatizing *Barometer Rising* on their trans-Canada network; MacLennan would appear on Morley Callaghan's radio quiz program for 13 April; large ads would go into American journals with wide circulation in Canada; *New Liberty* magazine would run a feature article for their April issue; booksellers were given postcards for customers and posters for display; specially bound volumes would go to reviewers; and press releases were scheduled for a large number of newspapers.[33]

Photographs for this extensive promotion campaign reveal that MacLennan's public image had not yet jelled into a single impression. It was almost as if his publishers wanted to present him from all angles at once to ensure that he did not turn on them, as he had turned on Duell, Sloan and Pearce. On the cover of *Saturday Night* on 10 April a glamorous Karsh photograph of his profile suggested that he was a highly sensitive aesthete. Inside the magazine, half a dozen photographs taken by Richard Arless at his home projected an entirely different image. These pictures show him sporting a moustache for the first time since he had been an Oxford undergraduate in Germany; complete with pipe and tweed jacket, he looked for all the world like an aristocratic English gentleman. Other pictures in the same magazine showed him at the typewriter in glasses, his shirt sleeves rolled up, his cigarette in a holder, looking like a dynamic and serious American journalist. Meanwhile, *Vogue* magazine on 15 May also ran an illustrated article with photographs taken at North Hatley by Mary McAlpine. These pictures show Dorothy and Hugh in working clothes in their garden; in one photograph he leans on a well-used hoe, wiping the sweat from his brow, his hair dishevelled by the wind, looking like the down-to-earth proletarian he had written about in the novel he never published, 'A Man Should Rejoice.' Where was the real MacLennan?

These spreads were but one aspect of the extensive publicity campaign mounted by Macmillan's. By radio, by poster, in journals and newspapers, and finally at parties in Montreal on 19 April and in Toronto on 25 April, *Each Man's Son* was confidently launched. Though MacLennan was strongly optimistic about its future, John Gray confided more cautiously to H. Lovat Dickson, director of Macmillan's in London: 'I don't really think it has the stuff of big sales, but at least we now feel that it will go over the 10,000 mark.'[34]

In the practical aspects of the publication of *Each Man's Son*, MacLennan showed a sound business sense. His previous experience gave him the knowledge and confidence to insist on alterations to the contract that was offered. Receiving a $1500 advance on royalties from Macmillan's and twice that amount from Little, Brown, he asked for a sliding scale of royalties based on a compromise between the usual British and American terms: 10 per cent to 2500 copies; 12½ per cent to 5000, 20 per cent thereafter. He also saw to it that the publisher got only a 10 per cent fee, rather than a fifty/fifty split, on all mass media income resulting from the book.[35] Much more assertive here than in the area of his writing itself, he acted firmly and with wisdom.

Meanwhile, Blanche Gregory had arranged with the American Literary Guild, a North American book club, to take on *Each Man's Son* as an alternative offering for August, assuring him that he and his publishers would make between $8000 and $10,000[36] as a result. In other areas, however, his long-time agent was proving to be redundant. Mass media representatives, book clubs, journals, and translators tended to approach MacLennan or his publishers directly, and Blanche Gregory showed little initiative in making the most of the new book. On the whole, she did not grasp the fact that the Canadian cultural network was then a small but accessible one; her contacts were all south of the border. Although later the Canadian branch of the Literary Guild also bought copies for their alternate choice in November, future deals with respect to *Each Man's Son* were handled directly by MacLennan or his publishers. John Gray was unable to interest Macmillan's in London in the book, partly because the readers' reports were only fair, but mainly because MacLennan's London agents, Pearn, Pollinger and Higham, had approached the firm too aggressively. By June, however, Wm. Heinemann Limited had accepted the book for publication in England. The Columbia Broadcasting System approached Macmillan's for the rights to a radio production and a newspaper syndicate headed by the *Montreal Standard* asked for serialization rights. This latter venture became too complicated for anyone to sort out, however; having two publishers with different contracts made it so difficult to know who had control over these rights that the matter was dropped. The television rights were sold to Ford Theatre for $600 with an eye to fall drama. As early as August 1951, MacLennan was approached for French translation rights.

But despite these outward signs of success, by the end of 1951 *Each Man's Son* had sold 10,500 copies through the Literary Guild, netting MacLennan much less than expected – $1181.25. In ordinary trade sales it sold the 10,000 copies that John Gray had predicted it would, earning MacLennan $2814.60. In other words, his total income from the book within the first year or so of its publication came to about $4600. Although this was not at all a bad total at the time, he was left with only $1500 after he had paid the $3150 needed for Dorothy's medical bills that year. It was two years before the National Film Board of Canada decided to make a film excerpt of the novel for $700 using MacLennan as a consultant. Eleven years were to pass before reprinting; fourteen years before the first paperback version of the novel appeared.

John Gray's caution about predicting the market was justified. *Each Man's Son* did not take off on high sales as MacLennan had hoped. A month after publication he was deeply upset. 'I've been shaken by news from Little, Brown,' he wrote to Gray on 14 May. 'It's not doing well down there, beyond universal praise from the critics.' Reviews did not, in fact, consist of unmitigated praise; more than one critic mentioned MacLennan's falling short of total success with his characters. Orville Prescott, who had given *Two Solitudes* a rave review in the *New York Times*, had actually echoed one of Harding's criticisms by writing that the book was 'never capable of stirring an emotional response.' Concentrating, as usual, on his themes – Calvinism, the pictoral presentation of Cape Breton, developing nationalism in Canada – only a few critics perceived what he hoped they would see beneath its surface. Except for one or two critics, among them his friend Bill Deacon who probably voiced more or less what MacLennan in conversation had told him of his intentions when he said the novel was 'expertly planned and executed,' the *literary* advance over his preceding work went unnoticed. Although Thomas Allen in the *New York Times* pointed out the universality of his themes and the controlled simplicity of the writing, George Woodcock in *Northern Review* merely mentioned the novel's sensitive and evocative passages and emphasized the theme of Calvinist guilt. Many reviewers criticized the ending over which MacLennan had laboured in revision as being artificial and too pat. One reviewer even theorized that in all his novels, the endings were weak. However, on the whole, reviewers thought this was MacLennan's best novel to date. Harriet Hill in the Montreal *Gazette*, for example, wrote: 'Now he returns to his native Nova Scotia for the setting of his new book which shows a rich maturity. All the old excellencies remain – the gift for narrative, the capacity to prison an unforgettable scene in a few words, the thoughtfulness marking everything MacLennan writes. But he has gained tremendously in the creation of character.' The *Chicago News* announced that it was 'unquestionably his finest work. It magnificently fulfills the promise of the earlier novels.'[37]

Why, then, were the sales of *Each Man's Son* so slack in both Canada and the United States? With excellent publicity and advertising, with reviews on the whole favourable, with a popular personal following such as he had by this time, sales were surprising. The truth of the matter seems to stand apart from these facts. The general North American public were at this point undergoing a broad cultural change as far as entertainment was concerned. With movies now readily within the budgets of many households and television beginning to appear in homes across the continent, reading as a source of entertainment seemed to be declining. Many are the articles from MacLennan and others protesting the replacement of reading time by watching time in a tone of voice bordering on hysteria. MacLennan protested not only because the shift to television implied cultural deprivation, unless television programs could be brought to the level of the world's literary masterpieces, but also because as a novelist he would no longer have a market. His publishers, too, were deeply concerned. 'The President of Macmillan, New York, was up here on Wednesday,' Gray wrote to him on 9 November 1951, 'with a pretty grim story to tell of the over-all result among American trade houses last year. Trade publishers generally throughout the United States lost money, that is the whole trade industry did on its book trading. It made up its losses slightly enough to give it about one-half per cent profit on the sale of secondary rights (movies, radio and the like) ... but it is still not a happy or healthy condition.'

Nor was the novelty of television and the success of motion pictures alone to blame for this. All publishers that spring were hit by the worst paper shortage ever. In addition, the increasing production of cheap paperbacks had taken the American market by storm. Novels such as *Each Man's Son* at three dollars had to compete with paperbacks of world classics, last year's bestsellers, and escape fiction selling for under a dollar in the bookstores. Times had changed for the worse, too, within the Literary Guild, which had chosen *Each Man's Son* as its alternate selection for August. Subscriptions had dropped from over 20,000 to half or a third of that number within the last few years. Though MacLennan could not see it at the time, however, another market, which would ultimately be one of his most profitable, had already begun. Claude Bissell's abridged school edition of *Two Solitudes*, with its glowing introduction, appeared in July 1951, following Macmillan's school edition of *Barometer Rising* (1948), the first of many later editions of his work to be used in classrooms across the nation. But at the moment this market did little to serve his practical needs. In the here and now, he had to face the cold fact that even a successful novel by a well-known novelist could not, under present conditions, earn one's keep: 'At least *Each Man's Son* settled one question – nobody can live by writing novels in Canada at the present time ... I'm grateful I was able to be free to do nothing but write for as long as six years. They were crucial years for me, but they are over now, and perhaps it's just as well ... A writer living alone in time begins to lose touch.'[38]

The winter of 1950-1 had been an expensive one. Dorothy, in mid-December, collapsed in a Montreal theatre with what appeared to be another embolism. Four days later she underwent an operation for a congenital twist in the small bowel. Sitting with her in the hospital for three days while her life teetered in the balance, MacLennan once more endured tremendous emotional strain. Her heart, stronger than it seemed, coped well, and she rallied on Christmas morning and recovered. MacLennan could manage only $50 a month towards the staggering bills and arranged terms. By 21 July 1951, however, he could not complete the payment of $450 the hospital demanded; so, distasteful as it was, he wrote to John Gray to inquire about Literary Guild payments, royalties, and so forth. Gray sent at once a cheque for $450 to cover the hospital expenses out of royalties already earned, but the larger financial problem remained. In humiliation he had to turn to his mother, who had remarried two years after Dr Sam died and was living in Halifax with her husband Clarence W. Anderson; from her he borrowed the $3000 he needed to pay his debts.[39]

Not only was Dorothy's illness expensive, her collapse that winter in which MacLennan had begun *Each Man's Son* really marked the point at which he realized her days were numbered. Later, he wrote of the novel to Marian Engel: 'It was written during one of the times in my life when I must say I was unhappy. I began the book about the time my wife's illness became fatal. I started the final re-write ... the day after she came out of the Ross after her second embolism ... Its undertones reflect my mood when I wrote it. I was learning to live with the condition which persisted until it ended.' For this reason, he considered the novel 'transitional,'[40] between an earlier period of his life in which there had been one kind of order and a much later period after Dorothy died when he was once again able to fit the fragments together into a coherent whole.

To earn money, he had continued to write as many articles for journals as he could commission. He wrote several pieces on Montreal for various magazines, and one on Nova Scotia; for *Saturday Night* he did a piece on Cape Breton. Each month he churned out an essay as well as a short editorial for the *Montrealer*, a magazine that was attempting to do in Canada what the *New Yorker* was doing in the United States; in one essay he turned his financial dilemma into a humorous situation, like the one in Leacock's 'My Financial Career': it began with the statement 'I was in the bank in the act of drawing out a small sum of money, and I mean small,' and went on to reveal the teller's assumption that all authors are rich. Eager to get on with another novel, about which he already had strong feelings and definite ideas, he confided to Gray on 14 May 1951: 'The new novel is clear in my mind and I'd like to plunge into it. However, the economic situation is too pressing and I doubt if I can do any fiction writing until I get some form of permanent or semi-permanent security. I don't particularly like the notion of returning to the academic fold and McGill and the University of Toronto are about the only places which would not be refuges from despair.'[41]

Writing directly to the principal and vice-chancellor of McGill University, F. Cyril James, he requested an interview. Fearing that this might be as fruitless as his application to McGill and to so many other places had been in the 1930s, he was pleasantly surprised to be offered, over the head of Harold Files, chairman of English, who was a friend and pleased to have him anyway, a part-time position. He accepted the job without protesting a salary so low that even his publishers were horrified.[42] For a mere $3000, the standard wage for such work, he was to teach two courses in English literature (five hours lecturing a week), one on seventeenth-century prose, the other on the modern novel. Meanwhile, for the summer months, he accepted an offer by Arthur Irwin of the National Film Board to work as a consultant, which involved spending several weeks in Ottawa; Dorothy's health was still such that this meant having her mother stay for the summer in North Hatley.

Staying alternate weeks in Ottawa with his friend Blair Fraser, he found he loathed this type of work. In the first place, he hated the travel, finding it disorienting. 'People move around too much in this century. Honestly, I think that's our principal trouble,' he told Gray. Secondly, he deplored the waste of time. Willing and eager to work, he refused a secretary on the basis that he had not yet been told what to do. After three weeks on the job he wrote 'Unless ... programs begin to get underway, I shall feel an imposter in this job.' Furthermore, he felt that he could not write scripts, though he was critical of the people who did: 'their work is weak in dialogue and story material.' Enjoying only those sessions in which creative ideas were exchanged with people like the historian Arthur R.M. Lower, the poet A.M. Klein, novelist Roger Lemelin, and radio commentator Lister Sinclair, he concluded that 'the novel trade has far more intrinsic integrity than these other mediums.' But, as he put it, 'with all its fiddle-de-dee this film board job has done better than pay my bills this summer.'[43]

Despite his apprehensions about entering the university world again, he found teaching greatly to his taste. Using his students as a sounding board, he really listened to their views on modern fiction – after all, they represented his future market. As early as two months after classes began, he was saying, as he maintained often from then on, that he was learning from his students. 'Their criticism of most current writing,' he told Gray, 'is that the characters are uninteresting because they are superficial ... I want to deal with deeper characters than I've handled heretofore. They should be the province of writers, for they are fundamentally more interesting. I have learned that much from my students.' Certainly the potential benefit of teaching fiction and prose to undergraduates was enormous. Not only could he acquaint himself with his future market but he was also himself forced to read, consider, and discuss the literary skills of other, more famous, writers. In so doing, he was likely to learn something himself. But this development, like all the other work he had taken on since the release of *Each Man's Son*, was not of his choosing. In fact, he refused to involve himself, as he had at Lower Canada College, in the life of the English Department. As he wrote to Gray: 'with a part-time job, my ambitions lying outside of the university, I can more or less keep free of politics. And if politics do mount, my resignation has been mentally written in advance.' Given his choice, he wanted to do nothing aside from the next novel that was germinating so actively inside him. However, as he was to write two years later: 'After that winter [1950-1] I decided absolutely that I must make myself financially independent of proceeds to come from fiction. Previously I had hoped that some day I would hit a jack pot, invest, and have that much of a backlog. It no longer was realistic to have that hope, I being the kind of writer I am and the market being what it is.'[44] His articles and essays, his work for the National Film Board, his teaching at McGill, were all forced upon him by the pressing need to earn money.

The fact that *Each Man's Son*, even though it did not sell enough copies to pay his bills, was enjoying greater critical success than *The Precipice* considerably influenced his career. It confirmed, once and for all, that he must confine himself to Canadian subjects and stick to the male point of view. If his 'gamble' with the theme and viewpoint in *The Precipice* had failed, his new departures with *Each Man's Son*, in which he attempted to correct the faults for which he had been criticized in his earlier fiction and to follow meticulously the suggestions of his editors, were more successful. 'I believe,' he wrote to Bill Deacon on 3 July 1951, 'that we in Canada must paddle our own canoe. We can't learn anything from the Americans for the simple reason that at the moment they have nothing to teach anybody. What we must resign ourselves to is the fact that the best we can do is to write good books and forget about making sales in the United States. Only by the sheerest accident is a Canadian writer likely to crack the American market today. From this it follows that a Canadian novelist might as well realize that he will have to do other work and carry on his writing simultaneously as best he can. My own career would seem to be as conclusive proof of this as one could wish to find.' He had been too ambitious with *The Precipice*; in trying to appeal directly to the larger American market he had had to back-track. 'Resigned' by the success of *Each Man's Son* to concentrating on the Canadian scene for both theme and market, he must also resign himself to working for his living.

Chapter nine

Plumbing the Depths: *The Watch That Ends the Night*

Tight with the tension that inevitably accompanied the completion of a novel, apprehensive especially about *Each Man's Son* on which he had staked his financial future, MacLennan abandoned himself in the summer of 1951 to the cool gales of North Hatley's sailing races and the fierce physical release of the week-long tennis tournament held there. He turned his attention as well to an assignment from *Holiday* magazine to write a piece on Montreal, which he had accepted mainly because it paid much more than the top Canadian magazines were able to pay for the same work. 'City of Two Souls,' like the many other articles about Montreal he would write over the next ten years or so, was filled with strong affection and loving, detailed observation of the city he had come to regard as the 'crucible of the nation's future.' To him, the mountain in the city's heart seemed 'utterly noble,' its forest park, through which riders spurred their horses each day, recalling the public parks in the great cities of Europe. But Montreal was also uniquely North American, evoking in him, as Halifax had done earlier, thoughts of the vast evolutionary process that had formed the land on which it stood: 'You can see how this world was scraped to its basalt bones by the glacier millions of years after it had been wrecked by such convulsions that a huge curved rent was made through which the waters of the Great Lakes could drain off into an ocean nineteen hundred miles away.' It boasted 'the greatest inland port in the world,' and its main artery, Sherbrooke Street, had become 'an emotion, an image in millions of minds ... a point of focus in

Dorothy's last painting, completed the day before she died in 1957 which the growth and meaning of Montreal as a cosmopolitan centre has at last become visible.' The dynamic mix of English and French, of European and North American, made the city seem to him 'a vital organism,' 'a covetous, bawdy, exciting place.'[1] To John Gray he remarked how thoroughly he was enjoying his assignment to describe it. As the tension dissolved and feeling flooded back, his unconscious mind threw to the surface the ideas that would take shape in his next novel. So it was of Montreal he was thinking – the city that by now was like part of his own soul – as he began to write *The Watch That Ends the Night*.

Even before the publication of *Each Man's Son* in April 1951 he had started work on his next book. 'Up to a fortnight ago,' he wrote in a lengthy letter to Gray on 7 December 1950, 'I had been making character sketches for a contemporary novel set in Montreal. I was right into it, feeling it strongly.' But this surge of creativity, he declared, had been interrupted by the crisis in Korea, which distressed him so deeply that he stopped writing to consider instead the larger implications of this event.

The outbreak of hostilities between South and North Korea in June 1950 had convinced him that 'we are closer to Dunkirk than to Munich ... The best we can hope for is that times will grow a lot worse before they get better.' For him personally, this meant that writing fiction at all might be a senseless activity: 'I have found it increasingly hard to believe that my projected novel of Montreal will seem important enough for me to make a good job of it.'

His confidence had been shaken also by the criticism his work had received in Toronto – a criticism that rankled sorely. With stubborn pride and more than a hint of truculence, he speculated to Gray: 'Perhaps I would have done better a long time ago to have argued with people criticizing my books as I did that night with Jim Scott. I had felt it was a little undignified to justify one's self, and so forth. But since that evening with you and Jim I feel I have come to certain conclusions, and I wonder what you think of them.'

He proceeded to throw out a bewildering series of theories on contemporary fiction and his own artistic problems in an attempt to rationalize his position as a modern writer. In doing so, he diverged both from his earlier opinions and from what he considered to be the mainstream of fiction at the time. As he later confessed to Gray, he was really groping in the dark: 'I'm not so sure that I'm right as that a lot of other people are wrong.'[2]

Certainly he thought Jim Scott and others were wrong in attacking his work on the grounds that he explained things too fully and brought national issues too much into his narratives; he could not, and would not, detach himself from the issues that had been the very means to his success as an author. Although he was more than willing to leave out those lengthy explanations that had encumbered his earlier work – indeed, he wanted even less explanatory background material in *Each Man's Son* than his editors were insisting upon – his emotional involvement with the Canadian nation had now become something akin to a commitment. In *Barometer Rising* he had tried to express the new nationalism by illustrating Canada's release from the bonds of colonialism and demonstrating the necessity for a 'non-committal' attitude towards both Britain and the United States. In *Two Solitudes* he had tried to show that in Canada's state of 'becoming' a modern state based on the co-operation of two different nationalities was a model that could be useful for the entire Western world. Both *The Precipice* and *Each Man's Son* had tried to put a finger on one of the central traits of the nation – an inflexible puritanism, different from the American version, which was both the nation's strength and its demon. Neither of these last two novels had quite captured what he wanted. Now he groped, as if in the dark, for something so elusive he could get at it only through theories that seemed somewhat preposterous. What indeed *was* the nature of Canada's national character? In his long letter to Gray on 7 December he made a preliminary attempt to answer this question:

It is a fact today that the destinies of millions of people are not affected by their own characters at all, but by the policies of nations ... Where individual character was destiny before, national character seems to be destiny now. I have felt this deeply for a long time, ever since before World War II began. And it was this feeling, probably more than anything else, which was responsible for the nature of at least two of my novels before *Each Man's Son*. People who don't feel this way about national character, naturally have thought that a book like *The Precipice* was cold and intellectual. At any rate it was a relative failure.

But if you look back on the great dramatic characters – Oedipus, Faust, Hamlet, Lear, Othello, Macbeth – only Hamlet is credible today, assuming Hamlet to be a modern man. No modern man could ignore so blindly the warning signs of impending danger as did the others unless he were mad, in which case he would not be tragic. The last great tragic heroes were Capt.

Ahab [*Moby Dick*] and Rubashov [*Darkness at Noon*], and it is significant that Rubashov was not so much the symbol as the incarnation of communistic intellectualism. But any other man intelligent enough to be a great general (Macbeth and Othello), or a great king (Oedipus) would inevitably have enough sophistication, enough knowledge of society and psychology, to withhold his decisive actions until he had verified the evidence. At least, any modern civilized man would so act.

On the other hand, this is not true of nations. Nations are apparently as incapable of heeding warning signs as were primitives like Othello and Oedipus. Nations succeed or fail according to their characters, and in the case of nation after nation, the individual tragic flaw has brought them to visible ruin before our eyes. Germany was Faust (the ablest and blindest of all the tragic heroes). The flaw in France is *La peur d'être dupé* – the over-trust in the intellect which enables France as a nation to be satisfied if she can analyze a situation in such a way as to uphold her intellectual vanity even at the cost of her existence. The flaw in the United States is the flaw of adolescent pride, which is constantly at war with the good side of that same adolescent who has received a very moral upbringing and can't understand why everyone doesn't like him, who doesn't want to grow up and – oh, God, the United States is so complicated and yet so transparent!

But a country like ours, at least up to the moment, is at best a sort of Horatio to Hamlet – though the U.S.A. is not much of a Hamlet.

This lengthy diatribe, not sustained particularly by internal logic and certainly not by reference to reality, reveals MacLennan's keen dislike of one assumption on which much fiction of the time was based: that character determines destiny. His own personal experience had been exactly the contrary, and it was out of this intense personal frustration that his aesthetic theories arose. Like an oyster, he was turning inward, going back again and again to the indigestible grit of his life experience, trying to make of it something with meaning and value.

In his quest he concentrated especially on defining a hero that might be called 'great' or 'tragic' without being old-fashioned and on presenting a novel that would strike the reader as contemporary without making it so narrow that the effect on human destiny of world events, such as the Korean War which now threw its shadow across his own path, would be overlooked. 'It is no accident,' he surmised, 'that the best contemporary novels have narrowed the field so that they deal with only a few individuals and probe the depth of those characters, yet have, on the whole, been unable to make the claim that these characters are "great" enough to be genuinely tragic.'

Up until this point, MacLennan had revered Shakespeare, along with the classical writers of Greece and Rome, as a writer in the 'heroic' tradition who struck 'universal' themes.[3] Now, for the first time, he called into question the validity of the term 'hero' in relation to Shakespeare's characters. In the context of modern society, with its extensive communications systems and universal scientific education, men like Othello, Lear, and Macbeth simply could not possess the 'tragic flaws' upon which their destinies pivot. Only Hamlet's dilemma had kept pace with the evolution of civilization.

In an essay he wrote in 1955 called 'Shakespeare Revisited,' he would refine this view to conclude that in Shakespeare's work there is a shocking absence of heroes: 'More than any other writer who ever lived, he took it for granted that decent men are dull. Worse still he assumed they were all dupes. He does not offer a single truly religious person in the whole folio, none who is at once steadfast, intelligent and competent.'[4] Although he no longer wished to use Shakespeare as a model for his characters, this did not mean that he had come closer to the literature of his own day. In the contemporary literature he was accused of ignoring, the fundamental premise seemed to him to be that 'character is destiny.' With this premise he could not agree, for to him the forces of fate lay beyond the control of the individual. Instead, the individual's life was subject, more than anything else, to the policies of nations – policies that were most dramatically enacted in wartime. The novel of civil life, if less dramatic, was nevertheless indistinguishable from the novel of military life; as the soldier was subject to the decisions of generals, themselves subject to the decisions of statesmen, so too were civilians tossed about willy-nilly on the ship of state. The trouble with following this modern trend in fiction was that it had already been done to death: characters had become too ordinary to be termed 'great' or 'tragic.' It became his personal challenge to find some concept of man's relation to the contemporary world that would reveal his role in the face of destiny yet avoid the depressing and, by now, trite conclusion that life is insignificant and man worthless. If neither Shakespeare nor modern English fiction provided suitable models, how were man's heroism and life's value to be dramatized in modern times?

Deeper still was the issue of national character, and he began to answer his question by shifting the theory of character as destiny to *national* character as destiny. 'Tragic flaws,' as he theorized to Gray, might seem improbable in individuals, but such flaws could easily be detected in the blindness of entire nations. Canada, he had concluded, 'is at best a sort of Horatio to Hamlet – though the U.S.A. is not much of a Hamlet.'[5]

MacLennan here stumbled on a theory of national identity the significance of which apparently eluded him. In casting Canada as Horatio to the United States' Hamlet, he did so at Canada's expense. His comparison suggested that Canada was at best a minor character in a world drama in which the United States played a starring role, Horatio being no more than a 'side-kick,' a willing collaborator, to the glamorous Hamlet. But he overlooked the fact that Canada had taken the lead in the North American contribution to two world wars, having entered both conflicts first – three years earlier in the instance of the First World War. Had he been able to see beyond his personal gripe that as a writer he had not been born into a country that was centre-stage, perhaps he might have grasped the wider implications of his remark: that Horatio was the better man, the wise, old counsellor who through his wisdom had outlasted the immature prince. Canada likewise had acquired sufficient experience at home and abroad to act with integrity and good judgement; what MacLennan had intuited in a flash was a far more apt analogy than he knew.

Canada's national 'flaw,' as he was on the verge of recognizing, was that it was curiously undramatic: in reaching nationhood gradually, without the suffering that usually accompanies such rites of passage, it did not lend itself to conventional heroics. He sensed that it was going to be inordinately difficult to create a hero who could at one and the same time be 'great' and yet represent the nation. 'It seems to me quite impossible,' he told Gray, 'to translate [my thoughts] into a contemporary novel.'

As he looked around him in the early 1950s he felt strongly that these years marked the end of that period of fundamental transition he had perceived from his Oxford years on. In an essay in 1955, 'The Transition Ends,' he analysed the new state of the world and the era of change which had ushered it in.

The agonizing transition which followed the end of the Victorian epoch has at last ended. What has resulted from the recent class war in the west and the struggle for power in Europe we can now see pretty clearly. It is unity – not the unity of the true believer, but the unity of disillusioned men who have settled for the mundane principle that life must go on regardless of the number of ideas which must be sacrificed. It is strange, it is almost fantastic, to compare the social atmosphere of twenty years ago to that of today. Who in 1935 could have believed that the European balance of power would count for so little in 1955? What socialist of the hungry thirties dreamed of the day when he would be a bureaucrat working for the Technical Assistance department of United Nations, relying gratefully on the capacity of General Motors and General Electric to produce a surplus? What tory of the Baldwin era foresaw the time when his party would be in power and popular, simply because it had adopted most of the views of its socialistic opponents? What prophet of the Hitler Decade guessed that Hitler's Beyond-This-Nothing War would result in unprecedented prosperity for the west? Was the cynic right when he said *plus ça change, plus c'est la même chose*? Does history always mock its makers? Did all those thinkers think irrelevantly, all those heroes die irrelevantly, all those prophets prophesy irrelevantly?

For MacLennan, the answer to these questions was 'Not quite.' 'The chief feature of this new age,' he argued, 'is the final acknowledgment by the West that the principles of democracy apply to all mankind.'[6] From his earliest notions of writing fiction in the 1930s, he had felt and seen that this violent transition in values had led to war. Even from his first unpublished novel, he had been attempting to demonstrate how this change was taking place: in 'So All Their Praises' Michael feels that the upheaval of the age is robbing the individual of significance and the creative imagination of a point of view from which to speak; the question that had hounded him as he wrote 'A Man Should Rejoice' had been 'Can a human being have and feel significance when he lives in such an age [of transition]?'; in *Barometer Rising* he had related the Halifax explosion in an earlier war to the wild devastation afoot in the Second World War once fascism and capitalism were unleashed; by the time he wrote *Two Solitudes* he had done his best to turn Canada's 'state of "becoming"' a nation out of its diverse elements into a reflection of a move towards unity throughout the whole Western world; in *The Precipice* he had analysed some of the forces behind the transition – capitalism in particular – and had shown the negative results of accelerated change; in *Each Man's Son* he had turned to questions of religious belief in such an age. Now, as the transition apparently came to an end in the uneasy truce between East and West known as the 'Cold War,' he combined a number of these earlier concerns in the widest consideration of human history he had yet attempted.

'It is not the new age,' he argued in 'The Transition Ends,' 'but the transition which stirs the passions.' Because of this, he surmised, the heroes of the transition had become increasingly more desperate and solitary. Since he believed that it was in 'the character of the fictional hero that an age reveals its inner meaning,' it was natural for him to look carefully at the representative heroes the transition had produced: Conrad's Kurtz, forerunner of Naziism, Galsworthy's Soames, along with the heroes of Proust, Mann, Joyce, Dos Passos, Koestler, Hemingway, and Waugh, all demonstrated the obsession with loneliness and escape from the haunted self that MacLennan believed was typical of the neurotic age that had spanned the first half of the twentieth century.

As far as his own book was concerned, he asked himself the question: 'What manner of man will the hero become in this new, more stable age?' 'It is almost certain,' he reflected, 'that he will be more intelligent than the haunted men of the transition, less desperate, less neurotic, and more willing to accept life as it is. As it is with men, so it is with nations. Only by accepting their own limitations can they become wise; only by facing down their own fears can they hope to be happy.'

In this summary of the kind of man who would likely be the new hero in the new age, he forecast the character of the man who would become his own hero, George Stewart. These speculations were called forth partly by a humorous book, well known at the time, entitled *Little Man, What Now*? by Rudolf Ditzen (1933). In this book, the question of 'what now?' specifically reflected the dilemma of all men who come to realize that they are 'just as little as all the other little men of the earth.' Later MacLennan was to incorporate this book's title into his novel's climax;[7] for the time being the speculations it prompted included the notion of a hero suitable for the characteristics of this new, more democratic age.

At first he had contemplated writing his autobiography, an idea he soon discarded because 'that would be far too cramping.' Next he thought seriously about reviving the notion he had used for his radio play in 1939 to present Augustus in Roman times as an allegorical comment on the modern era; the success of *The Egyptian* by Mika Toimi Waltari in 1949 had turned his attention to the possibilities of historical fiction, but this idea, too, he rejected within days after rereading the lives of Augustus and Augustine whose life he also considered dramatizing. Finally, he told Gray, he had decided to 'go back again to my own roots':

If *Each Man's Son* is authentic – of course we still don't know how it will fare with the public – I can continue in the pattern begun there. *Each Man's Son* is, I think, an entity; but the story doesn't come near ending there. It was written out of a profound compulsion to answer basic spiritual questions – no, question isn't the word – to meet the challenge of my own and other people's identity in a series of disintegrating worlds. Such, in effect, is the experience if not the story of my own life. I have lived in, and tried to accomodate [*sic*] myself to, four different worlds [Halifax, Oxford, Princeton, and Montreal], three of which for one reason or another became impossible for me to live in, and two of which have virtually disintegrated already.

I plan no autobiography ... but to try to create order out of the general pattern of the life and lives I've seen seems to me the fundamental challenge.[8]

All along, his greatest difficulty as a writer had been to find a focus for his material. On the one hand, he wanted to let what he called the 'great themes' shape themselves organically from within to reflect life. But, on the other hand, he did not want his novels to become shapeless. He had still not found a satisfactory resolution to this problem: the two unpublished novels contained more material than they could gracefully hold; *Barometer Rising*, while beautifully focused, had been too 'limiting' by leaving out so much he wanted to express; Athanase Tallard had run away with *Two Solitudes*, leaving the protagonist Paul far behind; in *The Precipice* he had lodged his point of view unwisely in his heroine; *Each Man's Son*, like *Barometer Rising*, was firmly focused, but again at the expense of the 'great themes.' To compound this dilemma, the attention critics and public alike had lavished on his so-called nationalism distracted his energies from this purely fictional problem. Basking in the praise his themes evoked, acutely responsive to the need Canada expressed for a spokesman in fiction, he had sometimes mistaken technical problems for cultural ones. Seduced from his wider ambitions by the more narrow success of national popularity, he had proceeded in an ambivalent way. While he was grateful for recognition and success no matter what form it took – to be acclaimed for the wrong reasons was, after all, better than not being acclaimed at all – his letters and essays reveal his discomfort and even his bitterness at not being recognized for what he really was: a writer who wished to give the world novels on the great universal and international themes, who simply happened to be a Canadian. He had recognized all along that the reviewers and critics usually missed this point. Too often his theories of fiction smacked of sour grapes as he tried to reason his way out of his predicament; underneath it all, he wished that he had been born elsewhere, where fiction had a base in tradition, a recognizable identity, and a ready market.

Because of the unique cultural situation in which he found himself, and especially because of the inadequacies of the critics he read so closely hoping to find clues that would aid in his success, his advance towards the resolution of his particular problem of finding a suitable focus for his unmanageable themes had been seriously delayed. Despite these difficulties, however, by the time he had finished *Each Man's Son* his self-confidence had increased and he was ready to come to grips with the problem that had always plagued him.

At first, he allowed those universal themes to ebb and flow organically. 'My next novel,' he wrote with self-assurance to Gray on 25 January 1951, 'has been working out in my mind. In odd moments I've already drafted the major scenes, and I will start work whenever things settle down so I can stay at my desk two hours at a time. Little, Brown call *Each Man's Son* "great" in their blurb. It isn't, not really ... But ... the next one will be, and I doubt if you've met anyone who uses that word so carefully.' Five months later, well after characters and scenes had started to surface, his perennial problem appeared: how to contain that amorphous mass of themes, settings, situations, and lives, which moved and shifted like some giant amoeba of the imagination? 'I'm looking for something new in my work and am not sure what form it is going to take ... I see life less and less conventionally, and the perfectly ordered book, the kind with classical structure like *Each Man's Son*, seems to me too rigid for me to release myself into. I'll have to find some way to discover the release without confusion. *Each Man's Son* was certainly better written, better ordered, more accurate and deep in its insights than anything else I ever wrote, but there is a real question whether it reflected life as well as *Two Solitudes* did, which has less deep insights into personalities, is ill-ordered and was written under such pressure of other work that it got out of hand.'

Somehow, he felt, *Two Solitudes* had come closest to expressing the view of life he wanted to convey. Afterwards he recognized that he had not quite captured his view. By submitting his manuscript too soon so that he could resign his teaching position at Lower Canada College, he had sacrificed the possibility of finding its true focus in one last revision. He had learned, however, from this mistake. Now he was determined to take his time. 'This is a book which will never move fast,' he stated categorically by the summer of 1953, a view he reiterated over the entire eight years it took to write it. He had come to recognize earlier that year that 'if a novelist feels himself desperate for time and money, and can't spend the energy to make a decent living, it shows in his work, making it narrow, cloistered and bitter.'

The part-time teaching job he had taken at McGill in 1951 was mainly responsible for this more relaxed approach to writing. Once he had adjusted to the disappointment of having to give up writing full-time, he characteristically made the best of a bad situation: 'I may not be able to produce so many novels in the future, now I have abandoned hope of supporting myself by them alone; but the chances are they may be better ones.' Not only were his lecture hours a great improvement over the gargantuan duties at Lower Canada College, but he saw that his students could actually provide him with a useful index of contemporary taste. And taking up a university post gave him the status and prestige he deserved. Above all, he could stop worrying about money; the pressure was off.

This relaxed attitude, combined with his greater self-confidence, allowed him to stand free of the influences that had restrained his creativity earlier. Again, he had learned by his mistakes. No longer would he slavishly try to join some 'American branch cycle' of literature as he had done with *The Precipice*. 'We can't learn anything from the Americans,' he maintained to Bill Deacon, for 'they have nothing to teach anybody.' Canadians must resign themselves to writing good books and forget about attempting to crack the United States market. 'We in Canada must paddle our own canoe,' he emphatically concluded in an image that found its way into the very heart of his novel.[9]

Curiously, even the slump into which fiction generally had fallen did not deter him; rather, it gave him a kind of philosophical detachment: 'Of course, in the interval, the market for novels may collapse, and if it does there's no way out. Meanwhile I propose to go on and do what I can. Writing is a gamble anyway, but I don't think you can beat the bank by trying to outguess the future.' At the end of 1951 a number of these changes had combined into a strongly optimistic outlook. 'Whatever this new book will be,' he wrote Gray, 'it will be pretty fundamental or nothing. One thing the state of the market and the rise of pocket books, combined with my sudden incursion into 17th century writing [preparing a course on English prose at McGill] has done, has been to convince me that by *trying* to be popular I'm not very likely to succeed. I want to deal with deeper characters than I've handled heretofore. They should be the province of writers, for they are fundamentally more interesting. I have learned that much from my students. Their criticism of most current writing is that the characters are uninteresting because they are superficial. The novel-reading market will never again be as large as it once was ... But maybe a good novel, written vividly with some depth in the writing, will have some sort of market.'[10]

In a number of speeches during the early 1950s he worked again at educating the public so that they would be more receptive to his work. In one such address, 'Fiction in the Age of Science,' which he delivered at McGill on 1 June 1951 to the Humanists' Association of Canada, he outlined the 'crisis' in the book trade. Serious fiction, he argued, was not paying its way. Since one peak year of 1945 the cost of printing was up 300 per cent while royalties remained at pre-war rates. The news media of television and radio dominated the modern scene even though the need for serious fiction was as great as ever. The best fiction now, he maintained, shows the soul of a man of goodwill: 'He is a lonely man, often guilt-haunted without knowing why, religious even in his agnosticism, deeply caring even when he shrugs his shoulders. He yearns desperately for a change from the technological nightmare in which he finds himself.' Later, in 1955, he spoke to the Royal Society of Canada's annual meeting on 'The Challenge to Prose,' analysing the various factors that provided obstacles to the prose writer of the day: a jaded audience, the rise in paperback sales, changes in literary taste, the adeptness of non-fiction writers since Lytton Strachey, and the influence of psychology. The novel, he asserted, must return to people again and a belief in the value of the individual.[11]

As he let his novel grow in its own time during the first couple of years after *Each Man's Son* was published, he made a conscious decision that was to prove of the utmost importance in resolving his perennial problem of finding a focus for his themes: he chose the first person point of view. Using John Gray now more as a 'sounding board' than as the ultimate authority, as he had with *Each Man's Son*, he wrote on 12 June 1952, almost immediately after he got word that the Lorne Pierce Medal for Literature had been awarded to him: 'Somehow the third person approach must presuppose, on the part of the audience, a more settled point of view [than] exists now. In times of chaos we fall back on the only thing we can know for sure – our own responses – and we trust a writer who at least appears to be doing the same. And the present time is surely chaotic, more than at any time I can remember, for at least in the 1930s and early 1940s a lot of people thought they had the answers and now nobody thinks that. However, it may turn out impossible to handle this in the first person way. There are always the two great problems – the limitations of the narrator and the character of the narrator.'

As always, he chafed at the thought of 'limitations' on the 'great themes' that concerned him. Two days later he was somewhat dubious about his decision. 'Do you think my guess is right,' he asked Gray, 'that at the present time the first-person approach has a better chance and seems more real than the third person? It may make no difference one way or the other to what I finally do. It is more than possible that I will have to return to the third person approach, and if I have to do it, I suppose I'll do it.' Gray's response, at once honest and encouraging, was largely responsible for reinforcing his choice: 'I think I agree with you about the first-person treatment. Undoubtedly it has more impact and probably for that reason comparatively few books can really bear up under it because unless the book itself is strong, the insistence of the first person claims too much attention. However, this is obviously just what your exploration is about and you will know presently whether the story can stand that strain. When it can, I think with you that it is a natural for these times.'[12]

MacLennan was late in recognizing what was by that time a commonly held theory – that the revolution from third person to first person fiction, begun by Joyce, Woolf, and Faulkner, was intimately related to the times. For this tardiness there were a number of reasons. In the first place he had himself experimented with the first person in his earliest novel 'So All Their Praises'; there too he had tried a stream-of-consciousness technique for some parts of the novel. But he had mixed his point of view, letting a third person omniscient narrator tell those parts of the story Michael couldn't know. Because that novel failed to find a publisher, he decided not to try that point of view again. In his later work his concerns had been elsewhere, at first for his themes, then for his characters. Finally, the writers who had used the first person were not to his liking; looking inward had so often meant narrowing the arena of human experience, and he had not looked to these writers for inspiration.

Now he was ready to try the first person for a number of reasons. Although he didn't see it himself, this switch was a direct result of his new self-confidence. The confidence that had taken such blows in the thirties was now revived to the point where an authoritative 'I' was possible. He had also been struck by the authenticity of much recent non-fiction, most of which had been written in the first person: Rebecca West, in particular, with her *Black Lamb and Grey Falcon* (1941), had gripped his imagination by showing how great themes could be elucidated from a single perspective. Dorothy's non-fiction, especially *Partner in Three Worlds*, had shown him the same thing. But it was actually Whittaker Chambers' *Witness* (1952), about the trial of the alleged communist agent in the United States Department of State, Alger Hiss, that provided the catalyst. In the same letter to Gray in which he first mentioned the possibility of using the first person, he prefaced those remarks as follows: 'I have an idea that at the present time the third person novel seems to lack authenticity with a public increasingly conditioned by non-fiction ... No novel, for example, could possibly be as exciting as Chambers' *Witness*, nor is it likely that a third person approach could achieve such an important result.' At the time he had just completed an essay called 'A Would-be Saint' about this book for the *Montrealer*.[13] Novels competing for the market with dramatized non-fiction, he saw, would have to adapt.

Above all, however, his choice of point of view resulted from the essays he was writing at the time. As he reached full stride both as a writer and as a public figure, his output was prodigious. Something of the enormous energy he was expending can be glimpsed in his own account of 'the heaviest month's work of my life,' December 1953, 'worse by a considerable deal than the month before Honour Mods. in Oxford.' In addition to his work on the novel, he accomplished the following: '(1) a 9,000 word piece on Canada for *Holiday* involving a lot of research, a jig-saw puzzle of a job when it came to getting it all in and making it readable. (2) A *Montrealer* piece. (3) A Montreal letter for Cooke's new *Saturday Night*. (4) McGill up to Dec. 21 (5) TV every Sunday night. (6) A paper on "The Artist in Society" as part of a series of panel discussion in Princeton at the meeting of their Graduate School alumni.' From all sources, these efforts netted him $2200. Financially, his worries were at bay. Over the years of the mid-fifties he averaged thirty articles a year; for the whole decade, 1950-9, his average was only slightly less. With a weekly letter to *Saturday Night*, along with the monthly articles (at $125) and frequent editorials (at $100) he wrote for the *Montrealer* between April 1951 and May 1959, he earned for himself and for Dorothy a small buffer of funds against disaster. By now, he had come a long way from his view at the time he wrote *The Precipice* that he was not so good as an essayist as he was at novels. 'I can write an acceptable essay now in two days,' he wrote to his graduate student Marian Engel in 1958: 'In 1946 I couldn't write a good one at all, and not even an acceptable one in under a month. That is technique, years of practice and training.'[14] Dorothy also had been busy thinking of ways to supplement their income, and she decided to put her editorial skills to work collecting the best of her husband's essays for a second collection; her proposal was encouraged by Macmillan's, and she proceeded to put together *Thirty and Three*, which came out in 1954. Although the financial security MacLennan's essays brought was important in itself for his sense of well-being, the writing of them had an effect far beyond his original aim of making money. In them he developed the habit of writing in the first person. It was in this arena that he experimented and practised with different subjects, a variety of characters, and, most important of all, different tones of voice.

The city of Montreal, which had provided the base of inspiration for the novel now under way, dominated his essays during the fifties. Over and over again he explored aspects of the city – its geography, its hospitals, its politics, its art shows, even its streetcar conductors. As he concluded in an article he did for *New Liberty* magazine in September 1952, cities allow the writer more freedom to tell the truth than small towns, a theory seen from the opposite point of view in his humorous rendition of North Hatley in 'Everyone Knows the Rules' (1951). In the city, he maintained, good and evil are juxtaposed in stark contrast and with greater intensity than elswhere. Above and beyond that, Montreal remained for him 'the heart of Canada' both politically and culturally. Although he concentrated, as a result, on an exploration of big city life, he paid tribute to the small towns of the nation as being the ideal environment in which the creative mind can grow up: in 'If You Drop a Stone' (1952), for example, he illustrated how the intimacy of small towns fosters the sense of an audience and a direct impression of life's realities.[15] Once again, in expressing these views, he revealed his growing self-confidence: making the best of circumstances he convinced himself that he had had the best possible environment for a writer – a childhood in small communities and now the anonymity of a large city, which allowed him not only the freedom to say whatever he wished but also located him at the hub of his nation's life.

The young man who had grown up a conservative and had flirted with Marxism in the thirties, toying with liberalism and socialism along the way, had become a reasonably independent political commentator, but with increasingly conservative leanings. After the Second World War, when events such as the Berlin blockade and the coup in Czechoslovakia had appeared to him to be part of a deliberate strategy of aggression on the part of the Soviet Union, he had come to oppose communist principles strongly, for communism in the service of Russian imperialism was a far cry from the society he imagined it might bring about two decades earlier. In articles like 'A Would-be Saint' and 'Damnatio Memoriae' (1956), about Krushchev's accession to power, he condemned communism in what he called its 'messianic' phase as a 'psychosis,' although under the new leader, he maintained, this psychosis would eventually be tempered into 'managerial development.' He even experimented during these years, quite unsuccessfully, with the science fiction mode for purposes of political comment; in both 'The Finding of the Way' (1955) and 'Remembrance Day' (1957) he took the competition between the West and the East in the 'space race' to bizarre, if logical, conclusions. But because he was also critical of United States imperialism in the Far East, he wrote articles such as 'The Albatross' (1955) arguing for peace and neutrality wherever possible. Reflecting the political orthodoxy of his day, he saw Canada's international role as that of 'middleman,' encouraging co-operation and compromise, but one in which, of necessity, ties with the United States formed 'the bedrock of our foreign policy.' On the whole, he preferred the British system of government to either republican democracy or communism: his pieces on the death of Queen Mary and on the eightieth birthday of Sir Winston Churchill amounted to outright panegyric. And when the Conservatives in Britain were returned once again in 1955, this time under Sir Anthony Eden, he was delighted, observing that at last 'moral health and economic stability' would return to the United Kingdom, an observation he had difficulty in reconciling a year later with Eden's blunders during the Suez crisis.[16]

At home, he felt little sympathy for the Liberal government, even though he voted for its return to power in 1953 on the grounds that its members were able administrators and the most likely to preserve national unity. But to him they seemed a dull lot, incapable of 'vision or vistas,' responsible for lulling the nation into a 'trance' of complacency. His disappointment with the Conservative party, with whom he felt more *en rapport*, occasionally surfaced, but it is no surprise to find him deeply moved by Donald Creighton's new biography of Sir John A. Macdonald, and excited at the first signs that the Liberal party was at last falling out of popular favour in 1956; for him, the Liberal government over the years had combined 'the worst features of socialism with the worst features of capitalism.' His essays on the swing to a Conservative government reflected his sense that the world was emerging from a transitional phase into a new age. Even the titles of the articles treating the political climate at the time of John Diefenbaker's election in 1957 expressed this notion: 'Canada's Revolution – WHY Did It Happen?' 'A New Era Is Recognized,' 'The Glacier Melts at Last,' 'Will the Trance End This Year?' As he approached his fiftieth year, he was becoming more and more conservative. 'I am waiting,' he had written in 1956, not entirely tongue-in-cheek, 'for the world to recover the kind of stability my Victorian ancestors took for granted.'[17] He was beginning to sound a little bit like Dr Sam.

In the course of writing these political commentaries, he was clarifying his own views as well as working out the political stage for his next novel. At the same time, he was testing his theories on other subjects. In an essay called 'The Homeric Tradition' (1955), he argued that contemporary sports writers had taken over the literary tradition of adventure stories. Sports columns introduced personalities whose physical prowess constituted a kind of heroism which made 'life larger than life.' He clung to an admiration of physical heroes, even though he was working out a quite different concept of the 'hero' for his novel. In 'Good Old Human Nature' (1952), 'Modern Tennis – A Study in Decadence' (1953), and 'Queen of Tourneys' (1955), for example, he paid tribute to the physical powers of his favourite tennis champions; in 'Fury on Ice' (1954) and 'Explosion and the Only Answer' (1955) he described the hockey matches he loved to watch. Even his nostalgic essay 'Orgy at Oriel' (1952) shows him practising the 'fast action' description he would eventually use in his novel, especially in the sections concerning the athletic 'transitional' hero Jerome Martell.[18]

His more relaxed attitude in general also freed his sense of humour. A number of the essays and articles he produced at this time tried out various styles of humour, with marked success. 'Laughter,' he had come to see, 'was the mark of civilized man.' Taking himself and his subjects in a much lighter vein than he usually did, he was witty, playful, and satiric by turns. Tongue-in-cheek pieces such as 'But Shaw Was a Playwright ...' (1951) and 'Everyone Knows the Rules' showed a new confidence in his audience. No longer did he feel the need to explain; at last he could assume the reader would 'get the joke.' Directly satirical pieces such as 'Remembrance of Men Past' (1955) revealed a refreshing ability to laugh at past events he had usually considered only in their serious, even tragic, aspects. Most successfully, he turned his playful side to the consideration of issues he really did take seriously, allowing them to reach the reader not as sermons but as subtle innuendoes. 'The Secret and Voluptuous Life of a Rose-Grower,' 'Divertimento for Males,' (1954) and 'By Their Foods ...' (1956) are excellent examples of this new direction.[19] Working from the most ordinary situations, his summer garden, a cocktail party, his experiences of foods from around the world, in which he whimsically explored the absurdity of his current preoccupation with national character, he deftly built his case by witty indirection.

He sometimes used an essay or short story to depict character. Blanche Gregory had urged him to put together a portfolio of short stories immediately after *Barometer Rising* had sold so successfully, and he had done his best to co-operate. However, when Earle Birney had written to him in 1942 asking for a contribution to *Story Magazine* he had replied: 'I should warn you that I have never felt at home in the short story medium.' The problem, of course, was that he found the short story, as he had found *Barometer Rising*, far too limiting. Eventually, none the less, he produced a number of short stories, centring on character, which were to hone his techniques considerably. 'The Lost Love of Tommy Waterfield' (1955), one of the best of these, recounts a near-disaster at sea which he had experienced as a boy in Halifax and draws to perfection the character of his boyhood friend Gordon Mackinnon. Most of these stories were autobiographical, many of them directly so. Again, using the first person point of view, he delved into the meaning of his past experience and into his own self in such stories as 'An Orange from Portugal' (1947), 'Christmas without Dickens' (1952), and 'October and Smoke' (1956).[20] Up to this point he had severely underrated his abilities in the essay form, but the very limitations against which he struggled gave a form and focus to his writing which had been wanting in some of his longer works.

In the best of his essays, such as 'Joseph Haydn and Captain Bligh' (1953), 'Confessions of a Wood-chopping Man' (1956), and 'The Curtain Falls on the Grand Style: A Dramatic Account of the English People' (1957), which he considered his best piece, he was sufficiently at ease in his writing to produce work that was beautifully structured, intellectually interesting, and deeply felt. Essays such as these moved with natural 'free-association' around a well-structured set of ideas, revealing character at every step. The facts that had sometimes detached themselves from character in his earlier fiction were now being drawn into relationship with theme and personality. He had come to see that the essayist 'uses facts as a catalyst to reveal his own personality.' In these, his best essays, he wrote with an authenticity that revealed not only his growing self-confidence but also his trust in his readers. His earlier pieces on writing in Canada had concentrated on the heavy responsibilities of the creative writer to define and interpret his society for readers both foreign and indigenous; now he saw that writing need not be 'like meeting strangers in a public place.' At last he had a sense of his audience; there was, in Canada, an educated reading public to whom he could address himself in the knowledge that he would be understood. This sense of 'decent intimacy' in communicating with his public changed the whole tone of his writing. As he himself realized when he took the decision to use the first person point of view: 'the essays I have been writing have made it easier for me to use that approach than formerly.'[21]

In this torrent of essays and addresses he turned again and again to the theories of fiction that were to mould and shape the novel that was under way. The most important of these ideas were expressed in a paper called 'The Artist and Critic in Society,' which he had been invited to deliver at a conference of what Dorothy called 'the big boys' at Princeton in 1953. Also on the panel were the physicists J. Robert Oppenheimer and Allan T. Waterman, the Catholic philosopher Jacques Maritain, and the art historian Erwin Panofsky. 'I couldn't approach this job,' he confessed to Gray, 'in the usual offhand manner of talking to the C.A.A.'[22] In his paper he outlined the theory of fiction he had been working towards for some years. For him, art had a purpose – it was useful. The artist's function and duty is this, he maintained, 'within a framework of truth to make compensation for the human predicament.' Thus he stated succinctly a moral view of literature in which he diverged from current trends. His reasons? The failure of much modern literature, he argued, 'lies in the fact that it has evoked terror without purging it, that too many modern writers, and painters too, purge *themselves* and not the audience.' By 'modern writers' he meant people like James Jones, whose *From Here to Eternity* he had panned on a CBC radio review in 1951, and Norman Mailer, whose work had come to epitomize for him the bleakness of modern materialism. Furthermore, his theoretical stance separated him from what he thought of as the 'intellectual' writers – T.S. Eliot in particular. As he was later to reflect sardonically in 'Sunset and Evening Star' (1955), 'Eliot's vision ... is utterly devoid of love of any kind, and even devoid of hate ... A poetry of the menopause it really is, and the Master himself has described it perfectly as "thoughts of a brain in a dry season."' This school of poetry contravened his belief that 'there must be some genuine emotion if the communication can be called an artistic one.' He termed much modern writing 'bruises without healing,'[23] and decided that for him such a lack of affirmation was unacceptable.

Having rejected so much contemporary writing as well as his earlier models, notably Shakespeare, to whom did he turn for literary models? Mainly he turned to Joseph Conrad, C.P. Snow, Tolstoy, and, interestingly enough, to Ernest Hemingway. Originally, he had regarded Hemingway with unqualified admiration, a sentiment that disappeared when he reacted strongly against his cynicism. Now, in his maturity, he sorted out what he as a novelist could truly take for his own use from the writer who had loomed so large in his younger days. Here, his new position at McGill helped him. In 1952 he was contemplating writing a college textbook out of the eleven hundred or so pages of lecture notes he had prepared for the course he was teaching on the development of English prose. He had written to Gray: 'I had to construct the whole picture myself, and found it both fascinating and enormously informative. It should pay off in future writing. I had never realized that there are certain clear, provable conclusions that can be drawn about the limitations and possibility of English prose expression. The professors are very well informed about poetry and drama and about the novel ... But the prose instrument they have taken entirely for granted and have also taken for granted a good many aspects of the novel and the prose drama as well.' Although no textbook resulted, his consideration of the history of English prose sharpened particularly his theories on Hemingway, whose true genius, he came to realize, lay in his revolution in *style*. In 'Homage to Hemingway' (1954), he stated: 'What Hemingway has done has been to restore order and clarity to our use of the English language. Out of our immediate inheritance of arty prose on the one hand and jargon on the other, Ernest Hemingway began to write with an aim which repudiated them both. He understood that between him and his reality lay a mountain-range of hackneyed words and phrases which had crushed the evocative powers of the English language.'

The only trouble for MacLennan was that Hemingway had used his powerful prose style for unworthy ends: he had portrayed only that side of life which is 'sensual,' ignoring the spiritual dimension; for this reason he 'is to a considerable extent responsible for the unhappy condition of the novel at the present time.' In his enumeration of the aspects of life Hemingway had regrettably overlooked can be seen his intentions for his own next novel: 'Thoughtful men cannot help living on mental levels that are distinct from physical ones. They are too rational, or too engrossed with the need of earning a living, to go to Africa to shoot lions or to Spain to watch bulls being killed. Liquor is apt to dull their perceptions instead of heightening them, as liquor seems to do for Hemingway's heroes. Rational men discuss their own neuroses, they are interested in science, they become involved in a multitude of activities for which the Hemingway style lacks an adequate vocabulary. They argue about communism and democracy, are concerned with the high cost of living and getting on in their jobs, they worry about their children's education and the danger of another depression. They show an interest in women as personalities, not as mere embodiments of a sensual dream. Their sexual lives are not ritualistic. In short, their minds, their ambitions, their awareness of themselves as coherent, complex personalities involved in a mundane existence make them entirely unsuitable as catalysts for Hemingway. Such men are even apt to wonder at times how they can save their souls.'[24]

While MacLennan was learning certain things about Hemingway from his English prose course, he was also picking up information in his modern novel course. There, he discovered, his students thought highly of Joseph Conrad, a writer he himself liked. 'Fiction,' he concluded, 'should aim at the younger generation; they derive more from it. Older people seem to prefer non-fiction and lighter work, stylized work. And if there is one thing I'm in a good position to know it's this younger generation ... I discovered in my course that the writer whose mood appealed most to them was Conrad. They are so digusted with the false optimism of western official society that this is one thing against which they can be relied on to react with violence. They are much more at ease with the subconscious. They probe rather deeply after motives.'

For a moral view that coincided with his own he turned to the South African writer Alan Paton, whose works he had for some time admired. Here was a writer in a position similar to his own, who lived and wrote in a country that was not then of prime significance in the world scene. It was not for Paton's nationalism, however, that he admired him; he had himself progressively lost interest in writing aggressively 'Canadian' fiction since *Two Solitudes*, and now he was saying to Gray: 'the "Canadian" aspect of my writing is now behind me, which will not mean I will be any less "Canadian" in my material.' Teaching a course in Canadian writing at McGill for the first time in the fall of 1953, he was confronted to the point of boredom with the opinion that the trouble with Canadian writers is that they are too self-conscious; to this he countered: 'Balls! It's the public that's self-conscious ... The public still feels unnatural when confronted with a real book about themselves.'[25]

It was rather Paton's artistic morality that attracted him. In a speech at the University of New Brunswick in 1952 he praised Paton's *Cry, the Beloved Country* as a novel of 'moral grandeur.' A later article, by its very title, disclosed his admiration for Paton's affirmation of life: 'Alan Paton – A Light in Darkness' (1954).[26]

In October 1954 MacLennan had met the British writer C.P. Snow after a few years of correspondence between them in which he had been assisting with the promotion of Snow's work in Canada. He had always admired his writing generally, but meeting him, becoming friends, intensified his admiration considerably. Both were sceptical of much modern fiction and tended to appreciate the great 'realistic' writers such as Balzac, Dostoevsky, Proust, and Tolstoy. Because of the interest sparked by their friendship, Snow's work constituted a partial model. He had found *The Masters* 'one of the saddest novels I have ever read. It may also be close to the greatest.' Admiring Snow's prodigious learning and technical skills, he nevertheless wished to be less 'cold' in his own work: 'But what of books like these? Is knowledge and insight and analytical power enough? Somewhere the soul rebels ... Reading Snow reminded me of the passage in Lucretius about the joys of standing on a promontory and watching the sailors struggling in the sea.'[27]

But it was Tolstoy to whom he finally turned for his foremost example of how to write fiction. During the last two months of 1956 he reread *War and Peace* with the profound admiration he had always felt for this novel, and he was reading it now with, as he put it, 'a kind of abstract indignation at the knowledge that if any novelist attempted to write today as Tolstoy did he would be so hopelessly out of fashion that the critics would tear him apart.' Comparing most modern literature with this masterpiece, he literally wrote himself into the conclusion that 'the most revolutionary course any artist can take now is to be conservative.' In an age when 'literary art has narrowed from a broad, open highway on which the sun shines to a narrow, probing incision made by an expert surgeon into the soul of a single patient,' he decided to emulate Tolstoy, even at the risk of critical disdain. Tolstoy, he had written to Gray in 1951, 'was ... the greatest novelist who ever lived.' Now, rereading *War and Peace* confirmed in him the belief that the modern novel had lost its scope and its sense of life's mystery through its 'obsession for neatness and technical perfection.' For him, the best scenes in Tolstoy's novel were the 'very scenes which the modern critic would condemn as extraneous.'[28] The stories of his own characters, he decided, like Tolstoy's, would be 'given their place in the historical events of the time' in the most 'natural' manner possible. Like Tolstoy, too, he would not shrink from making the moral pronouncements so unfashionable in the literature of his time.

When MacLennan, early on, had felt the challenge to negate modern trends in fiction, he did not underestimate his task. In a letter to Bill Deacon on 3 July 1951 he had confided: 'What the future of fiction will be I don't profess to know. I believe there will be a return to it soon. Perhaps – indeed probably – a new departure on the part of the novelists is required. Maybe a genius is needed. Certainly the trend that began in the 1920's has petered out into insignificance and I have been intensely hostile to books like Mailer's and Jones' because they seemed to me only to drag the art of fiction backward into the swamp of materialism from which there is no escape or hope – and here I speak artistically, not morally.' Two years later he protested to Gray: 'It's now not a question of advancing the Canadian novel but of advancing the novel itself – in other words of finding a way to express what I must express or fail.'[29]

At this time he had just finished reading Hugo McPherson's article 'The Novels of Hugh MacLennan' in *Queen's Quarterly* (1953), an article he thought, despite its jargon, was 'the only sensible thing of its kind I've read on my stuff in this country.' He agreed that in his last two novels his technique had been inadequate to his psychic needs. 'I had reached that conclusion myself,' he wrote to Gray; in fact, he added, 'the technique of almost all modern novels is inadequate to the needs of the writer and of the public.' Working on his new novel he firmly believed that he was reworking the novel form in a revolutionary way, negating the sterile dead-end of most modern fiction, returning fiction to an artistically moral path. To do this involved that organic process he had first tried with limited success in *Two Solitudes*. To find the right, the 'natural,' form for expressing modern life, that was the main difficulty; resolving this problem, as he saw it, could not be 'done entirely conventionally, but it must be done naturally, easily and without tricks.'[30]

The breakthrough occurred in September 1953. 'It came ripe,' he wrote Gray; 'at last I seem able to write the way I've always wanted to – with a great sense of release within a form which will contain it ... I think the story will be better [than *Each Man's Son*] and the appeal far wider, though I don't suppose any book I wrote will have the local appeal of [*Two Solitudes*] ... But I do seem to have more material here than I can handle. The thing grows and grows and I'm at last feeling at ease in its presence. Anyway, I hope for a publication in 1955.' A fortnight later he wrote further: 'It seems to be subtly different in method from most stuff that is being written, especially as regards the use of time sequences – a method which has imposed itself on me compulsively and in the earlier stages interfered with the writing. But it seems to reflect the shape into which my mind has grown and if that is so, I want to stick with it if possible, for it seems it is "different."' By July 1954 he had the whole novel drafted 'from beginning to end – this happened only once before [*Barometer Rising*] – and the only trouble is having to interrupt it to do the essays. I do find it's like losing the range and then having to re-find it every time I make these switches ... I'm still hoping to get the novel ready for a fall publication in 1955, but this is one book I simply can't afford to rush. Which doesn't mean writing – that in itself is no longer a problem to me – but grasping the meaning.'[31]

But by the end of 1955 the novel was still not finished; in fact, even a 1956 publication looked doubtful. 'Please God,' he wrote Gray, 'I'll finish it in 1956 even though not in time for a 1956 publication. I realize now that the essence of my problem was to work through to a new style – not so much in the sentence as in the broadest possible way, in the sense that painters use that word.' It was, in fact, his rereading of *War and Peace* at the end of 1956 that triggered the resolution of this problem. 'I've never written as well in my life as I'm writing now,' he told Gray. 'The last inhibition disappeared ... re-reading *War and Peace* ... every word of it, and some chapters several times over ... That book had acquired the absolutely perfect style for a novel, its utter naturalness never dominating the material, yet with always the right word, the right phrase, here or there on the page where it was needed to make the vital difference.'[32]

Finally, out of the welter of scenes and characters that reflected the inner changes he had felt in himself and perceived in others, the novel's form came clear in a dream that suggested an arrangement of the episodes he had written. In one strong burst of energy he began writing on Labour Day 1957, and finished the novel, like a racer breaking the tape, two days after New Year's. 'The only danger,' he wrote to Gray about a month before he finished, 'will be fatigue on the last hundred yards.' But he had found his form: 'the form (which was subtle and difficult and held me up for years, literally) seems to be so right that the latter half of the book just pours into it.'[33]

Earlier, when he had approached the writing of *Two Solitudes*, he had expressed considerable bewilderment: not really knowing whether to take a chronological approach or 'plunge in medias res,' he chose the former. Now, using a more truly organic method, he allowed the novel to find its own shape. The first person point of view gave a focus lacking in the earlier novel. By thinking of the whole as one man's story, the novel shaped itself more clearly. This time he chose the alternate method: he would 'plunge in medias res and then explain the background through flashbacks.'[34]

Although there is nothing radical about the structure of *The Watch That Ends the Night*, MacLennan was right in concluding that it was 'different' for him. Beginning in the present with Jerome's telephone call to George naturally stirs into action memories concerning both men which hinge on the pivotal character Catherine, to whom they are both actually married. It is natural that George thinks first of his own and Catherine's past lives, then that he should turn to the recollection of Jerome's account of his childhood. These two memory streams merge naturally into a common flow once all three lives intermingle. By the time the sequence of recollections reaches the present again, the reader can *feel* the truth of George's sense that an age has passed since Jerome's call that morning. MacLennan, for the first time in his fiction, successfully recreated mind-time by knocking the complacent George off course with the flood of memories that must inevitably ensue on Jerome's call. As George speculates on life itself: 'I thought about Jerome and wondered what he had done the night before, and I thought of him as I remembered him in the past. What is time anyway? The past seemed part of the present today. Time had lost its shape. Time is a cloud in which we live while the breath is in us. When was I living, now or twenty-five years ago, or in all those periods of my life simultaneously?'[35] After this 'cloud' of time is reproduced, in which past and present are lived simultaneously, the final progression of the story neatly and naturally resolves the conflicts into a satisfying affirmation. Later, on a CBC *Anthology* program eventually published as 'The Story of a Novel' (1960), MacLennan recounted the entire process by which he so slowly and laboriously wrote this book. His general theory about fiction stated here simply reflected his personal views, as it had so often before:

> Somewhere around 1950, it seems to have occurred to millions of readers that this kind of external action [Shakespeare's] – this drama played as a means of revealing the tragic nature of man – was apt to be both inaccurate and inadequate ... If they [modern novels] were tragic they usually dealt with outcasts, with men excessively violent, with men excessively primitive, with men excessively criminal.
>
> Around this time, it seemed to me, as it seemed to the educated public, that the basic human conflict was 'within' the individual. But how to find an artistic form for this concept? That was the question. Certainly the novelists failed who wrote clinically; they absolutely failed to purge the soul of pity and terror, which is art's supreme function ... Somehow I was going to write a book which would not depend on character-in-action, but on spirit-in-action. The conflict here, the essential one, was between the human spirit of Everyman and Everyman's human condition.

Considering that his visible career, with the publication of *Barometer Rising*, had begun on exactly the same day that Virginia Woolf's, with the posthumous publication of *Between the Acts*, had ended, these speculations must seem surprisingly naïve. Innovations in fiction during the early part of the twentieth century – those of James Joyce, William Faulkner, Woolf herself, to name but a few – had taken exactly the direction MacLennan had outlined. These writers, in far more experimental ways, had long since done their best 'to reveal the tragic nature of man' from 'within.' They, too, had tried to show, often with great success, the essential conflict 'between the human spirit ... and [the] human condition.'[36] Why, then, did he act as if none of this had happened, as if he were the first to discover this mode of writing fiction?

Certainly he was not in any way ignorant of the developments in fiction that probed deep within character in the early twentieth century. Not only does he mention such writers in his letters and essays but he had also been giving careful consideration to their works and methods in his course on the modern novel at McGill. In his first novel 'So All Their Praises' he had experimented with the stream-of-consciousness technique and had deliberately discarded it in his subsequent work. Now, much later, he still viewed 'stream-of-consciousness' as a method unsuited to his purpose, except for specific passages, and he found it, for him, too limiting. Looking as deep inside as Joyce, Faulker, and Woolf had done meant narrowing the novel's concerns from that 'broad, open highway on which the sun shines' to a surgical 'incision ... into the soul of a single patient.'[37] In other words, while stream-of-consciousness could certainly show 'within' the individual, it could not portray simultaneously 'the human condition.' To show one side of the 'essential conflict' without the other inevitably reduced both the dramatic and tragic conflict. Furthermore, the breakdown of structured language seemed to him to undermine that 'affirmation of life' he believed to be 'the supreme function of art.' So much stream-of-consciousness writing illustrated the alienation of human beings from life; structured language, on the other hand, was in itself evidence of communication between men. His synopsis in 'The Story of a Novel' of the changes in fiction about 1950, therefore, was really a highly personal account of changes in himself. It was *MacLennan* who then realized that he had been 'the unconscious slave of Shakespeare,' not writers of the modern novel in general; it was he who had found Shakespearean action 'inaccurate and inadequate' for his needs as a novelist, not novelists on the whole. Finding a form that would reveal his new sense of 'spirit-in-action' must, by his own admission, be 'done naturally' and must be accomplished 'easily and without tricks,' not 'entirely conventionally'[38] – that is to say, without undue stylistic artfulness such as stream-of-consciousness. At the same time, his novel must 'affirm' life by pitting inner forces ('the human spirit of Everyman') successfully against outer forces ('Everyman's human condition').

No greater example of the conflict between the human spirit and man's condition can be imagined than that with which he had lived daily for the decade just before he published *The Watch That Ends the Night*. Dorothy's condition had worsened during that time, by terrifying leaps and bounds. The horror of her oncoming death held MacLennan in its grip and seemed to taunt him into trying to make sense of a world in which such things could happen. When he wrote to John Gray in the early stages of his novel that he wanted to try 'to create order out of the life and lives I've seen,' it was primarily of Dorothy that he was thinking. How could he 'affirm' life at all when a woman as talented and energetic as she was existed on the edge of the abyss, victim of a fate she had no hand in making? As he recalled later in 'Victory' (1957), written shortly after her death, they both knew that from the weakening of her heart in 1947 through severe viral pneumonia 'she was like a city under seige, and the end of the seige was as sure as the last shot in a war ... For the last ten years she lived knowing that on any hour of any day she might die.' Here was an inner war as senseless as any conflict of nations. How could he find any meaning in it? The relentless series of embolisms so carefully documented in 'Victory' painfully demonstrate the humiliation and suffering Dorothy underwent: in 1948 bronchitis and an embolism in the brain left her paralysed on the left side and limping; in 1949 another embolism almost killed her; six months later another embolism in the brain and again a paralysed left side; in 1950 an embolism in the bowel and two abdominal operations she was scarcely fit to endure; in June 1955 another embolism; at Christmas 1956 an operation to remove a calcium growth from the arm joint, and, subsequently, jaundice; in November 1956 severe dizzy spells, a cyst on the kidney impossible to remove because by now surgery was too dangerous; finally, on Easter morning, one final embolism and death the next day, on 22 April 1957. It seemed at times to MacLennan that this long, drawn-out torture was a perfect example of flies to wanton boys. But the whole process also signified Dorothy's tremendous will to live. More than once she announced proudly: 'Well, I've fooled them again'[39] – a phrase Catherine Martell was to use frequently in *The Watch That Ends the Night*. Fittingly, the novel was dedicated to Dorothy: 'To you wherever and whatever you may be, my thanks and this book.'

But MacLennan was not only touched by Dorothy's tremendous privation over those last ten years. He, too, was under intense stress as she drew on his strength to keep herself alive. It was his ordeal too. He had also to find for himself some order in the chaos of his own life; more than once he must have wished, for his own sake as well as for hers, that it would all be over quickly.

In the characters of Catherine and George Stewart, he came to terms with the personal conflicts he was both observing and enduring. Through Catherine he shows the positive element Dorothy's example provided of inner strength in the face of staggering adversity. Dorothy had had to abandon her writing career at its height in 1948, before she had completed the novel she had begun; her doctor, Jack Howlett, had decided that it was simply too strenuous. A year or so later she attempted to fill her empty hours by painting, as Catherine does. To everyone's astonishment she showed genuine talent. By 1953, a few years after she had taken her first lessons from Marian Scott, John Lyman, Erik Goldberg, and Gordon Webber at the Montreal Museum of Fine Arts, she was herself exhibiting in the museum's Annual Spring Show, and her work was so good it was singled out for a whole column of newspaper comment. Unlike Catherine, Dorothy never dared try to have a child. Letters from the mid-1940s show that the MacLennans had considered the possibility then and that Dorothy had consulted a doctor about it. 'There's not a chance, so I'm told,' she had written to Bill Deacon on 29 January 1946. It was not only her health, however, but also Hugh's preference that they not try; as she admitted to Deacon some months earlier: 'No baby in this family ... don't need to keep press cameras ready. Too many boys all his life at school, Hugh says.'[40]

Like Catherine, to whom MacLennan allots particular paintings of his wife's, Dorothy in her painting revealed a wonderful sense of colour and line. Ironically her paintings epitomized a joy in life that was apparently incompatible with circumstances. As Catherine's paintings do, hers had amazingly grown 'richer and stronger all the time, a thing that has nothing to do with sentiment, for the early ones don't.' MacLennan singled out one of Dorothy's paintings and attributed it to his character: 'It was as close to being a self-portrait as Catherine had ever done. It was a picture of a fourteen year old girl on a swing lost in a joy of colors that sang like trumpets, the colors exuberantly gay. Yet the picture itself was inexpressibly poignant, for the girl had no recognizable features. She was simply all the young girls there ever were lost in a spectrum of spring and knowing themselves alone. The head drooped like a flower on a stalk. Even in beauty's very heart, even in the heart of life itself, this solitude.' Tragically, Dorothy died in the process of assembling her paintings for her first one-man show at the Galerie Agnès Lefort in Montreal, a show that was held posthumously the following week.[41]

In the spring after Dorothy died, and before that final surge of energy with which he was to finish the novel at the end of 1957, MacLennan had decided to name it 'Requiem' for his own 'lost generation': 'As I see it now, the title of the book will be "Requiem." And as you will see, a good deal of my own experience is involved in what, absolutely, is a work of fiction. It was impossible to keep these last ten years with Dorothy out of my work, but the main female character, though she could not exist without her, is not really her any more than any true fictional character is a real person. I seem quite at ease with the thing now. The title came to me the other day, and the requiem is only incidentally for Dorothy. As I see the novel, it is for our whole generation.'[42]

When John Gray first read the manuscript he was, for once, speechless. So close to the bone did it come that it was impossible for him to see it at first as anything other than an autobiographical record. 'It is more than a little hard,' he wrote to MacLennan on 4 February 1958, 'that at a time like this when as a friend and publisher I should like most to be of help, I am of so little use ... It is simply the shock of trying to see these people and this situation as fiction.' MacLennan continued to insist, despite this, that only a part of Catherine's character was based on Dorothy. 'Believe it or not, John,' he had written on 28 January, '"Requiem" is truer fiction than anything I have ever written. It is absolutely translated. It goes centuries and miles beyond Dorothy and me.' In this extraordinary letter to Gray he spelled out in considerable detail what he meant by this disclaimer; from it can be seen his conviction that in this novel, as in the 'apparition' or teenage daydreams that had committed him to writing, he had been 'guided' by a power other than his own, and that his characters had surfaced from so deep within that they might be called archetypes or memory traces far beyond any living individual.

It's a profoundly disturbing book, not for the obvious surface reasons but because of what (it's almost as though somebody else wrote it now) its uncanny handling of time. Forty years coverage? More than that, John. Flashes come up from the Neolithic, and those are universally applicable: they apply to the entire human race regardless of religious denomination, or colour or what have you. In places in this book art remembered several hundreds of thousands of years and disguised them. Only in the last week's sleep and solitude did I realize how surely I was guided – as I knew I was all fall and early winter.

Now there was no possible way in which this could have been handled except in the main first person by a narrator who partakes of some of my character (about 25% only) and with a main female character who had shared Dorothy's personal destiny in having a rheumatic heart, but otherwise differed vastly. Catherine is only about 20% her. But what was the point in employing any superficial disguises in an affair like this when the levels were so much more profound than I knew?

En effet, what other artist can you name who ever lived as I have? Or was so peculiarly equipped by inheritance and technical skill to deal with the real subject, which is good, evil and the possibility of justifying God's ways to man? What other disease but rheumatic fever could have produced a cyclic pattern of death and resurrection, not once but FIVE times? In the midst of life we are in death is a rhetorical phrase for most people. It was literal truth for me for TEN YEARS. How else could I live but live with it? And how else could I master it save through art? And how else do it but nakedly? And what else to say to the reader but 'what I now have to write fills me with dismay: naked it must be if it is to be true, but decently naked?' Where it is indecently naked, don't hesitate to tell me.

You see, this situation was very strange with us. We lived on a factual, clinical level, (we even re-lived) the conflux of the two basic myths of the human race: death and resurrection, both of which revert to the prehistoric origins of original sin. The world has been denying this for centuries. It has been murdering, tearing apart, all of those things for centuries and worst of all in our own century.

Over this scene the sexual sin is pinned as the fig leaf of disguise ...

All this far transcends anything personal in the lives of Dorothy and myself, yet without such an experience as we shared, as two citizens deeply loving each other, this extraordinary thing could not have happened. On the symbolic level of myth, ten years of my life died for her and she was haunted for guilt because of this even though I would gladly have given her any more years I had, and (thank God) she knew it at the end when she was far over the brink. It was her release from this haunting which gave her the final serenity which enabled her to paint those beautiful pictures at the end.

Contrariwise, when she died, she released the talent, the genius or whatever it was which produced 'Requiem.' For months it was my turn to be obscurely guilt-haunted. She died, in order that this book might be born; this book, if it's half as good as I think it, will make my name live, etc. The tension would have been intolerable if I had not surrendered entirely, drunk a little too much, and lived in a trance of activity until it was done.

Then I felt washed, clean and different. I had honoured her on the level of the person I loved; I had purged myself; I had done my duty. And still I was puzzled until the whole pattern emerged and I saw how I had been used by forces very mysterious ...

However, there is the public to be considered. I used to be timid, but nowadays I don't worry much about my moral courage. I am not ignorant of the things which will be said about me as a result of this novel. I am not unaware of the gossip, the ignorant, superficial guesswork it will cause. I feared this while she lived because it would have hurt her. It may possibly do me some passing damage next year. May I quote Luther: 'Since sin you must, sin bravely.' If the herd rejects me, a later herd will accept me. Although I deplore St. Paul's theology, I have always had a fondness for him personally. I feel now I have earned, in my own small way, the right to say: 'I have fought the good fight, I have finished the course,' and if I were a Catholic and believed in the survival of the earthly personality, I could meet Dorothy in the hereafter with level eyes. However, I am not so naïve as to believe for a moment, as Paul did, that for me is henceforth laid up a crown of righteousness. No, John, I have no illusions about that. I do believe that 'Requiem' will have a mixed reception, that it will make friends scared of me, that it will make some people want to murder me, that it will make others think all manner of things. But I have a hunch that it may sell quite a few copies.

Bless you, my dear friend, who have been so good and patient with me, and if you want to tell me I am a megalomaniac, a fool, a fanatic, a blunderer, or anything you may believe I am, please don't be correct, gentlemanlike and honourable, but just tell me. I promise you I will like you just as much as I ever did, and admire you just as much as I do now.[43]

This powerful letter reveals MacLennan's utter vulnerability under almost unbearable stress. So intense had his engagement been with the themes and characters of this novel, so vividly had he imagined himself into their world to resolve the pain of his own life into a triumph of art, that they had, at the moment of completion, become dearer to him than life itself. Not only had he felt 'guided' by 'mysterious forces' in an 'uncanny' way, he experienced in himself an almost god-like power which made him feel at the centre of the universe and above all men. He had not so long before written an essay imagining what Handel might have felt at the moment of creating *The Messiah* and had chosen that man and that moment as the most enviable in all human history. Now, he was experiencing the same flood of joy and reckless omnipotence himself.

John Gray's reply to this letter was full of reassurance and concern: 'Your recovery of strength, of shell for the purpose of going on living, is something your friends must hope for – perhaps more than you do.' None the less, having seen MacLennan for an evening just prior to writing his letter, Gray was convinced that he was mending a little 'after all the battering you have taken.' Above all, he was touched by MacLennan's exposure of his inmost self. 'Thank you,' he wrote, 'more than I would attempt to express for your letter. One might work a lifetime in the hope of half so much warmth and generosity of spirit. I never wonder why I am in publishing; for all its responsibilities it is a rare privilege.'[44]

In Jungian terms, MacLennan's character Catherine was a pure 'anima' figure. As such, for MacLennan, she reflected not only Dorothy but the essence of femininity in all the women who had affected him. Her name, like Kathleen's in *Two Solitudes*, derives from his mother's, as does the contralto voice so typical of all his heroines. Like his mother, like his youthful sweetheart Jean Shaw, like Nora Kaye whose performance so gripped him in *Pillar of Fire*, like Dorothy, and like all his heroines, she is dark-haired and opulent. In her is combined the positive force of a strong spirit, a spirit in tune with nature's cycles, and the negative power of what Robertson Davies has so accurately called the 'spiritual vampire.' Like the Sirens of Homer, to whom she is compared in the novel, Catherine is at once the power of the anima and a snare for all men. MacLennan came to agree with this theory; in a letter in 1979 to a professor at the University of Alberta who had consulted him about an article, E.D. Blodgett, he confessed: 'I never read a line of him [Jung] until nine years ago and discovered that I'd been something of a Jungian without knowing it. I realized then that of course Catherine was an *anima*, and it was Robb Davies who made it clear to me that to some extent she was also a spiritual vampire. She was not Dorothy Duncan, my first wife. Only the medical situation was similar there. She was, though I didn't know it consciously when I wrote the book, a girl I was in love with when very young who in her character had nothing of the guts of Catherine but for a very young man was in fact an anima for seven years.'[45]

In one sense, Dorothy too was a spiritual vampire, in the draining effect her illness had had on him. 'I realized,' he later told Gray, that the novel 'could not have been done while Dorothy was alive. But not,

I think, because of what it would do to her directly. Partially so, perhaps, but not entirely. Rather that the creative drive necessary to bring it off would not be available when she needed so much of that in me to keep her alive. In that sense, largely, she had to die in order that "Requiem" should be written.' Dorothy's grip on him was so strong that, as had happened with his father in 1939, he was unable to feel she was really gone for a long time after her death. Almost a year later, in March 1959, he confessed to Gray: 'This may sound a terrible thing to say, but I don't believe it is, really. Only in the last ten days have I been able to *feel* that Dorothy is no longer here. The sense of her presence was doubtless responsible for the intensity of much I wrote earlier, but it also kept me from any kind of objectivity.'[46]

Catherine, through these same powers for good and evil, by her sheer forcefulness and by the hold she has on both Jerome and George, exemplifies the 'spirit-in-action' MacLennan wanted to portray; the battle between her spirit and her fate partakes of a depth and universality that he had always tried to capture. But it is the character of Jerome Martell, also an archetypal figure, that he saw as the 'key figure' in *The Watch That Ends the Night*. Martell was the first of the novel's characters to materialize in a dream during the winter of 1956, he told Gray two years later: 'Martell, not Stewart is the key figure of the novel – by far the key figure. This I realized only last week when the book was off my hands. By what strange guidance was he nameless? Why that scene in New Brunswick which came to me, all of it vivid as if I were there, in the night two or three years ago? Ostensibly I had no part in the novel I was blundering along with, but some force caused me to know this was integral, and I spent a winter on it. Whence came the (to me at least) astonishing poetry of his escape down the river and his being accepted by a simple clergyman who instantly turned out not to be so simple after all? Whence the transference of the authority of the Father-God to the Mother-God who devoured men and was murdered by a wandering Cain? Whence, finally, the compulsion to revert these last eight months to the Scriptures and Johann Sebastian Bach?'[47]

The only model for the superficial aspects of Martell's character was a young man who came to Halifax just before MacLennan went to Oxford in 1928. That boy of sixteen had never been outside the New Brunswick lumber camp where his mother had been camp cook and his father reputedly the most brutal man in the camp.[48] Certainly, the model was not Dr Norman Bethune, as has been argued,[49] although the coincidental similarities are many: MacLennan never met Bethune, according to himself and to a number of people who also attended Popular Front meetings in the thirties. It would be more logical to suggest that Martell is modelled on the dynamic socialist poet Frank Scott, whom MacLennan knew well, and whose wife had first shown Dorothy the techniques of painting and introduced the MacLennans to a circle of artistic and political friends in Montreal in the thirties that resembles the Montreal bohemian community in *The Watch That Ends the Night*. The fact that Martell is a doctor was a result much more of MacLennan's transmutation of his father's occupation into fiction, as he had already done in *Barometer Rising* and *Each Man's Son*, than in any reflection of Bethune. The Martell family, who so kindly take Jerome into their home, were probably derived from a family story often told by MacLennan's grandmother, Mary MacQuarrie, about the Martell family in Glace Bay who harboured her and her family after a nightmarish trip from Pugwash.

More than any real life models, or combination thereof, MacLennan felt that Jerome Martell had swept into being on one of those waves of his own unconscious that washed over him from time to time. In Jerome, consequently, are combined all the qualities associated with the man of action. He is at once MacLennan's doctor father and all fathers – powerful, larger than life, courageous, intelligent, primitive. Just as Catherine is all women, Jerome is all the men of action MacLennan had admired and envied – not only his father but also Roger Ritter, the soldier; John Bassett, tennis champion; *Boys' Own Paper* heroes; Homeric heroes and Hemingway heroes; and his own heroes such as Stephen Lassiter and Archie MacNeil. Jerome's mysterious healing powers, like Catherine's creative virtues, are coupled with immense destructive capabilities. Both these characters illustrate ways in which human beings pit their energies against the force of the circumstances into which they are born.

Jerome's story also derives from a book called *Ten Heroes* by David Malcolmson. Duell, Sloan and Pearce had sent MacLennan a complimentary copy of this book in 1941, the same year they had published *Barometer Rising*. Malcolmson's central idea was that all literature could be categorized according to ten different types of heroes. In a chapter called 'The Escape from the Devouring Mother' he suggests that 'there is no real adventure without clutching hands ... The adventure lies in the difficulty of ... escape.'[50] Since Malcolmson had referred to a number of MacLennan's favourite authors as evidence for this theory – Hemingway, Homer, Melville, for example – he was attracted to the concept. This theme now surfaced in his dream about his own character Jerome.

It may have been MacLennan's own sense of quest, his determination to 'paddle his own canoe' as he had termed his endeavour with this novel, that inspired the seminal dream about Jerome which he thought formed 'the core' of his book. Jerome represents a side of MacLennan that found expression in athletics and in his rugged persistence with his writing, but that side of him stood in relation to his whole personality in somewhat the same way that a minor key reflects the major to which it is related. George Stewart is both the major key of MacLennan's self and the new hero he had been trying to define, a hero that would faithfully reflect the times. Against such a hero, men of physical prowess alone, like Jerome, would be set in a wider perspective than Homer or Shakespeare or Hemingway had seen them.

With George Stewart, MacLennan transformed the love triangle he had already used in each of his novels into a modern psychomachia, or drama of the soul. All three main characters merge inside George to some extent, dramatizing the choices he must make in life. Catherine, of course, has held sway in his soul from childhood; Jerome, in the extraordinary scene when Catherine recovers from her last embolism, actually seems to become one with George spiritually.[51] As dramatizations of forces within George, they represent the instinctive knowledge, female and male, that derives from the deepest memories of the human race. George must come to terms not only with the immediate situation of his wife's illness and imminent death but also with those feminine, creative instincts she represents. Similarly, with Jerome, he must adapt not only to the reappearance of this voice from the past, of a man back from the dead, but he must also reconcile himself to the destructive forces in himself that Jerome's actions represent.

Like so many of MacLennan's earlier heroes, George is the naïve, speculative man. Like Michael Carmichael, David Culver, Angus Murray, Paul Tallard, Bruce Fraser, and Dr Ainslie, George is the observer who is contrasted with the man of action. Although MacLennan was unconscious of it, his character George reflects well the national traits he had earlier thought might be represented by Horatio. George is both wise and innocent. Like Horatio, he outlasts the spectacular 'transitional' hero Jerome; heroism for him, as for his author and his nation, lies in his extraordinary powers of endurance. This time, MacLennan chose the most effective point of view to focus the psychomachia that had always attracted him.

In 'So All Their Praises' and 'A Man Should Rejoice' MacLennan had tried 'to show the significance of the individual in his own time.' Now, finally, the novel that had been brewing inside him for so long had been written. He had tried other, different combinations of the essential features of his time and of his quest, but it was really only with *The Watch That Ends the Night* that he was to find the right artistic form through which to present his story.

That story was essentially a religious one. Indeed, as he described it, the experience of writing this novel had been, in the deepest sense, a 'revelation.' As he declared to Gray: 'In absolute humility I felt that the Lord touched me at the end of this novel and I was only thankful I didn't quite break down under the final strain.' Or, as he wrote after travelling to Scotland: 'In the course of writing it I became a religious man, and the book is essentially religious in nature. One night in the Highlands its real theme came to me. It is contained in the [third] verse of the 90th Psalm: "Thou turnest man to destruction; and sayest, Return, ye children of men."'[52]

In the character of George Stewart, with new authenticity and sureness of touch, he worked out this personal view of life. George plumbs the depths of human despair and feels every lust and murderous impulse of which man is capable. Like Marlow in Conrad's *Heart of Darkness*, one model for the book, he travels down into his soul to find only the perversion of human energy; in the midst of this chaos, however, he ironically feels the spontaneous transformation of this energy into form, morality, and love. It is no accident that MacLennan, as he concluded the novel, turned to the religious music of Bach, Handel, and Beethoven and found there a reinforcement for what was happening to him and, through him, to his character George Stewart. In one of life's coincidences, it had been Easter when Dorothy's last embolism struck. In an essay written just about a month beforehand, called 'Triumph, the Story of a Man's Greatest Moment' (1957), MacLennan had scanned the course of human history searching for the man he most would like to have been. After surveying a vast panorama of military leaders, athletes, explorers, scientists, inventors, businessmen, writers, and composers, he fixed on the religious ecstasy of Handel during the period he wrote *The Messiah*. 'After Dorothy's death,' he wrote to Gray, 'I could listen to no music but Bach, and swam in him.'[53] The summer after Dorothy died he had spent in Halifax, going every afternoon to the mouth of the harbour to sit and watch the sea: 'The movement of the sea coming in and swirling about the rocks and coves, the internal currents and counter-currents of moving water, made me think of Bach's music ... While writing *The Watch* I played Bach every day ... and it helped solve many technical problems in the book.'[54] In Christian doctrine, which he nowhere slavishly followed, he found the *pattern* of death and resurrection that most closely approximated life's meaning for him. For George Stewart, the revelation of light arising out of darkness enables him to make sense of the mystery of human life and to affirm it: in Catherine he can see eventually the destructive power he had formerly associated primarily with Jerome; simultaneously he can see that the strength of virtue is equally in Jerome. 'There it was,' he reflects on one occasion, 'the ancient marriage of good and evil, the goodness of this day and the compulsive evil people must see and know, but the sky dominated in the end. Pale and shining, it told me that our sins can be forgiven.'[55]

Partly because it anticipated in miniature this great theme, MacLennan's earlier essay 'Joseph Haydn and Captain Bligh' (1953) remains his best short work. There, too, he had pondered the mystery of the human spirit, which in the same age could both inform the 'irresponsibility' of a Captain Bligh and the 'spiritual grandeur' of a Haydn. As he had shown as early as *Barometer Rising*, his deepest concern lay in the contrast between human energy misused and the purposeful direction of those same forces. Here, through George Stewart's psychomachia, through his descent into the heart of darkness and his discovery of the truth of resurrection, is the affirmation of life MacLennan thought so essential to art. This story is told not through a traditional hero like Jerome, but through 'Everyman,' through a hero more truly representative of the tragedy of the generation to which MacLennan belonged. As he wrote in 'Couth and Uncouth' (1955), his 'lost generation' had fought, suffered, and sacrificed in a special way, 'during those frightening days' of 'our age of transition.'[56] At last the time was ripe, his skill certain, his audience receptive.

'I wrote my heart out as I never did before,' he claimed of his novel 'Requiem.' I know so much now ... so much about life and pain and good and evil and love and hate, and at last I don't seem afraid to let it out.'[57] 'This book is probably my climax,' he declared on completing it. 'Everything in my life has led up to it.' With these words he forwarded his manuscript in mid-January 1958 to Craig Wylie of Houghton Mifflin Press in Boston, who, as his friend at North Hatley, was well aware that the novel was in the offing. A copy also went to John Gray at Macmillan's and to his new agent Diarmuid Russell of Russell and Volkening in New York. John Gray thought Russell, with whom MacLennan at last had been able to replace Blanche Gregory, the perfect reader for the manuscript; 'Diarmuid Russell coming at the book from right outside was exactly the kind of reader you needed,'[58] he wrote, explaining again that he himself was simply too close to the situation to be objective. Russell, who had been recommended by Craig Wylie, was quietly supportive, suggesting only that the final epilogue be shortened and changed to move Martell offstage quickly at the story's end.

Super-sensitive to criticism as he always was at the point of completing a novel, he was doubly vulnerable because of the wracking experience he had just gone through with Dorothy's death. Exhausted by the combined ordeal, he was in a highly nervous condition. It was in this state that his negotiations with Craig Wylie took place, negotiations that almost led to a breakdown. He had every reason to believe that Houghton Mifflin would more or less automatically take 'Requiem.' Wylie had told him that 'if he gets the script in February, he will be able to publish in September.'[59] As a friend, too, he had been encouraging, and MacLennan must have concluded that if his new novel were up to the standard of his others there would be no problem. Thinking as he did that it was better by far than his earlier work, he felt certain of Houghton Mifflin's approval.

This, however, was not the case. By 27 February, a little over a month after he had sent off the manuscript, MacLennan expressed some annoyance that Wylie had not written to him. His fears materialized at the end of the first week of March when Wylie came to his apartment in Montreal to talk to him in person. In a scene that must have been extremely painful to both men, but a crushing blow for MacLennan, the 'shock' of which 'nearly knocked me out,' Wylie told him that Houghton Mifflin would take the novel only as a gesture of friendship because they had 'faith in [him] as a writer.'[60] Just as he had often done on the tennis court when he lost a game, MacLennan lost control, throwing himself on the floor and tearing at pillows and furniture in his distress. Houghton Mifflin simply did not like it. MacLennan would accept no such charity and withdrew his book. As he wrote to Gray on 8 March:

> Their reaction was curious and contradictory. On the one hand they considered the novel almost perfectly constructed, full of powerful writing and remarkable insights, and their analysis of the handling of time convinced them that time was never more subtly handled than here. They thought Martell a remarkable character though nothing they said led me to believe they

understood him. They believed that no city – its atmosphere, feeling, appearance and reality – was more successfully shot through a book.

They reject it, and don't believe in it, because they don't think it comes off. Their reason is that the characters (except Martell) are too trifling as people to be equal to their destiny, especially George Stewart. This latter view, with one exception, seems very odd to me, when one considers the moral magnitude of characters in American fiction.

At the same time they are (or at least Craig is) deeply disturbed because they may be utterly wrong and may have missed a book which will be read a hundred years hence. They're not really too concerned about this, but this has been, I'd say, an uneasy rejection. They were quite unable to pinpoint any particular objection save the one of character, and there, in the broadest sense, their objection seemed to be moral. Craig quoted to me the old statement that in tragedy a man must be king to equal his destiny. I was forced to quote back that the reason for this, in antiquity, was that the Greek tragedies were founded on myths in which the hero was inevitably a king who was also a demigod.

Meanwhile, Isabel Dobell, a friend of MacLennan's from Montreal and North Hatley, who had done some work for the *New Yorker* and who would later become curator of the McCord Museum in Montreal, read the manuscript twice and 'structurally she wondered if the reader could keep up toward the end': she 'decided it did not quite come off because the characters kept crowding in with such pressure that the feeling of power was too much.'[61] Much later she recalled also that the novel was heavy with medical jargon at this point. The combination of these two criticisms – Wylie's and Dobell's – led MacLennan immediately to rework the manuscript along lines he described to Gray as follows:

I have therefore written to Russell asking him to hold up the manuscript until I have studied it again, and I would ask you to do the same and perhaps forget about a 1958 publication. I believe if there is any place where I can help out – apart from spelling out a few things *re* George Stewart – it is in the character of Catherine. If there is a real dead spot here I suspect it is there. Catherine is not Dorothy, but in many ways is too much like her. She may well be nothing but a symbol, and in her role she needs to be more than that.

I therefore plan to have a shot at creating a somewhat different character here, in the hope that it will come alive in its own right and not solely through the feelings of the people around her. What happens to her, her essential story, even a lot of what she says will not be changed. In my view of this book – character, *per se*, is not destiny except in Martell's case – such a change need not wreck the pattern or involve more than three weeks or a month's work.

Of course I can't be certain of this until I try. Maybe I can do nothing. If so, the thing will have to take its chances.

Although Gray was abnegating his responsibility as an editor for personal reasons, he did his best to be receptive to the novel. However, MacLennan sensed that he too had grave reservations about it: 'I can't believe that you are at all surprised by Houghton Mifflin's reaction, and I am inclined to believe that you share their view – though doubtless for different reasons – that the book does not come off. You have been infinitely kind, tactful and considerate. I wish therefore to say that I do not in any way hold you, even as a friend, to your statement that you would publish. If you don't believe in the book, then clearly you must not publish it.' Somehow, Gray's affection for MacLennan and his sympathy for his condition enabled him to say and do nothing that could jeopardize the friendship. Once again, MacLennan tried to explain what he had attempted in this novel: 'I agree entirely with Conrad that what is DONE is of small significance in comparison to the manner in which what is done is absorbed by human beings. The drama here is not of action, but within. The characters, as such, are secondary to the spirits they outwardly represent. In my experience chance – blind chance – plays an immense part, perhaps the largest part, in human EXPERIENCE. According to the traditional (I say mechanical) view of drama and art in the English-speaking world, character is destiny as regards action. I don't believe this to be true; I think it a legacy from Shakespeare's theatre. Anyway I know that the most [*sic*] of this novel, for me at least, is too true and too important for me to accept the view (which Craig with sincerity and sympathy would have me think) that it is wild because of the experiences I have had. This book was not written as a form of therapeusis.'[62]

Macmillan's criticisms of the novel ran directly opposite to the views of Houghton Mifflin. This was almost more than MacLennan could bear in his present state of mind. In exasperation and cold fury at the turn events were taking, he wrote back immediately to Gray before his better judgement took over. 'You must forgive me,' he began his long harangue, 'if my reply seems brusque in places. I have never felt so isolated in my life as I do now. It is not my fault; it is my perceptions; it is life which has done it. But clarity I must discover or all goes to pot.' He proceeded to summarize the opposing criticisms of his two publishers as they centred on his character Jerome Martell. To the readers at Houghton Mifflin, Martell was the only great character in the book; he, not George Stewart, won all the sympathy. The Macmillan readers, on the other hand, thought that Martell failed to win sympathy and that he was generally an inadequate character. As if to demonstrate by sheer logic what he thought any reader *must* see in his book, MacLennan went on to 'explain' the novel to Gray as to a simple-minded child:

> Now this is how I see this book.
>
> It is not a 'moral' novel in the ordinary sense. I believe it is as true a novel as anyone has had a chance of reading since God knows when. If the public can't feel any sympathy or pity for Martell, all I can say is that they refuse to look at their own souls. He is, in some ways, a great man. The same force which gives life also destroys it, and then it rebuilds it.
>
> I ask you, John, to look at the world we live in. Look at the murderous aggressions committed by good men. It is now an axiom of psychology that every man is a potential murderer. Who understands the twentieth century? Nobody. Yet it must be endured.
>
> Now about the Spanish War and Martell's going to it.
>
> Not a single person I ever knew in the Thirties had a genuinely pure motive about Spain. Not a single person I ever knew or read about had a genuinely pure motive about any war there ever was. Not even Jesus Christ had entirely pure motives. Wars don't just come, as well you know. Not one in a hundred is caused by economic circumstances. Wars are the direct results of pent-up aggressions and guilts, and the Spanish war was a prime example, because it was essentially a revolution.
>
> Connected with all revolutions is the basic Original Sin. Adam's sin was not sexual except indirectly. The paleolithic Adam, together with his brothers, rose against the Father-God, murdered him, ate his flesh in order to acquire his magic powers, and took his women. Centuries later his ancestors pleaded the lesser fault. There never yet was a case in which any but a fanatic like Lenin engaged in a revolution without there being some sexual deviation of some sort on the side. These things surge and seethe like the currents of the sea in every man who ever lives. The novels written by Anglo-Saxons almost never touch on any basic realities because they insist on presenting men either intellectually, or as sets of abstract principles, or as examples of 'There but for the grace of God.' I don't believe there is one instance in a hundred in which a man under great tension, in great perplexity, even knows why he does things.

It was simply beyond MacLennan's powers of endurance to think of major revision at this point.

So all I can do is this. I'm not going to change, alter or dress up the only really great character I think I have created. But in the Spanish War scenes it may be possible to have Stewart soliloquize here and there and make him a little more sympathetic than he seems to be. But I can't change the basic things in this book I know are true.

God, I'm sorry about all this. I am forced to believe the book will certainly fail, be torn asunder and thrown back in my face. I am also forced to believe it will one day be remembered. I am forced to go on to do the best I can with it. When it is done, and meets the fate which now seems probable, then I will possibly be able to stop wrestling with the Angel of Truth in Man and become ironical.

In an attempt to calm him down, Gray wrote reassuringly a few days later: 'Do we all sound like the blind men describing the elephant?'[63]

In the end, MacLennan's revisions were addressed to four main areas. First, he rewrote the opening section, clarifying the focus and removing a good deal of the medical jargon from it. Second, he combed Dorothy as thoroughly as he could from the character of Catherine. Third, he 'focused' the characters of both George and Jerome more sharply; John Gray had asked him for the 'provision of a chart' – a series of signs to help the reader follow his 'incorporation of modern psychology into fiction' – and MacLennan had responded by 'detaching himself' and by 'setting up many more signposts along the way ... virtually [to] tell the reader what the book is about, which before I left to his imagination.'[64] Fourth, he rewrote the character of Norah Blackwell.

Even though he had anticipated that this would be a 'disturbing book,' he would not forgive Craig Wylie, and explained away his criticism as follows: 'I keep recalling various things Craig said. They were so off-beam, most of them. Yet I believe his overall objection was a refusal to accept, or believe, a concept of fate which lies in the human condition – even in the human condition as related to God. He kept repeating that the characters "were not equal to their fate." That failed to make sense to me, especially when he went on to talk about Aristotle's insistence that only kings are possible as protagonists in tragic drama. He had a certain point there, but he seemed to forget that Greek drama was based on mythology in which the myth demanded that the protagonists should be tribal kings or tribal gods or demigods. At any rate I believe I have, in this revision made the characters *appear* stronger than they were.'

John Gray, however, he eventually thanked profusely for standing by him during this difficult time: 'You have been very kind to me, John. Thoughtful always, considerate, and fully aware of what an awful thing – the adjective is right – I dared to do in this book, just as you were fully aware that I had not succeeded in doing it as I had believed. Thank you for your whole attitude. You need not be concerned about me personally if you think this is a failure. I believe you would be ill-advised not to publish it now, and I don't think you will lose money on it. But feel free to express any opinion you choose. I am even able now to accept the implications of what I once said to you, not emotionally accepting them: that I may have written myself across a frontier into solitude and impotence to communicate in the novel-form. I am even able to accept the possibility – which Craig assumed was the fact – that my experience has destroyed my professional life, as many people believe it has done.'[65]

The revisions completed on 17 April 1958, after only a month's intensive work, MacLennan concluded that 'the overall burden of its meaning was the same as it seemed to be in January.' Still, he was convinced: 'It is a new kind of book. Conradian in its theme and mood, but like nothing Conrad ever did. The subconscious has been utilized now as no other novelist has ever utilized it: not clinically, but poetically, and I know true to experience.' He had only one regret about the novel – it had too much of 'The Ridge of Tears' about it: 'To a certain extent I regret the mood of sadness which pervades the whole. Toward the end – and this new Epilogue is divorced of its anti-climatic qualities – I believe a certain serenity has been achieved. But I'm afraid, perforce, the mood is that of Beethoven's Last Quartets. The title now does not apply merely to a single person, but to a whole generation and human epoch.'[66]

Revisions completed and sent off, MacLennan left Diarmuid Russell to negotiate an American publisher. Russell had already approached Harper's, but they had still not responded by the time MacLennan set off on 27 May for a much-needed holiday in Britain. After Dorothy's death, 'once the weeks of shock passed,' he had experienced 'a regurgitation of one crisis after another through which I had to live for ten years, and I used to wake tired out in the mornings from lying in a state of partial consciousness in which memory was active. It wasn't the loss last Easter that hurt so much, as the returning knowledge of the terrible loss to Dorothy in her own life, during all those years, which were half the time we were married.'[67] Before he left, the novel was already passing out of his system; he wrote to Gray on 23 May: 'Almost, it's out of me and gone. But art really is an obsession with some people, and I don't see how there can be any developing art without it. I talked as I did about the book not to justify it, not even to persuade you of any merits I feel it has which are not apparent to others, but because, I suppose, I still feel a slight duty to it as a father does to a child who appears one thing to him and another to somebody else. Also perhaps because I love the novel form, and know it is in acute danger of perishing and am stubborn enough to believe that IF what I have tried to do can reach even a small range of readers, it will help the novel stay alive.'

After the intense effort expended in plumbing the depths of his soul to write his novel, MacLennan felt like a miner coming back up the shaft into the light. Indeed, he had already turned his attention to other projects: two essays on the history of McGill University he had promised to Cyril James as editor of a book on McGill, and a series on the rivers of Canada commissioned by *Maclean's* magazine. Gray's predictions for the novel's success at this point were filled with caution. 'It will be published,' he wrote MacLennan on the eve of his departure, 'and it will sell at least reasonably well; but whether it gets the kind of reception you must hope for depends on a great string of unpredictables.'[68]

Once on board the *Manchester Regiment*, a name which amused him because of its close similarity to the *Manchester Battalion* on which Paul Tallard leaves Montreal in *Two Solitudes*, the sea voyage provided 'a paradise in which my mind went completely asleep for 11 days.' During his ten days in Scotland he stayed with a man named, oddly enough, Diarmuid MacLennan, a professor emeritus from McGill, also a widower, living in Kintail where the McLennan clan had originated. It was with this man, 'the only man,' he observed, 'who shares almost completely my own conception of God and religion,'[69] that he lost his sense of anxiety and pressure. A night at Oxford made him feel as if he had never left the place; dinners with C.P. Snow and his wife, the novelist Pamela Hansford Johnson, and with his friends Rache and Marguerite Dickson in London, all proved a rest and a solace for his troubles.

In July he flew back to Halifax to stay with his mother for a month. Then he travelled out to western Canada to collect information on the Mackenzie River, the first in his rivers of Canada series for *Maclean's*. The same magazine asked for an excerpt from the forthcoming novel, and he sent off the section about Jerome's escape by canoe. In a letter from his agent, which was waiting for him on his arrival in Halifax, he got the good news that Scribner's had decided to take 'Requiem'; their only requests were that the Montreal section about George's youth be cut somewhat and that the novel be given a new title. Within ten days MacLennan did the necessary cutting; by 4 August he sent off a suggestion for a new title, one with which he was not entirely happy, 'Sunrise at Evening.'[70] This interim title, however, suggested to one of Scribner's readers a line from the hymn *O, God, Our Help in Ages Past* – 'the watch that ends the night.' Hearing of this suggestion on 27 September 1958, MacLennan was delighted: 'This is the first time I've not titled one of my own books, but I do think it the best of them all.'[71]

Excitement was gathering at Scribner's about the novel; MacLennan heard from someone who had encountered some Scribner's people at a cocktail party that it is 'the best novel they've had in 20 years, excepting [*The*] *Old Man and the Sea*, which was a novella. Maybe true, maybe not, but anyway they're working very encouragingly on it.' Before the novel was even out, Carlos Baker, biographer of Hemingway, had read it for Scribner's and wrote a report which MacLennan sent on to Gray: 'I think it a distinguished novel, in many ways the best I have read for the last twelve-month, and I enjoyed it thoroughly from start to end. The author doesn't know me or anything about me, but you can tell him from me, if an occasion arises, that it's the best novel by a Canadian I have ever read, and that it surpasses in interest and importance most of the American novels I have read in the past year, and perhaps the past five.' MacLennan went on to comment: 'From people to whom I have given the book I have so far received a response I can only call overwhelmingly enthusiastic. They seem to have felt in it what I felt at its high moments while I wrote it, and I do believe if it once begins to move, it should move far.'[72] Finally, on a date MacLennan considered lucky, Friday the 13th, *The Watch That Ends the Night* was published in February 1959.

Reviews indicated that at last he was recognized and appreciated for exactly what he set out to do. While in the early stages of writing in 1953 he had predicted, as usual, that critics would misread his book: 'if the thing comes off, I'll be amused by the critics' reaction, for I'm damned sure they won't know what has been going on. They almost never do.'[73] But to most reviewers the novel was not merely a fictionalized essay on Canada and her history; he had succeeded in his aim to make universal themes out of an incidentally Canadian setting. This statement from the *Edmonton Journal* is typical: '[MacLennan's] faith that a figure of universal significance could be carved from the Canadian stone – and would eventually be recognized as universal – has been vindicated.' In his lead review in the *New York Times*, which appeared just after the novel went on the market, Orville Prescott praised it unreservedly for exactly those things MacLennan himself hoped to communicate: it is a 'penetrating psychological study'; it achieves a 'nice balance between intense drama and a sort of amused and civilized detachment'; it offers 'considerable humor'; it contains 'astute observation of all kinds of people'; it 'finds people lovable and life infinitely rewarding.' 'In its own way,' Prescott concluded, '[it] is a religious book.' Four months later he was still maintaining that *The Watch That Ends the Night* was one of only two books in the past year that he could recommend without reservation. One reviewer even sensed the influence of *War and Peace*: 'Mr. MacLennan jumps from one character to another and uses flashbacks in much the manner of the Russian novelists. But there is no confusion. His message is ringing clear.' Reinhold Niebuhr, the American theologian, called it a 'masterpiece.' With only one or two minor exceptions, the reviews were uniformly affirmative. One or two reviewers found the novel's conclusion sentimental or 'phoney'; the occasional reader found George Stewart insensitive; one felt that MacLennan showed no sense of humour;[74] but far and away the majority claimed that he had taken a huge step forward in his craft, that his characters were fused with theme and setting in a remarkable way, that the sense of the times in which they lived was given sensitively and with consummate skill, and that the novel was so 'readable' it could not be put down.

Only a few negative reviews spoiled this overwhelmingly positive response. In the *Kingston Whig-Standard* the reviewer admitted to a personal taste for 'Proustian self-analysis' and for Faulkner and Truman Capote: MacLennan's brand of 'realism' was therefore in no way pleasing to him, and he found the novel an unfortunate example of a peculiarly Canadian artistic heritage; for him, MacLennan 'never succeeds in bringing together the problems that involve all men and the impact of those problems on Canadians.' Other reviewers, too, expressed surprise that the novel took such a different path from much contemporary fiction. 'Morality? Duty? ... who can ask and who dares to utter these words?' one reviewer queried. Or, as Hugo McPherson put it more positively in the *Toronto Star*: 'Technically, its most stunning surprise is that Hugh MacLennan has dared to sound old-fashioned. In a decade that loves the artless confessions of children and the lusty incoherence of adolescents, he gives us a hero of mature years and good intelligence who writes a clear and vigorous prose.' McPherson also discussed the novel with Irving Layton and George Woodcock on CBC Radio: he argued that, while the novel was important and marked a technical advance over his earlier work, it was not 'great,' mainly because of the character George Stewart; Woodcock found Jerome Martell 'intolerable and incredible,' considered the novel uneven, and agreed with McPherson that it was not 'great'; Layton criticized what he considered to be MacLennan's distortion of the 1930s and thought the book attained only 'an admirable mediocrity.' MacLennan, after listening to this hatchet job, commented: 'I knew, regretfully, that jealousy was behind it, for one of them, Layton, had expressed to a mutual acquaintance an entirely different opinion two months ago before he discovered that the book would sell.'[75]

The success of *The Watch That Ends the Night* coincided almost exactly with a new feeling everywhere that Canadian literature had come of age. 'It is time we stopped talking about The great Canadian novel when books like *The Watch That Ends the Night* are being written,' Dorothy Dumbrille protested. Or, as the *Atlantic Advocate* declared: '*The Watch That Ends the Night* is Hugh MacLennan's best novel yet, and one that will be counted as of outstanding quality in any company.' Robertson Davies, in *Saturday Night*, urged that the novel be read not, as he had earlier done with *Barometer Rising*, as some kind of national duty but because the 'Canadianness' of this novel 'goes far beyond the [fact] that the setting of the book is Montreal ... it is rather that the thinking and feeling which give the book its weight and worth are Canadian ... Now, in his fifth book, he has gained a new mastery over the two strongest elements in his work: the story-teller and the self-explorer are one. The effect is virtually to double his stature. The Canadian novel takes a giant stride forward.'[76]

Something of the changes that had taken place in Canadian letters over the eighteen years since *Barometer Rising* had been published can be glimpsed in Bill Deacon's account of the lunch held by Macmillan's in Toronto to celebrate the book's publication on 17 February 1959: 'John M. Gray ... was host ... flanked by his editor Kildare Dobbs and promotion manager Mrs. E ... Weatherhill. Mr. MacLennan was ... in fine form. Perhaps the immediate enthusiasm that welcomed his book helped his mood. Also present were the critics Arnold Edinborough, Laurie McKechnie and Bob Fulford; Charles Bruce of Canadian Press, poet and novelist; Ralph Allen, editor and best-selling novelist; Pierre Berton, who does everything including the writing of an international best-selling book of non-fiction; and Ted Pope of *Tabloid*. This was the pleasantest literary-social event I have ever attended. Everybody present was up to his eyes in books; most were old friends of most of the others. There was no agenda. The 12 just sat around a big table for two hours of good food and good talk. The atmosphere was very Canadian and relaxed. Forty years ago no similar event could be held for lack of talent; 20 years back it could have been done by uniting individuals from different cities. Today, there is no lack of talent.'[77]

The novel was a solid success in Canada, the United States, and Britain as well. In an essay written with a good sense of fun, MacLennan exaggerated his own difficulty in believing his good fortune when he arrived in New York for the book's launching party to find Scribner's entire window display consisted of *The Watch That Ends the Night*.[78] A month after it was published, it appeared on the *New York Times* bestseller list, where it was ranked 13th for the week of 15 March; by the week of 10 May it was 8th (other notable books on the list were Pasternak's *Doctor Zhivago* in top spot, *Exodus* second, *The Ugly American* third, *Lolita* fifth, O'Hara's *From the Terrace* seventh, and Durrell's *Mountolive* from the *Alexandria Quartet* eleventh). By 12 July, after nineteen weeks on the *Times* list, it was still fourteenth place on the *Herald Tribune* list, and was bought for Doubleday's Book Club. In September it was selected for the Readers' Club of Canada. By November, sales in Canada reached 15,000 and the novel appeared in England published by Heinemann's. At the year's end it had sold 18,000 copies in Canada alone, and had earned MacLennan almost $4500. By 1975 it had sold 700,000 copies, and translations were under way into German, Swedish, and Estonian; the German edition alone sold 220,000 hard-back copies between 1960 and 1969. In late September 1959 MacLennan struck the financial windfall he had so long hoped for: he sold the movie rights to Eliot Hyman's Motion Picture Releasing Corporation for $70,000, with provision for profit sharing, to be paid in five separate annual instalments. In an eloquent plea to George Nowlan, minister of national revenue, in October 1959, he argued that the outright sale of film rights such as this should be regarded as a capital gain for income tax purposes. In his letter to Nowlan he argued cogently that the financial gains were demonstrably less for a successful writer in Canada than for his counterpart in the United States: a bestseller in Canada, which he defined as 5000 to 10,000 hard-back copies, netted a writer only $4000 as opposed to the $70,000 an American of relative popularity would gross in the United States. His breakdown of sales to date, of hard-back editions of his works, demonstrates clearly that although he had been successful by most standards his financial rewards had been slim:

	Canada	United States	United Kingdom
Barometer Rising (1941)	11,000	3,200	12,000
Two Solitudes (1945)	26,000	26,000	5,000
The Precipice (1948)	12,000	12,000	4,000
Each Man's Son (1951)	9,500	9,500	3,000
The Watch That Ends the Night (1959)*	13,000	26,000	–

* Figures on this last book are not yet final because it is still selling. Canadian sales will probably total, in cloth, 16,000. American sales, my publishers believe, may reach to 28,000, but they will be surprised if they exceed this.

In the seventeen years since *Barometer Rising* had first been translated, he pointed out, despite the fact that *Two Solitudes* had gone into six languages, he had earned a mere $1000 from translations of his publications. For total sales of *Barometer Rising* to date, including a paperback sale of some 50,000 copies for which he received only half a cent per copy, he had earned less than $600. For *Two Solitudes*, including the Book Club sales of 22,000 not included in the above columns, his Canadian receipts had been under $5000. With these facts in mind, he presented himself to Nowlan as sacrificing personal material gain on behalf of the nation: 'I assure you, Mr. Minister, that I profess sufficient professional competence to cash in on the American market. If I abandoned writing of Canada – as newspaper critics for years have expected me to do – and wrote of American scenes and situations from an American standpoint, I could have become a fairly rich man. A few Canadians have already done this. But by so doing, they turned their back on the rewarding and exciting opportunity of serving their own country as it deserves.'[79]

Even in the area of magazine articles there were odds against Canadians: while *Maclean's* paid $500, *Saturday Evening Post* in the States could afford $2000 per article. Although there is no doubt that MacLennan was putting his own case here as persuasively as possible, it would be cynical to say that his letter was in any way deceptive. He did feel tremendous allegiance to his country, even though it had not provided him with the opportunities he might have had from the beginning elsewhere. What he did not say, here, however, was that he did not really believe that anyone *could* write effectively out of a background other than his own; he had theorized for years that a writer *must* write out of his own context, and there is no reason to believe that he had changed his mind on that score. In whatever shade of grey the truth lay, MacLennan effectively slanted his argument to win the day; after long deliberation in Ottawa, his brief was successful. With only $3000 to his name eight months after the publication of *The Watch That Ends the Night*, he was certainly going to do his best to see that as little as possible of the $60,000, which would be his from the movie sale after commissions were paid, would go into income tax.

MacLennan had reached his full stature both as a writer and as a public figure. In the fullness of time, as more than one reviewer had predicted, he won the Governor-General's Award for fiction for *The Watch That Ends the Night*; in 1960, too, he was awarded the Alberta Medal and the Critics' Circle Award for his fiction generally. At no time had he really doubted that the novel would be a success: not when Houghton Mifflin rejected it, not when John Gray made cautious predictions for its success, not when reviewers like McPherson, Woodcock, and Layton turned up their noses at it. He had thought all along that it was going to be a sure thing. Now, after it was published and off to a flying start, he was authoritative. 'I'm not going to be modest about "The Watch,"' he told an interviewer a couple of months after the novel came out. 'I think it's a very good, very competent book. And you don't learn to write such a novel overnight ... The book was the result of 25 years of practising on the public.' Now, although he had earlier concealed the fact that he had been writing for some time before his 'first book' *Barometer Rising* appeared, he included those early unsuccessful years to add to his authority as a writer. He thought of himself as having effected a revolution in the novel at a time when the novel form itself was in serious difficulty. In the same interview, he stated: 'While "The Watch" doesn't avoid many of the basic tragedies of the human condition, still it doesn't "look back in anger." I felt a revolution of this sort was necessary if the novel as a genre was to live.'[80] Or, as he wrote privately to John Gray on 6 March 1959: 'Yes, the reception of *The Watch* is gratifying, but it also gives me a strange feeling. As you well recall, I was unashamedly sure of the value of this particular one, but at the same time I knew perfectly well that I had perpetrated something with it. It is a comfort, though a little unreal, to receive the kind of letters that come to me from readers now. *The Watch* quietly, and consciously, reversed the general trend of "serious" literature since the 1920s when Eliot and the others set a style and fashion which now has become petrified. I found out in New York that the chief reviewers and the Scribner's people realized this, and though the book may have any kind of fate in the current market, I believe it certain that it has already made a somewhat permanent mark. In New York I was told again and again that it had opened the door for Canadian writing down there somewhat as Paton opened the door to South Africans.'

Now fifty-two, MacLennan had confidence that 'the novel is still the subtlest and most accurate of all the literary forms invented, so long as it tells a story about real people and seeks to communicate and is written with a little love.' Looking back, he stated: 'As a novelist I know I've been lucky. I have crossed the half-century mark in my life and apparently I can still function and that seems remarkable to me, for it means I have survived the most bewildering transition in literary fashions there ever was. I survived it because I was a failure when I was young. Had I been successful in the Thirties, I believe I'd have been finished now.'[81]

The emotional and artistic feat of writing *The Watch That Ends the Night* left him empty. Looking ahead he had no immediate plans for another novel, as he always had before. 'A decline need not follow,' he wrote somewhat ominously to Gray just after finishing the novel, 'but non-fiction may.' Even earlier, he had commented: 'whatever may be essential in my own understanding of life has become something that only a handful of people would want to pay attention to even if I could express it extremely well'; 'this may well turn out [to be] my trouble in future: my kind of world is not like many other peoples' any more.' *The Watch That Ends the Night* was the novel that had been trying to write its way out of him from the very beginning; in it are all the 'great themes' he had already wrestled with, merged with all the significant life experiences he had since known, presented from a vantage point that, more than any other, spoke of his philosophy of life and art. Finally, he had got it right. He felt that he had written himself 'across a frontier' or through 'a sound-barrier.'[82] Possibly this novel would be his last.

In Halifax harbour in the 1960s

Chapter ten

Storm at Sea: *Return of the Sphinx*

The Watch That Ends the Night was acclaimed in Canada, the United States, Great Britain, and Germany, assuring MacLennan's reputation as a writer throughout the English-speaking world and beyond. His long-standing dream of becoming an internationally famous writer had been realized; anything he now wrote would automatically be treated with the respect and seriousness he had long thought he deserved. How could he cap this triumph?

Success of a similar kind, though on a smaller scale, had also come with the publication of *Two Solitudes* in 1945; but in more ways than he himself could have realized his present circumstances were profoundly different. For the last decade he had been progressively drawn inward by the demands Dorothy's illness had made on him and by the emotional energy he had needed to complete the novel that mirrored her tragic fate. Now, almost like Rip Van Winkle, he looked about him as if he had just awakened from a long sleep. While he had been involved in long, stressful vigils in the hospital and the arduous task of transforming the lives he had known into art, the world around him had undergone a sea-change. Literature in general had taken a new tack along lines he had consistently resisted, and the literary scene in Canada had come into its own; the changes in both these areas reflected the social and political theories of a new generation of writers.

The world was different after two world wars, and fiction was developing steadily in the same direction as its readers, away from the

Victorian standards of morality and aesthetics that had dominated it since its zenith in the nineteenth century. The appearance of Kinsey's first report on human sexuality in 1948 marked a new willingness on the part of middle class North Americans to discuss sexual matters with a freedom unthinkable a half-century before. Although James Joyce's *Ulysses* (1922) and D.H. Lawrence's *Lady Chatterly's Lover* (1928) had been written many years earlier, they were not allowed on sale in Canada until the end of the 1950s. The novel that probably most reflected the more open-minded attitude in Canada was J.D. Salinger's *The Catcher in the Rye*, which appeared in 1951. By 1956 Allan Ginsberg's poetry and Jean Genet's controversial play *The Balcony* had been published, to be followed three years later by William Burroughs' *Naked Lunch*. In 1962 Joseph Heller's *Catch-22* and Anthony Burgess' *A Clockwork Orange* were published, and by 1965 Norman Mailer had written *An American Dream*, followed in 1967 by *Why Are We in Vietnam*?

Whether MacLennan's puritanical upbringing had left him uneasy about the portrayal of sex or not, the severe criticism he had encountered over the sexual scenes in *Barometer Rising* and *Two Solitudes* had conditioned him to be cautious in his own depictions, a caution reflected in his literary theories. On the grounds that sex should not be used for sensational purposes or without a context that affirmed morality he had condemned writers such as James Jones and Mailer. Where such general affirmation existed he had no objection at all to sex or to forthright language. In fact, he had testified as an expert literary witness in obscenity trials on two occasions: in 1956 he spoke on behalf of Peter Denzer's controversial novel *Episode*, which documented life in a mental institution (and reads like an early version of Ken Kesey's *One Flew over the Cuckoo's Nest*), maintaining that the sexual scenes in it were 'an integral part and were not introduced for sensationalism'; although the defence lost this case, his testimony was more effective four years later, in 1960, when he testified on behalf of *Lady Chatterly's Lover*, declaring that Lawrence 'regarded this his most honest work in the statement of his philosophy of morals between man and woman that he could write.'[1] Despite these forays into the realm of public morals, the popularity of such aggressively obscene works as Mailer's later fiction was beyond his comprehension.

The expression of a burgeoning sexual freedom was not the only significant shift in the fiction with which he would now have to compete. Experiments with conventional form, initiated at first in the modern poetry of T.S. Eliot and Ezra Pound and then in the fiction of

James Joyce and Virginia Woolf, continued into the famous 'theatre of the absurd' school of drama with the writing of Samuel Beckett, Eugene Ionesco, and Harold Pinter. Although the general public often rejected these experimental works, exposure to such apparent formlessness prepared them for writers that did not follow the conventional plot structures of the nineteenth-century novel. It was possible by 1962, for example, for Vladimir Nabokov's *Pale Fire* to be a popular success.

In Canada the literary scene was dramatically different from the one MacLennan had surveyed in 1945. As Bill Deacon had noted in his comments on the lunch celebrating the publication of *The Watch That Ends the Night*, no such gathering could have occurred in Toronto at the time *Barometer Rising* was first published unless authors had been brought in from all across the country. By 1959, however, literature in Canada was well-established. Poetry continued to flourish with the addition of works by Irving Layton, Louis Dudek, Dorothy Livesay, James Reaney, Al Purdy, and a host of others. As for the vacuum in Canadian fiction, which had drawn MacLennan to its centre in 1941, an increasing number of capable writers had filled it. Ethel Wilson's *Swamp Angel* and Robertson Davies' *Leaven of Malice* were published in 1954, and the next year Mordecai Richler's *Son of a Smaller Hero* appeared. In 1956 Adele Wiseman and Mavis Gallant first had their work published, as did Leonard Cohen and Colin McDougall, both former students of MacLennan's, within the next two years. In 1963 Margaret Laurence brought out her first collection of short stories, to be followed almost immediately by her novel *The Stone Angel* in 1964. By the late sixties Alice Munro, Margaret Atwood, and Marian Engel had begun publishing fiction. Alongside this rapidly swelling tide of creative writing the critics Marshall McLuhan and Northrop Frye achieved international recognition, the former in 1951 with *The Mechanical Bride*, the latter in 1957 with *Anatomy of Criticism*.

These writers were already reaching markets in Canada that MacLennan could only have dreamed of in 1945. In 1957, the year in which he had commenced the massive rewriting that completed *The Watch That Ends the Night*, McClelland and Stewart had begun the New Canadian Library paperback series to get large numbers of Canadian books into the hands of students and the general public. It was no longer a lonely and frustrating business to be a Canadian writer. Reading engagements began to flourish in the early sixties, and universities acquired 'writers-in-residence,' if they could afford to do so, to act as consultants for creative writing courses. The Canada Council offered a number of grants and fellowships to assist writers in getting on with their work and also aided Canadian publishers in producing their books. The Governor-General's Award now carried with it an honorarium of $1000. Universities had begun to collect the letters and manuscripts of famous Canadians; although MacLennan told John Gray to destroy the manuscript of his novel once it was published, Gray sent it off to Robert Blackburn, chief librarian of the library at the University of Toronto, where it can still be found.[2]

In 1945 MacLennan had been a determined man of thirty-seven, with a wife his equal in intelligence and talent assisting him in crafting his career. Now, after Dorothy's death, he was desolate and depleted of energy; the completion of the novel so intimately linked with her fate had drained him of creative energy. Ironically, just at the time when the national tradition of writing he had earlier longed for was coming to pass, he was unable to take immediate advantage of it. Although the Canada Council offered him a senior fellowship shortly after he completed *The Watch That Ends the Night*, he had to refuse it because he had no ideas at all for another book. In a gesture that indicates how secure his national stature had become, the offer remained open for his future use. But as far as he could tell, he had written himself out.

Part of the process of recovering his equilibrium involved turning his attention to the non-fiction work at which he had become so adept. With two essays on the history of McGill and his several essays for *Maclean's* on the rivers of Canada, he kept well away from fiction writing, which he claimed made him feel 'like a man paddling a canoe down the rapids of a swirling changing river which nobody has charted or explored.' This time he would observe rivers from a decent distance, allowing the splendour of their vistas and the knowledge of their continuing history to heal his soul and enrich his sense of belonging. 'To bring this material alive to a present audience ... was my chief aim: to make people realize that time has been continuous and to make them see and feel the earlier life along the rivers'[3] was his stated purpose. So it was that he generalized once again from a strong personal need. When the rivers series was completed for *Maclean's* in 1960, he proposed to John Gray a revised and enlarged version in book form, a proposal that was eagerly accepted at Macmillan's. Within two years after publishing *The Watch That Ends the Night*, he brought out three non-fiction books: the third collection of his essays, *Scotchman's Return and Other Essays*, the title essay of which derived from his trip to Scotland after the novel was finished; *McGill: The*

Story of a University, which he edited in addition to writing the two main essays; and *Seven Rivers of Canada*, in which he collected his separate pieces from *Maclean's*.[4] All three were impressive, for he had become a consummate master of non-fiction prose.

In keeping with his need for peaceful stability at this time, he turned to a woman he and Dorothy had known and liked for more than ten years in Montreal and North Hatley. Frances Aline Walker, or 'Tota' as everyone called her, came from an old and wealthy Montreal family whose large stone house and expanse of garden had long graced the upper slopes of Westmount. Her family traced itself back several generations: on her mother's side to two Benson brothers, Yorkshire gentry who emigrated to Quebec City in 1810; on her father's side to a man who had also come to Quebec City from England about twenty years later. Her paternal grandfather had been a wealthy manufacturer who, for a time, had been mayor of Westmount, an independent rural suburb of Montreal at the time. He was eventually driven into near ruin by one of the more ruthless of the city's many tycoons, and by the time Tota was thirty the family had little money left. When she met MacLennan she was in her forties, just slightly older than he was. Her beauty was of exactly the type that appealed to him: small and vivacious, her hair was a rich sable brown; her skin, in striking contrast, was pale as alabaster. She loved dancing so passionately that she had hoped for a stage career, something her parents had firmly discouraged. Her grace and poise endeared her at once to MacLennan's mother and sister; in fact, with her natural kindness and warm charm she was not unlike the Katie of an earlier time. Despite her attractive and feminine personality she had never married; instead, she had become the classic 'maiden aunt' of her generation, called in by one branch of the family after another to give a hand with the children she adored. The emotional support she was able to give to MacLennan was the kind he most needed. She admired him greatly, as well she might at this stage of his career, and told him so. On 15 May 1959, three months after the publication of *The Watch That Ends the Night*, they were married at a small gathering in the home of a friend in Montreal. 'She danced like an angel; I like a clod,' MacLennan would later recall.[5]

Tota's companionship and support were instrumental in confirming his abilities as a non-fiction writer. After their marriage, the couple had made a honeymoon of his research trip to the Fraser River valley for the 'rivers of Canada' series. 'The real Hugh,' Tota later said, 'is found in his *Seven Rivers of Canada*.'[6] Her affectionate encouragement of his own deep response to the Canadian landscape helped him out of the 'valley of the shadow' in which he had landed. She enjoyed travel and, like Katie, had a fondness for picturesque description. In the loving descriptions of the land that characterize *Seven Rivers of Canada*, MacLennan surveyed the riches that awaited him as he awoke again to the beauty and challenge of the outside world; in a gesture of deep appreciation, he dedicated the book to his new wife.

At home in the Montreal apartment he and Dorothy had lived in for years, at 1535 Summerhill Avenue, Tota eagerly took up the round of social engagements that included several friends each of them had known independently before. Reaping at last the fruits of his labours, MacLennan moved out into the world once again, enjoying the round of dinners, cocktail parties, and informal gatherings that were his due. Tota proved to be a warm and capable hostess, arranging their social life with ease and authority. Both in Montreal and at North Hatley she saw to it that he had a stimulating and enjoyable life. She was also able to bond more firmly his relationship with his mother and Frances, a relationship that on more than one occasion had been strained by Dorothy's idiosyncracies. Tota was already close to her own family in Montreal; now visits to Halifax became increasingly frequent and pleasant.

With much greater peace of mind than he had known for years, MacLennan began to think about another novel. In letters to John Gray during the two years that lapsed after the publication of *The Watch That Ends the Night* he had sometimes been a little apologetic about not yet having begun another book.[7] Finally, on 21 December 1961, he wrote to say that a new novel was under way: 'I have no idea how it will turn out. As I get older and indeed ever since *Barometer Rising* – novels originate with me in a certain state of psychic unease akin to an overflow of water in a well. One has to wait for them. Now the general state of man's condition is a little more obvious, and therefore more difficult, than previously and the old problem of form comes up again. Or perhaps I should say, the proper form for whatever the feeling is ... 1961 was certainly one of the great watershed years of human history and it will be very hard to discover where the streams are really flowing and to plot a course in them. Anyway, one tries because one must.' While he let the creative waters ebb and flow, he tried with the rational part of his mind to come to terms with the changes in society that were becoming increasingly evident in that 'watershed' year.

The politics of the 1950s had generally bored him: he had not been excited by Diefenbaker or Eisenhower, and had noted in the summer of 1956 that, for once, his American friends at North Hatley had better things to discuss than elections. To him it had been a game, more or less, to write short articles on politics with an eye to predicting the future; occasionally he did so with spectacular success, calling the Conservative victory of 1957, for example, within a few seats.[8] On the whole, though, he saw the fifties as a time of relative stability, in which a good many of the social measures he had envied in the Scandinavian countries during the 1930s had gradually come about.

Now, however, with Quebec's 'Quiet Revolution' rapidly becoming quite noisy, his interest in politics, especially in Quebec, was fully revived. From as far back as the early 1940s, when he was writing *Two Solitudes*, he had thought of Montreal as 'the crucible of the nation's future.' In 'Quebec Forgets Its Old Fears' (1956), by no means his first article on the subject, he had compared the province to an iceberg: 'What lay under the surface – the hidden part of the iceberg – was the new Quebec created by the industrial revolution.' While on the whole his forecasts here had been inaccurate, he did recognize that the Québécois had become 'deracinated' and predicted that 'the influence of the Catholic Church will wane.' 'In the future,' he had concluded, 'French Canada will not so much appear as an island within the nation, but as its core and possibly as its conscience.'[9] His natural sympathy for the underdog, already expressed in *Two Solitudes*, along with a much deeper appreciation of the facts of the situation than had been possible for him in 1945, led him usually to take the side of French Canada on specific issues. When Donald Gordon had insisted in the summer of 1956 that the new CNR hotel in Montreal was to be named the Queen Elizabeth, for example, he had supported the indignant reaction of French Canadians who sent a fifteen-volume petition to Ottawa in protest. And, when Premier Maurice Duplessis had forbidden Quebec universities to accept federal aid, imposing a tax to enable the province to control its own education, he had sympathetically explained the logic of the move as follows: 'It is Canadien nationalism – the desire to preserve the state of mind generated by three centuries of hard history, the dread that its *mystique* may disappear if exposed to external influences – that has lain at the root of the whole controversy.' Analysing the Conservative victory of 1957, he had concluded that Quebec is 'the prize for which both parties must (in future) play.' By 1960 he was arguing that to speak French was a *must* for all Canadians; bilingualism seemed to him the means of keeping alive a nation with a dual culture, and to this end he suggested to English Canada the hiring of elementary school teachers who were bilingual, the introduction of French instruction for half of each school day, and the study of French literature in high school.[10]

By 1961, the year he began work on his next novel, he optimistically argued in *Maclean's*, in 'One Canada: The Real Promise of Quebec's Revolution,' that the dramatic changes in Quebec would in the long run strengthen Canada; English Canadians, he suggested, should welcome 'the Silent Revolution' as 'the most important development in many a year.' With particular attention to cultural advances, the break from the Roman Catholic church, the desire of the Québécois to control their own resources, and, especially, the new attitudes towards education, he believed that French Canada must be allowed to fulfil her natural destiny as one of the two founding nations: 'French Canada, though the English-speaking provinces seem unaware of this, has entered a climacteric which is causing her to search her inmost soul, and at last she is translating some of her aspirations into positive realistic action. Quite possibly, Quebec holds the key to the salvation of the Canadian identity about which the rest of us are concerned. This is one more reason why it has never been so important for English Canada to understand the mind of Quebec than it is now.' French Canada's growth into a new phase, he argued, contributed directly to a desirable resistance against United States influence: 'The French Fact in America ... has immense bearing on the very problem which has been worrying English Canada – the preservation of the Canadian Identity from American pressures.'[11] And, just as English Canadians feared assimilation by their neighbours to the south, so French Canadians understandably and logically dreaded absorption by their English-speaking compatriots.

Now that the British domination of English Canada he had so deplored in *Barometer Rising* had greatly moderated, he turned his attention to the increasing control of Canada's economy, natural resources, and communications networks by the United States. That this concern was as important to him as Quebec's future can be seen from a number of articles he wrote at the time. In an open letter to the newly elected president of the United States, John F. Kennedy, in the *Toronto Star* on 12 November 1960, he protested a variety of matters in which Canadians generally differed from Americans, including nuclear policy and the Far East; as well he decried the enormous effect the American style of living was having on Canada. The same month he wrote for *Maclean's* a strong article 'It's the U.S. or Us,' in which he outlined his theory that Canada was quickly becoming 'a spiritual slum' of the United States and urged Canadians to reject 'the huge brass bank of American salesmanship' in favour of their own national interests. By 1961 his ideas were reaching an American audience directly through *Harper's* magazine in an article called 'Anti-Americanism in Canada.' Characteristically he had a personal axe to grind: recently he had seen two of the Canadian magazines in which he had published extensively, the *Montrealer* and *Mayfair*, fold in the face of American competition, through the introduction of 'Canadian Editions' of American magazines such as *Time* free of advertising tax; his personal brief to the O'Leary Royal Commission on Publications in 1960 had helped draw attention to the implications of these new magazines for what he called 'our few remaining native voices.'[12] He disapproved of colonization, in any form.

Because he was so strongly opposed to American domination of Canada, he felt a certain sympathy for the aspirations of the separatist movement in Quebec – a sympathy that stopped well short of supporting violence, however. While recognizing that the movement was in earnest, even agreeing in print with a young separatist who maintained that English Canadians in Quebec were 'sitting on top of a bomb,' he could never condone the use of physical force to achieve political ends any more than he could accept war. In fact, he refused to believe that it might be necessary. To Pierre Bourgault's statement in *Exchange* – a controversial left-wing magazine in Montreal for which he himself wrote during these years – that 'No one has yet shown us how Quebec could achieve its independence peacefully,' he replied idealistically: 'French-Canadians are not a violent people and have always possessed a hard core of realism ... When these young people use the word "fight," they do not mean violence. They have ruled that out. They hope that if their movement catches on ... a Quebec government composed of separatists would be able to emancipate itself by democratic process.' Elsewhere he quoted André Laurendeau, a prominent Quebec spokesman soon to become co-chairman of the Royal Commission on Bilingualism and Biculturalism: 'It so happens that Anglo-Canadians are engaged in the same struggle as we are. They risk more than we do their identity as Canadians ... because geography and political institutions make us jointly responsible. Thanks to them, we are seventeen million instead of six million resisting Americanization.'[13]

In order to avoid being overwhelmed by the quick pace of change, which he termed 'the hurricane of the twentieth century,' MacLennan urged Canada to grasp the opportunity to become 'a model to the world in an epoch where the problems we have lived with here are causing murder and violence elsewhere.' Even when violence actually did break out in Quebec, he refused to consider acts of terrorism typical of the nationalist movement in general; as he demonstrated in 'Contemporary Events and Malraux's Novel' and 'When Montreal Refused to Hate,' both written in 1963, he saw such acts as emanating from a lunatic fringe who were in no way linked to the formal movement itself.[14] None the less, as bombings continued and tensions mounted during the late 1960s, finally culminating in the October Crisis of 1970, he became more and more anxious about his own safety: feeling that he might become a symbolic scapegoat for English Canada, he installed an iron grill across the windowed outside wall of his apartment which could be locked at night.[15]

For the time being, however, as he allowed his next novel to surface in the early 1960s, the emancipation of Quebec preoccupied his mind, along with the greater struggle of Canada to be free from the colonization of the United States. Pressing as these matters were to him, as far as the novel was concerned they were chiefly important because they were the local manifestations of sweeping cultural, social, and psychological changes in the larger world. This he made clear in an article called 'After 300 Years, Our Neurosis Is Relevant,' which he wrote in 1961 though it did not appear in print until it was collected in *Canada: A Guide to the Peaceable Kingdom* by William Kilbourn in 1970. In this essay he claimed that there are many elements in Canada likely to provoke neurosis, such as the harsh loneliness of the land and the tensions between English and French. In answer to the question 'Has Canada reached the point of cultural development when she can turn her neurotic character to creative purposes and, in healing herself, help to heal others?' he affirmed that this was so, and went on to make a statement that was crucial to his conception of his next novel: that maturity for individual and nation alike comes only when international interests are more important than local concerns. If he was to use the material uppermost in his mind for the novel he was to write, he would have to present in it the *universal*, an argument he elaborated on in a speech called *National Independence in the Modern World* which he gave to the Canadian Club in Toronto on 26 March 1962.[16]

He came to realize as well that the political unrest in Canada was part of another, much deeper movement that was sweeping the whole Western world. This 'psychic crisis,' as he called it, was taking place primarily among the young and was becoming evident in one university after another.[17] He was in certain ways well situated to observe this change, with a decade's experience at McGill to use as yardstick. Recognizing that he and Tota were too old to start a family of their own, he took a paternal interest in his students. Furthermore, since beginning to teach at McGill in 1951 he had had a strong curiosity about his students' tastes and attitudes, having seen in them a barometer of the market for his own fiction and having observed their behaviour with an eye to characterizations of his own: in *The Watch That Ends the Night* his portrayal of Catherine's daughter Sally and her boyfriend Alan Royce, both university students, reflected his perception that contemporary young people differed significantly from his own generation.

In a number of essays during the 1950s he had outlined his notions of the precise ways in which young people exhibited different attitudes to history, work, culture, sex, and education. In 'Fifty Grand: A Semi-Centenarian Takes Stock' (1957), the somewhat bitter assessment of his life written when he turned fifty, and even earlier in 'A Middle-aged Man Looks at Youth' (1954) and 'Couth and Uncouth' (1955), he had recognized the marked differences between young people then in their twenties and his own generation. One typical essay, 'It Pays to Pamper Our Children' (1956), had observed that the current generation was stable and happy, intellectually more mature, and wiser about sex in particular and about life in general because of the popularization of psychology that had not yet occurred at the time he was growing up. Contrary to the notion that they were spoiled and soft, he argued that they were simply not guilt-ridden as their parents had been and that they had their own brand of morality.[18]

With developments in the late fifties and early sixties, however, he began to change his views. 'The dim and tranced state of the 1950's is past,' he asserted.[19] Although in 1956 he had confidently maintained that the 'young people in post-war Canada are not decadent,' by 1959 he was deploring the breakdown of the family unit as illustrated in so much modern fiction, though he did not yet see evidence of such an attitude among the young. By 1960 he had turned once again to his old complaint about the misuse of modern technology as an explanation for the dissolution of humanist principles in education and for the psychological changes now becoming apparent.[20] In 1965, in a convocation address to the graduating students of McMaster University in Hamilton entitled 'More Important Than the Bomb,' he outlined briefly the theory he was to refine into a full-fledged analysis of the 'psychic crisis'; attempting to read their minds, he speculated that young people of these times must hate the dehumanizing effects of the technological society and must believe that no communication was possible with the older generation. In 1956 he had noticed that young people 'feel sorry for [their parents] in an amused way,' an emotion he found 'charming'; now, almost a decade later, he saw that this pity had become outright anger and disillusionment.[21] No common ground between the generations seemed possible.

In his attempts to come to terms with the social and political climate of the sixties, he laboured under certain disadvantages. Politically, he could not have been more badly situated to understand what was happening in Quebec. McGill was regarded by the new nationalists as the very bastion of English-Canadian myopia. The large government grants the university received, which for years had been out of all proportion to the number of English students in Quebec, had become a major issue. Had he wanted information from his colleagues in the French Department, he would have had lean pickings: most of the staff teaching French language and literature had been imported from France. Furthermore, his own attempts to master the French language after the success of *Two Solitudes* had been a relative failure, and although he had some reading knowledge of French he was far from being bilingual.

Nor was he better placed to understand the social changes that were taking place. As the son of a fairly elderly father, himself the son of an even more elderly father, he had been raised in a mid-Victorian context; although his father had done his best to broaden his interests, he had none the less been brought up in a relatively old-fashioned way, far from the centres of culture. Moreover, with no children of his own, his notions of what motivated young people could not be based on direct, emotional experience. Although he listened carefully to his students at McGill and observed them with more concern than did many professors, they could not substitute for the kind of knowledge he might have obtained from being a father himself.

Determined to overcome these disadvantages, he turned to books on psychology. One book above all drew together the various strands in his thinking at the time, G. Rattray Taylor's *Sex in History*. Although first published in 1953, MacLennan did not read it until late in 1960,[22] just before he began making notes for his new novel. Its importance to him cannot be over-emphasized.

Taylor had applied Freudian psychology to the study of history. Briefly, he saw history as moving in cycles between the two extremes of 'patrist' and 'matrist' societies, two forms of human culture taking their names from alternate methods of dealing with the classic Oedipal situation: the 'patrist' identifies with the father, assuming his authority and supporting his arrangements and laws; the 'matrist' clings to the mother in rebellion against the father, concentrating his energies on maintaining the comforts of life his mother represents. These two patterns are the extremes, he emphasized: 'when society is changing from patrism to matrism, or vice versa, there will be an intervening period in which the patterns will become confused. Moreover, there may be some happy periods in which people succeed in introjecting both parental figures in harmonious balance – but owing to the pressure of the Oedipal conflict, there is a natural tendency to fall off the fence on one side or the other.'[23] He discussed a number of eras in Western history to demonstrate this theory: Elizabethan England, a matriarchal society; Calvinism (the chapter that most engrossed MacLennan), a patrist reaction to matrism; Romanticism, a matrist period; and so on. The book ended with an analysis of contemporary society called 'Modern Morality' in which Taylor maintained that the world was becoming more and more matrist in reaction to the patrist society that was Victorian England.

MacLennan's imagination was seized immediately. For the most part Taylor's theories provided a meaningful framework for a number of separate views he already held: the cyclic view of history that had originated in his classical studies and was best expressed in Gibbon's *Decline and Fall of the Roman Empire* and Spengler's *Decline of the West* – a view that had lain behind his thesis *Oxyrhynchus*; a general feeling, mainly derived from his father, that the First World War had been one of the cataclysmic turning points in human history; his persistent notion that the technological advances of the twentieth century had thrown the times out of joint, diverting energy into destructive outlets like the neutron bomb while man's moral, humanitarian side lagged far behind; and his conviction that Calvin had been one of the most evil men, if not *the* most evil man, in Western history. Even his adaptation in *The Watch That Ends the Night* of David Malcolmson's type-hero 'The Escape from the Devouring Mother'[24] into the character of Jerome Martell had anticipated Taylor's views. The book also emphasized Freud, of course: in particular it drew attention to the Oedipus complex as the key not only to individual development but also to society's evolution. It was natural, consequently, that reading *Sex in History* led MacLennan back to a reconsideration of Freud.

Although he apparently did not reread Freud after his discovery of Taylor, the number of references to Freudian psychology in his letters and essays at the time suggests that, at the very least, whatever he already knew about him was recalled. Almost at once, for example, he wrote two versions of his leave-taking of his father when he went to Oxford, 'On Living in a Cold Country' and 'On Living with the Winter in the Country' (1961), in which he playfully 'analysed' his own remarkable decision to sleep outdoors in a tent for most of his youth, explaining it all as a manifestation of the Oedipus complex. In another article in 1961, 'The Thing We Are All Thinking About' (the bomb), he explored Freud's formula for mental health and happiness in the individual and applied it to civilization as a whole. In a letter to John Gray that same year he drew an analogy between Quebec's new nationalist movement and a patient under psychiatric treatment: 'I have the impression that the nationalists are nearing the state of mind of a psychiatric patient just before the treatment forces him to admit openly his real trouble – his hatred of his father or mother as the case may be, and his terror of punishment for feeling that way. In this case, of course, the Church.' And, in one of his periodic reassessments of Captain Bligh, 'Reflections on the "Bounty" Myth' (1962), he mused on the psychological significance of the *Bounty* for the present era; perhaps, he speculated, 'modern society, regimented into the service of its machines, secretly yearns for the primitive and for the overthrow of all authority.' During 1964 he saw the film *Phaedra*, based on the Greek myth about incest, three times because it impressed him as 'close to being the greatest movie yet.'[25]

In 1962 he wrote a short article on *Sex in History* for the Writer's Diary series in the *Montreal Star* and syndicated papers, to which he contributed weekly from July 1962 until October 1963. He praised Taylor's book and agreed that his own society was 'galloping hard towards matrism.'[26] By this time, with his novel scarcely begun, he had absorbed Taylor's theories almost as if they were his own, as the best framework within which to analyse current social trends. That the terms 'matrist' and 'patrist' were unlikely to mean much to the average reader seems not to have occurred to him; for him they explained everything, and they became an essential part of his vocabulary.

In 1963, four years after the publication of *The Watch That Ends the Night*, he decided he should wait no longer to take up the offer the Canada Council had so generously made him; although senior fellowships no longer existed, 'an arrangement of a special kind' was made to finance a year away from his duties at McGill. Partly because he felt himself too close to the political upheaval in Quebec, but more in imitation of James Joyce who had fled Ireland to gain perspective, he decided to spend the year in France. He would have done better, perhaps, to immerse himself in the daily life of any small French community in Quebec, but a letter to John Gray in September, explaining his decision, reveals a man admittedly at sea. Generalizing from his own sense of personal isolation in Quebec, he confided that he could not make any sense of the events taking place in Canada. For the first time, the ideas on which he would base his next book were not clear. Unlike Joyce, he had not formulated an aesthetic and national stance which had only to be written out; he admitted that he was setting off for France in the hope that his perplexing dryness of spirit would disappear:

> All I knew about the new novel is that I must get out of here to give it a chance to come. The world has become very queer to me lately, as I suppose it has to everyone our age. The change – in rapidity and degree – seems akin to the change in England between 1850 and 1870, though this is of a different kind ...
>
> I felt late last winter that there was nothing that I, personally, could do at this juncture. I've said my piece and I want to get out in the hope of gaining some perspective. Montreal used to be a fine place to live if you wanted to write. It would be good if you were young today. But the pressures [of] the past three years have been very bad, they make it hard to contemplate, and the English-speaking community is becoming more and more isolated even when, curiously enough, there is much more intercourse between them and the French than ever before. They have never behaved better than now, but they are paying for more than a century of indifference and arrogance in the past ... I can't understand or even sense the shape of things to come. I know nobody else who can, either.[27]

After a holiday in Greece and Italy, the MacLennans chose Grenoble in which to spend the winter of 1963-4. They lived in a single large room in the Hotel de Savoie, MacLennan writing hard five hours a day and spending the rest of the time trying to learn French – not the *joual* in which the Québécois were protesting their fate, but the language of the Continent. 'My own poor command of the French language has been the greatest cultural handicap of my life,' he had maintained two years earlier, and he bitterly regretted that at Oxford he had chosen German as his second language when he could as easily have acquired French. But language study had never been easy for him, and despite his assiduous and prolonged efforts to become bilingual he was never to master the French language beyond a basic working level. 'I hope to become fairly bi-lingual by the time I come home,' he wrote to Marian Engel, 'but my aural perceptions were never too good and I still miss a number of words per minute when people speak.'[28] For relaxation in Grenoble he restricted himself to short walks and a weekly drive into the neighbouring countryside.

In the Dauphiné he tried to see a parallel with Quebec's situation vis-à-vis the rest of Canada: a provincial society dependent on a central metropolis. This opinion he later expressed on his return home on a CBC Radio program called 'France and Its Provinces.'[29] Casting his new impressions persistently in the old moulds his mind had firmly established, he observed of the local people he met: 'I have become enormously fond of these French people in the Dauphiné. Their character more resembles that of the Scotch, even of non-Toronto, Ontario, than it does the French Canadians of Quebec. Their manners, I fear, are better and they have this curious sad French wisdom which English Canada possesses but feels guilty about possessing.' Lester Pearson's visit to France during his time there triggered further observations about Quebec, which suggest that he was becoming less sympathetic to the separatist cause; he thought the visit was 'one of the most subtle strokes of diplomacy Canada has ever worked': 'There can be no question that there was a small group in Paris fishing in our troubled waters, but the French as a whole want no part of trouble in Canada ... By getting de Gaulle to speak as he did, Mike [Pearson] pulled the rug right out from under not only the separatists, but a substantial body of French Canadians who over-estimated, out of wishful thinking, the role France could play for them. The truth is that France has more to gain from English-Canada than from Quebec ... Ironically, English-Canada has much more to offer France economically.'

As far as the novel itself was concerned, MacLennan worked slowly. The self-doubts that always plagued him at the outset were as usual present. 'The new novel goes well,' he wrote home to Gray; 'It will be a big one, and I write better than I have done before, though whether as popularly I don't know. It goes slowly at first, as all my novels do, but this time I see the general structure with much more clarity than ever before ... The question will be whether the writing – or my imagination – can meet its demands.'[30]

At this stage the book presented itself in the first person, with Gabriel Fleury, the old-worldly French immigrant from the Dauphiné in Montreal, as its narrator. Drafts of the novel from 1963[31] show that he began to write from much the same point of view as the one he had so successfully taken in *The Watch That Ends the Night*: a relatively low-key male narrator, Gabriel Fleury, relates the story about the man of action, Alan Ainslie, who is his friend. Furthermore the story definitely began as a tragic one: evidently Alan Ainslie, as MacLennan first conceived of him, was eventually to die. The characters who were to form the novel's cast were the Ainslie family: Constance, Alan's wife, tragically killed; Daniel, his son, an active separatist; and Chantal, his daughter, whose affair with Gabriel Fleury constituted one of the earliest scenes he drafted. Eventually, however, the novel started to break in two, as MacLennan noted in a scribbled message to himself on the front of one of these early drafts. The story seemed to be going in what he called a 'schizophrenic' direction, one part dealing with Gabriel's successful adaptation to events, the other part dealing with Alan's failure to do so. This binary movement led him away from the first person, which had so successfully focused *The Watch That Ends the Night*; even at this early stage he had abandoned the point of view that would most probably have given the novel an emotional tone, in favour of the third person narration that more accurately reflected his own sense of detachment from the events he was about to describe. By the end of 1963 he had completely switched the point of view, and had introduced the tycoon industrialist Herbert Tarnley into the opening scene, which had been exclusively Gabriel Fleury's before.

In one of the Writer's Diary columns he had written just prior to his trip to France, MacLennan had stated that since 'myth has been at the core of all the greatest art ... the artist who best fulfills his function is the one who contrives, no matter what his knowledge, to express it in some form akin to myth.'[32] Characteristically, this general statement concealed a deeply felt personal theory which he had recently worked out for himself. For *Sex in History* had not only sent him back to Freud, it had also revived his interest in the Oedipus plays of Sophocles. Sometime between his reading of Taylor's book at the end of 1960 and the writing of the early drafts of *Return of the Sphinx* in 1963, he had firmly decided to base his new novel on Sophocles' *Oedipus at Colonus*. This was the 'myth' that would give his novel its form, as he noted on the manuscript of one of these early drafts: 'The book seems slowly moving out of the depths into a schizophrenic form with Gabriel resolved out of the Complex while Alan, still trapped in it, will be destroyed. And to that extent, quite possibly, when the crack comes, it will be Gabriel who will play the role of Theseus in the O.C. – But this must rest for the working out of the novel. Structurally, as things proceed now, the plot is sound.' The 'Complex' here is the Oedipus complex on which Taylor had based his theory; the 'O.C.' is Sophocles' play. There is no reason to believe that he altered this general plan. In fact, with the single exception of the change in the outcome of Alan's life (he never is 'destroyed' as earlier intended), he remained faithful to this model until the novel's completion in the middle of September 1966.

In the fall of 1964, on his return from Grenoble, MacLennan was made a full-time faculty member at McGill after over a decade of part-time teaching. The progress of his novel was slowed considerably by his other duties, especially the following year when his new course attracted a huge influx of students. Expecting to finish the novel that winter, he was obliged to write to Gray on 25 October 1965 to say that he must rescind his prediction. 'A course planned as a seminar on the modern novel showed up 400 students,' he explained in dismay; 'I've now reduced the number to 250, but with two other over-sized classes, this is pretty rugged, especially as it's a new course. However,' he went on somewhat in the spirit of rationalization, 'this much good comes out of it. I believe I've made a break-through to the young generation at last and am seeing the present with the eyes of the present. I write with more concision and confidence, and I can manage at least three mornings a week.'

By 15 July 1966 he was still struggling to finish: 'The novel goes along as best it and I can. How I wish I could write an easy book! But I have a somewhat new vision of things these days – or rather, have understood the meaning of many things which previously emerged in disguise.' His means to understanding such things as the upheaval in French Canada, American intervention in Vietnam, and student unrest in the universities remained Taylor's analysis of history. Typically looking on the bright side of the delays in finishing the novel, in September 1966 he told Gray that it was on the verge of completion: 'Possibly the very difficulties I had may have sharpened the book's perspective. For me it was a frightening book to write, and how acceptable it will be God only knows, I can't let that concern me too much. I believe it to be far and away the most tightly written and dramatic novel I have ever written – more so than *Barometer* because the drama is internal.'

In the final weeks of writing he had at last experienced the heightened momentum he had come to associate with the completion of a novel: 'It flowed out to its end very fast in the final six weeks.' In fact, he claimed, he was even closer to his material than ever before: 'I had lived with the book so intensely for so long – much longer in that degree of intensity than with *The Watch*.' As he wrote the last page the title came to him, and he handed the manuscript to Tota with the despairing comment: 'This is the only one of my books I wish were not true.' A couple of weeks later he turned over the manuscript of *Return of the Sphinx* to John Gray, with the self-confident flourish of a writer who knows he is established: 'This present novel is much the most advanced thing I have done and it is a world book of the present time ... This one has broken through into the new generation and the new age, and as I work over it, I am rather frightened by its power. I never wrote so tightly or dramatically before ... Here the equations are tighter and I never before felt that any book of mine was so completely "finished."' Three weeks later he added somewhat superfluously: 'this book has struck the universal thing at the moment I know, and I also know that no other writer has grasped it.'[33]

MacLennan's purpose in *Return of the Sphinx* was two-fold, and can be traced back to the two primary influences on him at the time he was writing. First, as he later put it, he adapted Taylor's theories from *Sex in History* to 'use Freud as an art-structure'; second, he used the *Oedipus at Colonus* phase of the Oedipal myth to give dramatic qualities and structure, as well as universality, to his novel.

What did he mean when he wrote of Freud as 'art-structure'? In August 1967, after the book's publication, he wrote to Gray: 'Arthur Koestler, some twenty years ago, predicted that it would be at least forty years before any novelist who used the basic discoveries of Freud as an art-structure would be comprehensible to the critics. It so happens that this is precisely what I did in *The Sphinx*. I agree with Daniel Schneider that no art has a chance if it ignores scientific discoveries. Also, that to accept what I have accepted demanded a dramatic form which only on the arithmetical level is conventional. As the equations are right, they are bound to upset conventionally trained people who have to write about the book.'[34] In the most basic sense he was trying to incorporate, not ignore, the Freudian theories which by the fifties had filtered down into common parlance and were falling into disfavour among most intellectuals. But it was really *Sex in History* that had shown him how Freudian dynamics could be seen to structure all history. If man's reaction to the Oedipal situation could inform whole eras of human history, the same dynamics could be applied to the structure of a book, especially if that book dwelt explicitly on a historical period which Freudian theory could explain.

MacLennan was already well on his way to formulating a similar view of human history. In *The Watch That Ends the Night*, through George Stewart, he had recorded an opinion that was remarkably similar to the Freudian interpretations he was to consider: 'In my years of work as a political commentator I have come to a conclusion which shocks some of my friends who think of politics as a rational occupation. I believe that most international crises are like gigantic mystery plays in which obscure and absolutely irrational passions are handled by politicians, and viewed by the public, in a form of ritual akin to primitive religious rites. Hardly anything anyone says or thinks in a time of political crisis is likely to be rational or a representation of the facts. The crisis is almost never about the outward things with which it professes to concern itself. Also, no political crisis ever blows up quickly. It matures underground for years and months, the chemical ingredients are various and many. So it is within a nation, a human group or a city, and it often happens that the fulminate which fires the explosion is something nobody notices.' Even earlier, in *Two Solitudes*, his character Athanase Tallard states bluntly that 'perhaps all wars and revolutions and movements of history started from sources ... trivial and undignified.' A good many of his political essays in the fifties also reflected this view, especially his frequently stated theory that the shift to a Conservative government in the landslide victory of John Diefenbaker in 1958 had nothing to do with the surface issues but was rather the result of a massive psychic shift in the unconscious of the nation.[35] In his latest novel, his theories brought into crystalline focus by Taylor's theories and Schneider's Freudian reading of the *Oedipus at Colonus*, he concentrated his whole attention on the universal, unconscious psychic shifts of his time whose mere reflection had found its way into the surface events around him.

In *Return of the Sphinx* MacLennan illustrated that the current age was, as he had already put it, 'galloping hard towards matrism'; to do so he simply took wholesale the theories in Taylor's last chapter 'Modern Morality.' This present matrist era, as he depicted it, began as a reaction to the extreme patrism that had culminated in the two world wars. Thus, the earliest point of reference in the novel is the First World War, an event to which one of the characters, Tarnley, traces the beginning of all the current trouble: 'It was in the first one that it all started. I mean when it *all* started.' Tarnley's statement comes back to haunt Gabriel Fleury as he tries to make some sense of the present age: 'What had started then was surely the rebirth of a kind of man who had perished two thousand years ago, a man who knew there was no escape from his own nature into religion or politics or science or even into his own skill. That was certainly when it began for himself, and he was not even six years old when he understood it as a child understands certain things as final and absolute facts.' The First World War has broken the spirit of Gabriel's father, leaving him nothing to believe in or live for; the ideals and authority of the patrist era that was Victorian England had been exaggerated to an extreme that no human could tolerate. As for Gabriel and his slightly later generation, the Second World War remained the last gasp of a patrism that was being modified already by matrist influences. In one of the earliest scenes drafted, Gabriel recalls the sinking of his ship en route to Calcutta just before Pearl Harbor; the strange dreamy atmosphere he remembers as he drifts in a lifeboat afterwards illustrates the hiatus that follows the end of an era: 'All responsibility was gone. Without a single thing left to which he could sensibly attach his loyalty, with nothing he could even imagine himself doing to help anyone or anything, Gabriel felt a mysterious peace.'[36] The shark that hovers by his drifting hand is reminiscent of the monsters of the unconscious that Captain Yardley glimpsed at sea and that George Stewart experienced as the ocean of the unconscious threatened to overwhelm him after the structure of his identity temporarily disappeared.

For MacLennan, influenced by Taylor, this was the state of mind that resulted when the super-ego, even as bullying a one as that which expressed itself in two world wars, dissolved. *Return of the Sphinx* is full of such images as the Western world moves further and further away from the too aggressive patrism from which it is in revolt. Most dramatic is the image of the storm at sea, in which MacLennan so forcefully illustrated that 'hurricane which is the twentieth century' he believed was taking place. Based on 'Hurricane Ginny,'[37] which had ravaged the east coast of the United States in October 1963, causing thirty- to forty-foot high waves, and had caught the MacLennans en route to Grenoble on board the *S.S. Independence*, this storm rises out of the depths of the sea and knocks over Alan Ainslie, terrifying him with its violence: 'Then something loomed at him, something absolutely enormous came at him out of the dark shaped like Kilimanjaro with snow solid on a long, humped crest. A huge, soft-muscled something alive scooped the ship up, held her an instant, trembling, then threw her over on her starboard side with a roar of water and a crash of breaking gear.' This creature, at once the 'id' of Alan and all men, is also those forces MacLennan always imagined as being 'under the surface' of the ship of human progress and responsibility – the 'super-ego.' Here is the mysterious sphinx who returns periodically to puzzle man with the old, difficult questions to which man himself and the stages of his life are the only true answers. In this central symbol he had in mind also the writing of W.B. Yeats, whose cyclic view of history corresponded in some respects at least with Taylor's. 'Things are falling apart, the centre cannot hold,' Ainslie quotes from Yeats on one occasion, and indeed 'the great beast slouching towards Bethlehem to be born' is a part of that huge 'something alive' which ushers in MacLennan's new cycle of human history.

For Ainslie, the sensations he felt in that hurricane at sea are akin to those he feels years later in Ottawa as minister of culture aboard the ship of state seeing the province of Quebec, and the rest of the nation too, very close to chaos: 'The time he was living in was too fantastic for anyone to look it square in the eye. Hurricane weather but no hurricanes. Nuclear confrontations with serious-minded men seriously wondering whether there would be even a blade of grass left on the planet inside a few years, but so far no bombs. Full employment but no security. Knowledge in unknowable quantities but never so many people telling each other they could not understand. All the ideas that had guided and inspired Ainslie's life – socialism, education, the faith that science and prosperity would improve man's life, even the new psychology which everyone so glibly talked – the best he could say now of any of these hopes was that they had foundered in the ancient ocean of human nature ... He knew he was never seriously listened to by any of his colleagues when he repeated his storm warnings and implored them to do something before the storm broke.' Ainslie is a patrist in a matrist era, who feels he is 'unable to steer any true course of his own.'[38] No wonder his autobiography is called *Death of a Victorian*.

If the two world wars represent the final extreme of a patrist era in *Return of the Sphinx*, the decade of the fifties represents a time when the oncoming forces of matrism are temporarily in balance with the declining patrist values. But with the sixties comes the full sway and the decadence of matrism. This move into matrist extremes constitutes the present in the book, and it is this present which MacLennan, thanks to his students, claimed to be able to see 'with the eyes of the present.' Members of society are weak-willed consumers for whom personal pleasure is a dominant aim and whose education consists of advertising propaganda from the United States. Typical of this era – indeed personifying it – is the character Marielle, the older woman with whom Ainslie's son Daniel has a semi-incestuous affair. In an allegorical episode she sees her father killed during the war (again the death of patrism), and, consequently disillusioned in most ideals and principles, she exerts little if any authority in bringing up Clarisse, her illegitimate daughter. With a past history of several lovers, this luxurious Mediterranean woman is completely at home in the current matrist society, enjoying thoroughly the sight of so many young people having fun. To her it is nothing to sleep with Daniel, who is ostensibly her daughter's boyfriend. For both Chantal and Daniel, Ainslie's children, the Oedipus complex is a motivating force: each one has an affair with a parental substitute. In an earlier draft of the novel Chantal comments explicitly that 'this [is a] female age we live in now'; altered in its final version, the remark more specifically is applied to Quebec as 'behaving like a woman in the menopause.' MacLennan demonstrated on every level – individual, provincial, national, and universal – that the accelerating excesses of a matrist age were resulting in the kind of confusion, the inability to form any kind of super-ego, that Taylor had said was likely to follow as any historical cycle drew to its close. Chantal, who has herself seduced Fleury, her father's oldest friend, says in an early draft of the novel: 'Most of them [fathers today] look the other way when the kids tumble into bed with one another. Do you think that makes a boy like Daniel respect his father, or what his father stands for, or what he thinks his father stands for? ... It's in the air, Gabriel. This thing I'm talking about is in the air all around.' And, as Gabriel comments, also in one of the earlier drafts: 'I don't know much about history, but from the little I do know I have the idea that the termination of all regimes has the same symptoms. Everybody knows that the jig is up, but at the same time hardly anyone can accept what this is going to mean to himself personally.'[39]

One such symptom of a matrist phase is the breakdown of the family. This is represented in the novel symbolically by the death of Constance, Alan Ainslie's wife, who is killed, literally as MacLennan's friend George Barrett had been, by the acceleration of modern science and technology. In a senseless accident, in which a truck carrying a load of scientifically processed cheese goes out of control, the brakes fail and Constance Ainslie is crushed. Ainslie's family is consequently without a centre – things fall apart, and one of the novel's dramatized statements is the series of entrances and exits from the Ainslie apartment as Alan, Chantal, and Daniel careen in and out like random molecules, bumping into each other now and then as if by chance. Thus, MacLennan deliberately chose for the novel's present the last segment of the matrist era he believed was occurring throughout the world.

Return of the Sphinx illustrates that the change back to a patrist society is near at hand. Although Ainslie may hold that there are no hurricanes as yet, even though it feels like hurricane weather, the storm is about to break in his own family, in the nation, and throughout the world. His son Daniel is a separatist who increasingly moves towards the Quebec nationalist ideals and even towards violence. Like his separatist compatriots, he is a patrist. Furious at the decadence of the Americanized consumer society all around him, enraged at his father's ineffectual behaviour and his absence from home, disillusioned with Marielle for sleeping with him and abnegating her responsibility as Clarisse's mother, disgusted with his sister and his 'Uncle Gabriel' for their affair, he finds in the separatist movement a 'cause' with the direction, ideals, and sense of responsibility so clearly lacking in modern life. In its rebellion against the Roman Catholic church and against the Queen – both 'mother' symbols and hence representatives of matrism – the separatist movement promises a clean sweep, a new honesty, and male leadership. As Ainslie puts it in Parliament: '[Canada] is in terrible danger, and the danger comes from what well may be a change in its personality.' In his desperate hatred of the 'stinking world of cheating, corrupting, lying, selling-out and excusing themselves by telling you this is human nature,' Daniel models himself on his prize-fighter grandfather, Archie MacNeil from *Each Man's Son*, and sets out to bomb a building in the city his sister has earlier likened to 'a puritan when the bottom falls out of his character and all those polypy things that are inside of puritans come crawling out for a Mardi Gras.' Daniel's action, extreme though it is, is presented as normal, indicating the pressing need for the return to patrism. As Joe Lacombe, the French-Canadian policeman who catches him before he triggers the bomb, says: 'underneath you aren't crazier than anyone else ... That's what really scares me.' In a letter to Gray, MacLennan later explained his concept of Daniel: 'The tragedy of the western world today can be expressed pretty simply – the inability of the young men to identify with a father – i.e. with a creative superego, on account of what the patrists did in 1914, failed to do in the 1930s, repeated in 1939 and now are attempting to do in Viet Nam, big business and advertising ... Applied to French-Canada, Mother Church took the place of Father France for two centuries. Need one look any further than that for the rapprochement between that supreme Father-Image, DeGaulle, and the youth of today's Quebec which has rejected Mother-Church.'[40]

In structuring his novel between the last dramatic acts of a patrist era, through the ascension and decline of the matrist era that replaced it, up to the very point at which a new patrist revolution is to occur, MacLennan used Freudian theory to focus his individual, national, and universal themes. But *Oedipus at Colonus* gave him the tight dramatic structure and character patterns by which he could economically illustrate these Freudian views. In the arithmetical 'equations' to which he often referred when discussing the book – 'a symphonic harmony of individual characters, background, situation and story developments'[41] – Alan is roughly similar to Oedipus, his wife senselessly dead; Chantal, his daughter, resembles Antigone; Daniel, his son, resembles the traitorous Polynices; Gabriel Fleury is similar to Theseus. In his depiction of Alan, however, he changed his mind about following the pattern in *Oedipus*. Although Alan resigns from the government and for a time Chantal worries that he may kill himself, he does not die, as Oedipus did. At the outset Ainslie was supposed to have been killed; in fact, the riot with which the book opens originally featured the burning of Alan Ainslie in effigy, presumably to foreshadow what was to come. At some later date, however, MacLennan added the character of Moses Bulstrode, based in part on John Diefenbaker, and had him burned in effigy at the riot instead. His reasons for making this fundamental change probably had to do with his theory that art must *affirm*, that it must offer 'compensation for the human condition.' Whereas Sophocles could have the gods forgive Oedipus, and honour his place of death as a sort of shrine, no such option was open to MacLennan, and he resorted to an inner rebirth in Ainslie similar to that of George Stewart at the end of *The Watch That Ends the Night*. Through the land, which is elsewhere described as 'the only thing which will hold us together,'[42] Ainslie is healed. MacLennan used Gabriel as a foil for Alan, to indicate that stability is possible. At the end of the novel, when Ainslie is a broken man, Gabriel has managed to nurture his relationship with Chantal, which started out on such shaky ground, into a permanent and loving union. The novel also follows roughly the general scene arrangement of the play: scenes involving Ainslie's daughter and Gabriel are balanced by scenes involving his son Daniel and Marielle, and alternate with scenes centred on Ainslie either at home, at his Ottawa post, or at the cottage in the Laurentians. As in any Greek play the unities of time, place, and action are relatively stringent. As MacLennan later explained it: 'The intellectual ideas expressed in this particular novel of mine, are here articulated dramatically, so that they have a choric effect, unlike the outright exegesis which marred some of my earlier books.'[43]

Not only did he use *Oedipus at Colonus* as a general model for character and action, he also saw in it an allegory for the nation. In a letter to Gray on 31 August 1967 he wrote: 'the nation is still in an Oedipal dilemma. English-Canada for years refused to accept responsibility of the father's role however painful. She resents Father-England because he has lost his power. She tried, in the 1950's, to go to Uncle Creon (i.e. Uncle Sam) ... Today the pressure groups and the ethnic groups play the roles of members of royal families in Greek and Elizabethan tragedies ... In Greek tragedy the circumstances always make the characters static. It is a process in reverse of the "development" process of the Victorian novel. They do not develop outwardly: instead they go back into themselves and discover that what lay behind them has made them what they now are.' As far as he was concerned, *Oedipus at Colonus* was immensely relevant for the age.

There is no evidence that he thought that his two models might be so obscure to the general reader that the novel's significance might be missed. So real to him had Taylor's theories become, so compelling the truth of Sophocles' play since he had first translated it at Oxford, that it apparently did not occur to him that his world view might differ from that of other people. As he completed *The Watch That Ends the Night* he had worried that he might have trouble in future for this very reason, that 'my kind of world is not like many other peoples' any more';[44] but now, as the intensity of writing caught him up, he seemed to think that the universality of his models must be understood by readers everywhere. The truth was that models as remote as Sophocles and as intellectual as Taylor were far over the heads of his wide following. Even the ardent classicist Dr Sam, had he been alive, might have missed the point.

Although MacLennan had no worries about his sources, he did have other fears about the book. As he wrote it had crossed his mind that the book might not be 'popular' or 'acceptable'; thinking chiefly of the critics, and especially of those in Toronto, he was anxious about its reception: 'Toronto reviews of *Scotchman's* [*Return*] and *Seven Rivers* struck me, in general, as having been deliberately bad and loaded ... Our Anglo-Canadian reviewers, outside of *The Montreal Star*, are still pretty provincial, nor has the reality underneath the surface of this new book been as urgent elsewhere in Canada as it has been here, though I could just possibly be wrong about that.' Not even the announcement that he had won the Molson Award, given annually to an outstanding Canadian, which arrived just as he was sending off the manuscript, could put his mind at rest. Anxious to avoid the staggered publication that had, in his opinion, damaged sales of *The Precipice* almost twenty years before, he urged Gray to make sure that publication in Canada and the States would be synchronized, even though he recognized that 'Canadian readers and reviewers are not so slavish in regard to U.S. critics and best-seller lists as they were at the time of *The Precipice*.'[45] Such fears as he expressed suggest he had some substantial doubts about the novel itself.

His premonition that *Return of the Sphinx* would not find favour with the critics was dissipated by the response of Diarmuid Russell and Scribner's, according to whom the novel required almost no revision, only some slight textual alterations and an expansion of the 'Epilogue.' Perhaps understandably, his agent and his publishers let him down at this point. So secure was his status as a writer, so firmly was Canadian literature established, that criticism seemed superfluous. Virtually anything he produced now in the way of fiction was unlikely to find many obstacles at the publishing house. His own blindness to these new conditions prevented him from questioning the unaccustomed ease with which the novel was accepted. Never before had he been told that almost no revision of an original manuscript was necessary. The euphoria with which he completed the novel was fed by the predictable flattery he now encountered. On 23 October 1966 he reported excitedly to Gray that Russell and Charles Scribner 'call it "tremendous"': 'Also they think it both universal and topical at the very heart of today, as, to be immodest, I do myself. They envision practically no changes with the possible exception of a word or two and Burroughs [reader at Scribner's] described Bulstrode as "marvellous." He said – which pleased me most – that he seemed to him almost the quintessence of a modern politician, and the one he thought about was LBJ [President L.B. Johnson]. He even thinks Bulstrode will ring bells, locally, in England.' With uncontained enthusiasm he went on in this letter to discuss details of publication. Later, realizing that a spring launching was out of the question, he told Gray on 18 May 1967 that he had advised Scribner's to get together with Macmillan's to publish the novel in August in order to cash in on Expo 67, the world's fair held in Montreal to celebrate the centenary of Confederation. In a further attempt to give exactly the right presentation of the book to the Canadian market, he helped work over the blurb for the cover, giving the following as his reasoning: 'I am trying to kill this "little Canadianism" which, I think, has wrongly been hung around my neck by critics from the first book I wrote. It applies least of all to this particular one for from beginning to end the whole of it is contained within a single dramatic structure in which the surface conflicts are implicitly a part of the deeper ones hidden underneath.'

He even sent a copy before publication to Edmund Wilson, whose laudatory section on him in *O Canada*: *An American's Notes on Canadian Culture* had appeared in 1964. Wilson wrote back a most encouraging letter: 'I thought that your dramatization of the Canadian situation was masterly. It seemed to me a much better book than *Two Solitudes*, that you were hitting all the nails on the head, with no *longueurs* or boring episodes, and the descriptions, so much briefer than in your other books, touched in with a very sure skill ... At the end, I was a little disappointed, but this may have been due to my own exhaustion. I had expected something more climactic and some more definite upshot – though I suppose you were making the point that the issues don't come clear in Canada and that the forces put in motion were reduced to a kind of stalemate. And I don't think I understand about the Sphinx. What is the Sphinx's return? Do you mean simply that the situation is puzzling? If you do, I agree – and I agree that it is not confined to Canada. (Still, anyone who wants to know about Canada ought to read your book.)'[46]

Encouraging as this letter was, taken along with Gray's response on first reading that American readers might find Canada's problems 'outside their ken,'[47] it might have portended what was in store. Even highly educated readers would never see what he had intended. His mind at rest about its validity and appeal, however, with a cash advance of $12,500 from Scribner's and $2000 from Macmillan's, he sat back at his cottage in North Hatley and watched his book come out on 19 August 1967.

The signs were ominous. The first review he read was one he had dreaded, by David Legate in the *Montreal Star*. 'It was unfortunate, but unavoidable,' he wrote Gray, 'that Legate should have reviewed the novel in the *Star*. Never, since I have begun writing fiction has a reviewer of a book of mine more predictably misunderstood everything of value in the book itself. Even in Grenoble, I said to Tota, "when this book is finished, Legate will review it, and he never should allow himself to review any novel at all."' Legate panned *Return of the Sphinx* for 'going off at awkward tangents' and for displaying what he termed a 'painful "love interest."' Even so, he admitted that it displayed some of MacLennan's best prose and was compellingly topical. Just as he finished reading this review MacLennan received a telegram from Peter Newman of the Press Gallery in Ottawa: 'HAVE JUST COMPLETED THE RETURN OF THE SPHINX STOP FELICITATIONS ON A BEAUTIFUL BOOK FULL OF MEANING FOR THIS COUNTRY IN OUR CENTENNIAL AUTUMN.' This message helped to calm him down, but once again, as when writing the novel, he had the distinct feeling that he was going to raise the hackles of English-Canadian critics. In the letter to Gray he continued: 'I dare say, however, that in this case there will be a lot of sour reviews from English-Canada. The book is so contemporary, and I'm afraid it's so right in depth, that it cannot fail to create a lot of critical hostility here as it will not do ... in the States. However, I still believe it will be read, and already I have had reactions in depth from people more strongly favourable than from anything I wrote before.' In a hasty postscript he added information which had come by phone while he wrote: 'Tota just heard from her sister in Toronto that reviews there weren't so good. This doesn't surprise me much, but they need not reflect on sales.'[48]

Despite his offhand remarks, the degree of hostility that found its way into those Toronto reviews sent him reeling. As he read them during the next few days he was deeply upset. 'I'm half ashamed to say that the onslaught and malice of the first Canadian reviews upset me more than I ever knew,' he confided to Gray on 9 September. 'My brain told me they would all bounce, but they struck too many chords associated with earlier failures in my life, most of which were caused by my incapacity to make people in authority understand things which seemed very clear and simple to me.'

The three main reviews from Toronto, which constituted what MacLennan called 'a lynching party' (and Gray declared were 'so bad that I would hesitate to send them if I had not promised'),[49] were written by Robert Fulford for the *Toronto Star*, Barry Callaghan for the *Telegram*, and Peter Gzowski for *Maclean's*.[50] Fulford had been one of the Toronto critics who had given *Seven Rivers of Canada* a poor review; now he apparently thought that MacLennan's writing had served its initial function of putting Canada on the literary map and that he was not sophisticated enough to keep step either with the new schools of fiction arising throughout the nation or with the increasing competence of Canadian critics. His review began: 'Hugh MacLennan's new novel, Return of the Sphinx, is an essentially superficial and possibly a harmful book.' He argued that MacLennan's depiction of the situation in Quebec was often heavy-handed, at times even nonsensical, and, worst of all, irresponsible; the book was filled with 'mock-Freudian determinism' and was written in 'mock-poetic prose,' the characters superficially drawn, addressing each other 'as if they were dictating newspaper editorials.' He could not understand why MacLennan spent so much time in the novel describing the weather conditions, nor why he viewed Quebec as a woman. Quite opposite to Peter Newman, he concluded: 'This is the saddest book of our centennial summer. At this difficult, nervous moment in Canadian history, one of our most celebrated authors has attacked our most pressing issue and produced a book that contributes nothing to politics and less than nothing to literature. Even those who have always taken MacLennan lightly will be disappointed; those who have loved his books will be, I imagine, heartbroken.' If, as he claimed, MacLennan was 'one of our most celebrated authors,' it would seem, as far as Fulford was concerned, that he did not any longer belong in such company.

Without doubt, another 'celebrated author' was Morley Callaghan, who had never seen eye to eye with MacLennan's theories of fiction. While MacLennan had started out describing and defining the Canadian scene in his early work, Callaghan had been busy doing his best from the outset of his writing career, which predated the publication of *Barometer Rising* by thirteen years, to join directly an international stream of fiction by obliterating any specific references to Canada. Callaghan in Toronto, MacLennan in Montreal, had thus come to stand for two opposing views of fiction, at least to onlookers. Although they remained cordial in their personal dealings, the competition between the two men and the two major Canadian cities they represented none the less coloured their careers. To Torontonians, MacLennan had come to look parochial, old-fashioned, even absurd, in what they persisted in seeing as his 'nationalism' long after he had decided that he could afford to assume that readers would recognize his settings and society. It was Morley Callaghan's son Barry who wrote one of the three most scathing reviews of *Return of the Sphinx*.

His approach was different from Fulford's. For him it was 'an old-fashioned novel, and a second-rate old-fashioned novel at that.' 'Those who admire Hugh MacLennan's novels,' he began, 'never argue that he has achieved special insight into human psychology' – a statement that at one and the same time was patently incorrect (many critics of *The Watch That Ends the Night* had in fact praised him for exactly that) and announced that this reviewer at least was not one of MacLennan's admirers. He quoted Neil Macrae's patriotic speech from *Barometer Rising* to illustrate that such 'didactic enthusiasm now seems quaint, at very best.' The 'problems' dealt with in the novel he confessed he found 'too abstract, too artificial,' and argued that MacLennan 'curiously, in this story of nationalism and revolution ... makes no attempt to portray the riots and explosive emotions.' For him, 'the novel ends nowhere, for Ainslie ends as he began, out of joint with himself and his time.' Callaghan admitted that he did not understand the meaning of the novel's title: 'Perhaps – and it is not at all clear – this means a new cycle of violence and anarchy is upon us.' He did, however, throw a few crumbs MacLennan's way: the structure, he stated, is 'tight,' but what one really 'respects' in the end is 'MacLennan's effort.' Good try, he concluded, but a bad novel.

The review MacLennan thought 'most curious and incompetent'[51] appeared in *Maclean's*. Under the title 'Yes, But Can Our Major Authors Write?' the young critic Peter Gzowski began with a statement much like Callaghan's indicating that he too thought MacLennan had been vastly over-rated. He then proceeded to compare his work to that of Jaqueline Susann: 'Our own dear Hugh MacLennan, God knows, will never be blessed with the kind of mass popularity Miss Susann has achieved with her first novel.' This opener not only placed Gzowski firmly in Callaghan's camp, but it indicated an ignorance of MacLennan's publishing history and the immediate popularity of such novels as *Two Solitudes* and *The Watch That Ends the Night*. 'I can see little reason,' he went on, 'to treat MacLennan's newest work ... with any more respect than *Valley of the Dolls*,' wondering in passing whether a critic like himself, who had not 'had to sweat his shoulders off trying to write a major novel ... ought to have the right to write so flippantly about one man's year's work.' He approached the book with a set of prejudices which he all too easily found substantiated in the new novel. The 'contorted flashbacks' are 'a MacLennan characteristic, I suppose – remember the long passage out of Jerome Martell's boyhood?' he asked, then asserted that they get 'in the way of the story.' 'Another regrettable MacLennan habit,' he pointed out, was 'laying on the symbolism as thick as meringue'; for illustration he referred to Ainslie's war wound that has distorted half his face. In a devastating remark about the novel's content, he claimed: 'It is as if he has been looking at the events of recent years through a stained glass window in Westmount,' thus 'he turns his separatists into talking dummies.' In conclusion he wrote: 'He's written a very dull, impossible-to-believe book, falling far, far short of his pretensions ... It is a very bad book indeed: stilted, joyless and without insight ... The only misconceptions *Return of the Sphinx* casts any light on are those about whether our so-called major writers are, in fact, able to write.' Gzowski's review prompted John Gray to do something he had never done before; he wrote a letter to object: 'My protest simply takes the form of a suggestion: that you paste a copy of your review in a scrapbook and read it over once or twice a year, every year.'[52]

Nor were the three Toronto reviews the only negative responses. In a much gentler vein in the Toronto *Globe and Mail*, John Carroll, an associate professor of English at the University of Toronto, criticized the book almost reluctantly: 'MacLennan's compassion for the generations in conflict is enough (but barely enough) to save the novel from becoming a mere tract for the times. The exposition in the novel is wearisomely insistent and surprisingly heavy-handed when one considers the deftness with which MacLennan handled similar artistic problems in *The Watch That Ends the Night* ... MacLennan sacrifices the range and variety of mood and character that have always given a richness, like that of the Victorian novel, to his best work. *Return of the Sphinx* is perhaps more noteworthy for its topicality and its relation to MacLennan's earlier fiction than for its intrinsic value.' And Arnold Edinborough in *Saturday Night* suggested that MacLennan stick to essays in future, as he was a much better essayist than novelist. Much more strident was a review from Vancouver, where ever since *The Precipice* MacLennan had been unpopular in some circles. Charles Wolverton, critic for the *Province*, wrote a vitriolic assessment of the novel: 'It is what a poster is to a good painting'; he concluded that if MacLennan wished to put forth 'noble ideas of country and what it means to one' he should stick with the essay form: 'Somewhere, somehow, there is a story that will reveal the nation's anxiety over her division ... It could have a gutty humour, and a soul that is huge and warm. Hugh MacLennan will not write it.'[53]

Even in Montreal, beyond Legate's review, the novel fared badly. In the *Gazette* Joan Fraser treated the book as a poorly done portrayal of Quebec, out-dated by events even at the point of publication: 'To infer that the country will survive because the separatists are only lost young men is to ignore the Pierre Bourgaults of this world ... [and] a re-creation of the riot in which Donald Gordon was burned in effigy is not a picture of the Quebec of today.' She also criticized the dialogue in the novel: 'some of his conversations ring strangely.' Although 'the elements of the human drama are well-perceived,' she concluded, they are 'badly drawn.'

Similarly *Le Devoir*, without malice, found the novel unsatisfying. Naim Kattan, who had already shown himself to be a MacLennan supporter, wrote that although *Return of the Sphinx* was 'le roman le plus ambitieux de Hugh MacLennan ... il faut malheureusement dire que l'œuvre n'est pas à la hauteur de l'ambition de son auteur.' He did not find this new novel as convincing as *Two Solitudes*, now that the 'milieu,' 'traditions,' and 'religion' which gave meaning to the characters have disappeared from MacLennan's stage: 'Là où l'auteur a réussi c'est dans sa description de l'état d'esprit d'un certain milieu anglophone, milieu libéral qui est pris de court devant la montée d'une fièvre inconnue jusqu'ici.' His characters 'manquent de vie,' their love affairs 'semblent arbitraire, decidées à l'avance par l'auteur.' So, although the novel was a sincere 'cri du cœur, sa foi ne semble pas ébranlée, mais il montre du doigt l'accumulation des menaces.'[54]

The few Canadian reviews that did praise and recommend the novel – Leslie Roberts' radio reviews for CFRB in Toronto, CJAD in Montreal, and CKOY in Ottawa; a review in the *Calgary Herald*; a radio discussion in French between Philip Stratford and Gilles Marcotte; and, notably, a review by Dorothy Bishop in the *Ottawa Journal*[55] – fell by the wayside in the combination of virulent attack and melancholy disappointment that greeted it in Canada.

In the United States, however, the reception was entirely different. A fair number of American reviews took a line similar to that with which they had greeted *Two Solitudes* – that through MacLennan's novel they had much to learn about Canada. The *New York Times* review, written by a colleague of MacLennan's from McGill, for example, emphasized the importance of the novel for American readers: 'Millions of visitors have poured into Montreal this summer and flocked to the fabulous fair that was arranged to coincide with the 100th year of Canada's confederation ... The irony is that beneath all the celebration lies unbridged the deep chasm between the two cultures in Quebec ... *Return of the Sphinx* seriously explores [this] subject little known about in the United States and insufficiently known even in Canada.'[56] One review even emphasized the theme of anti-Americanism as a distant warning to which Americans ought to listen: 'we have every right to feel extremely uncomfortable when around these people [Canadians] since we are considered boorish, lacking in taste, materialistic ... vulgar, grasping, overpowering ... Is it possible that exposure to Princeton students engendered all that anti-Americanism? Whatever is behind his feeling we cannot be certain but it is deadly certain that if MacLennan's feeling about the United States becomes typical of the mass of Canadians, we're heading for a collision course some day with our "friendly" neighbour to the north.'[57]

Most American reviewers, however, did not take this parochial approach. They simply thought it was a magnificent novel. The *Book Buyer's Guide* in August, for example, singled out the four best novels of the season, placing *Return of the Sphinx* in first spot as 'the most finished and perhaps the most significant of [the three] – the most clearly "literature."'[58] Above all, and to MacLennan's delight, many American reviewers realized that his novel was about much more than the local scene in Quebec. Several titles showed this at once: 'Canadian's Sixth Novel Examines Moral Life of Modern Society'; 'Universal Timeliness'; 'If It Could Happen in Innocent Canada, Unrest is Universal.'[59] A high proportion of American reviews, in fact, saw far beyond the surface level of the story. As one reviewer put it: '[MacLennan] has hold of a clutch of important themes which he locates within an immediately contemporary Canadian context. He does this because it is his milieu and because ... he suggests through a key character ... Canada may "come very close to being the psychic centre of the world."' The *Saturday Review* agreed: 'It is astonishing that this novel about another country and people should be so rife with meaning for our country and us.' As Dorothy Tyler put it in the *Detroit News*: 'MacLennan sees the trouble and violence in his own Quebec as merely a cube in the mosaic of fury and destruction sweeping the world in our time ... He notes the sexual explosion that has always preceded a cataclysm in civilization. What, therefore, are we in for? So the Sphinx might be asking. Moreover, we live in a world in which both Marxian and post-Marxian ideas are at work.' Nor did Scott Donaldson in the *Minneapolis Tribune* have any difficulty realizing that 'MacLennan clearly intends for the reader to draw the analogy to unrest in American cities, and to war and forms of social disorder elsewhere.'[60]

Despite the general acceptance of the novel south of the border, two influential reviews found it less than excellent. *Newsweek* praised the book's timeliness and universality, but regretted that 'as fiction it fails to dramatize ... characters remain inert.' For *Harper's*, too, the book was 'a little disappointing,' despite the 'vigor' with which the story was presented, 'because it never deeply involves the emotions.'[61]

What caused this remarkable split in critical reception, a split MacLennan himself anticipated? As far as he was concerned it was partly the novel's truth that was responsible: 'It is not agreeable to be attacked like this, but after all I did write *The Sphinx* and I did know in advance that it would produce a psychic shock. I had, I admit, expected something less parochial and in this I was wrong.' Just as he had wished it were untrue when he had finished writing it, he thought that some readers had resisted facing the truth about the times: 'Fulford's was a psychological give-away that gives me hope for the country in spite of everything. It is axiomatic in psychoanalysis that just before the patient breaks through his neurosis he turns with savagery and hypocritical pity on his doctor. Perhaps English-Canada is really on the verge of doing what is essential to save the country.'[62] As he later exclaimed: 'How in God's name Fulford understood from the book that I wrote of the separatist movement as an adolescent hysteria beats me ... It is much more "about" what is now going on all around me at McGill.'[63]

He compared the response of Toronto reviewers at first to that of the South Africans against Alan Paton; later he stated bitterly that they 'are hicks trying to be hep.' To him, the reviews were shocking 'because some were inspired by malice while others were the product of the appalling parochial ignorance which is a vested interest in the press of Toronto and Vancouver and now can be ascribed to the Montreal *Gazette*. To turn over any book to a young girl like Joan Fraser, much less one like this, is a good measure of what the *Gazette* has sunk to.' As for Gzowski, he thought the main factor in this case was his age, and the fact that he was 'trying to curry favour with the radical young.' The young, he came close to saying, would be better understood by reading *Return of the Sphinx* than by pooh-poohing established writers: 'What is going on in McGill now is more frightening than the separatist movement and, without arrogance, I can say I understand it completely – or nearly completely. Anyone who works with hundreds of the youth as I do, who knows and accepts Rattray Taylor's *Sex in History*, knows the true causes underlying all this. I'll add another of my own: this drug taking, decadence and abandonment of all reason and principle in the west – government and radical young – is precisely what our ancestors meant when they spoke of the hand of the Lord. In modern times, it's the built in instinct of self-preservation within a living species. Only by complete decadence of will in the USA and western technological society can, apparently, the human race be spared for another try. THAT is what I mean by the Sphinx's return ... Nor need the decadence last longer than another decade before a patristic reaction sets in.'[64]

For all his psychoanalysing, what MacLennan apparently did not see was the degree to which the timing of the novel's publication was responsible for an unbalanced view of it in some quarters. The fact that it simply happened to coincide with Expo 67 did not help. Many reviewers assumed that he had deliberately produced his book as a kind of contribution to the general flag-waving activities of the centennial year.

To make this assumption was more than logical. MacLennan had been busy helping with the festivities in a fairly ostentatious way. He drew up the text for a brochure for the new Place des Arts theatre in

Montreal, which had been built with an eye to the tourists expected that summer. In addition, he wrote scripts that he himself performed for two brief television appearances on the CBC – one to introduce Expo, the other to sum up the celebrations. He also busied himself writing the text for *The Colour of Canada* in McClelland and Stewart's Canadian Illustrated Library series edited by Pierre Berton. Beyond that, and despite the fact that he had originally aimed for a 1965 or 1966 publication date, he expressed his genuine pleasure that the publication of *Return of the Sphinx* would occur at the same time as the nation's hundredth birthday.[65]

But this coincidence had been disastrous. Whereas he had intended to use his Quebec setting to get at the universal 'psychic crisis' underneath, critics concentrated more than they would have at any other time on the superficial 'Canadian' aspects of the novel. 'I wasn't trying to write the great Canadian novel,' he protested in an interview; 'I took an international theme – the crack-up between generations. It could have been written about many countries, but naturally a novelist is wise to use a milieu he himself knows well.'[66]

Although the hostility of the Canadian critics can be explained partly by the above reasoning, a better explanation came his way from Pamela Hansford Johnson, herself a novelist. Gray conveyed her message to him: 'She said, "Please give him my love and tell him that the Kicking Season comes around for every writer, usually right after a good or successful book. Just tell him it is the Kicking Season and I hope it doesn't get him down."'[67] With the plethora of new, younger Canadian writers in the ascendant, MacLennan seemed to be off course. It was indeed his 'Kicking Season.' In their enthusiasm for this new fiction, critics were all too quick to forget that his early novels had in part made it all possible by showing the way. A writer in Canada was now either 'in' or 'out,' and MacLennan was definitely 'out.' Certainly *Return of the Sphinx* was the exact opposite of Scott Symons' *Place d'Armes* or Leonard Cohen's *Beautiful Losers*, which both appeared the same year. Whereas MacLennan had stood back aghast from what he had called 'the hurricane of the twentieth century,' these two younger writers had embraced the chaos of the contemporary world and had found in it the dynamics of art itself. That hardly meant, however, that his offering of form and sanity had no place in the country's current literature; on the contrary, it provided a contrasting perspective that could well be played off against the next generation's point of view. Elsewhere there was room for both types of writing: in the United States, for example, not everyone was writing like Norman Mailer and Allan Ginsberg; older writers like Mary McCarthy and Saul Bellow were turning out fiction that could be called traditional. The literary nationalism MacLennan had done so much to incite had got somewhat out of hand.

He decided to fight back. As he had known even before he wrote the novel, the two main lines of attack in Canada were likely to be, first, that he was a nationalist writer, and, second, that he was Victorian and dated. In answer to these criticisms, which his novel had done nothing to confute, he wrote Gray on 22 August 1967: '"nationalist" is ambiguous. In the political sense it is a form of la trahison des clercs and that I have never been; that I detest. I am nationalist in the sense that Joyce and Yeats were, though deliberately more analytic because I have always been interested in history. As for "Victorianism," it is an inescapable fact that the novel just happens to be, fundamentally, a Victorian art form. It may be that non-fiction has superseded it. The evidence is strong that it has done so indeed. But a novel must tell a story, it must have a conscious social content, or it is pretty empty.'

On the principle that 'this image-making and breaking has become a kind of industry,' in short that sales were likely to need a boost, he did his best to launch indirectly a counter-attack on his critics, with Gray of course helping as middle man, for he had always thought it inadvisable and undignified to respond directly to critical attacks. The best he could do personally was to appear on CBC *Anthology* and 'say right out that this book is in the form of an *Oedipus at Colonus*' in order to 'spell out' the book's universality – as if this would clarify everything. But it was MacLennan himself who collected the better reviews and sent them, along with letters of praise from A.L. Rowse, the eminent historian of Elizabethan England, and from Edmund Wilson, to Gray, asking him to engineer as best he could a section of compensatory quotations. In the end Robert Fulford agreed to put together such a piece, which appeared in the *Toronto Star* on 14 November 1967. After quoting extensively from the best reviews, and from these two letters, under the rubric 'Other Views of Hugh MacLennan,' Fulford uncompromisingly added at the conclusion: 'None of this, of course, is likely to change the views of the Canadian reviewers. Certainly it doesn't change mine.' After reiterating his own views, he simply stated: 'but at the same time it seems to me important that Canadian readers should know there is another viewpoint, and that it is widely held outside Canada.'[68]

David Legate, whose review had been the first to upset him, had also come forward spontaneously: 'I hasten to come to MacLennan's defense in the light of the irresponsible onslaught meted out by Toronto reviewers, who seemed to be actuated by one or all of the following: (1) dislike of MacLennan's work in general; (2) fear and ignorance of the separatist theme; (3) the usual parochial outlook where Montreal is concerned. In any case, the crudeness of the almost conspiratorial attack can only serve to render their opinions valueless in future.' Also in Montreal, after conversations with MacLennan, his colleague at McGill the poet and critic Louis Dudek had come to the rescue in the most constructive way possible, by writing a serious critical study of the novel for the *Gazette*.[69] These rebuttals, like most such efforts, probably did little to help. The first reviews in Canada had seriously affected sales. By 20 February 1968, six months after publication, the novel had sold 11,000 copies in Canada, no mean figure; but in comparison with the sales of *The Watch That Ends the Night* for the same period they were less than half of what might have been expected. In the United States the novel did better, selling 16,000 copies in the first three months alone; but it was not commissioned by the Book of the Month Club until six months later. The final blow came when the Governor-General's Awards for 1967 were announced: there would be no award made for fiction in English that year.

Ironically, since *Return of the Sphinx* had dealt so openly and vehemently with anti-American sentiments in Canada, its greatest success lay south of the border. It was American critical reception and American sales that encouraged MacLennan to think about writing another novel. The Canadian reviews, on the other hand, came close to terminating his writing career: 'the kind of unchallenged label they put on me this time could last the rest of my life and come close to driving me out of writing in Canada. No kidding, it could.'[70]

Hugh and Tota at Englishtown, Cape Breton Island, 1964

Chapter eleven

Through Time and Space: *Voices in Time*

MacLennan's arrival at what he was soon to call 'the artist's third period' was a hollow triumph. Certainly the outer trappings of success were his. In 1952 he had become a Fellow of the Royal Society of Canada; with the publication of his latest novel *Return of the Sphinx* in 1967, he became a Companion of the Order of Canada and received the Royal Bank Award. He had garnered five Governor-General's Awards: three for his fiction – *Two Solitudes, The Precipice*, and *The Watch That Ends the Night* – and two for his collections of essays, *Cross-Country* in 1949 and *Thirty and Three* in 1954. In 1968 McGill University promoted him to the rank of full professor; he was invited far and wide to give speeches on a range of subjects including sports, education, the student revolution, literature, politics, and Canada. The nation's universities almost tripped over each other in their haste to thrust honorary degrees into his hands: by 1968 he had amassed seven D.Litt. degrees from the universities of Western Ontario, New Brunswick, Manitoba, Waterloo-Lutheran, McMaster, Sherbrooke, and British Columbia, as well as five LL.D. degrees from Dalhousie, Saskatchewan, Toronto, Laurentian, and Carleton. Tota framed them and hung them in his study at North Hatley, a small upstairs room already festooned with the photographs and awards she had proudly assembled. 'I am dying by degrees,' he quipped to his friend John Gray.

Within a few years, between 1969 and 1972, five critical books confirmed his status as the nation's literary pioneer; although his work had been the subject of dozens of academic articles since 1949, these were the first full-length studies devoted to his writing.[1] During these same years a number of film companies embarked on detailed negotiations to produce films of his novels, though none of these projects came to fruition; this not uncommon outcome of film companies' reactions to bestsellers disappointed him deeply, and must have puzzled his growing body of readers. Translations followed one another steadily until one or another of his novels eventually appeared in most of the languages of Europe (with the notable exceptions of Italian, Danish, Hungarian, and the South Slavic languages).[2]

Return of the Sphinx ought to have been the novel that consolidated the brilliant success of *The Watch That Ends the Night*. The fact that it had not sailed on smoothly to a similar success had cut him to the core. The momentum of his growing fame in Canada even while his latest novel was being badly received by Canadian reviewers was in sharp contrast to the critical acclaim that once greeted his earlier novels when he was comparatively unknown. It was not enough to mutter that the prophet goes unrecognized in his own land. He was being lionized, but for what?

Although he had been a reluctant nationalist when he started to write *Barometer Rising* so many years ago, he had now actually become, to a great extent, the man the public had then needed. His commitment to the nation that for better or worse had made his name had deepened into a bond that bore not the slightest resemblance to the flag-waving nationalism of electioneering politicians. His concern for education in general and for the well-being of the nation combined to propel him into the forefront of a movement to re-establish the Canadian identity of the universities. In 1969 he gave the keynote address to a Montreal symposium on the de-Canadianization of universities.[3] His speech expressed the bitter concern of one who had seen the gradual influx of non-Canadians, Americans in particular, into McGill University to the point where only 30 per cent of the staff in the humanities held Canadian first degrees and probably not more than about 35 per cent were Canadian citizens. He felt deep empathy for all those Canadian scholars who were being done out of jobs by these immigrants, partly because the situation was so similar to the one he had experienced himself during the Depression when Englishmen had been offered the university posts he sought. But his concern was larger than that. The take-over of the universities was but one aspect of the take-over of the country's economy, cultural institutions, and mass media by the more wealthy and aggressive United States. He particularly deplored the submissiveness of Canadians who had themselves brought such a situation about by undervaluing their own resources and culture. As one who had struggled so tenaciously to bring that culture into existence, he could not stand by silently while it drifted away.

His own essays and articles at this time gradually took on a different tone. Formerly he had written mainly of present and future concerns; now, increasingly, he looked to the past. Typically his titles became retrospective: 'Reflections on Two Decades' (1969) or 'Thirty Years of Canadian Writing' (1970) or 'Two Solitudes 33 Years Later' (1978). Although he still wrote vigorously on a number of contemporary issues – the federal election in July 1968, for example, which he forecast more accurately than any newspaper editor or politician in the country, mistaking only one seat – he assumed more characteristically the role of the older writer recalling 'the good old days.'[4] From this point on, he would think of himself as the wise old man who had reached maturity.

So it was that his own imagination was caught by a novel written by his compatriot Robertson Davies, *Fifth Business*, which appeared in 1970. He identified immediately with Davies' exploration of the Canadian identity from the point of view of a retired schoolmaster: 'Nobody has better put the problem of the older writer than you have here. As I have learned more from musical structures than from writing structures, I have not been afraid of what they call the artist's third period. It's of course a different thing to find a form for it, but you have found it perfectly in the interweaving of sudden drama with reflection.'[5] The notion of an older narrator and a form that mixed 'sudden drama with reflection' tied in perfectly with the novel he had himself begun to contemplate in his sixtieth year.

Although he had given in briefly to despair at the virulent Canadian reviews of *Return of the Sphinx*, he had not abandoned all thought of another novel. On the contrary, his own conviction that his novel's difficulties resulted from a combination of naïve, hostile critics and a public that had not as yet seen through the surface disruptions of the sixties to the decade's deeper psychic crisis, persisted well into the seventies. As late as 1973 he still asserted: 'I don't talk back to critics usually, but now I'm getting so I don't care, because in recent years so many of our critics have become cocksure and arbitrary ... If *The Sphinx* moved too fast for them, maybe it wasn't entirely my fault. I'll simply say that *The Sphinx* is the best book I ever wrote, formally.'

Once he had completed *Return of the Sphinx*, his mind had been off and away to another book. 'I'm still in the mood to consider another novel,' he wrote to Gray just after the book appeared. 'Paradoxically the consensus from U.S. reviewers encourages me to do this.'[6]

Between 1967 and 1972 he thought about the book and began drafting scenes for it. As usual, this initial stage was more or less a 'groping' which would lead to revision and focusing much later. The first scenes arose out of the experiences he had known in Freiburg, where he had spent one summer and three Christmas vacations from Oxford with the Holtzmann family. 'As I get older,' he recalled, 'scenes from that German city come back to me with great clarity and meaning.' But he thought of Freiburg not as it had been during the early 1930s but as it must have been even earlier during the First World War. 'Somewhat like the lumber camp river scene in *The Watch That Ends the Night*,' he wrote, 'I knew it was important, basic, but had no place [yet] in the ultimate form.' Germany had come to seem to him 'the touchstone country of the 20th century, so far as the so-called West is concerned. The Germans went the whole way in self-degradation, but just like the Highland clansmen, hardly any of them suffered the Oedipal guilt that comes from defying the father – which in that case was the total loyalty to the Germanic authority-principle. This may explain their astonishing recovery. It also explains their involuntary obliteration of the Hitler years, so that young Germans know hardly anything about them.'

These early drafts were interrupted in 1972 by an assignment to update and expand his *Seven Rivers of Canada*, originally published in 1961, into a magnificent illustrated edition with photographs by John de Visser. This endeavour was to have great significance for the forthcoming novel, because it helped resolve the problem that had been uppermost in his mind as he had set the novel aside, namely the handling of time. 'This book,' he wrote in August 1974, '[which] my publishers think ... is by far the best and most varied non-fiction prose I ever wrote ... enabled me at least to believe that I can finish the novel I pushed aside two years ago and resumed last winter. What I needed was a fundamentally new perspective in time, there being none at the moment anywhere, which is why modern fiction is in such chaos. A study of fluvial geology at least helped me gain that much perspective. It was encouraging, for instance, to learn that new dating methods have entirely altered our concepts of the duration of the ice ages ... We now know that they came and went, at least five distinct ones, between roughly 100,000 years ago and 8,000.'[7]

This comprehensive perspective on time did not constitute a radical change in his view of life. Even in his two unpublished novels he had recorded evidence of the vast panorama of the world's pre-history in the landscapes of Canada's east coast. That evolutionary view of Canadian geology had continued throughout his novels in landscape descriptions, reflecting the new nationalism of the thirties; Edmund Wilson had termed these descriptions 'meteorological,' 'the one feature of MacLennan's novels that does seem to me new and interesting.'[8] After his cross-country examination of the nation's rivers, however, this perspective deepened; not only did he respond with an almost primitive emotion to the epic vistas across the nation, he had also reached an age at which he could identify with natural history: just as Canada's river gorges and hill-encircled valleys marked epochs of geological time, stretching back millions of years, so too his own life seemed to him, in his sixties, like a series of 'ages' marked by violent and disfiguring transitions.

No one could have been more ripe to accept a set of theories that arose at about this time. Termed the New Biology, these theories gripped his imagination at once. Robert Ardrey, in particular, was a writer to whom he was instantly attracted: whether or not his theories withstand scientific examination is irrelevant; to MacLennan, his views of the evolution of man provided a convenient mythology to which he could link his already evolutionary view of the life process. 'When Keats first looked into Chapman's Homer,' he wrote in an extravagant letter of praise to Ardrey in May 1969, 'he could not possibly have felt more like Cortes than I do after looking into you. Everything has conspired to make the reading of your work the most exciting reading I ever did in my whole life.'[9]

The two aspects of Ardrey's books, *African Genesis* and *The Territorial Imperative*, that most impressed him were the notion of territorial boundaries and the necessity for respecting them, and the concept that man's nature was dual. Ardrey argued that men, like the apes from which they are descended, establish territories and are prepared to fight and die defending them; man's dual nature he had traced back to the emergence of *australopithicus africanus*, a flesh-eating ape that had used weapons such as the antelope bone to kill prey stronger than itself. According to him, the essential nature of these apes involved the proposition: '*The command to love is as deeply buried in our nature as the command to hate*.' For Ardrey, group survival in a state of nature just as frequently resulted in altruistic behaviour as it did in aggressive behaviour: the urge to kill was balanced by the urge to self-sacrifice in the interests of the group. This double impulse, he maintained, lives on in man today: 'We stand upon creatures lost in pre-Cambrian slimes. Our genes still reflect their ambitions.'[10]

MacLennan's contemplation both of the fluvial geology he had incorporated into his *Rivers of Canada* and of the theories of the New Biology clarified and strengthened his religious belief. Often in the letters, speeches, and articles he wrote from this time on he referred openly and specifically to his faith in God. He defined his personal notion of God in several places, notably in a speech he gave to the Canadian Club in Vancouver in May 1968: 'If this were a sermon, which it is not, the text I would choose would be this: "I believe in God – and that is what scares me." I mean it scares me now, in 1968, just as at other times – 1940 for instance – such a belief lifted up millions of people. The God I believe in is not the God of my Calvinist ancestors, though some of Him was present in that God, also. He is not the God of the ancient Jews, though even more of Him was present there. He is the God who manifests Himself in evolution, in all living creatures, and He moves in just as mysterious a way His wonders to perform as He did when the psalmist looked up to the hills and hoped for the best.' The extent to which this 'God of evolution' preoccupied him is evident in a slip he made in titling another speech he gave at the University of British Columbia that same month: instead of 'Convocation Address' he called it 'Congregation Address.'[11] Apparently sermonizing was very much on his mind.

While the enormous concerns of God, human nature, and evolution stirred in his mind and found their expression in early drafts of scenes set in Germany during the First World War, he was also responding intensely to the politics of the present moment in Montreal. The election of Pierre Elliott Trudeau as prime minister in 1968 had seemed to him like a dramatic turning point. In a personal note to Trudeau just before he officially became prime minister he had written: 'You have laid the ghost of Mackenzie King. Listening to you, I am reminded of Socrates.' To MacLennan, Trudeau seemed to be 'a philosopher king' whose 'reign' must signal a change for the better. He even considered using the occasion of Trudeau's victory as the concluding scene in a film of *Return of the Sphinx* that would incorporate flashbacks to *Two Solitudes*.[12]

While he had confidence that Trudeau's election 'was more important than all these negatives'[13] of 1968, and that it would turn the tide of political events into positive channels, nevertheless separatist activities in Quebec were steadily accelerating. When the kidnapping of the

British diplomat James Cross precipitated the October Crisis of 1970, terrorism reached unforeseen heights, and the subsequent kidnapping and murder of Pierre Laporte in Montreal by the Front de libération du Québec provoked Trudeau to suspend civil liberties in Canada through the War Measures Act. In the tense months of random bombings of public buildings that preceded this crisis, the MacLennans left their North Hatley cottage for the safety of their iron-grilled apartment in the city. 'I got out earlier than usual this year,' MacLennan confided to Don Sutherland at Macmillan's, 'because I had an absolute animal smell of acute danger. On that hillside we would have been completely helpless, and if some cell wanted to make a headline, a local Townships one could have done better with me than with anyone else in the region.'[14]

In a lengthy article for the Toronto *Telegram* on 21 November 1970, MacLennan turned back to his own novels about Quebec, *Two Solitudes* and *Return of the Sphinx*, in an attempt to analyse the horror of those few days in October. 'Quebec Crisis Bares the Agony of Youth' was far less a journalistic analysis of the October Crisis than an airing by MacLennan of the personal theories and artistic concerns he was currently struggling to express in his new novel. He still believed, as he had at the time of writing *Return of the Sphinx*, that to deal with the specific situation would be merely to skim the surface. In his article he tried to probe the deeper causes of recent events, causes that were universal and had led to other, similar political upheavals in other ages. With this in mind, he drew analogies between Quebec separatism and political unrest in ancient Rome and in Germany before the Second World War. The collapse of the influence of the Roman Catholic church in Quebec appeared to him to be a major factor in the appeal of violent nationalism to the young people of Quebec; similarly, he pointed out that it had been from Catholic Germany that the Nazis had come. 'And the FLQ are certainly national socialists,' he concluded.

Influenced by the New Biology he had so recently discovered, he theorized that underneath the entire situation in Quebec, and under what he now called 'the mid-20th century volcano' in general, were 'causes so mysterious [that] I am convinced they are lodged in the evolutionary process itself. What some New Biologists have called "The Keeper of the Kinds" permits no species to threaten the survival of all species, including itself, and this is what our military technocrats have been doing with gusto for more than 20 years, with promise of more to come. What wonder, then, that Canada which only 20 years ago seemed so innocent should now be in the vortex?' With this theory in mind, he speculated that responding to terror, such as that in Quebec, catapulted civilized men back thousands of years in time, evoking responses that were the instinctive reflexes of potential prey. 'Kidnapping and selective assassination touch memory traces on the subconscious; they go back to our primitive ancestors in their caves, knowing that at any instant the leopard may – or may not – come.' To him, Trudeau's invocation of the War Measures Act in response to the kidnappings and assassination in Quebec stood as a supreme example of 'The Keeper of the Kinds.' In preventing FLQ terrorism from destroying the nation, Trudeau had given evidence of MacLennan's 'God of evolution': 'the people of Canada and Quebec proved this fall that Canada is at the moment a true biological nation. Trudeau knew us better than we knew ourselves – or at least better than the intellectuals will ever know us. No matter what the differences of opinion, Canadians rallied to meet this threat to our national existence, to the defense of our intuitive knowledge of what is right.'[15] To Trudeau he wrote directly: 'The first time I met you I sensed that you might well have genius. Now I know you have it. So I hope you are not too lonely in your astounding understanding of men, history, evolution and action. Make no doubt you have the nation with you.'[16] As MacLennan saw it, overlooking with ease the inconvenience and injustice that so many innocent people suffered during the imprisonments and questionings, the War Measures Act had been an unqualified success. It had given evidence once and for all that Canada was a coherent, organic nation.

The force that most threatened to tear apart the nation, and mankind in general, was, in his eyes, the other side of man's inherent nature – the instinct to kill. In the same article in the *Telegram* he pointed his finger directly at the ascent of technology, as he had done so many times before, as enemy to the humanitarian attitude towards life he now believed necessary to preserve the entire human species. The war-mongering that had resulted in two world wars during his lifetime was an obvious example. Less obvious was the headlong rush of a technology that only seemed to benefit mankind. In a parody of the Apostles Creed, he derided this new 'god': 'I believe in Science, explorer and examiner of heaven and earth, and in Technology, its principal begotten son, who was born of the Virgin Mathematics, who descended into the hell of the Industrial Revolution, who rose again thanks to humane legislation, who ascended into the Welfare State where he sitteth on the right hand of Science the Father which is on earth, where he solveth the problems of all mankind, and will keep on solving them forever and ever, Amen.'[17]

What he saw in the weeks following the October Crisis confirmed his view that the most flagrant misuse of technology was now occurring in the mass media – especially in television – with the insidious manipulation of public emotion. As he remarked in the *Telegram* article:

> For nearly a decade, the TV screens have been inviting the most inflammatory irresponsibles to sound off and for entertainment purposes have given full exposure to anyone who wants to shock or propagandize.
>
> No student riot or sit-in was real unless the cameras were there. The egos of adolescents were fed and fattened until they believed the whole world stood in awe of them ...
>
> 'Student Power' was another word for student blackmail. The results of all this were happenings, and the media's sage had become famous for coining this word. However, the murder of truth, as always, leads to the murder of people.

The 'media's sage' here referred to is Marshall McLuhan, whose theories of the electronic village, the replacement of the written word by televised images, and the usurping of history by the philosophy of 'the medium is the message' appalled MacLennan. The immoral and irresponsible use to which technological aspects of the mass media were being put seemed to him a distortion of truth and a potential threat to human life. Not only did he condemn the over-stimulation of the technological society but he somewhat inconsistently accused it of being tedious. 'As for the new students,' he theorized, 'the technological society bores them. It seems romantic, even fun, for people who knew nothing of war to dream of dying on the barricades.'

The *Telegram* article marked an important step in the development of his novel. Somewhat in the same way that the essays he wrote during the 1950s sharpened his focus for *The Watch That Ends the Night*, this article forced him to get down on paper, in a way that could withstand public examination, the ideas that had still not jelled into any fictional form. As he wrote a couple of weeks later to Don Sutherland at Macmillan's, with whom he was now negotiating a Laurentian Library paperback edition of *Return of the Sphinx*: 'My article, I have just learned, has been syndicated through 14 papers from St. John's to Victoria. Drapeau [mayor of Montreal] wrote me to say he agreed "with it in every particular." To some extent I think the crisis of this fall, and the articles I wrote on it, has liberated me into the novel I have been brooding on for some time. Anyway, I am writing regularly and I think fairly well.'[18]

In 1974 he resumed work on the novel. If it were to incorporate the concerns uppermost in his mind, especially if it were to give some impression of vast aeons of time, it would be an ambitious project. How was it possible to incorporate First World War Germany and the near insanity of the 1960s in the same book? How could New Biology and fluvial geology throw any light at all on either of these settings? MacLennan, in this novel, took on a task as daunting as the one Milton had attempted in *Paradise Lost*: he, too, set out to justify God's ways to man!

Not surprisingly, the writing went slowly and revisions were extensive. Tota, during these years, developed a number of health problems that required his care. At some times more than others she was troubled by painful arthritis, an ailment for which they sought cure each summer in the mud baths of Italy. In 1979, after years of being restricted in her walking and standing, she underwent surgery for her ankle and was hospitalized for many months recovering. Personal letters between 1974 and 1980 often contain some reference to Tota's ill health, not in the form of a complaint but rather as an accepted fact of life at their ages. Nor was MacLennan himself exempt from the problems of physical aging: from time to time his back and neck were simply too stiff to spend many consecutive hours at the typewriter.

As usual, he had expectations of finishing long before he actually did. In August 1978, he wrote: 'It now seems possible that I will finish this novel by New Year's, though I have become so accustomed to interruptions I wonder if I will.'[19] It was to be almost two full years before publication.

During the decade or so in which he was writing this novel he thought further about theories of modern fiction. In his address to convocation at the University of British Columbia in May 1968, his scorn for much modern literature was intense: 'While fiction, like any other art, is often a true reflection of the times, it can also be a slavish follower of fashions, even an imitator of itself. If the novel is in trouble today, I think it clear that it is in trouble for much the same reason as that which causes many individuals to be certified and committed to asylums. The modern novel has followed to a dead-end this fashion of being totally self-centred. It has confused the search for truth with exhibitionism. It has forgotten what Shakespeare and Sophocles never forgot – that the best art must also be discreet. It has reduced love to various repetitive exercises in mechanical engineering and, with the acclaim of critics who have joined the bandwagon, it has abandoned, or turned over to non-fiction writers, its traditional role of occupying itself with human beings of personal value and with affairs of large and general importance ... Novel after novel leads the reader along the weary path of a joyless neurotic in his career from one girl to another, one guilt to another and so on and so on.' From this statement his literary tenets are clear. As before, he continued to insist conservatively that discretion, scope beyond the individual, and characters of 'personal value' were necessary aspects of 'the best fiction.' He was fed up with what he elsewhere called 'all the existential puzzles presented as fiction.' By 1971, in a letter to Robertson Davies, he made a remark which shows much more specifically what he had in mind for his own book: 'It seems to me there are two kinds of continuations from a basic mother-lode – the purely linear one chosen by Galsworthy and the other chroniclers, and the far more interesting one based, as it were, on the acknowledgement of relativity.'[20] Although this comment was intended as encouragement for Davies who had asked his advice about writing a sequel to *Fifth Business*, it reveals a significant change in MacLennan's own views. In *Two Solitudes* he had chosen the Galsworthy-style chronicle; now he was contemplating a new form which might reflect his wider perspective on time, one based 'on the acknowledgement of relativity.'

The only other novel in which he had attempted this sort of thing had been *The Watch That Ends the Night*. He still considered the form of *Barometer Rising* to have been 'artificial'; *The Precipice*, like *Two Solitudes*, had been cast in the traditional chronicle form, like Galsworthy's *Forsyte Saga*; both *Each Man's Son* and *Return of the Sphinx* had been 'dramatic' in form, modelled on the great tragedies of Shakespeare and the Greeks. But in *The Watch That Ends the Night* he had attempted and succeeded with what he called 'a very subtle form.' 'For one thing,' he explained in 1973, 'it's written in the first and third person ... by means of a little bit of timing and shading I found I could jump from the first person directly into the third.' Again he referred to the major concern he had with his current book: the handling of time. Apparently he was looking back to his most recent success for guidance; in the earlier novel he recalled: 'time ... is a continuum in which the action moves back and forth and up and down. This is something that ... one perhaps has to be older to be able to do. Because you're not *aware* of time when you're younger. Time to me now is like an expanding universe.'[21]

From his perspective in his sixties, time had expanded even beyond the scope that *The Watch That Ends the Night* had encompassed. Now, twenty years later, he searched for an even more subtle form that could range not just from the remembered past of history up to the present, but from the pre-history of the New Biology, through the present, and into the future.

In May 1979 he was finally freed of the onerous duties of teaching at McGill. That spring convocation marked his retirement and the honour of the title 'professor emeritus.' 'I'm grateful,' he wrote to his friend William Ready in Hamilton, 'for I love this truly marvellous university.' Although he would continue to teach one course in the development of English prose on a part-time basis, his time was much more his own than it had been for many years. This meant that he could work steadily on the novel, revising and focusing it in its last stages. By October he was almost finished; as he wrote to another acquaintance, the retired classicist Frank Leddy: '[my] novel ... could have no chance unless I could accept in my imagination and mind that 15,000 years ago is literally yesterday. I should finish it by the end of this present month. I doubt if anyone will like it and I may even have trouble finding publishers.' The final step involved extensive rewriting, as had every novel before: 'As always in a long novel, the first thirty or forty pages have to be somewhat revamped when the book is done,' he wrote in mid-November, 'even though I constantly edited and rewrote this one as I went along.' Finally, at the very end of 1979, he put the finishing touches on his book: 'It will run to about 170,000 words. If it hadn't been for *Return of the Sphinx* I might call it *Return of the Phoenix*, but so far no title has emerged.'[22]

The mood with which he completed the book could not have been less like the bursting energy with which he had finished *The Watch That Ends the Night*. 'In this present book,' he asserted, 'there is not the barest trace of nationalist sentiment on the part of myself. Nor did I feel any exhilaration when I finished it. Instead I was tired out.'[23]

The first reports from his new agent, Timothy Seldes in New York, and from Douglas Gibson, the editor at Macmillan's who had replaced John Gray after his death in the spring of 1979, were hopeful. Seldes thought the novel was wonderful and that it needed not the slightest revision; he was confident of finding an American publisher. Although Scribner's and Harper's both demonstrated short memories by declining it, St Martin's Press (the American house of Macmillan, London) agreed to bring out an American edition for the spring of 1981. Gibson also responded with decided enthusiasm, certain that this novel would be 'the literary event of the fall of 1980.'[24] He had a few revisions to suggest, however. Aside from a number of minor changes, he insisted MacLennan pay closer attention to the details of chronology: 'some damned reviewer is certainly going to spend a lot of time working out all of the details, so it makes sense for us to anticipate his work and make sure that his nit-picking expedition will prove fruitless. I'm convinced that this will prove a worthwhile [exercise] for us at this stage because the nature of the book – and especially its future setting – is going to cause the dates to be a matter of keen interest to every reader. So I have gone to some lengths to try to make sure that the dating is correct, and have drawn up two accompanying documents entitled Chronology of Future Events and Chronology of Characters.' In addition, Gibson called to his attention a few possible inconsistencies in the standard of technology represented in the book's present; he also recommended that he add an epilogue. None of these revisions, however, constituted serious criticism on Gibson's part. He was warmly complimentary about the novel: 'any problems in this manuscript are few and far between ... In fact, all my concerns are dwarfed by the manuscript's colossal ambitions – and achievements. This is such a thrilling piece of work in which even now, after four close readings, I continue to discover new delights and excitements.'[25] MacLennan agreed with the suggestions, especially the one concerning an epilogue. 'Now,' he said, 'the novel is completed in the manner of a fish prepared European-style, full circle, with its tail in its mouth.' By mid-June a date had been set for the launching of the novel: it would appear in the second week of October 1980.

The form in which MacLennan had finally cast the novel indeed outdid the scope and subtlety of *The Watch That Ends the Night*. 'It is a pretty bold [novel] in structure,' he had written in March: 'The book begins in 2039, drops back to the late 1960s, then to around 1909, then to 1918-1919, resumes in 1932 and continues in Germany till 1945. The story of the principal protagonists terminates in 1970, but the character who (within the novel) is putting the story together appears at the beginning as a "survivor" in his late seventies. This meant that I had to get away with quite a lot, and I had no wish whatever to write futuristically. I got into this situation because (so I believe) the reason for the collapse of the novel at the moment is that fiction requires a perspective in time and now there is no perspective because the changes are coming so fast. Critics will call the book "Orwellian," but I don't think it owes anything to Orwell, who died before the H-bomb.' 'The title,' he added, 'will be *Voices in Time*.'[26]

This futuristic setting was not without precedent in his work. During the mid-fifties he had written two essays for the *Montrealer* in which he had used a future setting as a springboard for his observations on the present. 'The Finding of the Way' (1955) was set at some unspecified future date after man has blown up the moon. The narrator is an elderly senator who still unaccountably has fits of nostalgia for the moon's absence, even though it has now become 'the golden Cosmic Age where no one has to think for himself.' Indeed, no man is allowed to think for himself, now that the giant computer Mec-Think rules the world. It takes only a short time for Mec-Think's companion computer Mec-Mem to brainwash the senator into a happy acceptance of the status quo – 'Our Way of Life which allows nothing to exist without a practical purpose.' With venomous satire, MacLennan concluded his essay with the senator's gleeful anticipation of explosions of planets and stars to come.[27]

The second piece, 'Remembrance Day: 2010' (1957), was even closer to the type of setting he would attempt in *Voices in Time*. Using the day on which silent tribute is paid to all those soldiers who died in battle from the First World War onwards with deep irony, he imagined a future world in which the Russians are established on Venus and the West has advanced to Mars. The moon has already been blown up in order to establish space platforms for further scientific experiments, and also, incidentally, to provide Earth with better television service. 'Remembrance Day' in the year 2010 is celebrated not as a tribute to self-sacrifice but for the purpose of showing the Russians that the West means business. As the tongue-in-cheek narrator concludes: 'We have just reached the outer fringes of the Solar System. Can any sane man possibly argue that we should stop there?'[28]

In these two essays, and in *Voices in Time*, MacLennan set the story in the future not so much to predict things to come but to get a meaningful perspective on the present. By the time he began his novel he had come to feel that 'History is the product of the fantasies of men';[29] it was for this reason, too, that he adopted the future: he tried to reflect the fantasies he now observed moulding the lives of men in his novel's form. By imagining that there has been an explosion of sufficient force to knock out almost the entire world, he dramatized his own theory.

Voices in Time interweaves the life stories of three men who are representative of three different generations roughly thirty years apart. John Wellfleet, the books' narrator, has survived the explosion that has wiped out all but a few hundred people along with most of the technology that has increasingly dominated the world. The 'Destructions' have been caused not by any war but by a sort of 'nervous breakdown' of the huge computer system that rules the world. Wellfleet is seventy-five when the story opens. From his birth in 1964 he has lived through several Bureaucracies, the Great Fear, and finally the Destructions. Now declared 'inoperative' and retired to a compound outside what used to be Montreal, he writes a book from the documents brought to his attention by a young man, André Gervais, who wishes to know more about the past so that he and his friends can rebuild the city.

The boxes of diaries, letters, and tapes that Gervais brings to the old man belonged to members of Wellfleet's former family, none of whom has survived. Two relatives in particular intrigue him: his older cousin Timothy Wellfleet and his even older uncle, the German Conrad Dehmel, who had married his aunt Stephanie, Timothy's mother.

Timothy Wellfleet's story traces the years from his birth in 1938, just before the Second World War, up to the Destructions. The climax of his career is a Montreal television news show he hosts during the October Crisis of 1970. As a result of his actions on this show, his stepfather Conrad Dehmel is assassinated.

Dehmel's story is almost entirely set in Germany where he was born to the wife of a German naval officer in 1910. His life experience includes a revulsion from the First World War enthusiasms of his father and his love for a Jewish girl, which is blighted by forces increasingly beyond their control as Hitler comes to power. Dehmel just barely survives the concentration camp at Belsen and recovers in North America where he eventually marries Stephanie and appears on Timothy's television show.

The clever meshing of these three stories presents a portrait of the artist as an old man. Nowhere else in his work had MacLennan so closely related the concerns of his characters to his own struggles to give literary shape to his perceptions. John Wellfleet, in his monumental task of composing the contents of the boxes of family papers into a story, dramatizes MacLennan's own attempts to come to terms with his time and the people he has observed.

In his second unpublished novel in 1937, 'A Man Should Rejoice,' MacLennan's protagonist the artist David Culver had embarked on his life story for the specific purpose of retaining his sanity: 'whether I can freeze a durable form out of a state of flux, I don't know. At least I shall write something of the life of my friends and myself, not because we were important personages, but because the chaos of our lives and ideas seem to me now to have been a pattern of our time. In ourselves, perhaps, is the form in the flux of things. We were not agents in a drama and we never changed things with our decisions, but we very consciously were participants in the ritual that was history ... A few years ago I could not accept this knowledge, but now I know that what happens to us can be greater than ourselves.' Fifteen years later, as he began to write *The Watch That Ends the Night*, MacLennan had set out, like Culver, 'to try to create order out of the general pattern of the life and lives I've seen.' Unfortunately Culver had been too young to grasp the full meaning of his experiences; even though he turns to 'the sense of space that goes far away to the horizon and whitens down to an unpaintable colour at the sea-rim' to 'make what happened to [him] in Europe seem proportionate,'[30] he cannot really get a satisfactory perspective or overview of the events that threaten his mental stability. In *The Watch That Ends the Night* the artist and the characters remain separate: although George Stewart, considered by MacLennan a 'modern' hero, and Jerome Martell, a 'transitional' hero, both reflect aspects of their creator, MacLennan remained the artist apart from his imagined world. Indeed, none of his earlier characters, except Paul Tallard, reflect his own agonies as an artist. Now, from his more mature perspective, he used his character John Wellfleet to dramatize the heroic struggle involved not only in history itself but more importantly in an attempt to 'freeze a durable form out of a state of flux' or to 'create order out of the general pattern of the life and lives I've seen.' *Voices in Time*, in expanding the time frame outwards, also probed inwards more deeply than MacLennan had ever done before.

For old John Wellfleet, as always for MacLennan, finding a form and a focus is the central difficulty. Confronted with the random bits of information in the boxes Gervais brings to him, he is temporarily overwhelmed, as MacLennan had been at the commencement of every novel he wrote. In an early conversation with Gervais he confesses: 'This material seems awfully patchy to me. I'm not sure I can find any real pattern in it ... The problem is where to begin.' To this Gervais replies: 'Why not at the beginning?' And Wellfleet goes on: 'But where *is* the beginning in all this stuff? ... I'm still confused about these papers. I don't know for sure whether there's a story in them or not, though I think there is. Voices in time, that's what they are, and who cares about any of them now?'[31] The voices out of which John Wellfleet must make sense come to him from several different time periods, from a number of lives, out of different countries, and in different languages. They even present themselves in different forms: a letter here, a taped telephone conversation there, a diary, the partial writing of memoirs, and a video-tape of a television show. Here was that giant amoeba of the imagination, which shifted back and forth, defying the artist to give it a shape that on the one hand would not betray its living reality, yet on the other could be sufficiently orderly to communicate that reality to others. In this metaphor of the flux of life out of which the artist must find some order and a form, MacLennan illustrated the problem that had haunted him from the beginning. As he had written in 'How Do I Write?' (1945), describing his experience writing *Two Solitudes*: 'As life grows organically, it can't be subordinated to a plan. At the same time, a novel without any plan at all is a shambles. Every novelist must somehow solve this dilemma, and generally he must solve it his own way.'

For MacLennan, the crucial decision of choosing a starting point had always been most difficult. 'Beginning a new novel,' he had written in that same article, 'I have never been able to know in advance whether to enter into a chronological narrative or to plunge in medias res and then explain the background through flashbacks.'[32] That is to say, he had always been torn between his rational mind, which preferred to order things logically in a chronological sequence, and his intuition, which grasped reality through the free association of luminous scenes. So far, his more rational side had tended to dominate. Not only were the majority of his novels written chronologically, but those that were not, such as *The Watch That Ends the Night* and *Return of the Sphinx*, had been begun with chronological drafts, even when those sections had become flashbacks out of sequence in the final version. Even now, with *Voices in Time*, he had started by writing chronologically the long section set in Germany which marks the earliest part of the story. At first, John Wellfleet, too, speculates that the beginning of his story may indeed be the tale of Conrad Dehmel's life: with a near-cynical selfishness he decides that he has no intention of catering to some imagined potential audience in the way MacLennan had earlier tried to do. 'If I write this I'll have to write it for myself. This will mean there'll be all kinds of things I'll talk about that nobody today can understand.' Feeling as if 'he had been living in a vast time-house divided into many separate rooms,' Wellfleet finally decides to throw caution and logic to the winds and 'to plunge in medias res,' not with Dehmel's story from 1910 but with Timothy's more recent saga from 1938: 'The more he thought about it, the more complicated his task became. In most parts he would have to weave this divergent material into some kind of form and he doubted if he would be able to do it ... Then panic seized him. What if he did not live long enough to finish it? ... "I'll have to begin somewhere," he muttered to himself, "and I'll have to begin now." He decided to begin with Timothy.'[33]

Wellfleet's choice of form was also MacLennan's. By plunging *in medias res* he was more conscious than before of abandoning the traditional chronicle form of Galsworthy, which he had used so often, in favour of the type of structure he had recommended so heartily in 1971 to Robertson Davies – one based on relativity. The decision to begin in this way raised problems of the handling of time, just as it had in *The Watch That Ends the Night*. MacLennan had even complained of his difficulty with time in *Two Solitudes* where he had used the simpler chronicle form, but, from his own point of view, the manipulation of time in the later novel had posed much greater problems. With *Voices in Time*, he attempted a setting that ranged far beyond the not inconsiderable scope of *The Watch That Ends the Night*. It is Wellfleet who raises this question as his central challenge in recording the history of his family: 'Before I began writing this history I told André Gervais that the handling of time was going to be very difficult. This material has come to me from so many segments of time, some of which I never lived in myself. Even Timothy's material comes from different segments.'

MacLennan implied that only an old man like John Wellfleet could see in the papers a pattern that would confront him and move him to tears. 'They've made me ask so many questions I should have asked when I was young,' he confesses to Gervais. 'Questions about myself. I'm involved in this too, and it troubles me.' By recording and interweaving the life histories from the boxes he comes to see the relationships, at times intricate, at other times profound, between himself and the men and women from whom he has felt remote.

Beginning with Timothy's story is at first an act of faith, for Wellfleet can see no connection whatsoever between his own life and that of his elder cousin. Timothy stands for everything John Wellfleet loathes. He has been one of the people whose immorality and irresponsibility has characterized the decade of the 1960s. At the height of his career he hosted the television show named 'This Is Now' in imitation of the momentary ecstasy of sexual orgasm. Somewhat in the style of the news program co-hosted by Patrick Watson and Laurier Lapierre in the sixties called *This Hour Has Seven Days*, Timothy's show features explosive interviews with public figures. One of the 'instant marriage, instant family, instant coffee, instant jobs' generation, Timothy has lustily taken his part in the consumer society first in advertising and then in television; like his entire generation, he has done his best to make the world like 'an international airport.' Nor is he troubled in his pursuit of selfish ends by any belief in God: his 'god' is technology, the powerful modern storehouse of scientific knowledge which he uses for irresponsible ends.

Timothy is a representative of the kind of modern artist neither MacLennan nor John Wellfleet can tolerate. Not surprisingly, since he is a product of the McLuhan age, Timothy cannot write coherently. His letters, tapes, and diaries are disconnected ravings, often wild and at times obscene. Through Timothy, MacLennan comes close to parodying the vision of life and the kind of art which he had deplored formerly in writers like James Jones and Norman Mailer. Self-centred stream-of-consciousness, to MacLennan, ultimately reflected nothing but chaos and dark night. Such writing, he had maintained for years, does nothing to affirm life and lacks the form which the true artist must provide. John Wellfleet decides that it is up to him to make sense of this material, so alien to himself. 'There was little continuity,' he complains of Timothy's contributions, 'and this meant it was impossible to let Timothy speak entirely for himself.'[34] With masterful ability Wellfleet arranges long quotations direct from Timothy into a meaningful sequence, linking them with his own recollections and observations.

With the two Wellfleet characters MacLennan returned to his most persistent theme: the use of power. 'The murder of truth leads to the murder of people,' he had stated in his article on the October Crisis of 1970. In the character of Timothy he dramatized the process by which this can happen. Creatively manipulating human responses through the technology he employs in the television studio, Timothy wields an enormous power over the lives of others. With purposes as trivial as mere entertainment or raw sensationalism, he carelessly makes and breaks reputations and lives with as little responsibility as that with which the *S.S. Mont Blanc* was loaded in Halifax harbour in 1917. To live with no other god than that of technology, with no sense of history and no purpose other than the selfish whim of the moment, is to court disaster. As MacLennan demonstrated in *Voices in Time*, such a philosophy does result in murder, has already caused political terrorism, and could lead to the near destruction of the entire world.

The innocent victim of Timothy's irresponsibility is the man who, unknown to him, has recently married his own mother in later life. Conrad Dehmel, formerly a German government official and now an historian, is a character who has lived through the same era as

MacLennan himself. Born in 1910 Dehmel, like MacLennan, has first idealized and then been repelled by the 'age of the hero' in the First World War. Like MacLennan, he has been dominated by a strong-willed father who has served in the war. Contrasting himself to his father, he at first feels considerable guilt, as George Stewart had in relation to Jerome Martell, at being a contemplative man rather than a man of action: 'During the early days of the war I played an ignoble part; my sole purpose was to survive.'

Like MacLennan, Dehmel thinks of himself as having been an innocent victim trapped in history. 'What should have been the prime of my life was blighted by the place and the time where I spent it,' he laments in his memoirs. 'It was the same for nearly all Germans of my age, and for hundreds of millions of others. We were robbed of our youth, of the best years of our lives, and this may explain why so many of us have failed the youth of today.'[35] The name 'Dehmel' comes from the German romantic poet whose *Weib und die Welt* had provided the story on which *The Precipice* had been based; Dehmel's poems in *The Oxford Book of German Verse* had epitomized the tragedy of the romantic for MacLennan ever since he first encountered them in Oxford. Named 'Conrad' by his father after Joseph Conrad, Dehmel combines in his life story both the tragic fate of the romantic and the blistering vision of man's 'heart of darkness' which Conrad recorded. His love for a strong Jewish woman, Hanna Erlich, draws Dehmel out of the security of his job at the Grosser Kurfürst Institute (based on the Kaiser Frederich Museum) into the pretense of being an officer in the Gestapo so that he can rescue her and her father from persecution. He is aided in this futile endeavour by Admiral Wilhelm Canaris, the head of German Intelligence, a figure who had fascinated MacLennan when he had read about him in Cornelius Ryan's *The Longest Day* (1959), and later in Anthony Cave Brown's *Bodyguard of Lies* (1975) and William Stevenson's *A Man Called Intrepid* (1976). Canaris is Dehmel writ large. As Canaris helps him to plan the rescue attempt he realizes 'that he was in the presence of a profound tragedy; that it was not a personal thing, but that Canaris was caught in a chain of mathematical equations from which there was no escape.' Like Canaris, he is 'trapped in the collapsing vaults of history.' Although Hanna has earlier realized that 'huge events and appalling personalities were poised to intervene in the personal lives of every living soul in Europe,'[36] the romantic streak in Dehmel refuses to accept this truth and for Hanna's sake he becomes a man of action whose interference in her life ironically leads to her capture, torture, and death. Having glimpsed the heart of man's darkness in this trauma, and also in his own torture and imprisonment in Belsen, he survives to take up a post in history at an American university through the efforts of the former Jewish director of the Grosser Kurfürst Institute, Erwin Rosenthal, a character based on Erwin Panofsky, the art historian who had taken part in the panel at Princeton with MacLennan in 1953.

To old John Wellfleet, Conrad Dehmel's life story is a forerunner of his own. Until he had attempted to rewrite Dehmel's story, he had thought that the Great Fear of the 1970s and the Destructions themselves had constituted the greatest tragedy in the history of mankind. Now he comes to see that Dehmel's generation lived through an even more tragic era: 'Now I am forced to link up my own experience of total destruction with his, and Germany is the touchstone ... For years I have taken it for granted that nothing that ever happened in this world was as terrible as what happened to us. Now I believe that on a purely personal level it was even worse for people like Hanna and Conrad.' Wellfleet eventually recognizes that the Destructions were 'so impersonal that there was no more malice in them than in a combined earthquake and volcanic explosion on a global scale ... To have your world annihilated by a computer balls-up is not the same as to be strapped naked to a table in a police basement and have your backbone and rib cage stripped by steel whips, your finger nails and genitals torn out with red-hot pincers, or your brain blown by electric shocks so powerful than an ignorant policeman can reduce the world's greatest genius to a screech of agony, all these things being done by men as human as yourself.'

The only positive role the individual can play in an era like this, Dehmel concludes, is to preserve something on which a new era can construct itself: 'My old dream of earning the right to belong to civilization as its interpreter vanished. What was needed now was not to belong to the old civilization, but to survive this nihilism in order to preserve the seeds of a new civilization.'[37] For John Wellfleet, this statement serves as an inspiring example. Just as Dehmel's records of the major landmarks of the German cities have played a constructive part in the rebuilding of urban centres after the war, so too will Wellfleet's record of these voices in time provide a potentially important moral guide to André Gervais and his friends in their reconstruction of Montreal.

Wellfleet's record, like MacLennan's *Return of the Sphinx*, shows human history moving through eras of patrist and matrist ascendancy. Eras of coherence, such as that in which Dehmel's mother grew up or the one Timothy's grandfather represents, hold matrist and patrist influences in a delicate balance that is usually short-lived. The extreme patrism of the 'millions of boy-men' responsible for imposing their fantasies of bigger and more powerful explosions on the world in two world wars is represented by two colonels reminiscent of the megalomaniac Colonel Wain in *Barometer Rising*: Colonel Gottfried Dehmel, Conrad's father, and Colonel Greg Wellfleet, Timothy's father. The matrist society of the sixties is spawned by a rebellion against the excessive patrism of such men, and is best represented by Timothy and the permissive society of which he is a part. In Gervais, MacLennan hopefully imagines the rebirth of a patrist society which, at least until it gets out of hand in its 'progress,' will constitute a coherent and moral era.

Such a view of history is cyclic, and MacLennan in *Voices in Time* refers back to the two historians whose work most influenced his own social history of the Roman Empire in his thesis at Princeton. Dehmel, who has also done a thesis on the lost civilization of Oxyrhynchus, agrees that the Russian progressive historian Rostovtzeff and the German philosopher Spengler were right in their notions of the rise and fall of empires.[38]

For MacLennan, such eras and the innate qualities of mankind that cause them to occur, stretch right back to the dawn of civilization and the emergence of man from the jungle. Through frequent images and comparisons drawn from the New Biology, he makes this theory explicit. 'A civilization,' Conrad Dehmel speculates on one occasion, 'is like a garden cultivated in a jungle. As flowers and vegetables grow from cultivated seeds, so do civilizations grow from carefully studied, diligently examined ideas and perceptions. In nature, if there are no gardeners, the weeds that need no cultivation take over the garden and destroy it ... During my lifetime too many of the men who thought of themselves as civilization's gardeners, in nearly everything they did from the promotion of superhuman science to superhuman salesmanship, devoted the ambiguous genius of their programmed brains to the cultivation of the weeds. They watered them with the jungle rains of the media. The klieg lights of the studios were their hothouses.' In this image, which derives in part from a juxtaposition of the Garden of Eden and the fallen world, MacLennan contrasted the two inherent sides of man's nature: the altruistic and the aggressive. In explaining Hitler's rise to power as the ultimate in aggression, he has Hanna's father, a psychiatrist, theorize that Hitler 'talks directly to the volcano underneath the rules' – that is to say, he touches the primitive tendency to self-seeking aggression that is one half of the genetic inheritance of every man. MacLennan speculates that in Hitler is the urge to gamble for tremendous stakes, a gambling instinct that probably accounts for the first emergence of man's jungle ancestors from the safety of their trees. As the world moves into the Great Fear, Timothy makes a comparison that recalls old Captain Yardley's observation of 'the ultimate solitude' in *Two Solitudes*. Just as Yardley had seen a terrifying nihilism in the aimless predatory beauty of the fish around his stranded boat in the tropics, so Timothy compares the state to which the world had come in the late 1960s to the underwater world of the Great Barrier Reef: 'a handful of young men ... had found the path to the powder magazine of Métropole. Unseen and with precision – my God, and with such beautiful haughtiness – they had moved out of the Great Barrier Reef of unidentified humanity to plant the bomb, to seize the hostages, then had faded back unseen into the Barrier Reef from which they were hurling their ultimatums like conquerors.' In the midst of the October Crisis, Timothy looks out over the city of Montreal and comments: 'This town is like a herd of zebras smelling leopards.'

But what the New Biologists had called 'The Keeper of the Kinds' ultimately balances this innate aggression. As the modern world moves toward almost certain annihilation, some mysterious force induces men to take steps to prevent the entire species from being wiped out. The bomb that eventually causes the Destructions is a modified version of the more lethal nuclear bombs which had earlier existed: 'Something profound and mysterious, something blessed and almighty in the genes of humanity, had created a taboo against these [nuclear] bombs ... They invented what were called 'clean bombs,' which had a destructive power less than that of the nuclears but nevertheless tremendous.'

For MacLennan, as for old John Wellfleet, this mysterious 'something' in the genes of man calls forth religious faith. In the long run, as Dehmel implies on one occasion, 'the creative energy of the universe will ... interfere with human ingenuity.'[39] These two forces which seem so similar – creativity and ingenuity – are in reality diametrically opposed: true creativity, MacLennan had come to believe, is the God-like ability to give form to chaos, to create a world out of the dark void as recounted in Genesis; human ingenuity, although it may seem to reflect an equal or even a superior power, serves in the end to endanger the species, if not to extinguish it utterly.

At the time he wrote *Two Solitudes* MacLennan had written: 'as life grows organically, it can't be subordinated to a plan. At the same time, a novel without any plan at all is a shambles.' That is to say, life had seemed unplanned to him and, consequently, he could see no clear way to reflect life in a planned novel structure. But now, as his religious faith deepened and his perspective expanded through time and space to survey man's entire history, now that the lives of others seemed to hold lessons as significant as his own, he had come to see that life is not unplanned. There is a God of evolution, he now believed, who works through all life to create even disorder. There is, in other words, a purpose to even the most purposeless human behaviour. The reason man himself has such difficulty grasping this truth is that each man lives his life in a set of specifics so overwhelming that he cannot step aside and see the overall pattern. Only in old age can a man hope to look back and out over his own life and that of others with sufficient detachment and insight to sense its purpose. The very form of *Voices in Time* dramatizes this process of detachment in John Wellfleet. Because he is now physically far removed from the life he has known and from that of the others he deals with, he is able to find a perspective from which he can see into God's purpose for the created world. MacLennan still thought that 'life grows organically,' but now he also believed that it was planned. This meant that a work of art did, in fact, reflect life by being planned too. With *Voices in Time* he successfully planned his universe with the same kind of purpose as his 'God of evolution,' still allowing for the organic growth of story and characters. As his epigraph from Goethe's *Faust* states: 'You draw near once more, swaying shapes / That once showed yourself to the clouded gaze.' Both for MacLennan and for Wellfleet, things have become clear in old age that in youth could not be comprehended.

Even in 1968, at the time he had started drafting the novel, MacLennan had arrived at the basis of this view. In his address to the students at the University of British Columbia he had said: 'We live in [a period] where it is possible to recognize an objective pattern within history itself. We live in a tragic time, certainly. So did Shakespeare. But there is not a single Shakespearean tragedy which does not end upon a note of renewal. Megalomania, egotism and blind wickedness run their courses in Shakespeare, but a Fortinbras, a Montano, a McDuff or an Edgar – previously almost bit-players – enter at the end to restore sanity and recover the state.' And, it could be added, Horatio. Once again, MacLennan identified himself and his country not with the heroes like Lear, Macbeth, and Hamlet, who by taking major decisions revealed their tragic flaws and precipitated disaster, but with the bit-players who survive and carry on.

The tone of this novel is one of resignation. It is almost as if, with Christian charity, he has forgiven his enemies. By taking a German of his own age and setting his story in wartime Germany, he recognized that the lives of the enemies were just as full of suffering as those he had known at home. There is no right or wrong side in war, only the terrible truth that man has it in him to behave so. Similarly, with Timothy Wellfleet, he at last could empathize with the kind of man he had most disliked and feared; he treats his immorality and irresponsibility with great understanding, showing in detail how forces beyond his control have conspired to make him what he is. By the time he wrote this novel, no fear of censorship confined him, as it had earlier; he was free to include the more explicit sexual scenes which were essential in creating characters like Timothy. This freedom was also made possible by the death of Katie, his mother, in 1971 at the age of ninety-four; no longer worried that he might upset her sensibility, as parts of his earlier novels already had, he was more relaxed to say whatever he pleased.

As he finished the novel, he had definite doubts about the way it would strike any reader but himself: 'I lived with the book so long that when it was over it did not seem real any more. Nobody but myself had read a line of it. I have said consistently that I didn't believe anyone would like it and I can only hope I'm wrong. Do I even like it myself? I'm making no comparison in point of quality and importance, but I've sometimes wondered if Shakespeare "liked" *King Lear* and *Troilus and Cressida*. If I was prophetic in earlier novels, it would not be pleasant if I'm prophetic in this one, except at the end where, many decades later, a new and much smaller human society begins to grow again.' When he had finished *The Watch That Ends the Night* he had speculated: 'this may well turn out [to be] my trouble in future: my kind of world is not like many other peoples' any more.' 'Whatever may be essential in my own understanding of life has become something that only a handful of people would want to pay attention to even if I could express it extremely well.'[40] If *Return of the Sphinx* had been as badly reviewed in the United States as it had been in Canada, he might well have thought that this forecast had been accurate; but because American reviewers in 1967 had understood and praised the universality of this novel he had been encouraged to try again. Would *Voices in Time* reach his Canadian audience; would it seem real? Or was he correct in stating that they were likely to miss the point again, putting down his book simply because younger Canadian writers were now in fashion?

The generally warm reception accorded *Voices in Time* when it was launched on 10 October 1980 fulfilled Douglas Gibson's prediction that it would be 'the literary event of the fall' and made MacLennan feel that he, like the phoenix that had originally been in his mind for the novel's title, was 'rising from the ashes of disfavor.'[41] Colin McDougall, a former student who had himself won the Governor-General's Award for his novel *Execution* in 1958, found *Voices in Time* 'compelling reading' because of its 'sheer narrative power.' His review in the Montreal *Gazette* on 11 October claimed that MacLennan 'used futurism as a device to show his poor bedevilled creatures suffering as God might see them.' Drawing attention to the very concern that had been central to MacLennan as he wrote – the handling of time – he went on to claim that MacLennan was 'a virtuoso in the use of time ... The shifts in time and point of view are deftly done and beautifully interwoven.' McDougall's tribute to the 'master-novelist' was equalled in Burt Heward's review for the Ottawa *Citizen* on 27 September, which praised his 'miraculously clear handling of eras and generations.' For Heward, he had summed up time 'with wisdom, humor and unalloyed artistry': 'MacLennan masterfully dramatizes mankind's ignorant abuse of technology, he never insults by preaching about such obvious evils as Hitler, destructive '60s radicals, and 21st-century nuclear holocaust. He need only describe his passionate lovers adrift in their smitten eras.' And Robin Mathews in *Books in Canada*, although he implied that MacLennan ought to have apportioned the blame to capitalism for the griefs of modern times, stated that *Voices in Time* reveals a deepening and intensification of his vision: 'The question MacLennan asks is of enormous importance: Has the modern world so bereft itself of personal and public values that it is doomed to disintegration? ... The question is the fundamental one of the century, the question that lifts the book out of national place and makes it a significant novel of Western culture.'

But praise such as this was not to go untempered. As Mathews had speculated, *Voices in Time* was likely to fuel not only 'the esteem of his admirers' but also 'the disdain of his detractors.'[42] Especially in Toronto, where *Return of the Sphinx* had come under severe attack, some reviews were scathing. William French in the *Globe and Mail*, for example, dismissed the novel as 'contrived and artificial,' having value only as a 'curiosity.' In contrast to Heward's assertion that MacLennan 'never insults by preaching,' French described this novel and all MacLennan's earlier fiction as 'unrelentingly earnest': he was possibly 'the last of the Victorians'; his novel nothing more than 'a sermon delivered in the guise of fiction.' Ken Adachi's review in the *Toronto Star* echoed French's: 'It *is* a sermon,' which 'trips up the novel which is contrived to bear its weight.' Although Adachi praised the intelligence with which MacLennan had constructed his novels like 'complex theorems,' he concluded: 'Intelligence is not an unmixed blessing; his mind casts more light than heat. And so his novel *as novel* suffers.' Comparing him to a street-corner evangelist entertaining passersby on their lunch hours, Adachi stated that MacLennan was 'a reasonable man apostrophizing the universe with a didacticism better left to the essay.' And, in a short radio review for CBC, Sam Solecki, editor of *Canadian Forum*, damned the novel outright as a dreary assembly of predictable stereotypes.

Other reviews fell between these two extremes. With puzzling inconsistency, Katherine Govier in *Maclean's*, for example, condemned the novel's 'dated psychology' and the use of fiction as 'a thin disguise for nostalgia,' but praised its display of 'all the fluid power of the best of his writing and the breadth of vision that came to us first with *Barometer Rising* almost 40 years ago.'[43]

Although on the whole these reviews did indicate a more receptive critical attitude towards MacLennan, a number of characteristic misconceptions about him had become ingrained. The categorization of him as 'old-fashioned' (or out of fashion) and Victorian surfaces in three of these reviews. Overlooking the entire section of the book dealing with Timothy's work in the mass media and his private life, which resembles that of Leonard Cohen's fictional characters, some critics continued to insist that MacLennan was ignorant of the morality, style, and insight of the mid-twentieth century. Such was the price he paid for setting such issues in a much wider context than a good many contemporary writers. As Heward accurately noted, while Mordecai Richler had moved from the 'bitter Holocaust humor of *St. Urbain's Horseman* to an accepting pro-humanity theme,' MacLennan had traced an opposite path until, with *Voices in Time*, he was venting 'a primal scream at man's monumental ignorance.'

For a number of these critics MacLennan deserved acclaim as a prophet. Typical of such statements is Heward's: 'MacLennan has evolved into virtually a national saint and prophet by nurturing Canada's self-image in his fiction and essays and by foreseeing French and Quebec alienation (*Two Solitudes*) and separatist violence (*Return of the Sphinx*).' Such assertions do not entirely bear examination. *Two Solitudes*, for example, actually described a situation already in existence, and in so far as it did make predictions it forecast the successful integration of the two language groups in Quebec through the evolutionary process of education and intermarriage. Similarly, *Return of the Sphinx* depicted FLQ acts of violence that had been occurring in Montreal since the early sixties but simply reached new levels and consequently international recognition with the October Crisis in 1970.

MacLennan himself actually fostered this notion of himself as prophet, perhaps understandably so. In the first place, it was part of his self-image as 'intuitive Celt,' part of the side of himself that experienced 'apparitions' and creative insights. Moreover, it has been sustained by the way in which life tends to imitate art. Often, after finishing a novel, he was struck by the way in which events in real life paralleled the events he thought he had invented. This was most notable, for example, when Quebec premier Daniel Johnson's son rebelled against him in public in much the same way as Alan Ainslie's son rebelled against his father in *Return of the Sphinx*. But such correspondences owe more to MacLennan's accuracy in drawing probable patterns of human relationships than to any 'second sight.'

At last MacLennan had attained the kind of success he had been waiting for. On his promotion tours across Canada in October and November 1980 he was approached by radio stations, bookstores, television programs, and magazine editors to give interviews and make a greater number of public appearances than he had ever been asked to do before. Exhausted, but in high spirits, he returned to Montreal to learn that after six weeks the original 7500 copies had been sold and the novel was off to press for a second printing.

Voices in Time is MacLennan's greatest novel. As in *The Watch That Ends the Night* he had found a form within which he could reflect the flux of a life that, after seventy-three years, seemed more unmanageable than ever. Even more than *The Watch That Ends the Night*, this novel harked back to those two unpublished novels 'So All Their Praises' and 'A Man Should Rejoice,' which, because they were set outside of Canada and even more because they were 'bulging at the seams,' had defeated him earlier. Now he had finally written an international novel that, as McDougall had noted, was 'not one book, but many.' To reach this point he had had to resolve his technical problems of finding a focus, and he had also had to fight free of those 'nationalist labels' that had hung uncomfortably round his neck since 1941. Ironically, it had been the rebuff of *Return of the Sphinx* that had finally released him. Since there was no pleasing the critics, why not write about what he wanted to, whether anyone understood it or not? With the additional freedom from fear of censorship, perhaps his mother's in particular, he had written about a subject of his own choosing, the same subject that had enticed him in the thirties, but from a vastly different perspective. Now, not only was his craft equal to the task, but his Canadian audience was more sophisticated. As Mathews rightly observed, he was able to address some of the fundamental questions of our society and thereby lift the novel 'out of national place' and make it 'a significant novel of Western culture.' Though critics would continue to insist that he had become a Canadian 'institution' and 'virtually a national saint,' his subject in *Voices in Time* had more than ever before become what he had always wanted it to be: universal.

And yet *Voices in Time* remains intensely Canadian, in a way far different from the aspirations of those critics who forty years ago forced him into the nationalist mould. As Katherine Govier offhandedly observed: 'The book is perhaps a lesson in how to live in unconscionable circumstances and keep the spirit alive.' MacLennan, in treating this theme through the ambivalence of power, especially as it is manifest in technology, is directly in one of the mainstreams of Canadian intellectual history. Unconsciously 'Canadian' too is the novel's form, which arose, after all, from MacLennan's contemplation of the great fissures that constitute our waterways in *Rivers of Canada*: it is vast, jagged, and strong. Nor did his energies fail him. The narrative power of the book indeed speaks everywhere of the experienced artist. Quoting André Malraux to describe his experience in writing it, he said: 'Jacob's struggle with the angels is what, really, I think writing a novel is ... Writing the writer, rather than writing the book.' Once he finished he confessed: 'I'll never write a serious novel again. It almost killed me.'[44]

Epilogue

As *Voices in Time* took off on solid and steady sales in 1980, MacLennan continued to lead the kind of life that over the years had become a set routine. Even after his retirement from McGill University he still taught one course on English prose to a predictably large group of undergraduates. Although his vigorous tennis games were now over, he swam regularly at the Montreal Amateur Athletic Association on Peel Street. His weight, he was fond of boasting, varied not a jot from that of his Oxford days. In the summers he was off with Tota to North Hatley, their lives only marginally slowed down by her difficulty in getting around.

In a retrospective written to mark the occasion of the fiftieth anniversary of the *University of Toronto Quarterly*, called 'Fiction in Canada – 1930 to 1980,' MacLennan cast his eye backwards over his own life. By his own bitter account his career – apparently so successful to outsiders – seemed to him a story of missed opportunities and bad luck: 'To be a native-born Canadian is to be born in ambiguity and to be a native-born Canadian writer is to be doubly ambiguous ... Whether we like it or not, we are stuck with one of the most ambiguous nations there ever was.'

More than any other writer of his time, MacLennan *was* stuck with Canada. From 1941, when *Barometer Rising* exploded into the national consciousness – which he now knew had then been 'innocent' – until 1967, when *Return of the Sphinx* had been misread and condemned as an unrealistic portrayal of the FLQ in Quebec, he had been somewhat

At McGill University, 1980

miscast as Canada's national spokesman. 'I doubt if my own background qualifies me as a spokesman for Canadian literature,'[1] he protested in 1980, as he had been protesting for over thirty years. But the public image of the man would not, and probably will not, budge even though with *Voices in Time* he produced the grand international novel he had always wanted to write.

MacLennan set out to be a writer, not a 'Canadian' writer. The detour he reluctantly took in 1941 from international to national subjects was both his curse and his blessing. On hearing that his seven novels have come to be associated with the developing stages of our national consciousness, he may chafe at the restraints and misconceptions surrounding his work; but fame, some small measure of fortune, and the opportunity to continue writing fiction have also been his to cherish. Though he has had his 'Kicking Season,' especially from journalists in Toronto, he has also savoured overnight popularity, high sales, and the genuine recognition by others of the obstacles in his course and their respect for his way of meeting them. As Margaret Laurence wrote, for example: 'Writers such as MacLennan, Callaghan, Buckler, Ross, O'Hagan, etc, and especially MacLennan, Buckler and Ross, in my view, were the heroic generation of our writers, for they were the first generation to write genuinely out of their own experience and the sight of their own eyes, and the first generation to write out of a non-colonial feeling ... i.e. they did not take for their models or mentors British or American writers, especially British, as had been the case with Can[adian] writing for so long before them. My generation of writers owes them everything, and I have said this many times, and keep on saying to the younger writers, now, that they must read MacLennan's writing ... and pay tribute to him, to know where they really have come from.'[2]

Not only in his novels but in his four hundred or so essays – several of which are brilliant – and in his even more numerous public appearances on radio, on television, or in person, MacLennan has concentrated 'whether he liked it or not' on matters of importance to this 'most ambiguous nation,' and in doing so he has elucidated many of them. In a number of purely practical matters – in particular, his demanding a Canadian contract for *The Precipice* in 1948, or his arguing successfully for better tax breaks for authors in 1959 – he charted a course from which all future writers in Canada would benefit.

His detour into Canadian nationalism, no matter how often and how fervently he may declaim its appropriateness, ironically drew him closer and closer to the country's heart. It was almost despite himself that he wrote in 1980: 'our nation is still worthy of love. She has not sold her soul outright to the men of greed and power. She still has a conscience and this may be why she finds it so difficult to make up her mind even about herself.' His emphasis, here and elsewhere, on 'soul' and 'conscience' as opposed to 'greed' and 'power' places him in one central tradition of Canadian intellectual history. Such concepts originated for him, as for others, in Christian principles, in self-sacrifice as opposed to selfishness, in humanitarian ideals as opposed to the 'advances' of technology. His concepts bear a striking resemblance to those of Canadians like his former Dalhousie professor Archibald MacMechan, or Maurice Hutton or Harold Innis or Donald Creighton or George Grant. On the bedrock of Presbyterian principles, using the scaffolding of the Classics, he erected his own personal indictment of technology and mass communications and his insistence that at life's core is a mystery that can only be called religious.

It was Harold Innis who defined the university as a 'centre where one has the right and duty not to make up one's mind.'[3] MacLennan might have said the same thing about the political arena. Eschewing any party affiliation, he has voted on at least one occasion for each of the main national parties. At any election, whether federal, provincial, or municipal, he has looked for the candidate who comes closest to his own ethical views and who seems most likely to implement them. Even his brief flirtation with Marxism in the thirties was really the expression of an idealized hope that altruism could replace the self-centredness of capitalism. His attacks on René Lévesque and the Parti québécois just prior to the separatist referendum in May 1980, predicting its defeat, were based on these same ethical principles: the policies of the separatists he characterized as 'fascist'; the pro-federalist argument he saw as self-sacrifice for the good of all. Such views reflect deeply held moral convictions rather than political acuity.

In his feeling for the vastness of this land, a feeling that first appeared in his unpublished novels and culminated in *Rivers of Canada*, and afterwards lay behind *Voices in Time*, he has expressed the peculiarly 'northern' character of his people. As the Canadian artist Homer Watson once wrote: 'no immortal work has been done which has not as one of its promptings for its creation a feeling its creator had of having roots in his native land and being a product of its soil.'[4] This same notion, which struck MacLennan consciously only after he had written much poetry and two unpublished novels, seemed to him by 1980 to have been 'the most important lesson of my literary life.'

It is not so much that his novels have signalled steps forward in our national consciousness, as critics would have us believe, but that the evolution of his own life and his inherent nature symbolize that process and the nature of the majority of people living here. The evolution he himself traced in his reminiscences, 'Fiction in Canada,' from innocent unconsciousness through national fervour to the experience of world citizenship, parallels Canada's development from colony to nation: that development relied on reserves of the very qualities he drew on in his career – strong moral principles, hard work, caution, altruism, and persistence. It is the demonstration of these qualities in his life and work that calls forth the admiration of those who respect things Canadian and attracts the hostility of those who find in things Canadian something inferior.

One of the characters in *Voices in Time*, thinking of the cast-iron containers full of the fragments of family history that John Wellfleet eventually arranges into an intelligible chronicle, comments: 'All our lives were in those boxes.'[5] This remark reverberates in the novel and beyond it into the life of its author. Almost continuously MacLennan has felt the constraints that bound him: not only the assumed 'role' of Canadian spokesman, but also the facts of his rigidly supervised childhood, his inflexible education, the stark realities he was forced to take as his context when he began writing. Even his initial successes, which ought to have freed him from those constraints, occurred at exactly the point at which his wife Dorothy began to spiral downwards towards death. It is not surprising that he so often imagined himself to be a Christ-like martyr. More than once his mother's favourite aria from *The Messiah*, 'He Was Despised and Rejected,' must have struck home with personal force. This image of himself, reinforced by the Calvinism he struggled so hard to overcome, has endured, quite at odds with the common view of his critics that he wears his reputation like an oversized coat.

The frustrations of being 'boxed-in' have deepened the temperamental sadness he inherited from his ancestors. 'So sad is Hugh MacLennan's vision of humanity,' observed one critic of *Voices in Time*, 'that you feel it in your bones – your very nerves ache.'[6] As with *The Watch that Ends the Night*, this last novel dramatized the view of life summed up in the MacLennan clan slogan 'The Ridge of Tears.'

The feeling of being cornered, of living within walls, once motivated the small boy to fantasies of heroic action; later it propelled the grown man to release his mind and emotions into art. Each and every novel has been an experiment for MacLennan. The ordinary round of activities in his daily life belie an extraordinary mind ranging further and further afield, intensely engaged in a world of its own making. In his continuing exploration into a world of words where he is free to create his own reality, he is a born artist. As his wife Dorothy once wrote perceptively: 'Hugh's originality of mind is *felt* in his unorthodox (though carefully considered) use of words, for he is neither a journalist nor an academician, but an artist.'[7] Or, as he himself commented in 1980: 'it was not economics that had turned me to writing fiction. It was a pure compulsion.'

Hugh MacLennan will continue to write for the simple reason that he can't *not* write. His mind, disdaining worldly limitations, will join the new waves of much younger chroniclers for whom he has prepared the way on the endless voyage out.

Notes

The following abbreviations are used throughout the notes for members of MacLennan's family: Hugh MacLennan H.M., Samuel MacLennan S.M., Katherine MacLennan K.M., and Frances MacLennan F.M. All family correspondence, unless otherwise indicated, is in the possession of Frances MacLennan.

The letters from Hugh MacLennan to George Barrett are located in the MacLennan Papers, Archives, McCord Museum, Montreal.

Letters from MacLennan and from Dorothy Duncan to William Arthur Deacon are in the Thomas Fisher Rare Book Library, University of Toronto, ms. collection 160; other correspondence found in this location is indicated in the notes by (UTL TF).

All correspondence between MacLennan and Dorothy Duncan and John Gray is located in the Macmillan Archive at McMaster University, Hamilton; other material from this collection is designated (Macmillan).

Items from the Hugh MacLennan Papers, Special Collections Division, University of Calgary Library, Calgary, are indicated throughout by (Cal); and from the Department of Rare Books and Special Collections, McGill University Libraries, Montreal, by (McG).

Various letters from MacLennan belong to their recipients: all letters to Marian Engel, for example, are in her possession; the letters to Gloria Ingraham belong to her.

Unless otherwise indicated, books and articles throughout the notes have been written by Hugh MacLennan.

1 From the Misty Island

Neil MacLennan, his wife Annie Mackenzie, and their son Duncan (ca. 1830-89) emigrated from Applecross in Scotland, just north of the MacLennan district of Kintail in Ross and Cromarty, to a farm in Malagawatch, Cape Breton Island, about 1840. Duncan, who became a tailor in Sydney, married Mary McPhee (1825-72) from Douglas, Nova Scotia, in 1855 (he later married Bessie Archibald in 1875): their daughter Annie Mackenzie (who eventually married Neil Ferguson) was born in 1856; their son Samuel John (1868-1939) was Hugh MacLennan's father.

William Hitchens and Martha Richards emigrated from Wales to a farm in Shelburne, Nova Scotia, about 1830. They had three sons (William, James, George): the middle one, James Edward (1829-91), who became a druggist, married Abigail Bigelow (1830-1925) in Pugwash in 1850; Abigail's father Amasa Bigelow, a U.E.L. ship-builder, had emigrated after 1776 from Boston with his wife Margaret Wood, who had come from Prince Edward Island. James and Abigail Hitchens had four children (Clifford, Mary, Hallie, Edward) of whom the second, Mary Killam (1855-1946), married Archibald MacQuarrie (1851-1915) in Glace Bay in 1873; Archibald was the son of Archibald MacQuarrie and Sarah MacInnes, who had emigrated from the Isle of Mull to Mira, Cape Breton Island, about 1840. Archibald and Mary MacQuarrie had twelve children (Gilbert, Nellie, Katherine, Abigail, an unnamed son, Flora, Frank, Alice, William, James, Marguerite, Ethel): the third, Katherine Clifford (1877-1971), was Hugh MacLennan's mother.

The impressions of mid-nineteenth-century Glace Bay in the opening paragraphs are taken from Mary MacQuarrie's 'Mother's Story,' in the possession of Frances MacLennan.

1 H.M. to author 7 Jan. 1976
2 F.M. to author July 1976
3 H.M. to author 7 Jan. 1976
4 F.M. to author July 1976
5 H.M. to author 7 Jan. 1976
6 'Voltaire Said ...' *Montrealer* 26 (Sept. 1952) 50
7 F.M. to author July 1976; written versions of her mother's stories, such as 'The Fairy Ship' and 'Carol's Story,' are owned by F.M.
8 Ewan Clarke, Katie's former accompanist, to author July 1976
9 Katherine Anderson [K.M.] *A Handful of Verses* 1956
10 F.M. to author July 1976
11 'My Surgeon Father' *Bulletin of the American College of Surgeons* 44 (1959) 214

12 H.M. to Marian Engel 10 July 1957
13 H.M. to author 14 April 1976
14 Robert Marsh, H.M.'s cousin, to author 17 Sept. 1976
15 H.M. to Susan Pellett 29 May 1975, as quoted in Gertrude E.N. Tratt *The Centennial History of Tower Road School* (Halifax: St Patrick's High School 1975) 60
16 This book is in the possession of F.M.
17 'Boys' Tales of Yore, British to the Core' *Montreal Star* 11 Aug. 1962
18 F.M. to author July 1976; H.M. to Ian Fraser in 'What Did You Read When You Were a Child?' *Montreal Star* 3 April 1977; 'The Books We Read When We Are Young' *Ontario Library Review* 45 (Nov. 1961) 226
19 Tratt *Tower Road School* 61-2
20 This medical unit, one of several such units raised by Canadian universities, was No 7 Unit. See Sir Andrew Macphail *The Medical Services* (Ottawa: F.A. Acland 1925) 44, 217. For H.M.'s account, see 'An Orange from Portugal' *Chatelaine* (Dec. 1947) 17, 72-5.
21 'Christmas without Dickens' *Mayfair* 26 (Dec. 1952) 45
22 Dr Harold L. Scammell to author 30 Nov. 1976
23 'My Surgeon Father'
24 F.M. to author July 1976; H.M. to author 7 Jan. 1976
25 Quoted in 'My Surgeon Father'
26 Dr C.J. Macdonald to author 9 Sept. 1976
27 H.M. to author 20 Aug. 1979, to John Gray 4 Jan. 1959
28 H.M. as quoted by Tratt *Tower Road School* 64
29 F.M. to author July 1976; 'On Living in a Cold Country' *The Other Side of Hugh MacLennan: Selected Essays Old and New* ed. Elspeth Cameron (Toronto: Macmillan 1978) 205-13
30 H.M. to S.M. 31 July 1919 (McG)
31 H.M. to author 7 Jan. 1976; reference to Milton in this context in H.M. to Gloria Ingraham 20 Nov. 1930
32 H.M. to author 7 Jan. 1976
33 H.M. to Engel 29 April 1959
34 Robert Marsh to author 7 Sept. 1977
35 Dr Scammell to author 1976
36 Records and Archives, Dalhousie University; H.M. to author 7 Jan. 1976
37 Ewan Clarke to author 1976
38 H.M. to Prof. E.D. Blodgett, University of Alberta 15 March 1979 (property of Blodgett)
39 Ewan Clarke to author 1976
40 'The Pleasures of Tennis' *Star Weekly Magazine* (22 June 1968) 21, 19; 'Confessions of a Wood-chopping Man' *Montrealer* 30 (Nov. 1956) 23; 'Fifty Grand: A Semi-Centarian Takes Stock' *ibid.* 31 (May 1957) 40

41 Ewan Clarke to author 1976
42 H.M. to Blodgett 1979
43 'Hugh MacLennan' OISE tape interview by Earle Toppings 1971
44 H.M. to Blodgett 1979
45 Dr Scammell to author 1976
46 'Jotham Logan: A Personal Tribute' *Dalhousie Review* 32 no 1 (Spring 1952) 15-18
47 F.M. to author July 1976
48 Records and Archives, Dalhousie University, 1924-8; H.M. to author 20 Aug 1979
49 'New York, New York ...' *Montrealer* 32 (March 1958) 34

2 The Voyage Out: Oxford and the Continent

1 'On Living in a Cold Country' *The Other Side of Hugh MacLennan* ed. Elspeth Cameron (Toronto: Macmillan 1978) 206
2 Details of this trip are taken from *ibid*. 205-13 and from K.M.'s journal 19 Sept.-11 Nov. 1928, in the possession of F.M.
3 K.M. to S.M. 30 Sept., H.M. to F.M. [5] Oct. 1928
4 Thompson to S.M. 4 Sept., H.M. to S.M. 3 Oct. 1928
5 H.M. to author 7 Nov. 1975
6 H.M. to K.M. 20 Oct., to S.M. 3 Nov. 1928, to author 7 Jan. 1976
7 H.M. to K.M. 20 Oct., to S.M. 8 Dec. 1928, to K.M. 4 Dec. 1929
8 H.M. to author 7 Jan. 1976, to K.M. 10 Dec. 1929
9 H.M. to author 7 Jan. 1976, to S.M. 3 Oct., to K.M. 17 Dec. 1928
10 H.M. to K.M. 26 May 1929 and 20 Oct. 1928, to S.M. 3 Nov. 1928
11 H.M. to F.M. 3 Sept. and 5 Oct., to S.M. 3 Nov. 1928
12 H.M. to S.M. 8 Dec. 1928
13 H.M. to K.M. 4 Dec. 1929 and 17 Dec. 1928, to S.M. 21 Dec., to F.M. 19 Dec. 1928
14 H.M. to K.M. 21 Dec., to F.M. 24 Dec. 1928
15 H.M. to S.M. 21 Jan. 1929
16 H.M. to K.M. 21 March, to S.M. 25 March 1929
17 H.M. to S.M. 11 and 17 April, to K.M. 16 and 21 April 1929
18 H.M. to K.M. 19 and 26 May 1929
19 H.M. to S.M. 30 May, to F.M. 3 June 1929
20 H.M. to K.M. Spring 1929
21 H.M. to K.M. 10 and 4 Dec. 1929
22 H.M. to S.M. 9 Dec., to F.M. 12 Dec., to K.M. 10 Dec. 1929
23 H.M. to K.M. 10 and 24 Dec. 1929

24 H.M. to K.M. 1 Jan., to S.M. 7 Jan. 1930; the quotation is from Shelley's poem 'Adonais,' stanza XXXVI.
25 H.M. to K.M. 21 Feb. 1930, to John Gray 28 March 1959
26 H.M. to K.M. 23 March 1930
27 H.M. to K.M. 27 March, to S.M. 31 March 1930
28 H.M. to S.M. 23 April 1930; Genner quoted in same letter
29 H.M. to S.M. 5 May 1930
30 H.M. to K.M. 18 May 1930; 'Orgy at Oriel' *Montrealer* 26 (Oct. 1952) 56-7
31 H.M. to K.M. 25 May, 2 and 26 June, to F.M. 21 June 1930
32 H.M. to K.M. 10 July 1930; 'Have You Had Many Wimbledons?' *Montrealer* 32 (Sept. 1958) 22-5
33 H.M. to F.M. 20 July, to S.M. 29 June 1930
34 H.M. to S.M. 17 Oct., to K.M. 23 Nov., 26 Oct., 9 Nov., 7 Oct. 1930
35 'My Last Colonel' *Montrealer* 33 (May 1959) 26-8, 'By Their Foods ...' *ibid.* 30 (March 1956) 29-30, and 'Must We Return to 1933?' *ibid.* 28 (Jan. 1954) 19; 'And Seeing the Multitudes' *Lower Canada College Magazine* (Feb. 1937) 9-14; 'Have You Had Many Wimbledons?' and 'Queen of Tourneys' *Montrealer* 29 (Aug. 1955) 21, 23, 25; 'Whose World Is This?' *ibid.* (Oct. 1951) 25-6, 'Remembrance of Men Past' *ibid.* 29 (March 1955) 25-7, 'October and Smoke' *ibid.* 30 (Oct. 1956) 20-2, and 'Oxford Revisited' *ibid.* 32 (Oct. 1958) 24; 'Footsteps of Genius' *ibid.* 28 (Oct. 1954) 25, 27, 29, 31
36 H.M. to K.M. 23 Nov., to S.M. 17 Oct. 1930
37 H.M. to S.M. 16 Nov., to K.M. 8 Dec. 1930
38 H.M. to Gloria Ingraham 20 Nov. 1930, 23 Feb. 1931, to author 7 Jan. 1976
39 H.M. to Ingraham 30 March, 23 Feb. 1931, 26 Jan. 1940
40 H.M. to author 7 Jan. 1976
41 H.M. to Ingraham 23 Feb., 31 March 1931
42 H.M. to K.M. 19 Dec. 1930, to Ingraham 23 Feb. 1931 and 20 Nov. 1930
43 H.M. to Ingraham 15 Dec. 1930, to K.M. 13 and 19 Dec. 1930, 15 Feb. 1931
44 H.M. to S.M. 8 Feb. 1931, to K.M. 23 Nov. 1930
45 H.M. to Ingraham 30 March, to S.M. 8 Feb., to Ingraham 23 Feb. 1931
46 H.M. to Ingraham 30 March 1931
47 Unpublished, n.d. (McG) box 2, part 1, folder 10, nos 84-5
48 H.M. to Ingraham 12 June 1931
49 H.M. to Leonard Cohen 15 Feb. 1957 (UTL TF ms. 122)
50 H.M. to K.M. 3 Nov. 1931, to S.M. 20 Jan. 1932 (McG), to F.M. 22 Jan. 1932 (McG)

51 Spender *World within World* (London: Hamish Hamilton 1951) 137; H.M. to Ingraham 12 June 1931. Samuel Hynes used the term 'watershed' year in *The Auden Generation: Literature and Politics in England in the 1930s* (London: Bodley Head 1976) 65.
52 H.M. to K.M. 11 Oct., to S.M. 23 Feb. 1931
53 H.M. to K.M. 11 Dec., to S.M. 16 Dec. 1931
54 H.M. to K.M. 30 Jan., to S.M. 20 Jan., to F.M. 22 Jan. 1932 (all McG)
55 H.M. to F.M. 22 Jan. 1932 (McG)

3 The Voyage Back: Princeton

1 Dorothy Duncan *Bluenose: A Portrait of Nova Scotia* (New York: Harper's 1942) 12-16
2 Duncan 'Portrait of an Author' *Mayfair* (Aug. 1955) 56; 'Portrait of an Artist: Dorothy Duncan' *Montrealer* 31 (June 1957) 36; H.M. to author 20 Aug. 1980
3 Isabel Dobell to author July 1976
4 'Portrait of an Artist' 36
5 Records and Archives, Northwestern University, Evanston, Ill.
6 'Portrait of an Artist' 40
7 Duncan *Here's to Canada!* (New York: Harper's 1941) 247-55
8 Duncan 'Portrait of an Author' 56; *Bluenose* 11, 13
9 H.M. to K.M. 30 Jan. 1932 (McG)
10 Robert Marsh to author 17 Sept. 1976
11 'How We Differ from Americans' *Maclean's* 59 (15 Dec. 1946) 49; H.M. to author 20 Aug. 1979
12 'How We Differ' 49
13 'In Praise of McGill' *Montrealer* 28 (July 1954) 23
14 H.M. to Edmund Wilson 15 June 1967 (Cal)
15 H.M. to author 7 Nov. 1975
16 H.M. to J.F. Leddy 3 Oct. 1979 (property of Leddy)
17 Israel Halperin to author 29 May 1979
18 Duncan *Bluenose* 67-8
19 H.M. to author 16 Feb. 1980
20 H.M. to Leonard Cohen 15 Feb. 1957 (UTL TF ms. 122)
21 Duncan *Bluenose* 66, 68-9
22 H.M. to K.M. 11 May 1930
23 'Couth and Uncouth' *Montrealer* 29 (Feb. 1955), 23; 'My Surgeon Father' *Bulletin of the American College of Surgeons* 44 (1959) 232
24 H.M. to K.M. 2 June 1930, to F.M. 3 June 1929 and 11 Dec. 1928
25 H.M. to K.M. 26 Oct. 1930

26 H.M. to author 24 June 1979
27 For a fuller discussion of these issues, see Corey *The Decline of American Capitalism* (New York: Corici-Friede 1934) 517-19, 525-6, 535-8, and John Tipple *Crisis of the American Dream: A History of American Social Thought 1920-1940* (New York: Pegasus 1978).
28 Col. Charles P. Stacey to author May 1979
29 See 'Miracle That's Changing Nova Scotia' *Mayfair* (July 1953) 30
30 'Sunset and Evening Star' *Montrealer* 29 (Oct. 1955) 23; H.M. to Leonard Cohen 13 Feb. 1955
31 Ronald Bottrall to author 9 May 1980
32 Duncan *Bluenose* 70
33 H.M. to author 16 Feb. 1980
34 'The Future Trend in the Novel' *Canadian Author and Bookman* 24 (Sept. 1948) 4
35 'So All Their Praises' unpublished ms. (McG) box 3, part 1, folders 1-2, pp. 32, 238, 245, 263
36 *Ibid.* 147, 154, 249, 112
37 *Ibid.* 147, 163, 165
38 H.M., notation on ms. of 'So All Their Praises'
39 Duncan *Bluenose* 69, 70
40 H.M. to author 24 June 1979
41 Duncan *How to Live in an Apartment* (New York: Farrar & Rinehart 1939) 10. Although Dorothy assigns her husband the pseudonym 'Michael' in this book, specific details of education, travel, job, and current residence are MacLennan's.
42 'So All Their Praises' 152-3
43 'History – What Is It?' *Montrealer* 30 (June 1956) 31
44 (Oxford: Oxford University Press 1926)
45 'History' 31
46 H.M. to Edmund Wilson 15 June 1967
47 H.M. to J.F. Leddy 3 Oct. 1979
48 H.M. to Wilson 15 June 1967
49 (Princeton: Princeton University Press 1935); (Amsterdam: A.M. Hakkert 1968, Chicago: Argonaut 1968)
50 H.M. to Wilson 15 June 1967
51 'History' 31; 'The Trained Mind in a Democratic Society' Graduate School Alumni Conference, Princeton University, 1-3 Jan. 1953
52 'Roman History and Today' *Dalhousie Review* 15 (1935-6) 67-79
53 For Beard's theory, representative of the New History, see Ellen Nore 'Charles A. Beard's Act of Faith: Context and Content' *Journal of American History* 66 no 4 (March 1980) 850-66

54 'Roman History and Today' 68-71
55 'A Man Should Rejoice' unpublished ms. (McG) box 3, part 2, folders 3-9, p. 2
56 H.M. to J.F. Leddy 3 Oct. 1979
57 'Rejoice' 56-9
58 H.M. to Barrett 5 March 1935
59 H.M. to author 16 Feb. 1980
60 Duncan *Bluenose* 69, 76, 77-8, 90-1, 78, 79

4 Becalmed: Lower Canada College

1 'A Message from Hugh MacLennan' *Program '70 for Lower Canada College* (1970) 1
2 'Montreal' *Montrealer* 31 (Aug. 1957) 28. His reference is to André Siegfried *Le Canada, les deux races: problèmes politiques contemporains* (Paris: Librairie Armand Colin 1906) [*The Race Question in Canada* (London: Eveleigh Nash 1907)].
3 'The Best-Loved Street in Canada' *Mayfair* (Oct. 1953) 35, and 'Montreal' 28
4 Penton *Non Nobis Solum* (Montreal: Corporation of Lower Canada College 1972) 53-5
5 H.M. to John Gray 15 Dec. 1960
6 *The Watch That Ends the Night* (Toronto: Macmillan 1959) 107-18, 103, 114
7 Walter McBroom to author 21 May 1976; Stephen Penton to author 17 May 1976
8 'The Thankless Profession' *Canadian Home Journal* (Nov. 1949) 29, 30
9 Storrs McCall to author March 1978
10 Penton *Non Nobis Solum* 147
11 H.M. to Block 24 Feb. 1942 (property of Victor Block)
12 Penton *Non Nobis Solum* 147
13 H.M. to Barrett 5 March 1935
14 'A Man Should Rejoice' unpublished ms. (McG) box 3, part 2, folders 3-9, pp. 32, 31, 7, 84, 86, 437, 452-3, 463, 2, chap. 14 first paragraph
15 *Ibid.* 318, chap. 25 second page
16 H.M. to Barrett 29 March 1936
17 Duncan *Here's to Canada!* (New York: Harper's 1941) 23
18 Duncan 'Portrait of an Author' *Mayfair* 29 (Aug. 1955) 59; 'The Torrents of Swing' *Lower Canada College Magazine* (June 1937) 23-8
19 Duncan *Bluenose: A Portrait of Nova Scotia* (New York: Harper's 1942), 109, 113, 106, 114
20 H.M. to author 3 Oct. 1980, Frank Scott to author May 1975. For a fuller discussion of the CCF at this time, see Walter D. Young *The Anatomy of a*

Party: The National CCF, 1932-61 (Toronto: University of Toronto Press 1969).

21 H.M. to Barrett 29 March 1936
22 H.M. to author Sept. 1975
23 'And Seeing the Multitudes' *Lower Canada College Magazine* (Feb. 1937) 9-14; H.M., notes made in Russia 1937 (McG) box 1, part 2, folder 4, no 3; H.M. to Barrett 29 Aug. 1937
24 Norman Penner to author Nov. 1979; *The Watch That Ends the Night* 286
25 H.M. to Barrett 29 Aug. and 26 Sept. 1937, 16 Feb. 1938
26 H.M. to Barrett 16 Feb. 1938
27 Anon. 'Reader's Report' 6 Nov. 1937 (McG)
28 H.M. to Barrett 16 Feb. 1938
29 H.M. to author 7 Jan. 1976
30 H.M. to S.M. 18 March, 31 July 1939 (Cal)
31 H.M. to author 7 Jan. 1976
32 H.M. to S.M. 16 Sept., 7 April, 18 March 1939 (Cal)
33 H.M. to author 4 Nov. 1977
34 'Roman History and Today' *Dalhousie Review* 15 (1935-6) 75
35 'Augustus' unpublished ms. (McG) box 3, part 1, no 11, pp. 6, 24, 31
36 H.M. to S.M. 18 March, 16 Sept. 1939 (Cal)
37 'Literature in a New Country' *Scotchman's Return and Other Essays* (Toronto: Macmillan 1960) 140-1

5 The Breakthrough: 'Barometer Rising'

1 'A Man Should Rejoice' unpublished ms. (McG) box 3, part 2, folders 3-9, pp. 62, 63-4, 66, 107-8, 120
2 'How We Differ from Americans' *Maclean's* 59 (15 Dec. 1946) 54; Duncan *Bluenose: A Portrait of Nova Scotia* (New York: Harper's 1942) 189-90
3 'Canada for Canadians' *Vogue* (15 May 1947) 136
4 Bissell 'The Novel' *Arts in Canada* ed. Malcolm Ross (Toronto: Macmillan 1958) 92
5 Callaghan *That Summer in Paris: Memories of Tangled Friendships with Hemingway, Fitzgerald, and Some Others* (Toronto: Macmillan 1963)
6 See Carl Berger *The Sense of Power: Studies in the Ideas of Canadian Imperialism, 1867-1914* (Toronto: University of Toronto Press 1970) 62.
7 Creighton 'Towards the Discovery of Canada' *University of Toronto Quarterly* 25 (1955-6) 276
8 Claxton, as cited by Margaret E. Prang 'Nationalism in Canada's First Century' *Historical Papers of the Canadian Historical Association* (1968) 116. For a full discussion, see C.P. Stacey 'Nationality: The Experience of Canada' *ibid.* (1967) 10-19.

9 Duncan 'Portrait of an Author' *Mayfair* (Aug. 1955) 59; *Bluenose* 68, 190; *Here's to Canada!* (New York: Harper's 1941) 3-4
10 The last chapters of 'A Man Should Rejoice' are reminiscent of Hemingway's ending in *A Farewell to Arms*. For a clear outline and diagrams of the events leading up to the explosion, see 'The Biggest Blast before the A-Bomb' *Popular Mechanics* (Dec. 1967) 81-3.
11 H.M. to author 7 Jan. 1976
12 *Barometer Rising* (New York: Duell, Sloan and Pearce 1941) 91, 82, 144
13 *Ibid.* 208
14 *Ibid.* 45. MacLennan himself believed something along these lines in relation to the Second World War; in a letter to George Barrett on 24 May 1940 he stated: 'even though Hitler may win, I believe there is bound to be a profound revulsion against him among his own people.'
15 *Barometer Rising* 4, 50-1, 6, 8
16 *Ibid.* 300, 311, 310, 325
17 G.M. Grant, for example, even before the turn of the century had said that Canada's '"divine mission" was to create a British North American nationality which would become a "living link" ... between Britain and the United States.' See Berger *The Sense of Power* 171.
18 J.S. Southron 'Latest Works of Fiction' *Times* 5 Oct. 1941; F.T. Marsh 'Barometer Rising' *Herald Tribune* 12 Oct. 1941
19 G.G. 'Montreal Writer Pens Stirring Novel of Wartime Halifax' *Montreal Standard* 18 Oct. 1941; McPherson 'Novel on Halifax Has Punch' *Windsor Daily Star* 11 Oct. 1941; Davies 'Disaster and a Canadian Family' *Saturday Night* (11 Oct. 1941); Deacon 'Critical Novel of Wartime Halifax' *Globe and Mail* 11 Oct. 1941; H.M. to Barrett 16 Nov. 1942
20 *Barometer Rising* 120. This analogy is noted and explored by Joan Coldwell 'Shakespeare in the Global Village' *Ideas* radio series (4 Feb. 1972) CBC Toronto 720204-1
21 Kenner as cited by Watt 'Nationalism in Canadian Literature' *Nationalism in Canada* ed. Peter Russell (Toronto: McGraw-Hill 1966) 247
22 *University of Toronto Quarterly* 11 (1941-2); *Canadian Forum* 21 (Dec. 1941); *McGill Quarterly* (Winter 1941); *Globe and Mail* 11 Oct. 1941; Montreal *Gazette* 11 Oct. 1941
23 Mackinnon to H.M. 17 Jan. 1942 (Cal)
24 H.M. to Marian Engel 8 July 1957, to author 29 Sept. 1976
25 Purkis 'Our Service Forces Enjoy These Canadian Books' *Book News from Collins* (1941)
26 Anon. 'Halifax TNT – Ship Explosion "Barometer Rising" Climax' *Toronto Star* 4 Oct. 1941
27 'My First Book' *Canadian Author and Bookman* 28 (Summer 1952) 3-4

28 H.M. to John Gray 27 May 1950
29 'A Boy Meets a Girl in Winnipeg and Who Cares?' *Montrealer* 33 (Feb. 1959) 18-20
30 Rand to H.M. 20 Feb., 19 March 1944 (McG)
31 Grove to H.M. 20 Nov. 1941 (Cal); see also *The Letters of F.P. Grove* ed. Desmond Pacey (Toronto: University of Toronto Press 1976) 415-16.
32 Bottrall to H.M. [16 March] 1944 (McG); H.M. to Barrett 20 Oct. 1941
33 Lewis 'A Notable First Novel by Hugh MacLennan' *The Book Society* (London) 15 July 1942
34 'Postscript on Odysseus' *Canadian Literature* 13 (Summer 1962) 86-97. This essay is sometimes quoted under the title 'Comments on a Nation's Odyssey.' MacLennan read Woodcock's essay on his novels, but explained that he was not conscious of the Odysseus myth while writing, as Woodcock had suggested; he was conscious rather of people he saw going away and returning from the United States after they had made money.
35 Woodcock 'A Nation's Odyssey: The Novels of Hugh MacLennan' *Canadian Literature* 10 (Autumn 1961) 7-18; O'Donnell 'The Wanderer in *Barometer Rising*' *University of Windsor Review* 3 (Spring 1968) 12-18
36 *Barometer Rising* 204
37 Sarah F. Adams 'Nearer My God, To Thee' *The Hymn Book of the Anglican Church of Canada and the United Church of Canada* (1971) Hymn 254
38 H.M., application for a John Simon Guggenheim Fellowship 26 Oct. 1942 (McG) box 1, part 1, folder 1, no 57
39 'The Discovery of Canada as a Literary Scene' address to the University of Rochester [1955], unpublished ms. (McG) box 1, part 1, folder 3, nos 1-9, p. 8
40 H.M., application for Guggenheim 4
41 H.M. to E.D. Blodgett 15 March 1979 (property of E.D. Blodgett)
42 'Culture, Canadian Style' *Saturday Review of Literature* 25 (28 March 1942) 3-4, 18-20; 'Anniversary of an Idea' *Montreal Standard* (27 June 1942) 1-3, 8
43 Ross '"Culture, Canadian Style" – Some Lucubrations on the Subject of Literature, Art and Culture in This and Other Countries' *Ottawa Journal* 11 April 1942
44 'Culture' 3-4, 18
45 'Anniversary' 3, 8, 2
46 'Culture' 3-4. The general theory of literature from which MacLennan derived this category to describe the 'Yankee tradition' originated in a book sent to him by his publishers: David Thompson *Ten Heroes* (New York: Duell, Sloan and Pearce 1941).
47 H.M. to Charles Duell 23 June 1942 (Cal)

48 'Taxation Retards Canadian Writing' address to Dominion-Douglas Ladies' Literary Society 19 Feb. 1943. It may be assumed that the triple taxation MacLennan refers to was caused by the fact that his contract was with an American publisher with North American rights. His royalty on copies sold in Canada would have been based on the export price to Wm. Collins and Sons, the Canadian distributor, a considerably lower base than the retail price on which American royalties would have been based. Since Canada was, in effect, an export market for books published in the United States, import duties would be levied at the border. Finally, on sales of the book in the United States, his royalty income would have been subject to taxation at the source (that is, in the United States) as well as in Canada.
49 'Anniversary' 8; H.M. to Barrett 20 Oct. 1941
50 H.M. to Barrett 16 Nov. 1942

6 On Solid Ground: 'Two Solitudes'

1 *Canadian Unity and Quebec* (Montreal: CBC pamphlet 1942) 1-16
2 H.M. to Barrett 16 Nov. 1942, 20 Oct. 1941
3 'The Genesis of *Two Solitudes*' [ca. 1972] unpublished ms. (Cal) 2, 11
4 'How Do I Write?' *Canadian Author and Bookman* 21 (Dec. 1945) 6-7; H.M. to Barrett 16 Nov. 1942
5 This theory corresponds to Paul's view near the end of *Two Solitudes* (p. 329): 'The background would have to be created from scratch ... He would have to build the stage and props for his play, and then write the play itself.'
6 H.M. to Marian Engel 19 June 1956
7 H.M. to author 6 Sept. 1980; Ringuet *Trente Arpents* (Paris: Plammarion 1938) and *Thirty Acres* (Toronto: Macmillan 1940); see also Ben-Zion Shek *Social Realism in the French-Canadian Novel* (Montreal: Harvest House 1977).
8 'The Genesis of *Two Solitudes*' 1
9 *Ibid.* 4
10 'Note' *Two Solitudes* [1945] ms. (McG) box 2, part 2, folder 1, no 1; *Two Solitudes* ed. Claude Bissell (Toronto: Macmillan 1951)
11 *Two Solitudes* (New York: Duell, Sloan and Pearce 1945) 301, 350, 328-9, 330
12 *Ibid.* 338-9, 370
13 *Ibid.* 61, 273
14 *Ibid.* 75, 126-7

15 H.M. to E.D. Blodgett 15 March 1979 (property of E.D. Blodgett)
16 W.L. Graff to H.M. 7 June 1944 (McG)
17 *Two Solitudes* 153, 28, 370
18 *Ibid.* 175-6, 61
19 *Ibid.* 103, 70. F.R. Scott felt that MacLennan had been 'too easy' on English capitalists in his novel (to author May 1975).
20 MacLennan was amused that the cover for Macmillan's Laurentian Library paperback edition of *Two Solitudes* showed McQueen with the features of Mackenzie King (H.M. to Gray 14 Nov. 1967); 'Culture, Canadian Style' *Saturday Review of Literature* 25 (28 March 1942) 4; H.M. to Dorothy Dumbrille, author of *All This Difference* (1945) 2 Jan. 1946 (Douglas Library, Queen's University); 'The Ten Greatest Canadians' *New Liberty* (Nov. 1949) 13 – the other nine were Samuel de Champlain, Count Frontenac, Joseph Howe, Donald McKay, Sir John A. Macdonald, Sir William Osler, Sir Wilfrid Laurier, Tom Thomson, and Sir Frederick Banting.
21 Duncan *Partner in Three Worlds* (New York: Harper's 1944) 339, 335, 339
22 Prescott 'Books of the Times' *Times* 17 Jan. 1945; H.M. to Deacon 22 Jan. 1946
23 H.M. to Dumbrille 26 Oct. 1945
24 'Literature in a New Country' *Scotchman's Return* (Toronto: Macmillan 1960) 140; H.M. to Barrett 20 Oct. 1941
25 *Morning Globe*, Boston 18 Jan. 1945; *Sun*, New York 23 Jan. 1945; *Dispatch*, Columbus 4 Feb. 1945; *Record* Philadelphia 4 Feb. 1945; *Saturday Review of Literature* 28 (10 March 1945); H.R. Pinckard 'Clashing of Worlds North of Border' *Advertiser* Huntington, West Virginia 11 March 1945; Stanley Anderson 'Novel by MacLennan Clarifies Dominion' *Press*, Cleveland 23 Jan. 1945; Michael Roberts 'Canada's Two Peoples' *People's World*, San Francisco 14 Feb. 1945; A.B. Parsons 'Near-Great Canadian Novel' *New Leader*, New York 28 April 1945; Lisle Bell 'Books and Things' *Hollywood Reporter* 17 Jan. 1945; Adams 'Speaking of Books' *Times* 19 May 1946
26 Kennedy 'Old and New Canada in a Major Novel; Quebec's Races, Creeds and Castes in Conflict and Cooperation' *Chicago Sun Book Week* 21 Jan. 1945; Denison 'Where Two Civilizations Meet' *Saturday Review of Literature* 28 (10 March 1945) – (Denison reviewed by H.M. in 'The Muse of Eloquence ... or ... the Eloquence of Money' *Canadian Author and Bookman* 42 no 2 [Winter 1966] 13-14); Wade 'Almost the Great Canadian Novel; the Best Yet Written' *Canadian Register* 28 April 1945; Eleanor McNaught 'Books of the Month' *Canadian Forum* (May 1945); Deacon 'French-Canadian Problem in Daring and Timely Novel' *Globe and Mail* 7 April 1945

27 Morgan Powell 'Problem of French Canada Is Discussed with Candour' *Montreal Star* 31 March 1945; G.J. Fitzgerald 'Racial Problem' *Gazette* 31 March 1945; Duncan to Deacon 21 April 1945; Jean Berand 'Le Roman "Two Solitudes"' *La Presse* 14 April 1945; Albert Alain 'Two Solitudes' *Le Devoir* 28 April 1945; Abbé Arthur Maheux 'A Masterpiece: Un Chef d'oeuvre' *Montreal Star* 15 Sept. 1945; H.M. to Deacon 8 April 1945
28 Anon. 'A Major Novel' *Saturday Night* 60 (7 April 1945); I.M.S. 'Reviews of New Books' *Queen's Quarterly* 52 (Winter 1945) 494-6; Woodhead, as cited in 'Is It Classical?' editorial *Gazette*, Montreal 29 Sept. 1945
29 Duncan 'My Author Husband' *Maclean's* 58 (15 Aug. 1945); *Two Solitudes*, 28
30 Trilling 'Fiction in Review' *Nation* 24 Feb. 1945; Deacon 'French-Canadian Problem'; Anon. *Saturday Night*; I.M.S. *Queen's Quarterly*
31 H.M. to Deacon 8 April 1945, to Dorothy Dumbrille 26 Oct. 1945
32 Michael Roberts 'Serious Novel of Modern Canada' *Daily Worker* 6 Feb. 1945; 'Two Solitudes' *Le Devoir*; M.G. Ballantyne 'The Two Religions' *Canadian Register* 28 April 1945
33 René Lévesque *My Québec* trans. Gaynor Fitzpatrick (Toronto: Methuen 1979) 138
34 Florence H. Bullock 'Conflict of Canada's Cultures' *New York Herald Tribune* 21 Jan. 1945; Anon. 'Editor's Choice' *Commonweal* 16 June 1945; Pinckard 'Clashing of Worlds'
35 H.M. to Deacon 9 Sept. 1945
36 H.M. to Eva-Lis Wuorio 'Man of Tremendous Sincerity' *Globe and Mail* 29 June 1946
37 Duncan, scrapbooks 18 April 1945 (Cal)
38 H.M. to John Gray 15 Dec. 1960
39 Concerning French translation, see H.M. to Mr. Provost 27 Oct. 1952 (Cal); Duncan to Deacon 12 and 21 April 1945
40 'Everyone Knows the Rules' *Montrealer* (Dec. 1951) 66, 68-9
41 Duncan to Deacon 21 April 1945; 'Rose-Grower' *Montrealer* 28 (Sept. 1954) 23, 25, 27, 29
42 'Background for Original Story on Halifax' [ca. 1946] unpublished ms. (McG) box 2, part 1, folder 10
43 H.M. to Deacon 9 Sept. and 8 April 1945

7 Charting a Course: 'The Precipice'

1 H.M. to Deacon 18 May, 7 March 1946
2 'Canada between Covers' *Saturday Review of Literature* 29 (7 Sept. 1946) 5-6, 28-30

3 'Canada for Canadians' *Vogue* (15 May 1947) 136; H.M. to Deacon 28 April 1946; see also H.M. to Deacon 7 March 1946.
4 H.M. to Charles Duell 5 March 1947 (McG)
5 H.M. to John Gray 27 Dec. 1961, to Duell 5 March 1947
6 H.M. to Deacon 5 Dec. 1948; 'April in Canada' *Montrealer* 26 (April 1952) 52-3
7 H.M. to author 29 Sept. 1976; see also Elspeth Cameron 'Ordeal by Fire: The Genesis of Hugh MacLennan's *The Precipice*' *Canadian Literature* 82 (Autumn 1979) 35-46.
8 H.M. to Deacon 12 Jan. and 7 July 1948
9 H.M. to author 29 Sept. and 6 Jan. 1976
10 Anthony Tudor to author 6 Sept. 1976
11 Balanchine *Great Ballets* ed. Frances Mason (New York: Doubleday 1968) 307
12 *The Precipice* (New York: Duell, Sloan and Pearce 1948) 7-8, 21, 39, 23, 96
13 'Do We Gag Our Writers?' *MacLean's* 60 (1 March 1947) 55
14 MacLennan uses here the concept and terms used by J.B. Brebner in *North American Triangle* (Toronto: Ryerson 1945).
15 'How We Differ from Americans' *Maclean's* 59 (15 Dec. 1946)
16 Frederic Wakeman *The Hucksters* (New York: Rinehart 1946). Bratian turned out to be singularly inappropriate as it belonged to one of the most aristocratic families in Romania; see H.M. to Gray 15 Nov. 1960.
17 'Do We Gag Our Writers?' 55; 'Canada between Covers' 6
18 H.M. to Deacon 7 July 1948
19 H.M. to Deacon 12 Jan., 5 Dec. 1948
20 'The Halifax Explosion' *A Pocketful of Canada* ed. John D. Robins (Toronto: Collins 1946) 25-7
21 H.M. to Deacon 18 July, Deacon to H.M. 11 July 1948; Deacon 'Canadian Performs Smoothly in a Canadian-American Story' *Globe and Mail* 26 June 1948
22 Hutchens 'Books and Things' *Herald Tribune* 8 Sept. 1947; Prescott 'Books of the Times' *Times* 10 Sept. 1948
23 Kennedy 'Canadian Cinderella, American Heel' *Chicago Sun and Times* 14 Sept. 1948; William DuBois 'Tensions in Two Lives' *New York Times* 12 Sept. 1948; George Austen 'Barometer Falling' *Mayfair* (Sept. 1948); Dorothy Michel 'Many-Sided ...' *Philadelphia Inquirer* 12 Sept. 1948; John A. Weigel 'Americans Learn ...' *Herald*, Dayton, Ohio 2 Oct. 1948; Eleanor Clarage 'Dashing ...' *Plain Dealer*, Cleveland 12 Sept. 1948; Merrill Denison 'Surmounting ...' *Saturday Review of Literature* 31 (18 Sept. 1948); Denham Sutcliffe 'Theme' *Christian Science Monitor* 23 Sept. 1948
24 Duncan to Deacon 12 April 1945, H.M. to Gray 5 Oct. 1966

25 H.M. to 'Don' [Sutherland] 22 April 1969 (Macmillan)
26 H.M. to Marian Engel 19 June 1956, to author 20 Aug. 1979
27 Claire Keefer 'Novel of the Week' *Journal* 19 June 1948; Deacon 'Canadian Performs'
28 'Changing Values in Fiction' *Canadian Author and Bookman* 25 no 3 (Autumn 1949) 15
29 'What Future for a Creative Elite?' Empire Day Dinner, Canadian Society of New York 24 May 1949, unpublished ms. (Cal) box 1, folder 1.1, no 43; 'Elephant,' *Maclean's* 61 (15 Aug. 1948) 50-3; 'Uncle Sam' *ibid.* 60 (1 April 1948) 7-8, 53-7
30 'The Future Trend' *Canadian Author and Bookman* 24 (Sept. 1948) 3-5; 'Do We Gag Our Writers?' 52; 'Changing Values' 14-17

8 New Departures: 'Each Man's Son'

1 H.M. to Deacon 5 Dec. 1948
2 H.M. to Gray 27 May 1950
3 H.M. to Gray 23 May 1950
4 H.M. to Charles Duell 31 Dec. 1948, 8 Jan. 1949 (Cal)
5 H.M. to Henry A. Laughlin 26 Jan. 1949 (Cal)
6 H.M. to Deacon 7 July 1948
7 'Do We Gag Our Writers?' *Maclean's* 60 (1 March 1947) 54
8 H.M. to Deacon 18 July 1948
9 Gray to author 21 Oct. 1977
10 H.M. to Gray 23 and 27 May 1950
11 Isabel Dobell to author Aug. 1976; H.M. to Gray 12 Aug. 1950
12 H.M. to Gray 30 Dec. 1960
13 H.M. to Gray 13 and 22 June 1950
14 'My First Book' *Canadian Author and Bookman* 28 no 2 (Summer 1952) 4
15 H.M. to Gray 13 June, 12 and 17 Aug. 1950
16 H.M. to Gray 27 May 1950
17 Cameron to Isabel Syme 31 Aug. 1950 (Macmillan)
18 Cameron to H.M. 27 July (Macmillan); Gray to H.M. 2 Aug. 1950
19 Cameron to H.M. 27 July (Macmillan); Gray to H.M. 2 Aug.; H.M. to Gray 11 Oct. 1950
20 Harding 'Reader's Report' Sept. 1950 (Macmillan)
21 H.M. to Cameron 1 Oct. 1950 (Macmillan)
22 Harding 'Memo re: Each Man's Son' Oct. 1950 (Macmillan)
23 Cameron to H.M. 27 Oct. 1950 (Macmillan)
24 H.M. to Gray 3 Oct. 1950
25 H.M. to Gray 3 Oct. 1950

26 H.M. to Gray 13 June, 3 Oct. 1950; Gray to H.M. 15 Aug. 1950, H.M. to Deacon 7 March 1946
27 H.M. to Gray 11 and 17 Oct. 1950
28 H.M. to Gray 17 and 12 Aug., 16 July, 17 Oct. 1950
29 H.M. to Marian Engel 8 July 1957, 19 June 1956
30 'Power and Love' *Montrealer* (April 1951) 27, 29; 'A Layman Looks at Medical Men' *Canadian Doctor* (Dec. 1952) 34-9
31 'Author-Layman MacLennan Draws Fire' *Canadian Doctor* (Jan. 1953) 35-7; 'My Surgeon Father' *Bulletin of the American College of Surgeons* 44 (1959) 232
32 H.M. to Gray 3 Oct., Gray to H.M. 17 Oct., Cameron to H.M. 27 July 1950 (Macmillan)
33 Publicity campaign described in detail in memo from M. McAlpine to Gray 27 Feb. 1951 (Macmillan)
34 Gray to Lovat Dickson 10 April 1951 (Macmillan)
35 H.M. to Gray 13 June, 16 July 1950
36 H.M. to Gray 10 Nov. 1950
37 Prescott 'Books of the Times' *Times* 9 April 1951; Deacon 'Doctor in Mining Town on Cape Breton Island' *Globe and Mail* 21 April 1951; Allen 'Wish and Fulfillment' *Times* 15 April 1951; Woodcock 'Each Man's Son' *Northern Review* (Oct.-Nov. 1951); Austin F. Cross 'Clever Fiction Writer Can't Finish Book' *Ottawa Citizen* 21 July 1951; Hill 'Calvin's Far Shadow' *Gazette*, Montreal 21 April 1951; V.A.B. 'A Story of Great Power by Canadian Novelist' *Chicago News* 11 April 1951
38 H.M. to Deacon 3 July 1951
39 H.M. to author Feb. 1980, to Gray 21 July 1951
40 H.M. to Marian Engel 8 July 1957
41 The First of these was 'City of Two Souls' *Holiday* 12 (Aug. 1951) 48-55; also 'Nova Scotia' *ibid*. 14 (Sept. 1953) 98-108; 'Cape Breton, the Legendary Island' *Saturday Night* 66 (3 July 1951) 12-13; 'But Shaw Was a Playwright ...' *Montrealer* (July 1951) 19; H.M. to Gray 14 May 1951
42 Frank Upjohn to H.M. 24 May 1951 (Macmillan)
43 H.M. to Gray 14 and 20 July, 4 Aug. 1951
44 H.M. to Gray 3 Nov., 21 Dec. 1951, 5 Jan. 1953

9 Plumbing the Depths: 'The Watch That Ends the Night'

1 'City of Two Souls' *Holiday* 12 (Aug. 1951) 48-55; 'Montreal: The Mountain in the City' *Mayfair* 26 (June 1952) 43-5, 74; 'The Best-Loved Street in Canada' *ibid*. 27 (Oct. 1953) 74. Over the years he also wrote: 'The Art of City Living' *Saturday Night* 66 (22 Dec. 1951) 7, 36; 'And This Is His

City' *New Liberty* (Sept. 1952) 28-9, 67-8; untitled *Saturday Night* 68 (10 Jan. 1953) 7-8; untitled *ibid.* 68 (31 Jan. 1953) 7-8; untitled *Montrealer* 27 (Jan. 1953) 54-5; 'Required: A Major Operation' *Saturday Night* 68 (15 Aug. 1953) 12-13; 'When the Evening Sun Goes Down' *ibid.* 68 (10 Oct. 1953) 12-13; 'The Forum and the Finer Things' *ibid.* 68 (21 Nov. 1953) 24-5; 'A Chill along the Backbone' *ibid.* 69 (9 Jan. 1954) 5; 'On Agreeing to Disagree' *ibid.* 69 (13 Feb. 1954) 12; 'Cherished Dream of a Hick Town' *ibid.* 69 (24 April 1954) 19; 'Thrift Tour of Montreal' *Holiday* 15 (Aug. 1954) 12-15; 'A Shiver When an Era Ends' *Saturday Night* 69 (9 Oct. 1954) 9-11; 'Jean Drapeau and his New Mandate' *ibid.* 69 (11 Dec. 1954) 9-11; 'Monument for the Mayor?' *ibid.* 70 (1 Oct. 1955) 11-12; 'Montreal on Wheels' *ibid.* 72 (16 Feb. 1957) 16-17; 'Montrealer' *Montrealer* 31 (Aug. 1957) 28-31

2 H.M. to Gray 7 Dec. 1950, 10 June 1951

3 'Do We Gag Our Writers?' *Maclean's* 60 (1 March 1947) 52

4 'Shakespeare Revisited' *Montrealer* 29 (May 1955) 23

5 H.M. to Gray 7 Dec. 1950; see also 'The New Nationalism and How it Might Have Looked to Shakespeare' *Maclean's* 70 (11 Feb. 1957) 8, 49-52, and 'Hamlet with the Features of Horatio' [1963] unpublished ms. (McG) box 1, part 1, folder 9, nos 1-8.

6 'The Transition Ends' *Montrealer* 29 (Nov. 1955) 25, 27

7 Rudolf Ditzen *Little Man, What Now?* trans. Eric Sutton (New York: Simon and Schuster 1933); *The Watch That Ends the Night* (Toronto: Macmillan 1959), 343

8 H.M. to Gray 10 Dec. 1950; Waltari *The Egyptian* trans. Naomi Walford (New York: Putnam 1949)

9 H.M. to Gray 10 June 1951, 10 July and 5 Jan. 1953, 24 April 1952, 3 July 1951. This image may have come from Dorothy; in *Partner in Three Worlds* (New York: Harper's 1944) she had given the following words to her narrator Jan Rieger (p. 237): 'It was as though I were in a canoe which I had pushed away from shore. The act of pushing had been mine, but once the small craft entered the current, it was no longer my own force which took me on. I could make a mistake and upset the balance of the boat and fall into the water.'

10 H.M. to Gray 10 Dec. 1950, 3 Nov. 1951

11 'Fiction in the Age of Science' *Western Humanities Review* 6 (Autumn 1952) 325-34, 333; 'The Challenge to Prose' *Transactions of the Royal Society* 49, series 3, section 2 (June 1955) 45-55

12 H.M. to Gray 15 Oct., 12 June, 14 June, Gray to H.M. 18 June 1952

13 West *Black Lamb, Grey Falcon* (London: Macmillan 1941) 2 vols. (New York: Viking Press 1941); Chambers *Witness* (London: A. Deutsch 1953)

and (New York: Random House 1952); H.M. to Gray 12 June 1952; 'A Would-be Saint' *Montrealer* 26 (Aug. 1952) 52-3

14 H.M. to Gray 5 Jan. 1953, to Marian Engel 16 Nov. 1958

15 'And This Is His City' *New Liberty* (Sept. 1952) 28-9, 67-8; 'Everyone Knows the Rules' *Montrealer* (Dec. 1951) 66, 68-9; 'If You Drop a Stone' *ibid*. 26 (July 1952) 50-1

16 'Montaigne's Law' *Montrealer* 30 (Jan. 1956) 21; see also, all in the *Montrealer*, 'A Telegram under the Door' 27 (Aug. 1953) 50-1; 'Damnatio Memoriae' 30 (May 1956) 19; 'The Transition Ends' 29 (Nov. 1955) 27; 'The Finding of the Way' 29 (April 1955) 23, 25, 69; 'Remembrance Day' 31 (Dec. 1957) 46-55; 'The Albatross' 29 (March 1955) 17; 'Must We Return to 1933?' 28 (Jan. 1954) 19; 'What Can We Do About It?' 28 (May 1954) 17; 'Whatever It Was It Wasn't Munich' 28 (Sept. 1954) 19; 'Barometer Rising' 28 (Dec. 1954) 23; 'The Inevitable Clash' 27 (March 1953) 21; 'Symbol of Reality' 27 (May 1953) 21; 'An Eightieth Birthday' 28 (Dec. 1954) 27; 'The British Election' 29 (July 1955) 17; 'The Cyprus Tragedy' 30 (July 1956) 19.

17 'Why I'm Voting Liberal' *Maclean's* 66 (1 Aug. 1953) 8-9; and, all in the *Montrealer*, 'The Listless Election' 27 (Sept. 1953) 21; 'Will the Trance End This Year?' 28 (July 1954) 15; 'The Problem of Having No Problems' 29 (Aug. 1955) 17; 'Sir John' 29 (Dec. 1955) 25; 'The Glacier Melts At Last' 30 (Sept. 1956) 13; 'Canada's Revolution – WHY Did It Happen?' 32 (May 1958) 20-2; 'A New Era Is Recognized' 31 (Nov. 1957) 37-45; 'A Scotchman's Thanksgiving' 27 (Oct. 1953) 56

18 'The Homeric Tradition' *Montrealer* 29 (Sept. 1955) 21, 23; 'Good Old Human Nature' *ibid*. 26 (May 1952) 58-9; 'Modern Tennis' *ibid*. 27 (Nov. 1953) 54-5; 'Queen of Tourneys' *ibid*. 29 (Aug. 1955) 21, 23, 25; 'Fury on Ice' *Holiday* 15 (Dec. 1954) 83-4, 86, 88, 90-1, 174, 176, 178-80; 'Explosion and the Only Answer' *Saturday Night* 70 (9 April 1955) 9-10; 'Orgy at Oriel' *Montrealer* 26 (Oct. 1952) 56-7

19 All in the *Montrealer*, 'Anatomy of Humour' (May 1951) 23, 25; 'But Shaw Was a Playwright ...' (July 1951) 19; 'Everyone Knows the Rules' (Dec. 1951) 66, 68-9; 'Remembrance of Men Past' 29 (March 1955) 25, 27; 'By Their Foods ...' 30 (March 1956) 29-30; 'The Secret and Voluptuous Life of a Rose-Grower' 28 (Sept. 1954) 23, 25, 27, 29; 'Divertimento for Males' 28 (March 1954) 35, 37

20 H.M. to Earle Birney 12 April 1942 (UTL TF ms. 49); 'The Lost Love of Tommy Waterfield' *Montrealer* 29 (Jan. 1955) 21, 23, 25; 'An Orange from Portugal' *Chatelaine* (Dec. 1947) 17, 72-5; 'Christmas without Dickens' *Mayfair* 26 (Dec. 1952) 45, 66-8, 70; 'October and Smoke' *Montrealer* 30 (Oct. 1956) 20-2

21 'Joseph Haydn and Captain Bligh' *Montrealer* 27 (July 1953) 50-1; 'Confessions of a Wood-chopping Man' *ibid*. 30 (Nov. 1956) 22-4; 'Curtain Falls' *ibid*. 31 (Feb. 1957) 28-31; H.M. to Gray 1 Jan. 1957; 'The Writer and His Audience' *Montrealer* 28 (June 1954) 29; H.M. to Gray 12 June 1952
22 'The Artist and Critic in Society' *Princeton Alumni Weekly* 53 no 14 (30 Jan. 1953) 85-91; Duncan to Gray 6 Jan., H.M. to Gray 5 Jan. 1953
23 H.M., radio review of *From Here to Eternity* CBC (15 April 1951); 'Sunset and Evening Star' *Montrealer* 29 (Oct. 1955) 23, revised in *Scotchman's Return* (Toronto: Macmillan 1960) 240; 'The Artist and Critic' 86; 'The Stuff That Dreams Are Made On' *Montreal Star* 22 Dec. 1962
24 H.M. to Gray 24 April 1952, 'Homage to Hemingway' in *Thirty and Three* ed. Dorothy Duncan (Toronto: Macmillan 1954) 92-5
25 H.M. to Gray 17 April 1958, 30 Dec. 1955, 16 Jan. 1954
26 'The Present World As Seen through Its Literature' Founder's Day Address, University of New Brunswick, 18 Feb. 1952; 'Alan Paton' *Montrealer* 28 (Jan. 1954) 52-3
27 H.M. to Gray 21 Dec. 1951
28 'Back to Tolstoy' *Montrealer* 30 (Dec. 1956) 37-40; H.M. to Gray 1 Jan. 1957
29 H.M. to Frank Upjohn 10 July 1953 (Macmillan)
30 McPherson 'The Novels of Hugh MacLennan' *Queen's Quarterly* 60 (Summer 1953) 186-98; H.M. to Upjohn 10 July 1953
31 H.M. to Gray 26 Dec. 1953, 16 Jan. and 6 July 1954
32 H.M. to Gray 30 Dec. 1955, 1 Jan. 1957
33 H.M. to author 20 Nov. 1970, to Gray 25 Nov. 1957
34 'How Do I Write?' *Canadian Author and Bookman* 21 (Dec. 1945) 6
35 *The Watch That Ends the Night* 90
36 'The Story of a Novel' *Canadian Literature* 3 (Winter 1960) 35-9
37 'Back to Tolstoy' 40
38 H.M. to Upjohn 10 July 1953
39 'Victory' *The Other Side of Hugh MacLennan* ed. Elspeth Cameron (Toronto: Macmillan 1978) 177-83; Dorothy Duncan as quoted in 'Portrait of an Artist: Dorothy Duncan' *Montrealer* 31 (June 1957) 37
40 'Spring Show: Confusion Compounded' *Saturday Night* 68 (11 April 1953) 11 (in this show, 6 April-6 May 1956, Dorothy exhibited 'Yankee Façade' and 'First Light'); Duncan to Deacon 29 Jan. 1946, 21 April 1945
41 H.M. to Gray 25 Nov. 1957; *The Watch That Ends the Night* 330; the show was held 6-18 May 1957.
42 H.M. to Gray 15 June 1957
43 H.M. to Gray 28 Jan. 1958

44 Gray to H.M. 4 Feb. 1958
45 Davies 'MacLennan's Rising Sun' *Saturday Night* (28 March 1959) 29; see Blodgett 'Intertextual Designs in *The Watch That Ends the Night' Canadian Review of Comparative Literature* (Autumn 1978) 280-8; H.M. to Blodgett 15 March 1979 (property of E.D. Blodgett)
46 H.M. to Gray 8 and 21 March 1958
47 H.M. to Gray 28 Jan. 1958
48 H.M. to author 29 Jan. 1980
49 Keiichi Hirano 'Jerome Martell and Norman Bethune – A Note on Hugh MacLennan's *The Watch That Ends the Night' Studies in English Literature* 44 (1968) 37-59
50 Malcolmson *Ten Heroes* (New York: Duell, Sloan and Pearce 1941) 161
51 *The Watch That Ends the Night* 364-7
52 H.M. to Gray 21 March 1959, 16 July 1958; the verse referred to is immediately followed by the verse in which the phrase 'a watch in the night' occurs.
53 'Triumph, the Story of Man's Greatest Moment' *Montrealer* 31 (March 1957) 53-8; H.M. to Gray 15 Jan. 1958
54 H.M. to Marian Engel 19 June 1967
55 *The Watch That Ends the Night* 168-9
56 'Couth and Uncouth' *Montrealer* 29 (Feb. 1955) 21
57 H.M. to Gray 21 March 1958, to Engel 31 Oct. 1957
58 Gray to H.M. 11 Feb. 1958; Russell was also Earle Birney's agent at the time.
59 H.M. to Gray 9 Dec. 1957
60 H.M. to Gray 27 Feb. 1958, 21 March 1948, 8 March 1958
61 H.M. to Gray 8 March 1958; Isabel Dobell to author Aug. 1976
62 H.M. to Gray 8 March 1958
63 H.M. to Gray 9 March, Gray to H.M. 14 March 1958
64 Gray to H.M. 14 March, H.M. to Gray 13 April 1958
65 H.M. to Gray 28 Jan., 17 and 13 April 1958
66 H.M. to Gray 17 and 13 April 1958
67 H.M. to Engel 4 Sept. 1957
68 H.M. to Gray 16 July, Gray to H.M. 26 May 1958
69 H.M. to Gray 9 May, 20 and 16 July 1958
70 'The High and Mighty Mackenzie' *Maclean's* 72 (11 April 1959) 18-21, 53-4, 56-60; 'The Testing of Jerome Martell' *ibid*. 71 (6 Dec. 1958) 16-19, 54-6, 58; H.M. to Gray 16 July, 4 Aug. 1958
71 'O, God, Our Help in Ages Past' *The Hymn Book of the Anglican Church of Canada and the United Church of Canada* (1971) Hymn 133. The fourth stanza is worded as follows: 'A thousand ages in thy sight / are like an

evening gone, / short as the watch that ends the night / before the rising sun'; H.M. to Upjohn 27 Sept. 1958

72 H.M. to Gray 5 Nov. 1958, to Upjohn 27 Jan. 1959 (with information to be forwarded to Gray)

73 H.M. to Gray 1 Jan. 1953

74 Dusty Vineberg 'Novelist Sees Triumph for "Canadian" Works' *Edmonton Journal* 21 Nov. 1959; Prescott 'Books of the Times' *Times* 14 Feb. 1959; Prescott, as quoted by J.S.K. 'Canadian Author at the Summit of His Narrative Powers' *Victoria Daily Times* 19 June 1959; Elizabeth C. Winship 'The Watch That Ends the Night' *Boston Globe* 8 March 1959; Niebuhr, as quoted by J.S.K. (as above); Anon. 'The Watch That Ends The Night' *New Statesman* 19 Dec. 1959; Hugo McPherson 'Long Night's Watch Ends with Wisdom' *Toronto Daily Star* 21 Feb. 1959; William Ready 'Canadian "American Tragedy"' *Milwaukee Journal* 31 March 1959

75 Robert A. O'Brien 'Canadian Types in Travail' *Kingston Whig-Standard* 7 March 1959; Anon. 'The Watch That Ends the Night' *In-Town Weekly*, Randolph, Mass. 28 May 1959; McPherson 'Long Night's Watch'; McPherson, Layton, and Woodcock *Anthology* CBC Radio review (24 April 1959); H.M. to Gray 27 April 1959

76 Dumbrille 'The Watch That Ends the Night' *Cornwall Standard-Freeholder* 28 Feb. 1959; Kermode Parr 'The Watch That Ends the Night' *Atlantic Advocate* (March 1959) 77; Davies 'MacLennan's Rising Sun' *Saturday Night* (March 1959)

77 Deacon 'MacLennan Launching Lunch' *Globe and Mail* 21 Feb. 1959

78 'New York, New York ...' *Montrealer* 32 (March 1958) 28, 31, 33-4. In an article in the *Winnipeg Free Press* in Aug. 1959, Thomas Saunders compared *Doctor Zhivago* to *The Watch That Ends The Night* to MacLennan's advantage.

79 H.M. to Nowlan 5 Oct. 1959 (Cal)

80 H.M. to Vineberg 'Novelist Sees Triumph'

81 H.M. to Maurice Dolbier 'A First Rate Canadian Writing Man' 9 Aug. 1959 (Cal) 5:52

82 H.M. to Gray 15 Jan. 1958, 8 July 1957, 13 April 1958

10 Storm at Sea: 'Return of the Sphinx'

1 Court proceedings, Carleton County Court (17 Feb. 1956) 197, and Superior Court of Quebec, Montreal (12 April 1960) 30; see also 'The Defence of Lady Chatterly' *Canadian Literature* 6 (Autumn 1960) 18-23

2 Gray to H.M. 15 Dec. 1961

3 'Hamlet with the Features of Horatio' [1963] unpublished ms. (McG) box 1, part 1, folder 9, nos 1-8; H.M. to Gray 19 Feb. 1961
4 *Scotchman's Return* (Toronto: Macmillan 1960); *McGill: The Story of a University* ed. H.M. (London: George Allen and Unwin 1961) – the articles are 'McGill Today' 15-25, and 'The Origins of McGill' 27-48; *Seven Rivers of Canada* (Toronto: Macmillan 1961)
5 H.M. to author 20 Jan. 1981
6 Tota MacLennan to author 2 May 1976
7 For example, he wrote to Gray on 29 Sept. 1961: 'The state of the world in August was not sympathetic to writing fiction.'
8 'Krushchev and the American Election' *Montrealer* 30 (Aug. 1956) 35; 'Why I'm Voting Liberal' *Maclean's* 66 (1 Aug. 1957) 8-9, 50-1
9 'The Genesis of *Two Solitudes*' [ca. 1972] unpublished ms. (Cal) 11; 'Quebec Forgets Its Old Fears' *Saturday Night* 71 (14 April 1956) 11-13
10 'Quebec vs Donald Gordon' *Saturday Night* 71 (July 1956) 10-11; 'Quebec Universities: Politics vs Need' *ibid.* 71 (8 Dec. 1956) 13-15; 'Is Quebec Still the Key to Canadian Politics?' *ibid.* 72 (20 July 1957) 10-11, 38; 'French Is a *Must* for Canadians' *Imperial Oil Review* 44 no 3 (June 1960) 2-5
11 'One Canada' *Maclean's* 74 (26 Aug. 1961) 15, 32-4
12 'It's the U.S. or Us' *Maclean's* 73 (Nov. 1960); 'Anti-Americanism in Canada' *Harper's* (March 1961) 16; 'Hugh MacLennan's Personal Brief to the Royal Commission on Publications' *Canadian Library Association Bulletin* 17 (March 1961) 235-42
13 'One Canada' 33; 'What the Non-Believer Believes' *Exchange: A Canadian Review of Contemporary Thought* 2 (Feb.-March 1962) 24; 'The Spirit of Contemporary Quebec' address to the Vancouver Institute, University of British Columbia (4 Nov. 1961) 15; Laurendau as quoted by MacLennan in this address
14 'Spirit' 2, 4; 'Contemporary Events and Malraux's Novel' *Montreal Star* 4 May 1963; 'When Montreal Refused to Hate' *ibid.* 15 June 1963
15 H.M. to author 20 Aug. 1980
16 'After 300 Years ...' *Canada* ed. Kilbourn (Toronto: Macmillan 1970) 8-13; '*National Independence* ...'pamphlet (Toronto 1962)
17 'More Important Than the Bomb' address, McMaster University 5 Nov. 1965 *McMaster News* 35 no 4 (Fall 1965)
18 'Fifty Grand' *Montrealer* 31 (May 1957) 37-41; 'A Middle-aged Man Looks at Youth' *ibid.* 28 (April 1954) 29, 31; 'Couth and Uncouth' *ibid.* 29 (Feb. 1955) 19, 21, 23; 'It Pays to Pamper Our Children' *Maclean's* 69 (21 July 1956) 4, 46-8

19 H.M. to Marian Engel 17 March 1961
20 'It Pays to Pamper' 4; 'The Collapse of the Family' *Montrealer* 33 (Jan. 1959) 16-18; 'The Classical Tradition and Education' *Scotchman's Return*, and *Horizon* (Nov. 1960) 16-24; 'The Artist in the 1960's' [1961] unpublished ms. (McG) box 2, part 1, folder 6, no 12
21 'More Important Than the Bomb' 8, 18; 'It Pays to Pamper' 47
22 H.M. to Gray 30 Dec. 1960
23 Taylor *Sex in History* (New York: Vanguard Press 1953) 83-4. For a full discussion of sources, see Elspeth Cameron '*Return of the Sphinx*: Oedipal Origins' *Journal of Canadian Fiction* (March 1980)
24 Malcolmson *Ten Heroes* (New York: Duell, Sloan and Pearce 1941)
25 'On Living in a Cold Country' *The Other Side of Hugh MacLennan* ed. Elspeth Cameron (Toronto: Macmillan 1978) 205-13, and 'On Living with the Winter in the Country' [1961] unpublished ms. (McG) box 2, part 1, folder 6, no 11, and folder 8, nos 14-25; 'The Thing We Are All Thinking About' [Sept. 1961] *ibid*. folder 7, nos 16-30, 32-7, 57-78; H.M. to Gray 17 May 1961; 'Reflections on the "Bounty" Myth' *Montreal Star* 29 Dec. 1962; H.M. to Marian Engel 24 Jan. 1964
26 'Reflections on Sex in History' *Montreal Star* 8 Sept. 1962
27 H.M. to Gray 3 Sept. 1963
28 'The Spirit of Contemporary Quebec' 2; H.M. to Engel 24 Jan. 1964
29 'France and Its Provinces' *Speaking Personally* CBC Radio (4 Aug. 1964) no 640804-2 and 640804-0(2)
30 H.M. to Gray 21 Jan. 1964
31 'Return of the Sphinx' [1963] unpublished ms. (Cal) box 3, folder 2, no 1
32 'The Stuff That Dreams Are Made On' *Montreal Star* 22 Dec. 1962
33 H.M. to Gray 15 July, 14 Sept., 5 and 27 Oct. 1966
34 H.M. to Gray 25 Aug. 1967; Schneider *The Psychoanalyst and the Artist* (New York: International Universities Press 1954). MacLennan appears not to have considered the much better study on the same subject: Ernst Kris *Psychoanalytic Exploration in Art* (New York: Schoken Press 1952).
35 *The Watch That Ends the Night* (Toronto 1959) 245; *Two Solitudes* (New York 1945) 176; 'A New Era Is Recognized' *Montrealer* 31 (Nov. 1957) 37-45; 'Canada's Revolution – WHY Did It Happen?' *ibid*. 32 (May 1958) 20-2
36 *Return of the Sphinx* (Toronto: Macmillan 1967) 5, 170, 34
37 For a full account of this storm, see Gordon E. Dunn and Banner I. Miller *Atlantic Hurricanes* (Louisiana State University Press 1964) 360-1
38 *Return of the Sphinx* 74, 51, 74-5, 76
39 *Ibid*. 43; 'Return of the Sphinx' [1963] 18, 23, 2
40 *Return of the Sphinx* 266, 258, 37, 293; H.M. to Gray 31 Aug. 1967

41 H.M. to Keith Gilley 16 June 1967 (Cal)
42 H.M. to Gray 13 Jan. 1965
43 H.M. to Gray 26 Dec. 1966; For a brief treatment of the Greek tragic pattern in the novel, see Louis Dudek 'Hugh MacLennan's New Novel' *Gazette* 9 Sept. 1967.
44 H.M. to Gray 8 July 1957
45 H.M. to Gray 14 Sept., 5 Oct. 1966
46 Wilson *O Canada* (New York: Farrar, Straus and Giroux 1964) 59-80; Wilson to H.M. 23 July 1967 (Cal)
47 Gray to H.M. 25 Oct. 1966
48 H.M. to Gray 20 Aug. 1967; Legate 'Point Counterpoint' *Montreal Star* 20 Aug. 1967; Newman to H.M. 20 Aug. 1967 (Cal); H.M. to Gray 20 Aug. 1967
49 H.M. to Don Sutherland 22 Aug. 1967 (Macmillan); Gray to H.M. 22 Aug. 1967
50 Fulford 'The Saddest Book of Our Centennial Summer' *Star* 19 Aug. 1967; Callaghan 'MacLennan's Latest: Stuffy, Lifeless, Platitudinous' *Telegram* 19 Aug. 1967; Gzowski *Maclean's* (Sept. 1967); Fulford's review of the earlier book is 'MacLennan Is Unsatisfying in "7 Rivers of Canada"' *Star* 9 Dec. 1961.
51 H.M. to Gray 23 Oct. 1967; MacLennan had praised Gzowski's article on French Canada in 1963 in *Maclean's* as 'accurate and balanced' (3 Sept. 1963 to Gray).
52 Gray to Gzowski 25 Aug. 1967 (Macmillan)
53 Carroll 'Compassion Saves a Tract for the Times' *Globe and Mail* 19 Aug. 1967; Edinborough 'The Unsynchronized Sphinx' *Saturday Night* (Oct. 1967) 49; Wolverton 'Return of the Jinx' *Vancouver Province* 18 Aug. 1967
54 Fraser 'Two Solitudes Updated' *Gazette* 26 Aug. 1967; Kattan 'Le Mystère des Deux Solitudes' *Le Devoir* 26 Aug. 1967
55 Roberts, radio review of *Return of the Sphinx* 9 Aug. 1967; Jamie Portman 'Gripping Debate on Canada Today' *Calgary Herald Magazine* 18 Aug. 1967; Stratford and Marcotte 'Des Livres et des Hommes' Radio Canada (French network of CBC) 8 Oct. 1967; Bishop 'A Novel of the Week' *Ottawa Journal* 31 Aug. 1967
56 Peter Buitenhuis 'Father and Son, French and English' *New York Times* 20 Aug. 1967; see also G.H. Pouder 'The Turbulence in Canada' *Baltimore Sunday Sun* 20 Aug. 1967; T. O'Leary 'Look to MacLennan If You Would Know Canada' *Kansas City Star* 27 Aug. 1967; Edmund Fuller 'The Bookshelf: Canada and Change' *Wall Street Journal* 12 Sept. 1967
57 Anon. 'Books in Review' *Citizen-Advertiser*, Auburn, New York 22 July 1967

58 *Book Buyer's Guide* (Aug.); see also James Powers 'Book Reviews' *Hollywood Reporter* 28 July 1967; C.B. Jones 'Top Fiction' *San Francisco Chronicle* 1 Aug. 1967; Seymour Raiz 'MacLennan's "Sphinx" Loud in Talent' *Cleveland Press* 1 Aug. 1967; Milton Crane 'On the Right Side of the Frontier' *Chicago Tribune* 27 Aug. 1967; Dayton Rommel 'Superb Tale of Canadian Conflict' *Chicago Daily News* 27 Aug. 1967

59 Charles A. Brady 'Canadian's Sixth Novel ...' *Buffalo Evening News* 5 Aug. 1967; Herbert L. Kreuger 'Universal Timeliness' *Worcester Sun Telegram* 20 Aug. 1967; Scott Donaldson 'If It Could Happen ...' *Minneapolis Tribune* 24 Aug. 1967

60 Brady *ibid.*; W.G. Rogers 'Book of the Week' *Saturday Review* (19 Aug. 1967); Tyler 'Of the Land Too Vast Even for Fools to Ruin It' *Detroit News* 20 Aug. 1967; Donaldson *ibid.*

61 S.M. 'Nation's Agony' *Newsweek* 28 Aug. 1967; Paul Pickrel 'A Stegner, a MacLennan and a Sontag' *Harper's* (Sept. 1967)

62 H.M. to Gray 23 Aug. 1967

63 H.M. to Jim Bacque 15 Nov. 1967 (Macmillan)

64 H.M. to Gray 23 Oct., 31 Aug., 17 Nov. 1967

65 [Place des Arts brochure] ms. [1967] (Cal) box 1, folder 1, no 33; 'The Night before Expo Opened' *Viewpoint* CBC TV 26 April 1967, and 'The Night Expo Closed' *ibid.* 30 Oct. 1967 (Cal) box 1, folder 1.1, nos 17-19, 20; *The Colour of Canada* (Toronto: McClelland and Stewart 1967); H.M. to Gray 12 Oct. 1966

66 H.M. to Dubarry Campeau 'Hugh MacLennan' *Telegram*, Toronto 18 Nov. 1967

67 Gray to H.M. 14 Nov. 1967

68 H.M. to Gray 23 Aug. 1967; Fulford 'Other Views of Hugh MacLennan' *Toronto Star* 14 Nov. 1967

69 Legate 'Man and His Literature' *Montreal Star* 30 Dec. 1967; Dudek 'Hugh MacLennan's New Novel' *Gazette* 9 Sept. 1967

70 H.M. to Gray 15 Nov. 1967

11 Through Time and Space: 'Voices in Time'

1 H.M. to Gray 25 Oct. 1965. The five books on MacLennan are George Woodcock *Hugh MacLennan* (Toronto: Copp Clarke 1969); Alec Lucas *Hugh MacLennan* (Toronto: McClelland and Stewart 1970); Peter Buitenhuis *Hugh MacLennan* (Toronto: Forum House 1971); Robert Cockburn *The Novels of Hugh MacLennan* (Montreal: Harvest House 1971); Patricia Morley *The Immoral Moralists: Hugh MacLennan and Leonard Cohen* (Toronto: Clarke Irwin 1972). The only previous full-length study was a

German doctoral thesis by Paul Goetsch, published as *Das Romanwerk Hugh MacLennans: Eine Studie zum Literarischen Nationalismus in Kanada* (Hamburg: Cram, de Gruyter & Co. 1961).

2 H.M. to Gray 25 July 1977

3 This speech was given 17 May 1969 and was later published in *The Struggle for Canadian Universities* ed. R. Mathews and J. Steele (Toronto: New Press 1969) 141-51.

4 'Reflections ...' *Canadian Literature* 41 (Summer 1969) 28-39; 'Thirty Years ...' Liberal Arts Lecture Series, University of Waterloo 20 Jan. 1970; 'Two Solitudes 33 Years Later' *Queen's Alumni Review* (March-April 1978) 4-9 (originally an address in French at the Université du Québec at Chicoutimi 3 March 1977); concerning the election, see Ron Haggart 'Which Star Did As Badly As You?' *Telegram*, Toronto 6 July 1968.

5 H.M. to Davies 14 Jan. 1971 (Cal)

6 H.M. to Donald Cameron *Conversations with Canadian Novelists* 1 (Toronto: Macmillan 1973) 140; H.M. to Gray 23 Oct. 1967

7 H.M. to author 29 May 1980, 20 Aug. 1979, 16 Jan. 1980, 25 Aug. 1974

8 Edmund Wilson *O Canada: An American's Notes on Canadian Culture* (New York: Farrar, Straus and Giroux 1964) 75

9 H.M. to Robert Ardrey 4 May 1969 (Cal)

10 Ardrey *African Genesis* (New York: Atheneum 1973) 173, 32

11 'The Crisis in the Human Psyche' Canadian Club, Vancouver 31 May 1968 (Cal); 'Congregation Address' University of British Columbia 29 May 1968 (Cal)

12 H.M. to Trudeau 7 April 1968 (Cal); Lester Cowan to Robert O'Brien 10 Oct. 1968 (Cal)

13 H.M. to Gray 6 July 1968

14 H.M. to Don Sutherland 22 Nov. 1970 (Macmillan)

15 'Quebec Crisis Bares the Agony of Youth' *Telegram*, Toronto 21 Nov. 1970

16 H.M. to Trudeau 1 Nov. 1970 (Cal)

17 'Literature and Technology or the Two Consciences' *Toronto Star* 'Other Voices' lecture series 29 Feb. 1972; also Sedgewick Memorial Lecture, University of British Columbia 1 March 1973

18 H.M. to Sutherland 9 Dec. 1970 (Macmillan)

19 H.M. to author 20 Aug. 1978

20 H.M. to Gray 23 Oct. 1967, to Davies 14 Jan. 1971 (Cal)

21 H.M. to Cameron *Conversations* 139

22 H.M. to Ready 29 May (property of Ready), to Leddy, 3 Oct. (property of Leddy), to author 17 and 2 Nov. 1979

23 H.M. to author 16 Jan. 1980

24 Douglas Gibson to author Feb. 1980

25 Gibson to H.M. 18 Feb. 1980 (property of Gibson)
26 H.M. to author 1 March 1980
27 'The Finding of the Way' *Montrealer* 29 (April 1955) 23, 25, 69
28 'Remembrance Day: 2010' *ibid*. 31 (Dec. 1957) 46-55
29 H.M. to author Sept. 1975
30 'A Man Should Rejoice' unpublished ms. (McG) box 3, part 2, folders 3-9, pp. 2, 3; H.M. to Gray 10 Dec. 1950
31 *Voices in Time* (Toronto: Macmillan 1980) 27
32 'How Do I Write?' *Canadian Author and Bookman* 21 (Dec. 1945) 6
33 *Voices in Time* 28, 29
34 *Ibid*. 78, 28, 78, 124, 29
35 *Ibid*. 261, 294
36 *Ibid*. 254, 173
37 *Ibid*. 241-2, 248, 207
38 *Ibid*. 137, 206-7
39 *Ibid*. 121-2, 176, 62-3, 302, 247, 122
40 H.M. to author 16 Jan. 1980, to Gray 8 July 1957, 10 Aug. 1955
41 H.M. to Burt Heward in 'Masterful Novel Protests Humanity's Ignorance' *Citizen*, Ottawa 27 Sept. 1980
42 Mathews 'The Night That Ends the Debauch' *Books in Canada* (Aug.-Sept. 1980)
43 French 'Unrelentingly Earnest' *Globe and Mail* 27 Sept. 1980; Adachi 'Voices: Game, Set and Match' *Toronto Star* 4 Oct. 1980; Solecki 'Arts Review,' CBC FM Radio 30 Oct. 1980; Govier 'The Collapsing Vaults of History' *Maclean's* (22 Sept. 1980)
44 H.M. to Heward in *Citizen*; to author 19 July 1980

Epilogue

1 'Fiction in Canada – 1930-1980' in a special edition of the *University of Toronto Quarterly*, published as *The Arts in Canada: The Last Fifty Years* ed. W.J. Keith and B.-Z. Shek (Toronto: University of Toronto Press 1980) 29-42
2 Margaret Laurence to author 22 Sept. 1977
3 *The Idea File of Harold Adams Innis* ed. William Christian (Toronto: University of Toronto Press 1980) 41
4 Homer Watson, as cited by J. Russell Harper *Painting in Canada: A History* 2nd ed. (Toronto: University of Toronto Press 1977) 208
5 *Voices in Time* (Toronto: Macmillan 1980) 153
6 Burt Heward 'Masterful Novel Protests Humanity's Ignorance' *Citizen*, Ottawa 27 Sept. 1980
7 Duncan to Miss Eayrs 29 Aug. 1954 (Macmillan)

Index

Picture credits

Unless noted below, photographs were provided by Hugh MacLennan (professional copying in most instances by Brian Merrett and Jennifer Harper, Montreal).

Katie MacQuarrie	Frances MacLennan
Jean Shaw	Jean Shaw
John Gray retirement	The late Finn Bay
Tudor's *Pillar of Fire*	Dance Collection The New York Public Library at Lincoln Center Astor, Lenox and Tilden Foundations
Halifax harbour 1960s	Hugh MacLennan Papers University of Calgary Library Special Collections Division
McGill University 1980	Coshof/*Atlantic Insight*

This book

was designed by

ANTJE LINGNER

of University of

Toronto

Press